BASIC
ECONOMETRICS

PRENTICE-HALL SERIES IN MATHEMATICAL ECONOMICS
Donald V. T. Bear, *Series Editor*

DENNIS J. AIGNER

University of Wisconsin

PRENTICE-HALL, INC., ENGLEWOOD CLIFFS, NEW JERSEY

Basic Econometrics

BASIC ECONOMETRICS
by Dennis J. Aigner

Printed in the United States of America

13-059014-2
Library of Congress Catalog Card Number 70-139411

Current printing (last digit)
10 9 8 7 6 5 4 3 2 1

PRENTICE-HALL INTERNATIONAL, INC., LONDON
PRENTICE-HALL OF AUSTRALIA PTY. LTD., SYDNEY
PRENTICE-HALL OF CANADA, LTD., TORONTO
PRENTICE-HALL OF INDIA PRIVATE LIMITED, NEW DELHI
PRENTICE-HALL OF JAPAN, INC., TOKYO

To Vernita

Series Forward

The Prentice-Hall Series in Mathematical Economics is intended as a vehicle for making mathematical reasoning and quantitative methods available to the main corpus of the undergraduate and graduate economics curricula.

The Series has been undertaken in the belief that the teaching of economics will, in the future, increasingly reflect the discipline's growing reliance upon mathematical and statistical techniques during the past 20 to 35 years and that mathematical economics and econometrics ought not to be "special fields" for undergraduates and graduate students, but that every aspect of economics education can benefit from the application of these techniques.

Accordingly, the Series will contain texts that cover the traditional substantive areas of the curriculum—for example, macroeconomics, microeconomics, public finance, and international trade—thereby offering the instructor the opportunity to expose his students to contemporary methods of analysis as they apply to the subject matter of his course. The composition of the early volumes in the Series will be weighted in favor of texts that offer the student various degrees of mathematical background, with the volumes of more substantive emphasis following shortly thereafter.

As the Series grows, it will contribute to the comprehensibility and quality of economics education at both the undergraduate and graduate levels.

DONALD V. T. BEAR, *Series Editor*

Preface

Much of the material contained in this text was developed over a period of two years for use in a specific course taught at the University of Wisconsin. As such, the sequence imposes the minimum prerequisites of a course in calculus and a knowledge of (not necessarily a course in) matrix algebra. The calculus preparation should include constrained maxima and minima and partial differentiation, though only limited use is made of calculus. At one point in an early chapter, multiple integrals appear, but facility in evaluating them is not required. It is but a matter of taste that the exposition rests primarily on continuous variables and not discrete ones. The elements of matrix algebra are included in a brief Appendix.

Also included, but relegated to Appendix status, is a review of the principles of classical and Bayesian statistical inference. This review should allow the reader an opportunity to conveniently refresh his memory on such matters when they arise in the text.

The book's organization is, in the mind of its author, quite a natural one. After an introductory chapter, the basic theory of linear regression is presented in Chapters 2 and 3. Some sections of Chapter 3 actually "apply" the theory, but by and large, applications come through the problems (and their answers) at the end of this and other chapters. Chapter 4 considers the regression model under various permutations of its underlying assumptions, and discusses alternative estimation methods whenever appropriate. Chapter 5 covers the incorporation of qualitative factors in regression analysis through the use of so-called "dummy" variables. The final chapter contains a discussion of system models—models that contain several equations.

The burden of synthesis—making the theory relevant—is on the "Problems and Answers" sections of Chapters 2–5. It is assumed throughout that the reader has access to a computer and reliable regression programs; very little space is devoted to the mechanics of regression calculations.

The book is short by current standards (500–600 pages being quite a moderate length for econometrics texts). This is a positive feature because the book is *succinct*. Because the level of rigor attempted is not the highest, however, many arguments are intuitive; hopefully, the reader's intuition will correspond to the author's.

Many individuals made contributions to the book, in various capacities. My colleagues at Wisconsin, L. Christensen and A. S. Goldberger, read and commented on the entire manuscript, as did R. Ramanathan of the University of California at San Diego. D. V. T. Bear of UCSD offered many helpful suggestions on matters of exposition and substance. Two graduate students at Wisconsin, V. Galbis and Y. S. Lee assisted in working out problems. The manuscript typing was accomplished with great skill and speed by Linda Anderson and Alice Wilcox.

DENNIS J. AIGNER

Contents

BASIC
ECONOMETRICS

1 Introduction to

Quantitative Analysis

1.1 INTRODUCTION

The subject matter of this book forms part of what may broadly be called *econometrics*—the observation and measurement of economic variables and relationships. In other social sciences similar terms and definitions appear, as in *psychometrics* and *sociometrics*. And, specializing perhaps to an extreme, the economic historians have produced *cliometrics*, loosely defined as the quantitative analysis of the economic past.

Indeed, it is with a view to the past that the economist hopes either to establish credible explanations of observed behavior—usually referred to as *model-building*—or to gain confidence in an economic relationship with which he hopes to predict future behavior. These two pursuits are linked, of course, by the fact that confidence in a predictive relationship or "theory" depends on its verification (absence of refutation), on the basis of its ability to explain the past. The role of the econometrician is to deal with procedures for objectively determining when an economic theory may reasonably be refuted as an explanator of past behavior.

1.2 THEORY, MODEL-BUILDING, AND PREDICTION

Under what conditions may a theory be refuted by empirical methods of testing? And what constitutes a proper test?

The traditional theory of consumer's behavior provides a familiar and, for present purposes, an adequate illustration of the movement from theory to testing. It proceeds deductively from the proposition that a consumer has a utility function for goods with sufficiently nice properties that it can be maximized. As a result of the maximization operation, given the consumer's fixed money income for the short period under consideration, a system of first-order "marginal conditions" or *structural* equations is generated that conceptually may be solved to obtain the main objects of interest: the set of demand equations. In each of these, the optimal consumption level of a good (in physical terms) depends functionally on the set of given prices and money income. The demand equations are the *reduced form* of the structural system: they relate each *endogenous* or *dependent* variable (optimal consumption quantities) to the set of *exogenous* or *independent* variables (given prices and income). Analysis of the set of demand equations yields further logical consequences for the theory, or "deductions."

First, it is demonstrated that the partial derivative of the optimal consumption quantity of any good with respect to the price of that good is a sum of two components, commonly referred to as the "substitution effect" and the "income effect." The sign of this derivative, which is the slope of the demand function for the commodity in question, is negative for any "normal" good—one with a positive income effect. The substitution effect alone must always be negative, which is again a mathematical consequence of the theoretical framework. Further, the demand equations must each be homogeneous of degree zero in money income and prices: a proportional increase in all prices and money income will not affect optimal consumption quantities, according to the theory. Finally, the cross-effects of price changes on optimal consumption levels (again, in the sense of a partial derivative) must be symmetric.

Which of these conclusions forms a testable hypothesis? For example, the theory states that "normal" goods ought to have downward-sloping demand curves. Given that we can identify a "normal good" and meet all the assumptions used in the theoretical framework, a series of price-quantity observations on this good for some consumer should fall in a downward-sloping pattern. Otherwise, we would have refuted the theory. To make this test is not so easy as it may seem, however. For example, prices of other goods and money income must have remained constant through the period of observation, because the slope in question is a *partial* derivative. Obviously these required circumstances could be met in the real world only by extreme coincidence; what is called for is a controlled experimental situation—which the economist almost never has.

The theory also asserts that the substitution effect on the optimal consumption of any good from a change in its price, ceteris paribus, must be negative. It would seem difficult to operationally separate the income from the substitution effect. For all we can hope to observe for a given consumer unit are various quantity-price points, which reflect already the optimization process involving both substitution and real income effects of price changes. Apparently, even if we could run a controlled experiment, in this instance we would find it difficult to construct the "ideal" circumstances sufficient to allow separation of the two effects. But some recent advances have suggested means by which the two effects *can* be separated out in empirical work.

We could also conceive of ideal conditions under which the zero homogeneity of each demand equation might be tested. And, since the sign of the income effect is determined by the sign of the partial derivative of quantity with respect to money income, we may test the hypothesis of "inferiority" with an estimate of this derivative. Symmetry of the cross-substitution effects is more difficult to frame as an empirically testable hypothesis, and requires that we consider the system of demand equations rather than any single one.

Theories need not be so formal as the theory of consumer behavior in order to be interesting. Much of the applied economic literature is, in fact, devoted to consideration of tests of economic "intuition." For example, it has been suggested that as an economy (nation) develops, incomes become more equally distributed. Proposing an adequate test of this hypothesis involves not only certain "controls," or ceteris paribus assumptions (as in the previous example), but some basic measurement problems in moving from a *concept* such as income equality to an *observable quantity*. While we will not dwell on this latter problem in this book, the movement from concepts or "theoretical variables" to observables is a major effort in most empirical research in economics. Prominent examples include the measurement of *the* "price level" and *the* "aggregate capital stock."

In a related way, one's interest in quantitative relationships may direct the testing aspect of model-building to be replaced by a desire to *estimate* certain quantities. An elasticity of demand is a good example. An oligopolistic firm may desire to forecast the impact of a pending price change on its revenues, profit position, and the industry in general; knowing the relevant demand elasticity would thus be of great usefulness. The government each year sets support levels for certain agricultural commodities. At what values should they be fixed? Whatever objective the answer to this question is to serve, the elasticity of demand for the commodity will almost certainly be of importance.

For such a problem in estimation, theory still plays a major role. It suggests (as in the demand-function case) the relevant relationships to consider and the *conditioning* variables that must be controlled if one is to obtain an estimate of the required quantity (for example, a price elasticity) rather than some hybrid quantity that mixes the effects of price changes with population shifts or income changes or something else.

Finally, suppose our major concern is with the prediction of some economic variable into the future. What role *should* theory play in obtaining a good predictive relationship? Obviously our theory or intuition cannot be ignored in the pursuit of an adequate predictive relation. On the other hand, correspondence to a theoretical relationship is not the appropriate test of a forecasting equation. The proper criterion is simply: how well does it forecast?

If I had been able to predict the level of GNP in the United States over the past ten years within one percent, you likely would judge that I was a successful forecaster. Now I ask you to back me financially in a forecaster's derby for next year. Is my past performance enough to entice you? Past performance *is* enough for a statistical validation of my prowess. Perhaps

Des Jan. Feb. Mar. Apr. Mei Jun. Jul. Ag.

you would like to know exactly what my forecasting equation looks like? If it had the predicted value of GNP as a function of the price of beer in Havana, Cuba, and the team batting average of the Dodgers, I would probably be better off not telling you.

The point is that the ability to forecast accurately an economic variable that is somehow structurally related to a set of other variables should be dependent on one's ability to reproduce the structure. You may be envious of my past forecasting performance, and statistically it is outstanding, but yet you hesitate to put money behind me because my equation has apparently very little to do with the set of *causal* relations you believe to exist in the economy that generated the observed values of GNP. Clearly we have just moved into the area of subjective and out of the realm of objective judgment. But our *belief* is that if a forecasting equation is to be an accurate predictor of GNP *forever*, it must be a proxy for the underlying economic structure. Then we can be assured that so long as the structure remains stable, the predictive equation will perform well.

1.3   REGRESSION, MODEL-BUILDING, AND PREDICTION

The goal of this book is to show how the regression model may be used to make predictions with an estimable margin of error, to obtain estimates of desired quantities, or to perform tests of hypotheses of the sort discussed above. In this section our purpose is to present a capsule view of the text that follows, establishing the regression framework and its goals by analogy to a familiar case of estimation and testing. We will also take this opportunity to review briefly some of the principles of statistical estimation and inference theory along the way.†

BRIEF REVIEW OF THE PRINCIPLES OF ESTIMATION AND INFERENCE

Given a population upon which a variable, y, is measurable, how should the mean of y, μ, be estimated from a simple random sample of observations taken from the population? That is, how should sample observations on y be combined into a single number, the *estimate* of μ? One important quality of any proposed *sample statistic* or *estimator* of μ is whether the chosen estimator of μ is, "on the average," equal to μ. Here the "average" refers

† A more extensive review is contained in Appendix B.

to an average taken over all samples of the same size, n. This property is called _unbiasedness_. Formally, $E(.) = \mu$, where E stands for mathematical expectation.

A second desirable property is small variance. An estimator that possesses the smallest possible variance among a group of alternative estimators is said to have the property of "bestness," or "efficiency," or "minimum variance." Among estimators that are formed as linear combinations of the sample observations,† the sample mean, $\bar{y} = \sum_{i=1}^{n} y_i/n$, possesses the property of unbiasedness. Within _that_ class of alternative estimators it also possesses minimum variance. It, then, is the usual choice for estimating μ.

The _variance_ of $\bar{y}$ over samples of like size is, in a descriptive sense, a measure of how precise $\bar{y}$ is as an estimator for μ, since $\bar{y}$ is unbiased. In terms of the population variance, σ_y^2, and assuming that either the population is large or the sample is drawn with replacement, the variance of $\bar{y}$ is given by the familiar formula

$$(1.3.1) \qquad \sigma_{\bar{y}}^2 = \frac{\sigma_y^2}{n}.$$

Generally speaking, of course, we do not know σ_y^2 and thus cannot use (1.3.1) operationally. But an unbiased estimator of σ_y^2 is also available from the sample. It is the _sample variance_,

$$(1.3.2) \qquad s_y^2 = \frac{1}{n-1} \sum_{i=1}^{n} (y_i - \bar{y})^2,$$

where y_i is the ith observation on y in the sample. For a measure of the precision of $\bar{y}$ in estimating μ we would use $\sqrt{s_y^2/n}$, the estimated standard error (deviation) of the estimate, $\bar{y}$.

In this development, the suggestion of $\bar{y}$ as a potentially useful estimator was by analogy to the construction of μ in the population. Now we shall approach the same estimation problem from a different—and more formal— vantage point. The idea is this: any of the n sample observations considered as a random variable has the frequency distribution of y in the population, $f(y)$, given independence of observations in the sampling procedure; that is, for the ith observation y_i (before it is actually selected) under these sampling specifications, $f(y_i) = f(y)$ for all i. The mean of y_i is μ, its variance is σ_y^2, and so on. A way of formally stating these specifications is to write the following statistical model,

---

† To review the terminology used here, a "linear" estimator has the form $\sum_{i=1}^{n} w_i y_i$, with the w_i's known weights. So, for a sample of size two, both $\bar{y} = y_1/2 + y_2/2$ and $\bar{y} = y_1/3 + y_2$ are linear estimators.

(1.3.3) $y_i = \mu + \epsilon_i,$

where ϵ_i is an unobservable random variable with mean zero and variance σ_y^2. ϵ_i might be called "sampling error" on the ith observation. To repeat, what (1.3.3) "says" is that y_i is a random variable with mean μ and variance $\sigma_{\epsilon_i}^2 = \sigma_y^2$.

Now we ask the important question: with a sample of n observations, how *should* the observations be combined to "best" estimate μ or to "best" predict y? One suggested criterion for determining which estimator to use is to select the one that makes $\sum_{i=1}^{n} (y_i - \mu)^2$ smallest. This can be interpreted as minimizing a sort of "prediction-error variance" defined over the sample observations with respect to μ, the unknown parameter. The reader is likely already aware that the sum of squared differences between the sample observations and an arbitrary constant is smallest when the constant is chosen to be $\bar{y}$. If not, simply minimize $\sum_{i=1}^{n} (y_i - \mu)^2$ with respect to μ, to find $\hat{\mu} = \bar{y}$.

From before we know $\bar{y}$ is unbiased. Forming $\bar{y} = (1/n) \sum_{i=1}^{n} y_i$ as an estimator for μ is, therefore, also "optimal" in the sense that this estimator has the smallest variance of all unbiased linear estimators. This optimization process is an elementary application of the method of *least squares*. The selection of $\bar{y}$ as an estimator of μ is thus seen to rest both on a definite rationale of predictive usefulness and the analogy principle, which suggests possible sample statistics on the basis of their analogous construction to the population parameters of interest.

For accomplishing formal hypothesis tests about μ based on the sample statistic $\bar{y}$ a further assumption is required. It is an assumption about either the frequency distribution of y in the population, or of $\bar{y}$ in the population of random samples of size n. In some instances the sampling distribution of $\bar{y}$ is available theoretically. This is the case, for instance, when $\bar{y}$ is the sample proportion of elements possessing a particular attribute. With independence in sampling n times this proportion would follow a binomial distribution. Otherwise, if sample size is large enough the *central limit theorem* of statistics may be invoked to argue that no matter what the distribution of y is in the population, $\bar{y}$ will follow the normal distribution in large samples, because it is a weighted average of presumed independent random variables. Finally, the distributional form of $f(y)$ may be assumed. If the normal distribution is used, $\bar{y}$ will also follow a normal distribution for any given sample size. As is well known in this latter case, if the population variance must be estimated, it is the "t" distribution on which the classical forms of inference about μ—hypothesis tests and confidence intervals—would be based.

AN INTRODUCTION TO REGRESSION

Now we consider a modification of the underlying statistical model (1.3.3) that will take account of the *possibility* that y is *statistically related* to another variable defined over the same population. (Following our earlier remarks, the words "statistically related" should not be taken to mean that y is related to x in any particular cause-effect sense.)

The sense in which the phrase "statistical relationship" is meant is summarized in (1.3.4):

(1.3.4) $$y_i = \mu(x_i) + \epsilon_i,$$

which, under the specification that ϵ_i has zero mean, says the average value of y_i is known to be related to the level of another variable, x_i. The form of this relationship is unspecified in (1.3.4), $\mu(x_i)$ simply meaning $E(y_i) = \mu(x_i)$: the expected value of y_i is $\mu(x_i)$. We expect, a priori, to be better able to predict the average level of y using knowledge of its relation to another variable, x, than without such knowledge. As we will see shortly, even if y *is not* related to x, considering that it might be does not penalize us: the worst we can do is revert to estimating μ by $\bar{y}$.

Pictorially, the estimation situation is depicted in Fig. 1.1. Suppose there are four observations on y in our hypothetical sample, taken at different observation "points," x_1, x_2, x_3, x_4. We assume that the x-values can be preselected, and that repeated observations on y may then be taken. For example, if y is reaction time for some chemical reaction, x might be

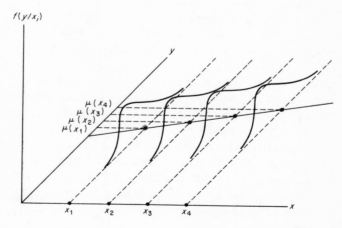

Fig. 1.1

The Conditional Distributions of y Assuming a
Positive Relation Between y and x

temperature. Our "experiment" consists of controlling temperature at four different levels and taking one observation on reaction time at each temperature level. The frequency distributions of y at different x-values drawn in Fig. 1.1 embody these assumptions.

The *linear regression model* supposes that the means $\{\mu(x_i)\}$ lie on a straight line. That is,

$$(1.3.5) \qquad\qquad y_i = \alpha + \beta x_i + \epsilon_i.$$

In addition, it is required that we say something about the variance in each of the distributions of Fig. 1.1 in order to say much about matters of prediction error. The classical regression model assumes that in each distribution the variance is identical, a constant, σ^2.

To recapitulate briefly before continuing, in the linear regression model the mean of y is assumed to be linearly related to x, the *conditioning* or *independent* variable, so that any sample observation, y_i, can be viewed as consisting of two parts: an average value defined when $x = x_i$ and an unobservable sampling error, ϵ_i. Observations are assumed to be mutually independent, and possessive of identical variances, σ^2. While this particular "model" is generally not satisfactory to describe economic relationships, it is the beginning point for more elaborate schemes. Its shortcomings for economic data should be obvious. Usually economic data are not generated from such a "controlled experiment." Moreover, it may not be possible to "replicate" the experiment as it is assumed above. For instance, one could not conceive of repeating the "experiment" that yielded a Gross National Product of $861 billion in 1968.

The estimation problem posed is to "best" estimate $\mu(x_i)$ for *each* distribution. If there were no regression hypothesis, the "best" we could do would be to group our sample observations according to x and compute the several subsample means. But with (1.3.5) we can do better than that, *if* (1.3.5) is an adequate statement of what the true model should be. As is usual in statistical analysis, inference is accomplished within the context of an assumed model. Generally speaking, statistical tests are not designed to choose between alternative models, only to test hypotheses about population parameters given a model.

The usefulness of the previous development now becomes apparent, for a similar situation presents itself in the current problem. Prediction error is epitomized by the sum of squared differences between the actual y_i's and their respective means, the latter to be estimated from the sample. Under the specifications laid down, the least-squares criterion function is just

$$\sum_{i=1}^{n} [y_i - \mu(x_i)]^2 = \sum_{i=1}^{n} (y_i - \alpha - \beta x_i)^2,$$

to be minimized over the sample observations with respect to α and β, the unknown population parameters. The *method* of least squares is again used, therefore, and produces linear estimators of α and β, say a and b, which are unbiased. They are also "best" in a dual sense. They minimize estimated prediction error and have minimum variance among alternative linear unbiased estimators.

Inference is accomplished within the regression framework with an additional assumption about the distributional form of $f(y)$. Without a priori information to the contrary, a normal distribution is usually assumed. Since the least-squares estimates of regression coefficients are formed as linear combinations of the observations, they too will possess normal distributions. The distribution theory is complete with the t-distribution used for inference purposes when the variance, σ^2, is estimated from the sample.

The usefulness of the regression model for forecasting purposes is clear. If y *is* related to a variable x by an equation such as (1.3.5) and a value for x is known before $\mu(x)$ must be estimated, we can generally do a better job of forecasting by using the fitted regression line than by forecasting $\mu(x)$ at $\bar{y}$. For model-building, however, it is important to be able to test hypotheses that are often characterized by statements about the sign of some derivative. For our simple, two-variable example (1.3.5), we find that $dy/dx = \beta$, so that a hypothesis about the slope dy/dx can be tested by standard statistical techniques applied to the least-squares estimate of β. If y were the quantity purchased of some good by a certain household and x that household's income, we would expect the least-squares slope estimate, b, for a linear regression model to be positive if the good was "normal."

In our example on the theory of consumer's behavior, it is apparent that a two-variable model will not do. Indeed, the derivatives of interest there are partial derivatives. What is required to accommodate this problem within the regression framework is merely to add additional independent or conditioning variables. While not as easy to visualize, the same essential problem is involved, finding estimators for the parameters in a model such as

$$y_i = \beta_0 + \beta_1 x_{i1} + \cdots + \beta_k x_{ik} + \epsilon_i,$$

that minimize

$$\sum_{i=1}^{n} (y_i - \beta_0 - \beta_1 x_{i1} - \cdots - \beta_k x_{ik})^2.$$

The resulting *multiple regression* "line" has all the same properties it did for the two-variable case, with the estimated slope coefficients being the respective estimated *partial* derivatives, $\partial y/\partial x_j$.

FROM THEORY TO REGRESSION

The application of the classical regression framework is not always straightforward. In particular, applications in economics often give rise to situations where the least-squares method will not produce good estimates of the coefficients in a model. Theoretical considerations may lead us to believe that the underlying assumptions of the classical model are not met. For example, it may be that certain causal relations exist in the explanation of a particular phenomenon that cannot be expressed via a single mathematical equation (of any form). In these situations modifications in the classical framework must be made or alternative techniques for estimating the model must be used. Moreover, the supposed model is assumed to be *linear* in parameters. Otherwise, the aforementioned optimal properties of the least-squares estimators do not, in general, hold. Again, theoretical considerations may generate models that are nonlinear in parameters, so that other methods of estimation become more appropriate. Models that are specified as nonlinear in conditioning variables are compatible with the classical framework so long as the nonlinear functions are known. In any event, the complete analysis of a model (note that we are now not primarily concerned with forecasting) is a worthy task. It requires competence in both economics and regression theory.

To get some feeling for this last statement, let us consider the implementation of a model of demand for some good, written as the linear multiple regression equation

$$(1.3.6) \qquad y_i = \beta_0 + \beta_1 x_{i1} + \beta_2 x_{i2} + \beta_3 x_{i3} + \epsilon_i,$$

where y_i is aggregate quantity demanded of the good in year i, x_{i1} is its average annual price, x_{i2} is aggregate income in year i, and x_{i3} is the average annual price of a close substitute. Theory has suggested the important variables to use, and we have, for convenience, put them in linear form with constant coefficients, β_1, β_2, and β_3. The least-squares estimates of these coefficients will yield insights into many interesting questions concerning the commodity in question—or will they? First, since the data are a time series, can we be sure that we have captured the underlying structure satisfactorily? Aside from the "theoretical" variables, are any other variables operating on y over time that may be confounded in $x_1, x_2,$ or x_3 if they are not controlled for? An obvious oversight is the neglect of population changes as they affect demand—that is, as they *shift* the demand schedule. A convenient way to incorporate them is to put the quantity and income variables on a per capita basis.

Next, if the traditional demand theory is to be represented by (1.3.6), does (1.3.6) satisfactorily conform to any and/or all the conditions of the theory? There is first the question of how a theory articulated for a micro unit carries over to a relation expressed in terms of aggregate quantities. This *aggregation problem* we will not consider in this book. Throughout it will be assumed that the model set out for analysis is well defined in terms of the units of observation—which may not, in fact, be the case.

One question suggested by the theory is whether (1.3.6) is homogeneous of degree zero in prices and income. Clearly, it is not. So, either another functional form must be selected that *is* homogeneous of degree zero in prices and income [without the constant term, (1.3.6) would only be homogeneous of degree one], or a means of capturing this effect in the present linear form must present itself. The homogeneity property may be proxied for by suitably deflating the price and income series to some appropriate base year. Then an increase of 3 percent in all prices and income in one year will not be compared to an increase of 2.5 percent in some other year, since the deflator will effectively cancel out these varying price effects.

A number of other variations on the classical assumptions arise commonly. Are the residual variances constant? In time-series analysis often they are not, a condition which can be tested statistically; if not rejected, this means that the least-squares estimates probably do not possess their announced properties. The framework is very flexible, though, allowing many problems to be couched in a form like (1.3.6). For example, suppose quarterly data for (1.3.6) were available. The quarterly demand structure reacts seasonally for many products, another demand "shifter" to be accounted for. The regression model can be adapted easily to incorporate nonquantitative variables such as "season" with the introduction of so-called "dummy" variables.

Given time series data on quantity demanded, prices, and income, it is not necessarily clear that (1.3.6) should appropriately be viewed as a demand equation. The observed relation between quantity and own price over time is the result of many equilibrium determinations by the "market," and as such may trace out a demand equation (if the supply curve has remained fixed over time), a supply equation (if the demand equation has remained fixed over time), or neither (when neither schedule has remained fixed over time). This is the *identification* problem, where the underlying phenomenon being modeled involves jointly determined or interdependent variables rather than the simpler relationships suggested by the categorization into one "dependent" variable and one or more "independent" variables.

To conclude this introduction we emphasize that throughout the book statistical models will be used in an attempt to capture the essence of complex real-world relationships between economic (and other) variables. Because we simplify our models in order to make them tractable, many assumptions are used that must be checked in any given application; otherwise no inferential technique can be used effectively. The emphasis on theory in the text is an attempt to force the user of regression methods to consider carefully the assumptions underlying particular statistical models as they relate to the data at hand and the economic phenomenon that generated the data—to enable him to move beyond a "cookbook" approach to the use of statistical methods, toward bettter inference and richer economic models.

2 Classical

Two-Variable Regression

2.1 INTRODUCTION

Our approach in this book will be to move in this chapter through the complete set of ideas for a two-variable regression model, including the relevant inference theory, and then to extend them to the multiple regression case. Obviously, an alternative way to proceed would be to consider the more general model first, treating two-variable regression as a special case. Hopefully, our more deliberate, less elegant approach will yield greater intuitive understanding of the fundamental ideas of the regression framework, since for two variables ordinary algebra will serve the purposes of development and derivation, and the entire framework can be discussed with the aid of two-dimensional graphics.

An important preliminary to the algebraic development and statistical analysis of sample data within a regression framework is to develop a set of relations about the expected values of a random variable conditional on one or more other random variables. In our introductory chapter the regression model was posed as if a controlled experiment could be accomplished, generating sample values for y, the dependent variable, at selected values for another variable, x. In this sense we might refer to x as a *fixed variate*. It is our independent or conditioning variable: a *regressor*.

As also pointed out previously, economic data generally *do not* correspond to the fixed variate specification for x. Rather, x will usually be a random variable in the fullest sense, and our data body is to be interpreted as a set of joint observations on y *and* x.

Most of the available theory refers to the fixed-variate regression model. In that case, the regression hypothesis is about the expected value of y in its *unconditional* distribution—that is, $E(y)$. When x is a random variable, however, *all* these same results go through only when we concentrate on the *conditional* distributions, $f(y \mid x)$. Then the regression model is about the *conditional means* $E(y \mid x)$ relating to the value of x. In the stochastic-x case, to generalize to the unconditional distribution of y presents some difficulties we shall discuss later on.

For the bulk of the book, in particular this and the following chapter, we will either consider the fixed-variate case or assume the analysis is being accomplished in the conditional distribution of y. For purposes of exposition we concentrate on the conditional analysis, because x as a fixed variate is just a special case of this situation. Until the latter part of Chapter 4, *any* use of the concepts expected value and variance should be interpreted as conditional on the independent variables, even though in the notation the "condition" is often ignored.

2.2 CONDITIONAL EXPECTATIONS

Let us begin with a brief review of the important rules of calculating unconditional expectations—that is, the expected value of a random variable or a particular function of it in its unconditional or marginal distribution. There are four:

(a) The expected value of a sum of random variables is the sum of their respective expected values. Letting the random variables in question be denoted by $z_1, \ldots, z_n$ and with E the expectations operator, $E(\sum_{i=1}^{n} z_i) = \sum_{i=1}^{n} E(z_i)$.

(b) The expected value of a constant is the constant itself. With k a constant, $E(k) = k$.

(c) The expected value of a constant *times* a random variable is the constant *times* the expected value of the random variable. $E(kz_i) = kE(z_i)$.

(d) The expected value of a product of two random variables is the product of their expected values *if* the random variables are statistically independent. With independence, $E(z_i z_j) = E(z_i)E(z_j)$.

Conditional expectations are developed along similar lines, except that the observed value of another random variable is held as background information. If y is the main variable of interest and x is the "conditioning" variable, it is their joint distribution, $f(y, x)$, that is the basis for deriving marginal (unconditional) and conditional distributions for y (or x). Thus, we have the familiar relationships:[†]

$$(2.2.1) \qquad f(y) = \int f(y, x)\, dx, \text{ the marginal distribution of } y,$$

$$f(x) = \int f(y, x)\, dy, \text{ the marginal distribution of } x,$$

$$f(y \,|\, x) = \frac{f(y, x)}{f(x)} \qquad \begin{array}{l} \text{whenever } f(x) \neq 0, \text{ the conditional} \\ \text{distribution of } y \text{ } given \text{ } x.[\ddagger] \end{array}$$

And as the unconditional expected value of y is computed as

$$(2.2.2) \qquad\qquad E(y) = \int yf(y)\, dy,$$

its conditional expectation is

$$(2.2.3) \qquad\qquad E(y \,|\, x) = \int yf(y \,|\, x)\, dy.$$

[†] In what follows, y and x are assumed to be continuous random variables for convenience only. The derived relations also hold when either y or x or both are discrete.

[‡] It may be helpful to recall the analogous formulas for the case of discrete variables,

If we expand (2.2.2), we discover an important fact linking conditional and unconditional expectations—namely that the unconditional expected value of y is the expected value of its conditional expectation. Expanding,

$$(2.2.4) \qquad E(y) = \int y f(y) \, dy = \int y \int f(y, x) \, dx \, dy$$

$$= \int y \int f(y \mid x) f(x) \, dx \, dy \qquad \text{[by (2.2.1)]}$$

$$= \int \left\{ \int y f(y \mid x) \, dy \right\} f(x) \, dx \qquad \begin{array}{l}\text{(interchanging the order} \\ \text{of integration)}\end{array}$$

$$= \int E(y \mid x) f(x) \, dx \qquad \text{[by definition (2.2.3)].}$$

That is, taking the expectation of $E(y \mid x)$ over the conditioning variable, x, yields $E(y)$.

The other important rules for conditional expectation follow along similar lines.

---

making use of a joint probability table. Let y take on values, $y_1, \ldots, y_n$ and x take on values $x_1, x_2, \ldots, x_m$ according to the joint distribution $f(y, x)$ displayed as follows:

The Joint Frequencies $f(y_i, x_j)$, $\sum_{i=1}^{n} \sum_{j=1}^{m} f(y_i, x_j) = 1$.

y \ x	x_1	x_2	$\cdots$	x_m	"Marginal"
y_1	$f(y_1, x_1)$	$f(y_1, x_2)$		$f(y_1, x_m)$	$\sum_{j=1}^{m} f(y_1, x_j) = f(y_1)$
y_2	$f(y_2, x_1)$	$f(y_2, x_2)$		$f(y_2, x_m)$	$f(y_2)$
$\vdots$					
y_n	$f(y_n, x_1)$	$f(y_n, x_2)$		$f(y_n, x_m)$	$f(y_n)$
"Marginal"	$f(x_1)$	$f(x_2)$		$f(x_m)$	

To obtain the marginal or unconditional distributions we note that summing the table entries along a given row, say the first, gives the probability that $y = y_1$ given $x = x_1$ or $x = x_2$ or ... or $x = x_m$. That is, $\sum_{j=1}^{m} f(y_1, x_j) = f(y_1)$. Similarly, the remaining frequencies required to complete the distribution of y are available as row "margins," and the frequency distribution of x is given by the column "margins." These summations are, respectively, the counterparts of $f(y) = \int f(y, x) \, dx$ and $f(x) = \int f(y, x) \, dy$ written for continuous variables.

The conditional frequencies (probabilities) $f(y_i \mid x_j)$ are obtained by dividing each cell entry by the appropriate marginal entry. So, $f(y_1 \mid x_2) = f(y_1, x_2)/f(x_2)$, and so on until the entire distribution $f(y \mid x)$ is developed. The notation $f(y \mid x) = f(y, x)/f(x)$ describes exactly this operation.

Note also that $f(\cdot)$ is used to mean many different things: while it always represents a probability density or frequency function as appropriate, it does *not* mean, for example, that $f(y, x)$ and $f(x)$ are the *same function*.

RULE 1

IF c IS A CONSTANT (GIVEN x), THEN
(a) $E[(y + c)|x] = E(y|x) + c,$
(b) $E(cy|x) = cE(y|x).$

PROOFS:

(a) $E[(y + c)|x] = \int (y + c)f(y|x)\,dy$

$$= \int yf(y|x)\,dy + \int cf(y|x)\,dy$$

$$= E(y|x) + c.$$

(b) $E(cy|x) = \int cyf(y|x)\,dy$

$$= c\int yf(y|x)\,dy$$

$$= cE(y|x).$$

RULE 2

IF $E(y|x) = $ CONSTANT, THEN $E(y|x) = E(y)$ ("MEAN INDEPENDENCE").

PROOF:

$$E(y) = \int yf(y)\,dy = \int y\int f(y, x)\,dy\,dx$$

$$= \int\int yf(y|x)f(x)\,dy\,dx$$

$$= \int E(y|x)f(x)\,dx \qquad [\text{as in (2.2.4).}]$$

If $E(y|x) = k$, then

$$E(y) = \int kf(x)\,dx = k\int f(x)\,dx = k = E(y|x).$$

RULE 3

IF $E(y|x) = $ CONSTANT, THEN $E(yx) = E(y)E(x)$ ("UNCORRELATEDNESS").

PROOF:

$$E(yx) = \int\int yxf(y, x)\,dy\,dx$$

$$= \int x\int yf(y|x)f(x)\,dy\,dx = \int E(y|x)xf(x)\,dx.$$

If $E(y|x) = k$,

$$E(yx) = \int kxf(x)\,dx = kE(x).$$

From Rule 2 above,

$$E(y \mid x) = k \Longrightarrow E(y \mid x) = E(y).$$

Therefore,

$$E(yx) = E(y)E(x).$$

Some interpretation of these results is as follows. Just as statistical independence can be stated $f(y, x) = f(y)f(x)$ or $f(y \mid x) = f(y)$, so, in an analogous fashion, can *mean independence*. This is the essence of Rules 2 and 3 above. Statistical independence is a much *stronger* relation to hold between random variables, since it implies mean independence. In fact, statistical independence implies that *any* moment of $f(y \mid x)$ does not depend on x—that is, $f(y \mid x) = f(y)$; whether an observed value for x is available or not as a "condition" has no effect on the entire frequency distribution of y, including all its moments. To see that this line of implication holds for the mean, write

$$(2.2.5) \qquad E(y \mid x) = \int y \, \frac{f(y, x)}{f(x)} \, dy = \int y \, \frac{f(y)f(x)}{f(x)} \, dy = E(y).$$

The next line of implication moves us from mean independence to *uncorrelatedness*. To say two random variables are uncorrelated is to say that their covariance is zero. It is clear from the conclusion of Rule 3 for conditional expectations that mean independence implies $\text{Cov}(y, x) = 0$, since

$$(2.2.6) \qquad \text{Cov}(y, x) = E\{[y - E(y)][x - E(x)]\}$$
$$= E(yx) - E(y)E(x).$$

The line of implication in this instance is again not reversible; uncorrelatedness does not generally imply mean independence, just as it was found that mean independence did not, in general, imply statistical independence. An illustration that demonstrates these irreversibilities is included as Problem 2 at the end of the chapter. Finally, we might now modify the traditional rule (d) for calculating unconditional expections (p. **18**) to read: "... *if* the random variables are mean-independent," as a weaker but still (only) sufficient condition for the expectation of a product to equal the product of expectations.

2.3 THE POPULATION REGRESSION FUNCTION

With y and x both random variables, the population of interest is a set of elements giving rise to measurements jointly on y and x. But it is also to be assumed that x is known; that is, the analysis is to be conditioned on x taking a particular value, say x_i. The general representation for all such possible values is the generic symbol, x, and the distributions of interest are the conditional ones, $f(y \mid x = x_i)$, which we simply denote as $f(y \mid x)$. Now, the characteristics of these distributions that form the basic point of inquiry for regression analysis are the conditional means, $E(y \mid x)$, and the *regression model* is a specification of how these conditional means are related to each other *through* x.

The classical analysis of regression assumes that the conditioning variable, x, is fixed in repeated samples. With this assumption there is no need for the introduction of notions of conditional expectations to capture relationships between y and some related continuous variable, x. The sort of experimental situation implied by the classical assumption allows for multiple observations on y to be taken at "controlled" values for x, and using the assumption implies that the data under consideration were gathered in this way. So, for example, laboratory measurements on the activity levels of a certain bacteria strain taken at various temperature levels may fit the classical assumption, if other factors affecting activity levels are held constant. Observations on aggregate consumption and income levels for the United States over time most certainly cannot. It is for this latter case of joint observations on y and a stochastic conditioning variable whose value cannot be controlled that the conditional expectations formulation of the regression model is appropriate.

Often the regression framework is interpreted strictly in terms of the observed sample, even though this is patently incorrect. Indeed, the most important conceptual foundation of regression analysis is the *population regression function* (PRF). We think of a population of elements on which measurements y and x are to be taken. Our inference problem comes about because we presumably have only a sample of these elements. The sample is assumed to have been selected randomly—another assumption we will want to scrutinize carefully later.

In the population, we speak generally of a *population regression function* (PRF), g, written

$$(2.3.1) \qquad\qquad E(y \mid x) = g(x).$$

This PRF simply says that the means of the conditional distributions of y over the conditioning variable, x, are functionally related to x. Even from this seemingly innocent specification some properties of the PRF appear.

Because $E[y - E(y)] = 0$, by definition of the mean, we define ϵ by

$$(2.3.2) \qquad\qquad \epsilon = y - E(y \mid x) = y - g(x),$$

so that $E(\epsilon \mid x) = E[y - E(y \mid x)] = 0$. ϵ is called the *residual*, or *disturbance*, or *random error*. To show formally that $E(\epsilon \mid x) = 0$, we can use the rules for conditional expectations developed in Section 2.2. First, we know that $E(y|x)$ is a constant *given x*—that is, $E\{[E(y|x)]|x\} = E(y|x)$. Thus by Rule 1 for conditional expectations, $E(\epsilon|x) = 0$, which result will not hold everywhere if $g(x)$ is defined in any other way than as $E(y|x)$.† Since $E(\epsilon|x) = 0$, a constant, by Rule 2, it follows that $E(\epsilon) = 0$. The error term, ϵ, is mean-independent of the conditioning variable in the PRF. Finally, $E(\epsilon x) = E(\epsilon)E(x) = 0$; that is, ϵ is uncorrelated with x in the PRF. These results lead to the main object of interest, the *population regression model* (PRM):

$$(2.3.3) \qquad\qquad y = g(x) + \epsilon.$$

$g(x)$ so far is unspecified. In a particular application its form may be suggested by theory. But by far the most convenient a priori specification in the absence of such knowledge is as a linear function—not necessarily linear in x, but linear in its unknown parameters. The so-called *linear regression model*, then, takes the form

$$E(y|x) = \alpha + \beta x$$

or

$$(2.3.4) \qquad\qquad y = \alpha + \beta x + \epsilon,$$

with $E(\epsilon) = 0$ and $E(\epsilon x) = 0$, expressed for our two-variable case. To re-iterate, the "linearity" of the model is in the fact that *parameters* (α, β) appear raised to the first power. A model $y = \alpha + \beta x^2 + \epsilon$, therefore, is still a linear model, while $y = \alpha + x^\beta + \epsilon$ is not. We shall have more to say on this in Chapter 5.

Before continuing, we should remark that the regression model $y = g(x) + \epsilon$, whatever the form of g, suggests that our interest centers on y *conditional* on x, as if x in some sense *causes* y. Certainly we may *consider* $E(y|x)$ without *believing* that x causes y, but in modeling economic phenomena there will be inherent lines of causation, although some may not be *known* or suggested by theory. If the line of causation is from y to x, or if y and x are simultaneously determined, a conditional analysis of the model $y = g(x) + \epsilon$ is *inappropriate*. These matters are taken up in later chapters of the book.

Secondly, the model says that the relationship between y and x is not perfect *in the population* because, although $E(\epsilon) = 0$, for any *particular* population element the residual need not be zero. What interpretation is to be put on ϵ, then, if the model is supposed to be an empirical representation of a theory that *explains* behavior?

---

† A proof of this statement is required of the reader in Problem 1 at the end of the chapter.

There are several points of view on this matter. One suggests that there most probably are important conditioning variables left out of the model. No doubt few, if any, models of economic behavior are complete with only one independent variable, as in (2.3.4). We can easily add more independent variables to the two-variable framework of this chapter, however, so what is at issue is whether or not economic behavior can conceptually be captured completely in an empirical relationship. This is a matter of philosophy. If it is believed that *conceptually* we can write down a relationship that determines the behavior of some variable y on the basis of one, several, or very many independent variables, then the residual ϵ is a "practical" proxy for some set of left-out variables. To fit within the context of regression, the left-out variables must act together in such a way that $E(\epsilon) = 0$. If the left-out variables point of view is unacceptable, a second interpretation suggests that ϵ represents an inherent randomness in the behavior underlying the model at hand.

The third primary interpretation of ϵ in the population regression model does not have this philosophical overtone. It is that measurement error in y is responsible for ϵ, which for economic data in particular is probably a very appropriate statement. The problem here is that x is an economic variable too, generally subject to errors of observation on the same grounds. Unfortunately the regression framework cannot cope well with the assumption of errors of measurement on *both* y and x.†

2.4 THE SAMPLE REGRESSION FUNCTION

We assume that a simple random sample from the population of interest has been taken, yielding observations (y_i, x_i) for $i = 1, \ldots, n$, and consider the construction of a *sample regression model* (SRM),

$$(2.4.1) \qquad y_i = a + bx_i + e_i, \qquad i = 1, \ldots, n,$$

where a and b are coefficients to be computed, and e_i is the *calculated residual*, $y_i - a - bx_i$. Our goals are to estimate accurately $E(y \,|\, x = x_i)$, and hence α and β of the PRF. The question now is, how should the *sample regression function* (SRF), $a + bx_i$, be constructed? We shall consider two approaches to the calculation of a and b, one rather informal, the other a technique of estimation that guarantees certain results if its prerequisite assumptions are met.

The first possible approach is to construct the SRF by analogy. As the sample mean is suggested by analogy as an estimator for the population

---

† The problem of errors of observation in both y and x is treated briefly at the end of this chapter, and again in Chapter 4.

mean, let the SRF have properties analogous to the PRF. Once the analogy tells us how a and b might be calculated, we can analyze them more formally as estimators of α and β, or investigate the relationship between predictions from the SRF and the actual values of y.

What properties does the PRF have? There are two fundamental ones: $E(\epsilon) = 0$; $E(\epsilon x) = 0$. By analogy, in the sample the average of the calculated residuals should be zero, as should the sample correlation of e_i with x_i. Thus we must determine a, b so that

$$(2.4.2) \qquad \frac{1}{n} \sum_{i=1}^{n} e_i = 0 \quad \text{or} \quad \sum_{i=1}^{n} e_i = 0$$

and

$$\frac{1}{n} \sum_{i=1}^{n} e_i x_i = 0 \quad \text{or} \quad \sum_{i=1}^{n} e_i x_i = 0.$$

For convenience, let us drop the i-subscript and operate with the understanding that sums are taken from $i = 1$ to $i = n$. The two equations in (2.4.2) are easily written [using (2.4.1)] in terms of the observed quantities (y_i, x_i). They appear in (2.4.3):

$$(2.4.3) \qquad \sum y = na + b \sum x,$$
$$\sum xy = a \sum x + b \sum x^2,$$

which solves to:

$$(2.4.4) \qquad b = \frac{\sum xy - n\bar{x}\bar{y}}{\sum x^2 - n\bar{x}^2}, \qquad a = \bar{y} - b\bar{x},$$

where $\bar{x}$, $\bar{y}$ denote the sample means of x and y, respectively.

As a check on the properties of the SRF, consider

(a) $\qquad e_i = y_i - a - bx_i,$
$$\sum e = \sum (y - a - bx)$$
$$= \sum y - na - b \sum x$$
$$= \sum y - n\bar{y} + nb\bar{x} - b \sum x = 0,$$

and

(b) $\quad \sum ex = \sum yx - a \sum x - b \sum x^2$
$$= \sum yx - \bar{y} \sum x + b\bar{x} \sum x - b \sum x^2$$
$$= [\sum yx - n\bar{y}\bar{x}] - b[\sum x^2 - n\bar{x}^2]$$
$$= 0$$

by (2.4.4).

Some additional properties of the SRF follow easily. First, writing $\hat{y}_i$ as the estimated value of $E(y \mid x = x_i)$—that is,

$$(2.4.5) \qquad\qquad \hat{y}_i = a + bx_i$$

—we find that the means of the predicted and actual values are equal in the sample: $\sum \hat{y} = \sum (y - e) = \sum y$ because $\sum e = 0$ always. Thus, $(1/n) \sum \hat{y} = \bar{\hat{y}} = \bar{y}$, and at $\bar{x}$, $\hat{y} = \bar{y}$ because $\hat{y} = a + b\bar{x} = \bar{y} - b\bar{x} + b\bar{x} = \bar{y}$.

Next we note that the predicted values are uncorrelated with the calculated residuals. This result is quite intuitive, since a and b are constants in the sample, and e_i is forced to be uncorrelated with x_i. It is therefore reasonable to expect $\sum \hat{y}e = 0$, which can be seen from $\sum \hat{y}e = \sum (a + bx)e = a \sum e + b \sum xe = 0$. Finally, because of this last property, $\sum y^2 = \sum (\hat{y} + e)^2 = \sum \hat{y}^2 + \sum e^2$, and since y and $\hat{y}$ share the same mean and the mean of e is always zero,

$$(2.4.6) \qquad \sum (y - \bar{y})^2 = \sum (\hat{y} + e - \bar{y})^2$$
$$= \sum (\hat{y} - \bar{y})^2 + \sum e^2 + \sum (\hat{y} - \bar{y})e$$
$$= \sum (\hat{y} - \bar{y})^2 + \sum e^2.$$

The sum of squared deviations or total variation in y is partitioned into two distinct (exclusive) sources, the sum of squared deviations of the predicted values of y from their mean and the sum of squared deviations of the calculated errors from their mean (zero). For evaluating the SRF as a predictive model, (2.4.6) is the key result. If *all* the points in the sample lie on the SRF as calculated by this *analogy principle*, then for every i (observation), $\hat{y}_i = y_i$ and $\sum e^2 = 0$. This case corresponds to *perfect prediction*, as $\sum e^2$ is an indicator of the "badness" of fit of the regression line. At the other extreme, if in the sample $b = 0$ and $a = \bar{y}$, then $y_i = \bar{y}$ for all y and $\sum (y - \bar{y})^2 = \sum e^2$. This corresponds to the situation *in the absence of a regression hypothesis*; that is, in this case we would predict y at $\bar{y}$ *unconditionally*—without knowledge of x. This result, were it to occur in a given sample, says that knowing x does not improve our ability to predict y. So, we revert to the practice of predicting y in its unconditional distribution, at $\bar{y}$.

The usual statistical notion of "relation" between two variables is the *correlation coefficient* of x and y, defined by

$$(2.4.7) \qquad r_{xy} = \frac{\dfrac{1}{n}[\sum xy - n\bar{x}\bar{y}]}{\sqrt{\dfrac{1}{n}[\sum x^2 - n\bar{x}^2]}\sqrt{\dfrac{1}{n}[\sum y^2 - n\bar{y}^2]}},$$

the numerator of which is the *sample covariance*

(2.4.8)
$$S_{xy} = \frac{1}{n}\left[\sum xy - n\bar{x}\bar{y}\right]$$

and the denominator of which is the product of the sample standard deviations of x and y—that is, the square roots of their sample variances,

(2.4.9)
$$S_x^2 = \frac{1}{n}\sum (x - \bar{x})^2 = \frac{1}{n}\left[\sum x^2 - nx^2\right],$$

$$S_y^2 = \frac{1}{n}\left[\sum y^2 - n\bar{y}^2\right]\dagger$$

There is a simple relation between r_{xy} and b. Since b can be written [see (2.4.4)] as $b = S_{xy}/S_x^2$, we have

(2.4.10)
$$r_{xy} = \frac{S_{xy}}{S_x S_y} = \frac{bS_x^2}{S_x S_y} = b\left(\frac{S_x}{S_y}\right)$$

and

(2.4.11)
$$b = r_{xy}\left(\frac{S_y}{S_x}\right).$$

If $b = 0$, $r_{xy} = 0$ and vice versa. If the scatter of points is instead a *vertical* line, b and r_{xy} are of the indeterminant form $0/0$.

Note also that the correlation coefficient between y and x is always the *same* as the correlation coefficient between x and y, whereas it is not generally true that the regression coefficient of y on x is the reciprocal of the regresssion coefficient of x on y.

An important step toward a full understanding of correlation and two-variable regression is to elaborate on the interpretation of (2.4.6). Written in terms of sample variances the relation is simple:

(2.4.12)
$$S_y^2 = S_{\hat{y}}^2 + S_e^2,$$

where $S_{\hat{y}}^2 = (1/n)[\sum \hat{y}^2 - n\bar{y}^2]$, $S_e^2 = (1/n)\sum e^2$. The last term on the right of (2.4.12) measures variation in the sample residuals. That is, *after* the regression line has accounted for the relationship between y and x, the sample residual at each i measures what is left unaccounted for, or unexplained. S_e^2 is the average squared residual, the *unexplained* variation in y after regression. The $S_{\hat{y}}^2$ term naturally, then, is called the *explained* variance. These two sources of variation must add to S_y^2 if a and b are calculated according to (2.4.4).

---

† This is somewhat unconventional, in that $(1/n)[\sum x^2 - n\bar{x}^2]$ is not, for example, an unbiased estimator of the population variance of x. $[1/(n - 1)][\sum x^2 - n\bar{x}^2]$ is, and for that reason is usually called "sample variance." For purposes of this exposition this discrepancy is unimportant.

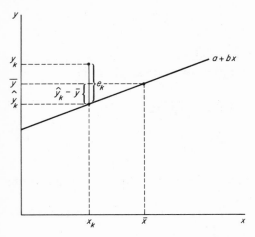

Fig. 2.1

Sources of Error in the Regression Model

Geometrically, the partitioning of S_y^2 into $S_{\hat{y}}^2$ and S_e^2 can be viewed in Fig. 2.1. The regression line accounts for variability of the estimated conditional means from the grand mean, $\bar{y}$, which is given in the sample by terms like $(\hat{y}_k - \bar{y})^2$ for all values of x, not just the kth. Thus $S_{\hat{y}}^2$ is the sample average variation in $\hat{y}$, averaged over the n observations. For each value of x there is a deviation in the y-direction of the actual observation, y_k, from its estimated conditional mean, given in the sample by $(y_k - \hat{y}_k)$. If there were more than one observation at each x_k, we could produce a sample estimate of the conditional variance of y at x_k. Otherwise, if all conditional variances are assumed to be equal, a pooled estimate is possible. Saving a more definitive discussion until later, S_e^2 in this sense measures conditional variance.

A forecaster who was fortunate enough to find all the sample points lying on his sample regression line would estimate prediction error at zero in the range of data.† Alternatively, he would have "explained" 100 percent of S_y^2 by $S_{\hat{y}}^2$. A suggestive measure of how well the SRF does in accounting for the variability in y, as measured by S_y^2, is the ratio $S_{\hat{y}}^2/S_y^2$. (This ratio describes the proportion of variance explained.) Notice that by substituting first $\hat{y} = a + bx$ and then $a = \bar{y} - b\bar{x}$ into the definition of $S_{\hat{y}}^2$ we get

$$(2.4.13) \quad S_{\hat{y}}^2 = \frac{1}{n} \sum (\hat{y} - \bar{y})^2 = \frac{1}{n} \sum (a + bx - \bar{y})^2$$

$$= \frac{1}{n} \sum (\bar{y} - b\bar{x} + bx - \bar{y})^2 = \frac{1}{n} \sum b^2 (x - \bar{x})^2$$

$$= b^2 S_x^2,$$

† There are two pathological cases that do not correspond to this statement. They are the vertical line and horizontal line scatters mentioned previously.

and

$$(2.4.14) \qquad \frac{S_{\hat{y}}^2}{S_y^2} = \frac{b^2 S_x^2}{S_y^2} = r_{xy}^2$$

from (2.4.10). The squared correlation coefficient of y and x measures the proportion of explained variance in a two-variable regression model of y on x. The notion of "degree of relationship" frequently alluded to in discussions of simple correlation is just this. In passing we should note again that whether y is regressed on x, or x on y, r_{xy}^2 is the same. Thus, while different causal meaning may be introduced by the regression of x on y, from a forecaster's point of view this simple two-variable model is symmetric with respect to its ability to forecast y from x or x from y.

Moreover, it is not generally true that the calculated regression coefficients in these two regressions will bear a reciprocal relation to one another. Letting b_{yx} be the coefficient calculated by equation (2.4.11) in the regression of y on x, and b_{xy} the analogous coefficient in the regression of x on y, though b_{yx} and b_{xy} must have the same sign, we find that

$$(2.4.15) \qquad b_{yx} = \left(\frac{1}{b_{xy}}\right) r_{xy}^2.$$

Generally, b_{yx} and b_{xy} are inversely related with factor of proportionality r_{xy}^2. They are mutual reciprocals only if x and y are perfectly correlated.

We may speak of the proportion of unexplained variance also, S_e^2/S_y^2. Because S_y^2 may be partitioned into $S_{\hat{y}}^2$ and S_e^2, we see that r_{xy}^2 may equivalently be defined by

$$(2.4.16) \qquad r_{xy}^2 = \frac{S_{\hat{y}}^2}{S_y^2} = 1 - \frac{S_e^2}{S_y^2}.$$

Equations (2.4.2) through (2.4.16) are the basic relations of two-variable regression consistent with the analogy principle.

Calculation of the SRF may be approached alternatively through an application of the technique of least-squares estimation. The key theoretical result that guarantees desirable properties for least-squares estimates in linear models is the Gauss-Markov theorem, which states that for a PRF $E(y|x) = \alpha + \beta x$, linear in parameters, if the conditional variances are all identical—that is, $\sigma_{y|x}^2 = \sigma^2$—then the method of least squares (LS) supplies *best linear unbiased estimates* (BLUE) of α and β.

The method of LS was discussed briefly in Chapter 1. It directs us to find "values" for the unknown parameters α and β that minimize $L = \sum [y - E(y|x)]^2 = \sum (y - \alpha - \beta x)^2$.

Using the calculus, a minimum for this function is found at values $\hat{\alpha}$ and $\hat{\beta}$ for which

(2.4.17)
$$\frac{\partial L}{\partial \alpha} = -2 \sum (y - \hat{\alpha} - \hat{\beta}x) = 0,$$

$$\frac{\partial L}{\partial \beta} = -2 \sum (y - \hat{\alpha} - \hat{\beta}x)x = 0,$$

if the appropriate second-order condition is met.† Solving these equations simultaneously clearly leads to solutions for $\hat{\alpha}$ and $\hat{\beta}$ that are identical to the a and b of (2.4.4). Hence all the relationships developed before are relevant under least-squares estimation. If the constant-variance assumption is a reasonable one, moreover, the a and b of (2.4.4) have BLUE properties as estimators of α and β. The goal of good prediction is also served by the minimization of the LS criterion function, since with the LS estimators inserted, the minimized value of L, $\sum (y - a - bx)^2 = nS_e^2$, minimizes sample unexplained variance.

When is the constant-variance assumption not reasonable? This is a question best reserved until later, when we take up "applications" of the regression model. Approaching this question only briefly, the constant-

Fig. 2.2

A Scatter Diagram Where the Conditional
Variance of y Apparently Varies with x

---

† The second-order criterion for a minimum in this instance is that the determinant of

$$\begin{bmatrix} \dfrac{\partial^2 L}{\partial \alpha^2} & \dfrac{\partial^2 L}{\partial \alpha\, \partial \beta} \\[2ex] \dfrac{\partial^2 L}{\partial \beta\, \partial \alpha} & \dfrac{\partial^2 L}{\partial \beta^2} \end{bmatrix}$$

be positive *and* that $\partial^2 L/\partial \alpha^2$ and $\partial^2 L/\partial \beta^2$ be positive. Clearly $\partial^2 L/\partial \alpha^2$ and $\partial^2 L/\partial \beta^2$ are positive. As the reader can readily verify, the condition

$$(\partial^2 L/\partial \alpha^2)(\partial^2 L/\partial \beta^2) - (\partial^2 L/\partial \alpha\, \partial \beta) > 0$$

is equivalent to requiring that $S_x^2 > 0$. Since a variance is always positive so long as the variable in question *varies* and $n \geq 2$, this requirement will generally be met.

variance assumption would be questionable if the scatter diagram of sample observations (y_i, x_i) looked like Fig. 2.2, for example, where the dispersion of y in its conditional distributions seems to increase with x. Also, there may be theoretical reasons for suspecting that the conditional variances are not constant over x.

2.5 STATISTICAL PROPERTIES OF *a, b*

The BLUE properties of least-squares estimators can be easily demonstrated in the two-variable case. To review briefly, a *linear* estimator is one formed as a linear combination of the observations on the random variable in question—in this instance $y_1, y_2, \ldots, y_n$. To see that b is a linear estimator, we note that it can be written in the form $b = \sum_{i=1}^{n} c_i y_i$.

The property of *unbiasedness* says, $E(a) = \alpha$ and $E(b) = \beta$. Since under simple random sampling each sample has an equal chance of being selected, the meaning of this expectation is that viewed over all possible samples of a given size, n, the average value of the estimate is the numerical value of the parameter being estimated.

The "bestness" property is a minimum-variance property. Among all unbiased linear estimators, the least-squares estimators have minimum variance. Now we shall proceed to show unbiasedness and bestness.

For future convenience, let any variable expressed as a deviation from its sample mean be written with a star notation—that is, $x_i^* = x_i - \bar{x}$. Upon noting $\sum x^* = 0$, we see that

$$(2.5.1) \qquad b = \frac{\sum xy - n\bar{y}\bar{x}}{\sum x^2 - n\bar{x}^2} = \frac{\sum x^* y^*}{\sum x^{*2}} = \frac{\sum x^* y - \bar{y} \sum x^*}{\sum x^{*2}} = \frac{\sum x^* y}{\sum x^{*2}}.$$

Thus, b is linear in the y_i's with weights $c_i = (x_i - \bar{x})/\sum_{i=1}^{n} (x_i - \bar{x})^2$.

Using (2.5.1), we can directly express b in terms of β by substituting the PRF for y. This gives

$$(2.5.2) \qquad b = \frac{\sum x^* y}{\sum x^{*2}} = \frac{\sum x^* (\alpha + \beta x + \epsilon)}{\sum x^{*2}}$$

$$= \frac{\alpha \sum x^* + \beta \sum x^* x + \sum x^* \epsilon}{\sum x^{*2}}$$

$$= \beta + \frac{\sum x^* \epsilon}{\sum x^{*2}},$$

since $\sum x^* = 0$, and $\sum x^* x = \sum x^{*2}$. While $\sum x^* e = 0$ in the sample, $\sum x^* \epsilon$ involves the population random variable ϵ_i for which e_i is merely an observed value. On the average, however, over all possible simple random samples of size n, ϵ will be uncorrelated with x and hence with x^*. Formally, $E[\sum x^*\epsilon] = \sum [E(x^*\epsilon)] = 0$. Thus, $E(b) = \beta$.

Clearly a is also a linear estimator for α, since $a = \bar{y} - b\bar{x}$, and $\bar{y}$ and b are linear in the y_i's. $E(a) = E(\bar{y}) - \bar{x}E(b) = (\alpha + \beta\bar{x}) - \bar{x}\beta = \alpha$, which proves unbiasedness. Since $E(a) = \alpha$ and $E(b) = \beta$, $E(\hat{y}) = E(y|x) = \alpha + \beta x$.

As for the variance of b (given x), we have

$$(2.5.3) \qquad \sigma_b^2 = \text{Var}\left[\beta + \frac{\sum x^*\epsilon}{\sum x^{*2}}\right] = \text{Var}\left[\frac{\sum x^*\epsilon}{\sum x^{*2}}\right].$$

Assuming independence in sampling, the residual ϵ_i is statistically independent of the residual ϵ_j. Our assumptions also include $E(\epsilon) = 0$ and $E(\epsilon_i^2) = \sigma^2$. Using the rule for variance calculations that states that the variance of a sum of independent random variables is the sum of their variances and the rule that states that the variance of a constant times a random variable is the constant squared times the variance of the random variables, we find that

$$(2.5.4) \qquad \sigma_b^2 = \left[\frac{1}{\sum x^{*2}}\right]^2 \sum x^{*2}\sigma^2$$

$$= \frac{\sigma^2}{\sum x^{*2}}.$$

Note that as a matter of experimental design, if we could control the placement of values for x in its range, we should put them at the extremes of the range in order to make $\sum x^{*2}$ as large as possible and thus minimize σ_b^2.

To see that among alternative linear unbiased estimators b is best, consider a general linear estimator $\tilde{b} = \sum_{i=1}^{n} c_i y_i$, whose variance is given by

$$(2.5.5) \qquad \sigma_{\tilde{b}}^2 = \text{Var}\left[\sum c_i y_i\right] = \sum c_i^2 \text{Var}(y_i)$$

$$= \sigma^2 \sum c_i^2.$$

For $\tilde{b}$ to be unbiased, $E(\tilde{b}) = \beta$, which will be so only if $E(\tilde{b}) = E[\sum c_i y_i] = E[\sum c_i(\alpha + \beta x_i + \epsilon_i)] = \alpha \sum c_i + \beta \sum c_i x_i + \sum [E(c_i \epsilon_i)] = \beta$. (Since the c_i's are scalars, $E(c_i \epsilon_i) = c_i E(\epsilon_i) = 0$, so $\sum [E(c_i \epsilon_i)] = 0$.) Then $\sum c_i = 0$ and $\sum c_i x_i = 1$ are required conditions for $E(\tilde{b}) = \beta$ whatever are α and β. Subject to these conditions we wish to show that (2.5.5) is a minimum when $\tilde{b} = b$.

To minimize $\sigma_{\tilde{b}}^2$ is to minimize $\sum c_i^2$, subject to $\sum c_i = 0$ and $\sum c_i x_i = 1$, a straightforward Lagrangean problem. To begin, define the Lagrangean function

(2.5.6) $$H = \sum c_i^2 + \lambda_1 [\sum c_i x_i - 1] + \lambda_2 [\sum c_i].$$

We require the minimum of $\sum c_i^2$ at a point where $\sum c_i x_i = 1$ and $\sum c_i = 0$, which is found by differentiating H with respect to each c_i, λ_1, and λ_2. The resulting system of first-order equations is

(2.5.7) (a) $$\frac{\partial H}{\partial c_i} = 2c_i + \lambda_1 x_i + \lambda_2 = 0, \qquad i = 1, \ldots, n,$$

   (b) $$\frac{\partial H}{\partial \lambda_1} = \sum c_i x_i - 1 = 0,$$

   (c) $$\frac{\partial H}{\partial \lambda_2} = \sum c_i = 0.$$

Solving this system of equations yields the result $c_i = x_i^* / \sum x^{*2}$.† Plugging these c_i's into $\tilde{b} = \sum c_i y_i$ gives $\tilde{b} = b$. What we have proved is that under the assumptions of classical regression in a two-variable case the unbiased linear estimator with smallest variance is the least-squares estimator. This result is the Gauss-Markov theorem.

The implications of all this are that finding the b that minimizes $\sum e^2$ (the least-squares criterion) also yields the "best" (most precise) linear unbiased estimator of β. By minimizing S_e^2, which measures in some sense the "badness-of-fit" of the regression line (assuming a line is the proper population relation), we have coincidentally maximized the precision of estimation.‡

To show "bestness" for a as an estimator of α is now straightforward. The development is as follows:

(2.5.8) $$\sigma_a^2 = \text{Var}\{\bar{y} - b\bar{x}\}$$
$$= \text{Var}(\bar{y}) + \bar{x}^2 \text{Var}(b) - 2\bar{x} \text{Cov}(\bar{y}, b)$$

conditional on x. The expansion is the result of a theorem on variances, which states that for a difference between random variables, say $z = x - y$, $\sigma_z^2 = \sigma_x^2 + \sigma_y^2 - 2\sigma_{xy}$ with σ_{xy} the covariance between x and y. Now since $\bar{y} = (1/n) \sum y$, and $\sigma_y^2 = \sigma^2$ conditional on x, we see again the familiar expression for the variance of the sample mean, that $\sigma_{\bar{y}}^2 = \sigma^2/n$. From (2.5.4), $\sigma_b^2 = \sigma^2/\sum x^{*2}$. To complete (2.5.8) it remains to show $\text{Cov}(\bar{y}, b) = 0$.

A brief digression will serve our intuition about $\text{Cov}(\bar{y}, b)$. Consider the SRM $y_i = a + bx_i + e_i$ with the *solved* value for a inserted. Putting $a = \bar{y} - b\bar{x}$ into the SRM gives $y_i = \bar{y} + b(x_i - \bar{x}) + e_i$, or by transforming $\bar{y}$

---

† From (2.5.7a), $c_i = -(\lambda_1 x_i + \lambda_2)/2$, which when inserted into (2.5.7c) gives $\lambda_2 = -\lambda_1 \bar{x}$, or $c_i = -(\lambda_1/2)(x_i - \bar{x})$. Using this in (2.5.7b), $-(\lambda_1/2) \sum (x_i - \bar{x}) x_i = 1$, or $-\lambda_1/2 = 1/\sum x^{*2}$. Finally, $c_i = (x_i - \bar{x})/\sum x^{*2}$.

‡ There are other linear estimators—though not unbiased ones—with smaller variance. For example, the estimator $.5b$ has variance $.25\sigma_b^2$.

to the left side of the equation, $y_i^* = bx_i^* + e_i$. The restriction that determines b is $\sum ex = \sum ex^* = 0$. The fact that the point of sample means *always* lies on this SRF (a consequence of $\sum e = 0$) allows us to view the estimation problem in two ways: either we use $y_i = a + bx_i + e_i$ and solve for a and b to satisfy $\sum e = 0$ and $\sum ex = 0$, or we restrict the myriad of possible regression lines to a choice between those which pass through $(\bar{y}, \bar{x})$ and find the one (determined by its slope) that minimizes the sum of squared vertical deviations of actual values from it. Considered this way, we should expect the determination of b given x (and thus $\bar{x}$) not to depend on $\bar{y}$, so that Cov $(\bar{y}, b) = 0$.

More formally, we can make use of another theorem on variances to prove the result. The theorem says that for two arbitrary linear functions of the same variables, say $C = \sum c_i y_i$ and $D = \sum d_i y_i$, their covariance is given by

$$(2.5.9) \qquad \text{Cov}\,(C, D) = \sum_{i=1}^{n} \sum_{j=1}^{n} c_i d_j \,\text{Cov}\,(y_i, y_j).$$

For our problem, $\bar{y} = \sum d_i y_i$ with $d_i = 1/n$, and $b = \sum c_i y_i$ with $c_i = x_i^* / \sum x^{*2}$. Also, by the random-sampling assumption Cov $(y_i, y_j) = 0$ for $i \neq j$, and by the constant-variance assumption, Var $(y_i) = \sigma^2$ for all i. Using this information in (2.5.9),

$$\text{Cov}\,(\bar{y}, b) = \sum_{i=1}^{n} \left(\frac{1}{n}\right)\left(\frac{x_i^*}{\sum x^{*2}}\right)\sigma^2 = \frac{\sigma^2}{n} \sum_{i=1}^{n} \left(\frac{x_i^*}{\sum x^{*2}}\right) = 0$$

because $\sum x^* = 0$.

As a result of this conclusion, (2.5.8) can be completed. In its final form, we find

$$(2.5.10) \qquad \sigma_a^2 = \frac{\sigma^2}{n} + \bar{x}^2 \frac{\sigma^2}{\sum x^{*2}} = \frac{\sigma^2}{n} + \bar{x}^2 \sigma_b^2.$$

Since σ^2, n, and $\bar{x}$ are fixed, σ_a^2 is minimized when σ_b^2 is at a minimum. This occurs when the least-squares estimator, b, is used.

A final matter of interest is the presentation of an appropriate measure of precision for a conditional mean estimate at some arbitrary x-value, say x_0. The predicted conditional mean at x_0 is $\hat{y}_0 = a + bx_0$, with variance

$$(2.5.11) \qquad \sigma_{\hat{y}_0}^2 = \text{Var}\,(a + bx_0)$$
$$= \text{Var}\,[\bar{y} + b(x_0 - \bar{x})]$$

by inserting $a = \bar{y} - b\bar{x}$. Now this variance determination looks very much like the one involved in (2.5.8) for σ_a^2. Since Cov $(\bar{y}, b) = 0$,

(2.5.12)
$$\sigma^2_{\hat{y}_0} = \text{Var}(\bar{y}) + (x_0 - \bar{x})^2 \text{Var}(b)$$
$$= \frac{\sigma^2}{n} + (x_0 - \bar{x})^2 \frac{\sigma^2}{\sum x^{*2}}.$$

Viewed through (2.5.12), precise estimation of a particular conditional mean is obtained through least-squares estimates of the parameters α and β. The sample-design comment made previously is relevant here also. To make $\sigma^2_{\hat{y}_0}$ as small as possible, $\sum x^{*2}$ should be made as large as possible. Otherwise, without control over the observation points on x, (2.5.12) is a minimum at $x_0 = \bar{x}$. At $\bar{x}$, $\hat{y} = \bar{y}$ and $\sigma^2_{\hat{y}} = \sigma^2/n$. Movements away from $\bar{x}$ symmetrically increase $\sigma^2_{\hat{y}_0}$ in proportion to $(x_0 - \bar{x})^2$, the square of the difference between the prediction point x_0 and the sample mean, $\bar{x}$.

Visually, if we plot bands of prediction error, $\hat{y}_0 \pm \sigma_{\hat{y}_0}$, as in Fig. 2.3, we see the suggested relationship clearly. The "sense" of why our ability to predict $E(y \mid x)$ precisely trails off as x_0 moves from the point of means $(\bar{y}, \bar{x})$ derives from the fact that the difference between any given conditional mean and the grand mean of y is estimated from the sample. As the regression model partitions the total variance in y into variation within each conditional distribution and variation of the conditional means around the grand mean, at the point $\bar{x}$ this second source of variation is zero: the conditional distribution at $\bar{x}$ has $E(y)$ as its expected value. Prediction at points away from $\bar{x}$ involves an estimation of the slope of the regression line *in addition* to the calculation of $\bar{y}$, the unbiased estimate of $E(y)$. Succinctly put, our ability to estimate precisely from the regression line falls off greatly as we move out of the range of the sample data. In particular, it is best at the "fulcrum point" of the sample, the point of means $(\bar{y}, \bar{x})$.

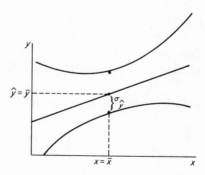

Fig. 2.3

One-Standard-Deviation Prediction
Bands for the Estimated Conditional
Mean in Two-Variable Regression

2.6 ESTIMATION OF σ^2

Before we can hope to develop an inference theory for the regression model, the variance formulas of the previous section must be made operational. Referring again to the classical inference problem for a population mean based on the mean of a random sample, recall in that case also the population variance is generally unknown, to be estimated from the sample. The important relationship that ties the variance of the sampling distribution of the mean for samples of a given size to the variance of the population frequency distribution is $\sigma_{\bar{y}}^2 = \sigma_y^2/n$.† If we can estimate σ_y^2 precisely, we will also estimate $\sigma_{\bar{y}}^2$ precisely.

The development of an appropriate estimator for σ_y^2 in this example situation usually is presented as follows. By the analogy principle, the sample variance, say $s^{*2} = (1/n) \sum (y - \bar{y})^2$, is suggested as a possible estimator for σ_y^2. And, it is a straightforward matter to show that s^{*2} defined in this way is a biased estimator of σ_y^2. In fact,

$$E(s^{*2}) = \left(\frac{n-1}{n}\right)\sigma_y^2.$$

So by the simple alteration $s^2 = [n/(n-1)]s^{*2}$ we can easily produce an unbiased estimator of σ_y^2, namely s^2.

S_e^2 in the regression model provides an estimator for σ^2 by analogy, as did s^{*2} for σ_y^2 in the example above. Because the sample must be used to calculate a and b, however, S_e^2 can also be expected to be a biased estimator of σ^2 for the same reason as in the case of s^{*2}, above. The key concept involved in these relationships is the notion of "degress of freedom" in estimation, a matter we will take up more formally in the next section.

For the two-variable regression model it is not difficult to prove directly that $E(S_e^2) \neq \sigma^2$ and to find an alternative estimator in the sample that is unbiased. To begin, write S_e^2 in terms of $y_i = \alpha + \beta x_i + \epsilon_i$ and $\hat{y}_i = a + bx_i$, as

$$(2.6.1) \quad S_e^2 = \frac{1}{n} \sum (\alpha + \beta x + \epsilon - a - bx)^2$$

$$= \frac{1}{n} \sum \{(\alpha - a) + x(\beta - b) + \epsilon\}^2$$

$$= \frac{1}{n} \sum \{(\alpha - a)^2 + x^2(\beta - b)^2 + \epsilon^2 + 2x(\alpha - a)(\beta - b)$$

$$+ 2\epsilon(\alpha - a) + 2x(\beta - b)\epsilon\}.$$

† Under the assumption of sampling with replacement or from a population of "infinite" size.

Upon taking expectations, (2.6.1) becomes

$$(2.6.2) \qquad E(S_e^2) = \frac{1}{n} \sum \left\{ \sigma_a^2 + x^2\sigma_b^2 + \sigma^2 - 2\frac{\bar{x}x\sigma^2}{\sum x^{*2}} - 2\frac{\sigma^2}{n} \right.$$
$$\left. + 2\frac{x^*\bar{x}\sigma^2}{\sum x^{*2}} - 2\frac{xx^*\sigma^2}{\sum x^{*2}} \right\}.$$

Of the last four terms, $-2\bar{x}x\sigma^2/\sum x^{*2}$ is the expected value of $2x(\alpha - a)$ $\cdot(\beta - b)$, the next two terms form the expectation of $2\epsilon(\alpha - a)$, and finally, $E[2x(\beta - b)\epsilon] = -2xx^*\sigma^2/\sum x^{*2}$, all of which the reader may verify. Upon summing, $\sum (2x^*\bar{x}\sigma^2/\sum x^{*2}) = 0$ by virtue of the fact that $\sum x^* = 0$. The remaining terms yield

$$(2.6.3) \qquad E(S_e^2) = \sigma_a^2 + \sigma_b^2\left(\frac{1}{n}\sum x^2 - 2\bar{x}^2\right) + \sigma^2 - 4\frac{\sigma^2}{n}.$$

When σ_a^2 and σ_b^2 are appropriately substituted for in terms of σ^2, (2.6.3) simplifies to

$$(2.6.4) \qquad E(S_e^2) = \sigma^2\left(\frac{n-2}{n}\right).$$

Hence, S_e^2 is not an unbiased estimator of σ^2. However, if we form $\mathscr{S}^2 = [n/(n-2)]S_e^2$, it is clear from (2.6.4) that *it* is unbiased.

There are elegant and more general ways to demonstrate this result, but they rest on more than elementary algebra and the calculus of expectations. We return to this matter in the next chapter, when we consider the multiple regression model.

To put the main result of this section to use, we would unbiasedly estimate σ_b^2 [from (2.5.4)] by

$$(2.6.5) \qquad \hat{\sigma}_b^2 = \frac{\mathscr{S}^2}{\sum x^{*2}},$$

σ_a^2 [from (2.5.10)] by

$$(2.6.6) \qquad \hat{\sigma}_a^2 = \frac{\mathscr{S}^2}{n} + \bar{x}^2\frac{\mathscr{S}^2}{\sum x^{*2}},$$

and $\sigma_{\hat{y}_0}^2$ [from (2.5.12)] by

$$(2.6.7) \qquad \hat{\sigma}_{\hat{y}_0}^2 = \frac{\mathscr{S}^2}{n} + (x_0 - \bar{x})^2\frac{\mathscr{S}^2}{\sum x^{*2}}.$$

The prediction bands of Fig. 2.3 can therefore be estimated with (2.6.7).

2.7 DISTRIBUTION THEORY
AND INFERENCE

Up to this point nothing has been assumed or said about the *form* of the conditional distributions, only about their first two moments. By inserting $\mathscr{S}^2$ into the variance formulas for σ_a^2, σ_b^2, or $\sigma_{\hat{y}_0}^2$ operational measures of precision for the regression model are obtained, and for forecasting purposes we may appropriately stop at that point, relying for statements of precision on r_{xy}^2 and the estimated version of $\sigma_{\hat{y}_0}^2$. In order to *infer* something about a particular conditional mean, α, or β, however, such descriptive measures are not enough. For example, one may want to make assertions about the value for β, or test a formal hypothesis about one or more of the model's parameters. Such pursuits require a knowledge of the distribution of the relevant sample estimators, $\hat{y}$, a, and b. Since these sample statistics are all random variables related to ϵ, however, a distributional theory for the regression model rests solely on the distribution of ϵ. As is the case in classical (and other) statistical inference, inference about an unknown parameter (or parameters) takes place in the context of a *given* distribution. There are no procedures that *imply* the appropriate distribution for a particular problem.† Thus the *distribution assumption* for a statistical model is critical.

For large samples, sample estimators formed as weighted averages of independent random variables are, under very general conditions, distributed according to the normal distribution. This result is best known as the *central limit theorem*. It does not require the set of variables involved to possess the same distributions, nor do we need to know their form. But for any given problem it is difficult to predict when the sample size is large enough to allow use of this theoretical result.

In many instances the problem itself, the sampling procedure, or a combination of factors may meet the prerequisite conditions for some theoretical distribution to be the appropriate sampling distribution. For example, sampling for a binary attribute in a population using sampling with replacement yields the binomial distribution for the sample proportion of individuals possessing the characteristic of interest. Under sampling without replacement, the correct theoretical distribution is the hypergeometric. The normal distribution, on the other hand, except from the central limit theorem, is not *derived* as the appropriate theoretical distribution of anything. Often it is assumed to be the appropriate distributional form, sometimes on the basis of empirical correspondence to observed data and

---

† There are tests of "goodness-of-fit," by which an a priori distribution can be refuted as the appropriate underlying distribution for an observed sample. No objective procedures exist for "choosing" among distributions, however.

other times "on faith." It is referred to traditionally as the "normal distribution of error," hence its connection with the regression model and its "error," ϵ.

As a distribution of errors, the normal distribution requires certain things of the process generating the "errors." For instance, the range of errors implied is $(-\infty, \infty)$, and the distribution is symmetric. It is just as probable that an error of two standard deviation units (from a mean of zero) or more will be made in the positive direction as it is in the negative direction, under a normal distribution. The old idea of human errors in a long sequence of arithmetic calculations "canceling out" is just this symmetry notion. Rules for rounding numbers are similarly based on the symmetry of the distribution of errors.

A simple specification giving rise to a regression model for which the normal distribution is not clearly inappropriate is to assume that were two variables Y and x both to be measured accurately, there would be a "perfect" (nonstochastic) relation between them, $Y = \alpha + \beta x$, but because of measurement error in observing Y, we observe $y = Y + \epsilon$, where ϵ is "measurement error."† With the appropriate substitution, the PRM is $y = \alpha + \beta x + \epsilon$. So long as it is reasonable to expect measurement errors to cancel out "on the average," to assume that they are distributed symmetrically and that the likelihood of error is inversely related to the magnitude of error, the normal distribution is a plausible model for the distribution of ϵ.

Since the regression model in economics is generally an expression of some economic "structure" or set of causal relationships flowing from the independent to the dependent variable, in this two-variable case the question arises whether the model has been adequately specified with respect to other important independent variables, so that measurement error is the only remaining source of disturbance of the relationship between y and x. This raises the further points of whether the lines of causation are appropriately drawn, since it *does* make a difference in the determination of the slope coefficient (not the correlation coefficient) whether y is regressed on x or x on y—the least-squares slopes so obtained are not generally their mutual reciprocals—and whether there is joint causation, in which case a single equation cannot be expected to adequately capture the underlying structure. These specific questions can be analyzed rather well with regard to how such problems affect the properties of least-squares estimates. Their effect on a normal specification of the error distribution is less clear.

With these cautions noted, suppose we assume that the normal distribution does characterize the conditional behavior of ϵ. By specification, then, $\epsilon \sim N(0, \sigma^2)$, where the notation $\sim$ means "distributed as," and $(0, \sigma^2)$ are the parameters needed to completely specify the distribution, namely its mean and variance. Since ϵ is now regarded as a normal random variable

---

† Recall, however, our earlier remarks on this specification.

conditional on x, the conditional distribution of y is likewise normal because $y = \text{constant} + \epsilon$. So, $y \sim N(\alpha + \beta x, \sigma^2)$. y is a very elementary *linear* function of ϵ, and although it is clear that adding a constant to ϵ has no effect on the form of the distribution in moving from $f(\epsilon)$ to $f(\text{constant} + \epsilon)$, other transformations of ϵ are of interest to us here, whose distributions may not be so obvious.

The set of transformations of interest and their distributions are contained in five distribution theorems, and represent the normal "family" of distributions. We present them here without proof.†

THEOREM 1

IF y_i ($i = 1, \ldots, n$) ARE NORMALLY AND INDEPENDENTLY DISTRIBUTED RANDOM VARIABLES WITH MEANS $E(y_i) = \theta_i$ AND VARIANCES $E(y_i - \theta_i)^2 = \sigma_i^2$, THEN THE WEIGHTED SUM $\sum w_i y_i$, WHERE NOT ALL $w_i = 0$, IS NORMALLY DISTRIBUTED WITH MEAN $\sum w_i \theta_i$ AND VARIANCE $\sum w_i^2 \sigma_i^2$.

THEOREM 2

IF z_i ($i = 1, \ldots, m$) ARE NORMALLY AND INDEPENDENTLY DISTRIBUTED RANDOM VARIABLES WITH MEAN ZERO AND UNIT VARIANCE, THEN $\sum z_i^2$ IS DISTRIBUTED ACCORDING TO χ^2 (CHI-SQUARE) WITH m DEGREES OF FREEDOM, WRITTEN χ_m^2. IF ONLY $q \leq m$ OF THE z_i'S ARE INDEPENDENT, $\sum z_i^2 \sim \chi_q^2$.

THEOREM 3

IF u_i ($i = 1, \ldots, n$) ARE INDEPENDENTLY DISTRIBUTED RANDOM VARIABLES, EACH ACCORDING TO χ^2 WITH m_i DEGREES OF FREEDOM, THEN $\sum u_i$ IS ALSO χ^2 WITH $m = \sum m_i$ DEGREES OF FREEDOM.

THEOREM 4

IF z IS NORMAL $(0, 1)$, u IS χ_m^2 AND INDEPENDENT OF z, THEN

$$t = \frac{z}{\sqrt{\dfrac{u}{m}}}$$

HAS THE "t" DISTRIBUTION WITH m DEGREES OF FREEDOM.

THEOREM 5

IF u_1 AND u_2 ARE INDEPENDENTLY DISTRIBUTED χ^2 VARIABLES WITH m_1 AND m_2 DEGREES OF FREEDOM, RESPECTIVELY, THEN

† Most books on mathematical statistics will contain these proofs. See, for example, A. M. Mood and F. Graybill, *Introduction to the Theory of Statistics* (New York: McGraw-Hill, 1963), or John E. Freund, *Mathematical Statistics* (Englewood Cliffs: Prentice-Hall, 1962).

$$F = \frac{u_1/m_1}{u_2/m_2}$$

HAS THE "F" DISTRIBUTION WITH m_1 AND m_2 DEGREES OF FREEDOM.

To begin, let us deduce from these theorems the distribution of b, the least-squares slope, beginning with the initial assumption $\epsilon \sim N(0, \sigma^2)$. b is a linear function of the $\{\epsilon_i\}$, namely $b = \beta + \sum x^*\epsilon/\sum x^{*2}$, from (2.5.2). Because of our random-sampling assumption, the ϵ_i's are independent, so Theorem 1 can be used to conclude $b \sim N(\beta, \sigma_b^2)$. The normal distribution can therefore be used to produce a confidence interval around β with knowledge of σ_b^2,

$$(2.7.1) \qquad \Pr\{b - z_{\alpha/2}\sigma_b \le \beta \le b + z_{\alpha/2}\sigma_b\} = 1 - \alpha,$$

where $z_{\alpha/2}$ is the abscissa on the standard normal distribution (mean zero, unit variance) which cuts off $\alpha/2$ proportion of the area in one of the tails; that is, $\Pr\{z \ge z_{\alpha/2}\} = \alpha/2$.† A formal hypothesis test of $H: \beta = \beta_0$ versus an appropriate alternative may be carried out as well, using $z = (b - \beta_0)/\sigma_b$ as a test statistic, and comparing its observed value in the sample to the appropriate "critical" values taken from the standard normal distribution. For a two-sided alternative, $H_A: \beta \ne \beta_0$ at level of significance $\alpha = .05$, for instance, the rejection points are ± 1.96.

As a practical matter, of course, σ^2 and hence σ_b^2 are unknown. The development of the distribution for $z = (b - \beta)/\sigma_b$ with an estimate of σ_b inserted is as follows. Since $b \sim N(\beta, \sigma_b^2)$, $(b - \beta) \sim N(0, \sigma_b^2)$ and $(b - \beta)/\sigma_b \sim N(0, 1)$. Next, we consider the distribution of the sum-of-squares $\sum e^2$, or

$$(2.7.2) \qquad \sum e^2 = (n - 2)\mathscr{S}^2 = \sum(\alpha + \beta x + \epsilon - a - bx)^2$$

as in (2.6.1). Writing out each sample residual e_i in this way makes it easy to see that $E(e_i) = 0$, because $E(a) = \alpha$, $E(b) = \beta$, and $E(\epsilon) = 0$. Also, the variance of each e_i is determined on the basis of the development of (2.6.1) and (2.6.2) to be σ^2. Finally, each e_i possesses a normal distribution because it is formed as a linear combination of other normally distributed variables. To make use of Theorem 2 we need only convert each e_i to a standard normal basis by dividing by σ and ascertain the number of independent variables in the set $\{e_i\}$. Specifically, we form

$$(2.7.3) \qquad \frac{(n - 2)\mathscr{S}^2}{\sigma^2} = \sum_{i=1}^{n}\left(\frac{e_i}{\sigma}\right)^2 = \frac{1}{\sigma^2}\sum_{i=1}^{n}e_i^2,$$

---

† The reader should not confuse this use of the symbol α with the α of the linear PRF. Each is "conventional."

which is a sum of n squared standard normal variables. According to Theorem 2, (2.7.3) is χ^2 with a number of degrees of freedom equal to the number of independent variables in the sum. This is the definition of degrees of freedom. "Independence" in this sense can usefully be thought of as follows: the sampling procedure insures independence for the $\{\epsilon_i\}$, but our *use* of their observed values imposes two effective constraints or restrictions on them, namely $\sum e = 0$ and $\sum ex = 0$. So, not *all* the $\{e_i\}$ are really free to vary; two of them are subject to restriction in order to calculate $\mathscr{S}^2$ from the sample. The number of degrees of freedom in $\mathscr{S}^2$ is $(n-2)$; hence

$$(2.7.4) \qquad \frac{(n-2)\mathscr{S}^2}{\sigma^2} \sim \chi^2_{(n-2)}.$$

The final step is to form the ratio of $(b-\beta)/\sigma_b$ to the square root of this χ^2 variable divided by its degrees of freedom. According to Theorem 4,

$$(2.7.5) \qquad t = \frac{(b-\beta_0)/\sigma_b}{\sqrt{\mathscr{S}^2/\sigma^2}} \sim t_{(n-2)}.$$

Simplifying (2.7.5),

$$(2.7.6) \qquad t = \frac{b-\beta}{\sigma/\sqrt{\sum x^{*2}}} \bigg/ \frac{\mathscr{S}}{\sigma} = \frac{b-\beta}{\mathscr{S}/\sqrt{\sum x^{*2}}}$$

$$= \frac{b-\beta}{\hat{\sigma}_b}.$$

A formal hypothesis test or an interval estimate of β can be made using the t-distribution, substituting, for example, in (2.7.1) the correct "t" cut-off points and $\hat{\sigma}_b$ for σ_b. By the central limit theorem, as sample size becomes large the t-distribution can be satisfactorily approximated by the normal so that at some point (usually taken to be $n \geq 60$) normal cut-off points may be used with nominal error.

The most popular hypothesis test involving β in economic models is the hypothesis of "no relation," or $H: \beta = 0$. For this test the proper statistic is [from (2.7.6)] $b/\hat{\sigma}_b$, the ratio of b to its estimated standard error, the so-called "t-ratio."

A parallel development to our inference results for b yields an inference theory for a as an estimator of α. $a \sim N(\alpha, \sigma_a^2)$, since $\bar{y}$ and b are normally and independently distributed.

An argument parallel to the one used in moving from (2.7.2) through (2.7.4) concludes that $(a-\alpha)/\hat{\sigma}_a \sim t_{(n-2)}$. Again, the t-distribution is used to do inference for α, either in terms of a confidence interval or a formal statistical test. Previously we showed that $\text{Cov}(\bar{y}, b) = 0$. While zero covariance does not generally imply independence, statistical independence implies zero covariance. An exception to the first part of the statement is the normal distribution. Under the joint normal distribution which governs the behavior of $\bar{y}$ and b, their zero covariance implies their statistical independence.

Finally, another parallel development gives inferential content to Fig. 2.3, and allows us to interpret the one-sigma confidence bands there as an interval that contains a given conditional mean $E(y|x_0)$ with probability .68 for large samples (from the normal distribution) and slightly smaller probability (depending on sample size) in general (from the t-distribution).

2.8 CONSTRUCTION OF F-TESTS

Although in two-variable regression the hypothesis of "no relation" or "no regression" is equivalent to the hypothesis $H: \beta = 0$, the multiple regression framework invites other tests which cannot be characterized with a single parameter. So, while of no immediate consequence, we introduce here an alternative method for testing $H: \beta = 0$ which will be of great usefulness later. The development is of an F-test, making use of Theorem 5.

To make at least some attempt at paralleling conventional statistical notation and development, the F-test is the main inferential technique in the *analysis of variance*, of which regression is a special case. Generally speaking, in analysis-of-variance problems primary interest focuses not on the estimation of regression coefficients but on the significance of the independent variable, or variables, in explaining variation in y. In testing $H: \beta = 0$, for example, a comparison is made between the amounts of unexplained variation or error variance, allowing the value of β to be unspecified and under the hypothesis $\beta = 0$. Thus two *models* are compared, $y = \alpha + \beta x + \epsilon$ and $y = \alpha + \epsilon$, with all other characteristics identical. If the hypothesis is true, one would *expect* sample-error variance under both models to be the same. Otherwise, one model will have substantially smaller unexplained variance in the sample. To tell when this difference becomes "large enough" to reject the hypothesis at some predescribed level of significance is the role of the test procedure.

The regression model under "no restrictions" consists of several specifications and relevant results, which we shall put under the mnemonic Ω.

(2.8.1) Ω: Model under no restrictions: $\begin{cases} y = \alpha + \beta x + \epsilon, \\ E(y|x) = \alpha + \beta x. \end{cases}$

$$SS_\Omega = (n-2)\mathscr{S}^2 = \sum_{i=1}^{n} e_i^2.$$

$$E[SS_\Omega/(n-2)] = \sigma^2.$$

The notation SS_Ω is read: "error sum-of-squares under Ω." The statement $E[SS_\Omega/(n-2)] = E(\mathscr{S}^2) = \sigma^2$ is the result given in Section 2.6.

Under the hypothesis $H: \beta = 0$ a different model is supposed to hold, whose specifications are given as Ω with H imposed. A popular way of characterizing this is, from set-theoretic terminology, $H \cap \Omega$. For brevity we shall just use "H" to mean Ω with whatever modifications are imposed by the hypothesis. So,

(2.8.2) H: Model under H: $\beta = 0$: $\begin{cases} y = \alpha + \epsilon, \\ E(y) = \alpha. \end{cases}$

$$SS_H = \sum_{i=1}^{n} (y_i - \bar{y})^2 = nS_y^2.$$

$$E[SS_H/(n-1)] = \sigma^2.$$

The results reported under H are just the familiar definition of sample variance and the statement that it is an unbiased estimate of the population variance σ^2. In this model, note that the population variance and the so-called error variance coincide. The sample mean, $\bar{y}$, is the least-squares estimate of $\alpha = E(y)$.

Now if H: $\beta = 0$ is true, we would expect $SS_H = SS_\Omega$. SS_H will generally be greater than SS_Ω. The reasoning here is the same used to argue $S_y^2 \geq S_e^2$ for the regression model. The objective is to construct a test for determining when SS_H is "too much" larger than SS_Ω. In both instances, if a normal $(0, \sigma^2)$ distribution for ϵ is assumed, we know:

(2.8.3) $\dfrac{SS_\Omega}{\sigma^2} \sim \chi^2_{(n-2)}, \qquad \dfrac{SS_H}{\sigma^2} \sim \chi^2_{(n-1)}.$

We would like to apply Theorem 5, but it so happens that these two χ^2 variables are not independent. The demonstration of this fact is not easy, and we will not attempt it here. Some insight is obtained, however, if we consider $SS_H - SS_\Omega = nS_{\hat{y}}^2$. We see that this SS *is* independent of SS_Ω because of the partitioning of S_y^2 into S_e^2 and $S_{\hat{y}}^2$. Since $\text{Cov}(e, \hat{y}) = 0$ and e and $\hat{y}$ are normally distributed variables, they are independent variables. Therefore the variables $[\sum (\hat{y} - \bar{y})^2]$ and $[\sum e^2]$ will be independently distributed. That $\sum (\hat{y} - \bar{y})^2$ is a sum of n squared normal variables each of which has zero mean should be clear. That each of the variables $\hat{y}_i - \bar{y}$ has variance σ^2 is also obvious from (2.8.3). Accepting this fact we know that $\sum (\hat{y} - \bar{y})^2/\sigma^2$ has a chi-square distribution independent of SS_Ω.

The one remaining detail prior to an application of Theorem 5 is to determine the number of degrees of freedom in $SS_H - SS_\Omega$. Unfortunately, the development of the important theoretical result needed at this point is beyond the scope of this book. The result asserts that SS_H in fact contains SS_Ω as a "proper subset." That is, in light of Theorem 2 the $(n-2)$ squared independent standard normal variates in SS_Ω/σ^2 also appear in the $(n-1)$ squared independent standard normal variates of SS_H/σ^2. Thus their difference contains only *one* squared standard normal variable, and the distribution of $(SS_H - SS_\Omega)/\sigma^2$ is χ_1^2. As a general rule, the degrees of freedom in $(SS_H - SS_\Omega)/\sigma^2$ *whatever* H will be given by the difference in the degrees of freedom in SS_H/σ^2 and SS_Ω/σ^2.

Using the above result in our current problem, by Theorem 5

$$(2.8.4) \qquad\qquad F = \frac{(SS_H - SS_\Omega)/1}{SS_\Omega/(n - 2)} \sim F_{1,\,n-2}.$$

By substituting $nS_\hat{y}^2 = nb^2S_x^2$ and $SS_\Omega/(n - 2) = \mathcal{S}^2$, we find

$$(2.8.5) \qquad\qquad F = \frac{nb^2S_x^2}{\mathcal{S}^2} = \frac{b^2}{\left(\dfrac{\mathcal{S}^2}{\sum x^{*2}}\right)}$$

$$= \frac{b^2}{\hat{\sigma}_b^2}.$$

This F-statistic is the squared t-ratio from before, and as a general proposition, the square root of an F-ratio with one degree of freedom in the numerator is distributed according to "t". Under H we would expect $(SS_H - SS_\Omega) = 0$. Rejection of H is on the upper tail of the F-distribution (corresponding to a two-tailed t-test of $H: \beta = 0$ versus $H_A: \beta \neq 0$).

2.9 PROBLEMS AND ANSWERS

GENERAL PROBLEMS

1. (Section 2.2) Consider the following set of conditional distributions of y given x:

x \ y	1	2	3	4	5	Σ
-1	$\frac{1}{3}$	0	$\frac{1}{3}$	0	$\frac{1}{3}$	1
0	0	$\frac{1}{3}$	$\frac{1}{3}$	$\frac{1}{3}$	0	1
1	0	$\frac{1}{2}$	0	$\frac{1}{2}$	0	1

and the marginal distribution of x: $f(x = -1) = f(x = 0) = f(x = 1) = \frac{1}{3}$.

    a. Calculate the conditional means $E(y\,|\,x)$.

    b. Calculate the unconditional means $E(x)$, $E(y)$, and $E(xy)$.

    c. Are y and x stochastically independent? Are they mean independent? Uncorrelated?

    d. Tabulate the conditional distribution of $\epsilon = y - E(y\,|\,x)$, and note that $E(\epsilon\,|\,x) = E(\epsilon) = E(x\epsilon) = 0$.

e. Consider an alternative to the population regression function, say $g^*(x) = \{2$ if $x = -1$; 3 if $x = 0$; 4 if $x = 1\}$, and compute $E(\epsilon^* \mid x)$, $E(\epsilon^*)$, and $E(\epsilon^* x)$.

ANSWERS:

(a) Conditional means, $E(y \mid x)$:

$$E(y \mid x = -1) = (1)(\tfrac{1}{3}) + (3)(\tfrac{1}{3}) + (5)(\tfrac{1}{3}) = 3,$$
$$E(y \mid x = 0) = (2)(\tfrac{1}{3}) + (3)(\tfrac{1}{3}) + (4)(\tfrac{1}{3}) = 3,$$
$$E(y \mid x = 1) = (2)(\tfrac{1}{2}) + (4)(\tfrac{1}{2}) = 3.$$

(b) Unconditional means:

$$E(x) = (-1)(\tfrac{1}{3}) + (0)(\tfrac{1}{3}) + (1)(\tfrac{1}{3}) = 0.$$

Joint distribution $f(x, y) = f(y \mid x)f(x)$:

x \ y	1	2	3	4	5	$f(x)$
-1	$\tfrac{1}{9}$	0	$\tfrac{1}{9}$	0	$\tfrac{1}{9}$	$\tfrac{1}{3}$
0	0	$\tfrac{1}{9}$	$\tfrac{1}{9}$	$\tfrac{1}{9}$	0	$\tfrac{1}{3}$
1	0	$\tfrac{1}{6}$	0	$\tfrac{1}{6}$	0	$\tfrac{1}{3}$
$f(y)$	$\tfrac{1}{9}$	$\tfrac{5}{18}$	$\tfrac{2}{9}$	$\tfrac{5}{18}$	$\tfrac{1}{9}$	1

Therefore

$$E(y) = \sum yf(y)$$
$$= (1)(\tfrac{1}{9}) + (2)(\tfrac{5}{18}) + (3)(\tfrac{2}{9}) + (4)(\tfrac{5}{18}) + (5)(\tfrac{1}{9}) = 3,$$

and

$$E(xy) = \sum \sum xyf(x, y)$$
$$= (-1)(\tfrac{1}{9}) + (-3)(\tfrac{1}{9}) + (-5)(\tfrac{1}{9}) + (2)(\tfrac{1}{6}) + (4)(\tfrac{1}{6}) = 0.$$

(c) y and x are not stochastically independent, since $f(y \mid x) \neq f(y)$ (from given tables). y *is* mean-independent of x, since $E(y \mid x) = E(y) = 3$. Is x mean-independent of y?

Consider the conditional distributions of x given y—that is, $f(x \mid y)$. They are, by using $f(x \mid y) = f(x, y)/f(y)$,

x \ y	1	2	3	4	5
-1	1	0	$\tfrac{1}{2}$	0	1
0	0	$\tfrac{2}{5}$	$\tfrac{1}{2}$	$\tfrac{2}{5}$	0
1	0	$\tfrac{3}{5}$	0	$\tfrac{3}{5}$	0
Σ	1	1	1	1	1

Using $E(x|y) = \sum xf(x|y)$, we have

$$E(x|y = 1) = -1,$$
$$E(x|y = 2) = \tfrac{3}{5},$$
$$E(x|y = 3) = -\tfrac{1}{2},$$
$$E(x|y = 4) = \tfrac{3}{5},$$
$$E(x|y = 5) = -1.$$

Therefore, x is *not* mean-independent of y, since $E(x|y)$ is not a constant but varies with y.

y and x are uncorrelated, since

$$\text{Cov}(y, x) = E(yx) - E(y)E(x) = 0 - 0 = 0.$$

(d) Define $\epsilon = y - E(y|x)$, for $x = -1, 0, 1$. Recall from (b) above, we have

x	$E(y|x)$
-1	3
0	3
1	3

Also note that $f(\epsilon|x) = f[y - E(y|x)|x] = f(y - \text{constant}|x)$, so that

ϵ $(x = -1)$	$f(y|x = -1)$	ϵ $(x = 0)$	$f(y|x = 0)$	ϵ $(x = 1)$	$f(y|x = 1)$
-2	$\tfrac{1}{3}$	-2	0	-2	0
-1	0	-1	$\tfrac{1}{3}$	-1	$\tfrac{1}{2}$
0	$\tfrac{1}{3}$	0	$\tfrac{1}{3}$	0	0
1	0	1	$\tfrac{1}{3}$	1	$\tfrac{1}{2}$
2	$\tfrac{1}{3}$	2	0	2	0

Arranging these results in a conventional two-entry table, we have the conditional distribution of ϵ given x—that is, $f(\epsilon|x)$:

x \ ϵ	-2	-1	0	1	2	Σ
-1	$\tfrac{1}{3}$	0	$\tfrac{1}{3}$	0	$\tfrac{1}{3}$	1
0	0	$\tfrac{1}{3}$	$\tfrac{1}{3}$	$\tfrac{1}{3}$	0	1
1	0	$\tfrac{1}{2}$	0	$\tfrac{1}{2}$	0	1

Now,

$$E(\epsilon|x = -1) = (-2)(\tfrac{1}{3}) + (0)(\tfrac{1}{3}) + (2)(\tfrac{1}{3}) = 0,$$
$$E(\epsilon|x = 0) = (-1)(\tfrac{1}{3}) + (0)(\tfrac{1}{3}) + (1)(\tfrac{1}{3}) = 0,$$
$$E(\epsilon|x = 1) = (-1)(\tfrac{1}{2}) + (1)(\tfrac{1}{2}) = 0,$$

so that

$$E(\epsilon \mid x) = 0$$

and

$$E(\epsilon \mid x) = 0 \Longrightarrow E(\epsilon) = 0.$$

To check this, find the joint distribution of ϵ and x by using $f(\epsilon, x) = f(\epsilon \mid x)f(x)$:

x \ ϵ	-2	-1	0	1	2	$f(x)$
-1	$\frac{1}{9}$	0	$\frac{1}{9}$	0	$\frac{1}{9}$	$\frac{1}{3}$
0	0	$\frac{1}{9}$	$\frac{1}{9}$	$\frac{1}{9}$	0	$\frac{1}{3}$
1	0	$\frac{1}{6}$	0	$\frac{1}{6}$	0	$\frac{1}{3}$
$f(\epsilon)$	$\frac{1}{9}$	$\frac{5}{18}$	$\frac{2}{9}$	$\frac{5}{18}$	$\frac{1}{9}$	1

from whence the marginal distribution of ϵ is obtained; then

$$E(\epsilon) = \sum \epsilon f(\epsilon)$$
$$= (-2)(\tfrac{1}{9}) + (-1)(\tfrac{5}{18}) + (0)(\tfrac{2}{9}) + (1)(\tfrac{5}{18}) + (2)(\tfrac{1}{9}) = 0.$$

Since $E(\epsilon \mid x) = E(\epsilon) = 0$, we have

$$\text{Cov}\,(\epsilon x) = E(\epsilon x) - E(\epsilon)E(x) = 0$$
$$= E(\epsilon x)$$
$$= \sum \sum \epsilon x f(\epsilon, x)$$
$$= (2)(\tfrac{1}{9}) + (-2)(\tfrac{1}{9}) + (-1)(\tfrac{1}{6}) + (1)(\tfrac{1}{6}) = 0.$$

This result agrees with the general proposition that mean-independence implies uncorrelatedness,

$$E(\epsilon \mid x) = \text{constant} \Longrightarrow E(\epsilon x) = E(x)E(\epsilon).$$

(e) Take as an alternative to the population regression function, $g^*(x)$, where

x	$g^*(x)$
-1	2
0	3
1	4

Define $\epsilon^* = y - g^*(x)$. Then the conditional distribution of ϵ^* given x is [same procedure as in (d) above]:

x \ ϵ^*	-3	-2	-1	0	1	2	3	Σ
-1	0	0	$\frac{1}{3}$	0	$\frac{1}{3}$	0	$\frac{1}{3}$	1
0	0	0	$\frac{1}{3}$	$\frac{1}{3}$	$\frac{1}{3}$	0	0	1
1	0	$\frac{1}{2}$	0	$\frac{1}{2}$	0	0	0	1

from which we find

$$E(\epsilon^* \,|\, x = -1) = (-1)(\tfrac{1}{3}) + (1)(\tfrac{1}{3}) + (3)(\tfrac{1}{3}) = 1,$$
$$E(\epsilon^* \,|\, x = 0) = (-1)(\tfrac{1}{3}) + (0)(\tfrac{1}{3}) + (1)(\tfrac{1}{3}) = 0,$$
$$E(\epsilon^* \,|\, x = 1) = (-2)(\tfrac{1}{2}) + (0)(\tfrac{1}{2}) = -1,$$

but

$$E(\epsilon^*) = (1)(\tfrac{1}{3}) + (0)(\tfrac{1}{3}) - (1)(\tfrac{1}{3}) = 0.$$

The joint distribution of ϵ^* and x is $[f(\epsilon^*, x) = f(\epsilon^* \,|\, x) f(x)]$:

x \ ϵ^*	-3	-2	-1	0	1	2	3	$f(x)$
-1	0	0	$\frac{1}{9}$	0	$\frac{1}{9}$	0	$\frac{1}{9}$	$\frac{1}{3}$
0	0	0	$\frac{1}{9}$	$\frac{1}{9}$	$\frac{1}{9}$	0	0	$\frac{1}{3}$
1	0	$\frac{1}{6}$	0	$\frac{1}{6}$	0	0	0	$\frac{1}{3}$
$f(\epsilon^*)$	0	$\frac{1}{6}$	$\frac{2}{9}$	$\frac{5}{18}$	$\frac{2}{9}$	0	$\frac{1}{9}$	1

and again

$$E(\epsilon^*) = \sum \epsilon^* f(\epsilon^*)$$
$$= (-2)(\tfrac{1}{6}) + (-1)(\tfrac{2}{9}) + (1)(\tfrac{2}{9}) + (3)(\tfrac{1}{9}) = 0.$$

But

$$E(\epsilon^* x) = (1)(\tfrac{1}{9}) + (-1)(\tfrac{1}{9}) + (-3)(\tfrac{1}{9}) + (-2)(\tfrac{1}{6}) = -\tfrac{2}{3}.$$

2. (Section 2.3) "Deviations from the population regression function have zero expectation conditional on the conditioning variable; this will not be so for any other function." Demonstrate this proposition.

ANSWER:

Definition: Population regression function:

$$E(y \,|\, x) = g(x).$$

Definition: Deviations from the population regression function:

$$\epsilon = y - E(y \,|\, x) = y - g(x).$$

So, we can write $y = g(x) + \epsilon$, where $E(\epsilon) = 0$. This is because

$$E(\epsilon \,|\, x) = E(y \,|\, x) - E[E(y \,|\, x)x]$$
$$= E(y \,|\, x) - E(y \,|\, x) = 0$$

and clearly $E(\epsilon \,|\, x) = 0$ for all x implies $E(\epsilon) = 0$.

Now, take any other function, say $g^*(x) \neq g(x)$, and prove that $E[y - g^*(x) \,|\, x] \neq 0$ in general. By definition, $\epsilon^* = y - g^*(x)$, so that

$$E(\epsilon^* \,|\, x) = E[y - g^*(x) \,|\, x]$$
$$= E(y \,|\, x) - E[g^*(x) \,|\, x]$$
$$= E[g(x) + \epsilon \,|\, x] - E[g^*(x) \,|\, x]$$
$$= E[g(x) \,|\, x] - E[g^*(x) \,|\, x]$$
$$= g(x) - g^*(x) \neq 0 \qquad \text{by assumption.}$$

Thus,

$$E(\epsilon^* \,|\, x) \neq 0 \qquad \text{in general.}$$

3. (Section 2.4) For the following set of sample observations calculate the sample regression function, graph it in the scatter of points, and do numerical checks of its properties.

Obs.	y	x
1	1	−1
2	−1	0
3	1	2
4	−1	3
5	3	3

ANSWERS:

Obs.	y	x	xy	x^2	$\hat{y}$	$e = y - \hat{y}$	xe
1	1	−1	−1	1	$\frac{3}{33}$	$\frac{30}{33}$	$-\frac{30}{33}$
2	−1	0	0	0	$\frac{10}{33}$	$-\frac{43}{33}$	0
3	1	2	2	4	$\frac{24}{33}$	$\frac{9}{33}$	$\frac{18}{33}$
4	−1	3	−3	9	$\frac{31}{33}$	$-\frac{64}{33}$	$-\frac{192}{33}$
5	3	3	9	9	$\frac{31}{33}$	$\frac{68}{33}$	$\frac{204}{33}$
Σ	3	7	7	23	3	0	0
Means	$\frac{3}{5}$	$\frac{7}{5}$	$\frac{7}{5}$	$\frac{23}{5}$	$\frac{3}{5}$	0	0

$$b = \frac{\sum (x - \bar{x})(y - \bar{y})}{\sum (x - \bar{x})^2} = \frac{\sum (x - \bar{x})y}{\sum (x - \bar{x})x} = \frac{\sum xy - [(\sum x)(\sum y)/n]}{\sum x^2 - [(\sum x)^2/n]}$$

$$= \frac{7 - [(7)(3)/5]}{23 - [(7)(7)/5]} = \frac{35 - 21}{115 - 49} = \frac{14}{66} = \frac{7}{33}$$

$$a = \bar{y} - b\bar{x} = \frac{3}{5} - \left(\frac{7}{33}\right)\left(\frac{7}{5}\right) = \frac{33(3) - 49}{33(5)} = \frac{50}{5(33)} = \frac{10}{33}.$$

Therefore, the SRF is

$$\hat{y} = \frac{10}{33} + \frac{7}{33}x.$$

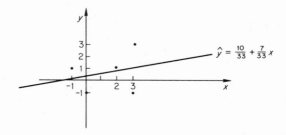

4. (Section 2.5) The random variables x_1 and x_2 are independently distributed with the same variance, σ^2, but different means:

$$E(x_1) = 2\theta \quad \text{and} \quad E(x_2) = 4\theta,$$

where θ is an unknown parameter. Two estimators of θ are proposed:

$$\hat{\theta}_1 = \frac{x_1}{4} + \frac{x_2}{8}, \quad \text{and} \quad \hat{\theta}_2 = \frac{x_1}{10} + \frac{x_2}{5}.$$

Which estimator would you prefer and why?

ANSWER:

$$E(\hat{\theta}_1) = \frac{2\theta}{4} + \frac{4\theta}{8} = \theta,$$

$$E(\hat{\theta}_2) = \frac{2\theta}{10} + \frac{4\theta}{5} = \theta.$$

Therefore both estimators are unbiased.

$$\sigma_{\hat{\theta}_1}^2 = \frac{\sigma^2}{16} + \frac{\sigma^2}{64} = \frac{5}{64}\sigma^2,$$

$$\sigma_{\hat{\theta}_2}^2 = \frac{\sigma^2}{100} + \frac{\sigma^2}{25} = \frac{5}{100}\sigma^2.$$

Therefore $\hat{\theta}_2$ has the smallest variance, and would be preferred for that reason.

5. (Section 2.5) Outline the assumptions required for b to be a BLUE of β in the classical regression model and show how each contributes to bestness and/or unbiasedness.

ANSWERS:

The assumptions required are the Gauss-Markov assumptions, namely that in the model $y_i = \alpha + \beta x_i + \epsilon_i$, linear in parameters α and β, where either x can be fixed at each observation or analysis conditional on x is appropriate, the error term ϵ_i has the following properties:

$$E(\epsilon_i) = 0, \qquad E(\epsilon_i \epsilon_j) = \begin{cases} \sigma^2, & i = j, \\ 0, & i \neq j. \end{cases}$$

As a result of the first assumption on ϵ_i it also follows that ϵ_i and x_i are unrelated in any statistical sense. This latter property yields unbiasedness [see Eq. (2.5.2)]. "Bestness" for the least-squares estimators is provided by the assumption

$$E(\epsilon_i \epsilon_j) = \begin{cases} \sigma^2, & i = j, \\ 0, & i \neq j. \end{cases}$$

Were it not for this assumption, minimizing the least-squares criterion would not automatically guarantee unbiased linear estimators of minimum variance. See the development of Eqs. (2.5.3) and (2.5.4) for details.

6. (Sections 2.4, 2.6, 2.7) For the following data:
   a. Compute a, b, $\mathcal{S}^2$, r_{xy}, $\hat{\sigma}_b^2$
   b. Test $H: \beta = 0$ against $H_A: \beta \neq 0$.
   c. Develop a 95 percent confidence interval for the conditional mean of y given $x = 36$.

$$\bar{x} = 51.2, \qquad\qquad\qquad\qquad \bar{y} = 42.6,$$

$$S_x^2 = \frac{1}{n}\sum_{i=1}^{n}(x_i - \bar{x})^2 = 778.8, \qquad S_y^2 = \frac{1}{n}\sum_{i=1}^{n}(y_i - \bar{y})^2 = 779.4,$$

$$S_{xy} = \frac{1}{n}\sum_{i=1}^{n}(x_i - \bar{x})(y_i - \bar{y}) = 343.1, \qquad n = 10.$$

ANSWERS:

$b = .44$, $a = 20.1$, $r_{xy} = .44$. $S_{\hat{y}}^2 = 150.8$, $S_e^2 = 628.6$; $\mathcal{S}^2 = \frac{10}{8}S_e^2 = 785.8$; $\hat{\sigma}_b^2 = .10$, $\hat{\sigma}_b = .32$, $b/\hat{\sigma}_b = 1.38$.

   Since $t_{.95,8} = \pm 2.306$, the hypothesis is not rejected. $\hat{\sigma}_{\hat{y}_0}^2 = 101.7$; $\hat{\sigma}_{\hat{y}_0} = 10.1$. $\Pr\{36.9 - 23.2 \leq E(y \mid x = 36) \leq 36.9 + 23.2\} = .95$.

PROBLEMS ON SPECIAL TOPICS

1. *An Introduction to the "Errors-in-Variables" Problem.* Suppose we have "true" variables X_i, Y_i related deterministically as:

$$Y_i = \alpha + \beta X_i,$$

but we observe $y = Y + v$ and $x = X + u$. That is, the sources of error in the model are due to errors of observation. We assume $E(u) = E(v) = 0$, and that X and Y are independent of u, v; also, u and v are independent. Further we assume that they each have constant variance over the observations in a random sample of size n.

a. First develop the correct regression model in terms of observed values y_i, x_i.

b. Is the usual least-squares estimator of β in this model unbiased?

ANSWERS:

(a) Writing Y_i and X_i in terms of their observed values and respective observation errors,

$$y_i - v_i = \alpha + \beta(x_i - u_i),$$

or

$$y_i = \alpha + \beta x_i + w_i,$$

where $w_i = -\beta u_i + v_i$.

(b) Since $E(u) = E(v) = 0$, $E(w) = 0$, but $E(wx) \neq 0$. This can be easily seen:

$$E(xw) = E[(X + u)(v - \beta u)] = E(Xv - \beta Xu + uv - \beta u^2)$$
$$= -E(\beta u^2) = -\beta \sigma_u^2.$$

The implication of this result is that $E(b) \neq \beta$, because in (2.5.2),

$$E(b) = \beta + E\left\{\frac{\sum x^* w}{\sum x^{*2}}\right\},$$

the second term is not zero. In other words, the least-squares slope estimate, b, is a biased estimator for β.

Intuitively, there are sources of error in both the vertical (y) direction *and* the horizontal (x) direction in this model. Least squares accounts for only a vertical source of error, and for this reason we may expect it not to produce estimates with the most desirable properties.

2. *An Introduction to the Consumption Function.* Collect two aggregate series covering the period 1929–64, personal consumption expenditure (including durables) per capita in constant prices (y), and personal disposable income per capita in constant prices (x).

a.   Draw a scatter diagram of the (y, x) points.

b.   Calculate the least-squares regression line $\hat{y} = a + bx$ and draw it in.

c.   Compute r_{xy}^2 and $\mathcal{S}^2$.

d.   Calculate the average propensity to consume (apc), marginal propensity to consume (mpc), and income elasticity of consumption (evaluated at the point of means, $[\bar{y}, \bar{x}]$).

e.   Friedman's permanent income hypothesis suggests that for long time series the income elasticity of consumption is one. Formulate a test of this hypothesis in the regression framework, and test it with your data.

f.   Also, reproduce items (b), (c), (d), (e) for the period 1929–40. Conclusions?

ANSWERS:

The table below presents data collected in the *Economic Report of the President* (Washington, D.C.: January, 1968), from Table B-16 (p. 227).

Per Capita Personal Consumption Expenditure (y) and Per Capita Disposable Personal Income (x) in the United States, 1929–64 (in 1958 dollars).

Year	y	x	Year	y	x
1929	1145	1236	1947	1431	1513
1930	1059	1128	48	1438	1567
31	1016	1077	49	1451	1547
32	919	921	50	1520	1646
33	897	893	51	1509	1657
34	934	952	52	1525	1678
35	985	1035	53	1572	1726
36	1080	1158	54	1575	1714
37	1110	1187	55	1659	1795
38	1079	1105	56	1673	1839
39	1131	1190	57	1683	1844
40	1178	1259	58	1666	1831
41	1240	1427	59	1735	1881
42	1197	1582	60	1749	1883
43	1213	1629	61	1755	1909
44	1238	1673	62	1813	1968
45	1308	1642	63	1865	2013
46	1439	1606	64	1945	2123

(a)   The scatter of points and regression lines for the periods (1929–40) and (1929–64) are shown in the graph below.

(b), (c)   For 1929–40:

$$y = 214.9 + .7574x,$$
$$(5.86) \quad (22.74)$$

with $r_{yx}^2 = .981$, $\mathscr{S}^2 = 13.53$. t-ratios for the coefficients appear in parentheses.
   For 1929–64:

$$y = 77.21 + .8583x,$$
$$(1.24) \quad (22.24)$$

with $r_{yx}^2 = .9320$, $\mathscr{S}^2 = 88.25$.

(d)   For 1929–40, $a\hat{p}c = (\bar{y}/\bar{x}) = .9537$, $m\hat{p}c = .7574$, whereas the required elasticity is

$$\hat{\eta} = \left(\frac{\widehat{dy}}{dx}\right)\left(\frac{\bar{x}}{\bar{y}}\right) = \frac{m\hat{p}c}{a\hat{p}c} = .7942.$$

For 1929–64, $a\hat{p}c = .9077$, $m\hat{p}c = .8583$, $\hat{\eta} = .9456$.

(e)   First, a digression on an incorrect test. Suppose part (e) is interpreted as suggesting a test of the hypothesis that the income elasticity of consumption evaluated at the point of sample means $(\bar{y}, \bar{x})$ is one. Let the elasticity by denoted by $\eta = (dy/dx)(\bar{x}/\bar{y})$. From the population regression equation, $dy/dx = \beta$. The required test says, then, that β is determined by the equation:

$$1 = \beta\left(\frac{\bar{x}}{\bar{y}}\right) \quad \text{or} \quad \beta = \frac{\bar{y}}{\bar{x}}.$$

An income elasticity of one at $(\bar{y}, \bar{x})$ occurs when (at that point) the mpc and apc are equal. Presumably one would then test $H: \beta = \bar{y}/\bar{x}$ against $H_A: \beta < \bar{y}/\bar{x}$ using the standard t-test, with the statistic $t = (b - \bar{y}/\bar{x})/\hat{\sigma}_b$.
   Now consider a test of $\alpha = 0$. If $\alpha = 0$ in the population regression function, then $\beta = \bar{Y}/\bar{x}$, where $\bar{Y} = E(y) = E[E(y \mid x)]$ —that is, the "grand" population mean of y. The appropriate statistic for this test is $a/\hat{\sigma}_a$, and it is clear that the difference between this and the first test mentioned is that the first test uses the sample mean $\bar{y}$ in setting $\beta = \bar{y}/\bar{x}$ as the hypothesis of interest, while the intercept test deals in population quantities, $\beta = \bar{Y}/\bar{x}$.[†]
   The problem is that the statistic t defined above is *not* the cor-

---

[†] Recall, the classical assumption is that observations on x are "fixed," so that reference to "population quantities" refers to the population of y *given* the x_i's,

rect statistic with which to test $\beta = \bar{Y}/\bar{x}$; it depends on a further sample random variable (besides b), namely $\bar{y}$. In constructing t, σ_b is *not* the standard deviation of $(b - \bar{y}/\bar{x})$; therefore we have not met the requirements of Theorem 4, which state that the numerator of the t-statistic must be $N(0, 1)$.

The correct variance of $(b - \bar{y}/\bar{x})$ is easy to determine, however, since $\bar{x}$ is the conditioning variable and b is uncorrelated with $\bar{y}$. It is

$$\operatorname{Var}\left[b - \frac{\bar{y}}{\bar{x}}\right] = \sigma_b^2 + \frac{1}{\bar{x}^2}\frac{\sigma^2}{n}.$$

To see now that the tests are equivalent, compare the relevant statistics:

$$t_{(1)}^2 = \frac{a^2}{\left[\dfrac{\mathscr{S}^2}{n} + \dfrac{\mathscr{S}^2}{\sum x^{*2}}\bar{x}^2\right]} \quad \text{and} \quad t_{(2)}^2 = \frac{\left[b - \dfrac{\bar{y}}{\bar{x}}\right]^2}{\left[\dfrac{\mathscr{S}^2}{\sum x^{*2}} + \dfrac{1}{\bar{x}^2}\cdot\dfrac{\mathscr{S}^2}{n}\right]}.$$

If we factor $(1/\bar{x}^2)$ out of the denominator of $t_{(2)}^2$, we get

$$t_{(2)}^2 = \frac{\left[b - \dfrac{\bar{y}}{\bar{x}}\right]^2\bar{x}^2}{\left[\dfrac{\mathscr{S}^2}{n} + \bar{x}^2\dfrac{\mathscr{S}^2}{\sum x^{*2}}\right]} = \frac{a^2}{\left[\dfrac{\mathscr{S}^2}{n} + \bar{x}^2\dfrac{\mathscr{S}^2}{\sum x^{*2}}\right]} = t_{(1)}^2.$$

Thus, testing that the regression slope β is the ratio of *population* means is equivalent to testing $\alpha = 0$. It is *not correct* to use the standard t-test setting $\beta = \bar{y}/\bar{x}$ as the hypothetical value, but an appropriate modification can be made in the estimated standard deviation in the denominator of the t-ratio for $(b - \bar{y}/\bar{x})$ to make this test valid.

Then, for 1929–40, at 95 percent ($t_{.95, 10} = \pm 2.228$) the appropriate test statistic is $t = 5.85$ and the hypothesis $H : \eta = 1$ is rejected. For the longer time series, $t = 1.24$, which when compared with the appropriate tabled value ($t_{.95, 36} = \pm 2.030$) directs a decision not to reject H.

(f)   As expected, the income elasticity of consumption is greater for the long time series.

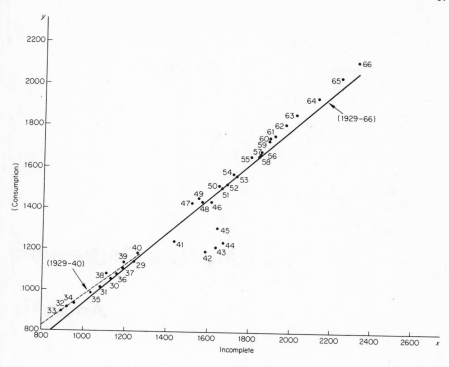

3 Multiple Regression

Analysis

3.1 INTRODUCTION

It is difficult to think of an economic variable that relates to but a single causal factor. Moreover, even if some such relation is plausible, the question remains how to isolate it among the myriad of variables that are not directly relevant but that cannot be controlled. In the context of demand analysis quantity is expected to depend jointly on own price, the prices of other goods, and money income. However, if the data source is a time series, we will want to separate the demand relation from increases in and variations due to population changes. In this sense we want to *control* population in order to look at the demand relation suggested by theoretical considerations.

The word "control" ought to be carefully interpreted to indicate that most economic data are not derived from a laboratory experiment. In particular, we cannot really control the level of population so as to generate numerous observations on the relevant variables with population held constant. What we can do is either account for population shifts by dealing with per capita quantity and income, or else include it as an additional "independent" or *exogenous* variable. In either instance, note that we are at the mercy of the sample—of the particular set of observations used in the analysis. While the statistical procedures we will now discuss allow us to speak of the demand relation after allowance for population effects, the possibility remains that the relation itself—its form, and so on—is different at different population levels. Without the ability to perform a laboratory experiment we can only hope that this distortion is small. Otherwise, we must build a model for population, which then interacts with the demand relation. But it presumably would contain other variables worthy of "explanation" in terms of the socioeconomic structure. In the end, this process leads one to consider everything as dependent on everything else in a huge system of interdependent relations.

And the problem of control should not be taken lightly. In fact, the notion that empirical analysis in economics is dependent on "sample" data that often (as in the case of time-series information) *cannot* be replicated forms the basic objection to classical methods of statistical inference in such uses raised by the "modern" or "Bayesian" school of statistics.

Our focus in this book is on single-equation models with a single *dependent* variable related to a number of so-called *independent* variables. We will consider briefly, however, the estimation problem for a single equation containing mutually dependent variables that has been extracted from a system of interdependent relations.

Even in the face of these issues there is much that can be accomplished with the least-squares regression framework. In what follows the object is to outline carefully the basic assumptions and methodology underlying multiple regression, and to proceed with some rigor. For when we begin discussing regression "applications" it will become clear that intelligent use of the methodology requires the user to have an ability to adapt the framework to his problem, after first ascertaining whether it applies at all.

3.2 CONDITIONAL EXPECTATIONS REVISITED

Our development of multiple regression will parallel the previous chapter, with appropriate additions and embellishments. First, as we previously spoke of a regression model that posits a relationship between the conditional expectation of y and a single conditioning variable or *regressor*, x, now we consider the distribution of y conditional on a *set* of independent variables, $\{x_1, \ldots, x_k\}$. For the purpose of discussing the PRF and its properties some extensions to the rules of conditional expectations are required.

The underlying frequency distribution of interest in the multiple regression model is the joint distribution $f(y, x_1, \ldots, x_k)$, from which the conditional distribution of y can easily be written:

$$(3.2.1) \qquad f(y \mid x_1, \ldots, x_k) = \frac{f(y, x_1, \ldots, x_k)}{f(x_1, \ldots, x_k)},$$

where $f(x_1, \ldots, x_k)$ is the "marginal" distribution (a joint distribution) of the set of x's. It is formed by

$$(3.2.2) \qquad f(x_1, \ldots, x_k) = \int f(y, x_1, \ldots, x_k) \, dy.$$

Stochastic (statistical) independence of y and the set of independent variables $\{x_j\}$ is defined when the conditional frequency distribution of y does not depend on any x_j. Equivalently, under independence $f(y)$ does not change over the myriad of possible *observed* points $\{x_1, \ldots, x_k\}$. It is also constant over the range for any one of the variables $x_1, \ldots, x_k$. As before, the derivations are in terms of continuous variables, while the results carry over to the discrete case.

The conditional expectation of y is given by

$$(3.2.3) \qquad E(y \mid \{x_j\}) = \int y f(y \mid \{x_j\}) \, dy,$$

and it is easy to see that the unconditional expectation is just the expected value of this conditional expectation, although it looks quite formidable were we to consider *doing* the operations indicated. For, the marginal distribution of $y, f(y)$, is not so simply written as before, although its *sense* is unchanged. To wit:

$$(3.2.4) \qquad f(y) = \int\int \cdots \int f(y, x_1, \ldots, x_k) \, dx_1, \ldots, dx_k,$$

which is simply an extension of the two-variable relationship of (2.2.1), computed over k "margins" rather than one. Using (3.2.4) and the definition of $E(y)$,

$$(3.2.5) \qquad E(y) = \int y f(y) \, dy$$

$$= \int y \int\int \cdots \int f(y, x_1, \ldots, x_k) \, dx_1, \ldots, dx_k \, dy.$$

By substituting (3.2.1) and rearranging, however, (3.2.5) becomes

$$(3.2.6) \quad E(y) = \int\int \cdots \int \left\{ \int y f(y \,|\, x_1, \ldots, x_k) \, dy \right\} f(x_1, \ldots, x_k) \, dx_1 \cdots dx_k$$

$$= \int\int \cdots \int E(y \,|\, x_1, \ldots, x_k) f(x_1, \ldots, x_k) \, dx_1 \cdots dx_k.$$

That is, the unconditional expected value of y equals the expectation (over the k variables $x_1, \ldots, x_k$) of its conditional expected value.

Parallels to Rules 1–3 of Section 2.2 follow directly.

RULE 1

IF c IS A CONSTANT (GIVEN $x_1, \ldots, x_k$), THEN

(a) $E[(y + c) \,|\, x_1, \ldots, x_k] = E(y \,|\, x_1, \ldots, x_k) + c$,

(b) $E(cy \,|\, x_1, \ldots, x_k) = cE(y \,|\, x_1, \ldots, x_k)$.

RULE 2

IF $E(y \,|\, x_1, \ldots, x_k)$ IS CONSTANT (DOES NOT DEPEND ON $x_1, \ldots, x_k$), THEN

$$E(y \,|\, x_1, \ldots, x_k) = E(y) \qquad \text{(MEAN INDEPENDENCE)}$$

and FOR ANY x_j,

$$E(y \,|\, x_j) = E(y).$$

RULE 3

IF $E(y \,|\, x_1, \ldots, x_k)$ IS CONSTANT, THEN

$$E(yx_j) = E(y)E(x_j) \qquad \text{(UNCORRELATEDNESS)}.$$

Formal proofs of these theorems are left to the reader. Rule 3 follows directly from the corollary included in Rule 2, namely, $E(y|x_j) = E(y)$, and requires nothing more than the proof of Rule 3 in Section 2.2. The key to the corollary was mentioned previously, in the discussion on stochastic independence.

3.3 THE POPULATION REGRESSION FUNCTION

Consider now a PRF

$$(3.3.1) \qquad E(y|x_1, \ldots, x_k) = g(x_1, \ldots, x_k),$$

and define the residual $\epsilon = y - g(x_1, \ldots, x_k)$. As was argued in Section 2.4, this regression function has the following properties:

$$(3.3.2) \qquad E(\epsilon|x_1, \ldots, x_k) = 0$$

from an application of Rule 1 for conditional expectations. Given the point $(x_1, \ldots, x_k)$, $E(y|x_1, \ldots, x_k)$ is constant, hence (3.3.2). Since the conditional expectation of the residual is a constant, from Rule 2 we have

$$(3.3.3) \qquad E(\epsilon|x_1, \ldots, x_k) = E(\epsilon) = 0.$$

The unconditional expectation of ϵ is zero. Finally, from Rule 3 and the corollary to Rule 2, the residual is mutually uncorrelated with each of the conditioning variables, because $E(\epsilon|x_1, \ldots, x_k) = 0$ implies $E(\epsilon x_j) = 0$ for $j = 1, \ldots, k$.

Now suppose the population regression function is linear (in parameters), by which assumption we write

$$(3.3.4) \qquad y = \beta_0 + \beta_1 x_1 + \cdots + \beta_k x_k + \epsilon.$$

We may proceed to obtain estimates of the β's as in the simple regression case, via the analogy principle or by least squares.

3.4 THE SAMPLE REGRESSION FUNCTION

Given a random sample of n joint observations $(y_i, x_{i1}, \ldots, x_{ik})$, write the SRM as

$$(3.4.1) \qquad y_i = b_0 + b_1 x_{i1} + \cdots + b_k x_{ik} + e_i, \qquad i = 1, \ldots, n.$$

The calculated residuals must by analogy to the PRM possess the properties:

(3.4.2)   (a) $$\sum_{i=1}^{n} e_i = 0,$$

(b) $$\sum_{i=1}^{n} e_i x_{ij} = 0, \qquad j = 1, \ldots, k,$$

or

$$\sum (y - b_0 - b_1 x_1 - \cdots - b_k x_k) = 0,$$
$$\sum (y - b_0 - b_1 x_1 - \cdots - b_k x_k) x_1 = 0,$$
$$\vdots$$
$$\sum (y - b_0 - b_1 x_1 - \cdots - b_k x_k) x_k = 0,$$

where the summation is understood to be over the sample observations, $i = 1, \ldots, n$. The above is a system of $k + 1$ linear equations in the $k + 1$ unknowns, $b_0, \ldots, b_k$, the computed *partial regression* coefficients of y on the x's. Rearranging, we have

(3.4.3) $$b_0 n + b_1 \sum x_1 + \cdots + b_k \sum x_k = \sum y,$$
$$b_0 \sum x_1 + b_1 \sum x_1^2 + \cdots + b_k \sum x_k x_1 = \sum y x_1,$$
$$\vdots$$
$$b_0 \sum x_k + b_1 \sum x_1 x_k + \cdots + b_k \sum x_k^2 = \sum y x_k.$$

Matrix notation will facilitate the ensuing analysis greatly, so define

$$\mathbf{y} = \begin{bmatrix} y_1 \\ \cdot \\ \cdot \\ \cdot \\ y_n \end{bmatrix} \qquad \mathbf{X} = \begin{bmatrix} 1 & x_{11} & \cdots & x_{1k} \\ \cdot & & & \\ \cdot & & & \\ 1 & x_{n1} & \cdots & x_{nk} \end{bmatrix}$$
$$(n \times 1) \qquad\qquad [n \times (k+1)]$$

$$\mathbf{e} = \begin{bmatrix} e_1 \\ \cdot \\ \cdot \\ \cdot \\ e_n \end{bmatrix} \qquad \mathbf{b} = \begin{bmatrix} b_0 \\ \cdot \\ \cdot \\ \cdot \\ b_k \end{bmatrix}$$
$$(n \times 1) \qquad\qquad [(k+1) \times 1]$$

Now the original SRM may be represented by

(3.4.4) $$\mathbf{y} = \mathbf{Xb} + \mathbf{e},$$

and the set of "normal" equations in (3.4.3) by

(3.4.5) $$(\mathbf{X'X})\mathbf{b} = \mathbf{X'y}.$$

The unique solution (if it exists) to this set of equations is given by

(3.4.6) $$\mathbf{b} = (\mathbf{X}'\mathbf{X})^{-1}\mathbf{X}'\mathbf{y}.$$

What is meant by the "if it exists" qualification is that we must be able to form $(\mathbf{X}'\mathbf{X})^{-1}$: the inverse matrix must exist. Other (equivalent) ways of saying this are: (1) the rank of $(\mathbf{X}'\mathbf{X})$ must be $k + 1$; (2) $|\mathbf{X}'\mathbf{X}| \neq 0$; and (3) the columns of $(\mathbf{X}'\mathbf{X})$ must be linearly independent. Since $(\mathbf{X}'\mathbf{X})$ is a product of $\mathbf{X}'$ and $\mathbf{X}$, we know that its rank will equal the rank of $\mathbf{X}'$ or $\mathbf{X}$, whichever rank is smaller. But: rank $\mathbf{X}$ = rank $\mathbf{X}'$, so that for $(\mathbf{X}'\mathbf{X})$ to be of *full rank* $(k + 1)$, $\mathbf{X}$ must have rank $(k + 1)$. For this to be so the columns of $\mathbf{X}$ must be linearly independent, a necessary condition for which is $n \geq k + 1$.†

The characterization of conditioning variables as "independent" variables comes from just this usage: that in order to form $(\mathbf{X}'\mathbf{X})^{-1}$ the *observed* values of any particular conditioning variable cannot be formed as exact linear combinations of the *observed* values of other conditioning variables. This meaning of independence, "linear independence," is not statistical independence. If one random variable is an exact linear transformation of another, the two are very much dependent in the statistical sense. Note, however, that two conditioning variables that are perfectly correlated *in the sample* make the columns of $\mathbf{X}$ linearly dependent. The reader should verify that a correlation coefficient of one between two independent variables, x_h and x_l, implies that x_h is a scalar multiple of x_l. Anything less than perfect correlation will allow $(\mathbf{X}'\mathbf{X})^{-1}$ to be formed, but "near perfect" correlation presents an additional difficulty in that the precision of estimated coefficients diminishes with high intercorrelations between "independent" variables, as we shall soon see.

To get some feeling for the formula $\mathbf{b} = (\mathbf{X}'\mathbf{X})^{-1}\mathbf{X}'\mathbf{y}$, let us consider the two-variable problem in this more general context. First, the appropriate notation is

$$\mathbf{X} = \begin{bmatrix} 1 & x_1 \\ \cdot & \cdot \\ \cdot & \cdot \\ \cdot & \cdot \\ 1 & x_n \end{bmatrix}, \qquad \mathbf{y} = \begin{bmatrix} y_1 \\ \cdot \\ \cdot \\ \cdot \\ y_n \end{bmatrix},$$

$$\mathbf{b} = \begin{bmatrix} b_0 \\ b_1 \end{bmatrix} = \begin{bmatrix} a \\ b \end{bmatrix} \quad \text{in our previous notation.}$$

Then:

---

† If $n < k + 1$, there are *many* sets of coefficients that will satisfy the normal equations. For a review of these concepts in matrix algebra the reader is referred to Appendix A.

$$\mathbf{X'X} = \begin{bmatrix} 1 & \cdots & 1 \\ x_1 & \cdots & x_n \end{bmatrix} \begin{bmatrix} 1 & x_1 \\ \cdot & \cdot \\ \cdot & \cdot \\ \cdot & \cdot \\ 1 & x_n \end{bmatrix} = \begin{bmatrix} n & \sum x \\ \sum x & \sum x^2 \end{bmatrix}$$

and

$$\mathbf{X'y} = \begin{bmatrix} 1 & \cdots & 1 \\ x_1 & \cdots & x_n \end{bmatrix} \begin{bmatrix} y_1 \\ \cdot \\ \cdot \\ \cdot \\ y_n \end{bmatrix} = \begin{bmatrix} \sum y \\ \sum xy \end{bmatrix}.$$

Forming $(\mathbf{X'X})^{-1}$,

$$|(\mathbf{X'X})| = n \sum x^2 - (\sum x)^2 \quad \text{(a scalar)},$$

$$\mathbf{\Delta} = \mathbf{\Delta}' = \begin{bmatrix} \sum x^2 & -\sum x \\ -\sum x & n \end{bmatrix},$$

the adjoint matrix, so that

$$(\mathbf{X'X})^{-1} = \frac{1}{n \sum x^2 - (\sum x)^2} \begin{bmatrix} \sum x^2 & -\sum x \\ -\sum x & n \end{bmatrix}.$$

Solving for $\begin{bmatrix} b_0 \\ b_1 \end{bmatrix}$ in $\begin{bmatrix} b_0 \\ b_1 \end{bmatrix} = (\mathbf{X'X})^{-1} \begin{bmatrix} \sum y \\ \sum xy \end{bmatrix}$,

$$b_0 = \frac{\sum x^2 \cdot \sum y - \sum x \sum xy}{n \sum x^2 - (\sum x)^2}$$

and

$$b_1 = \frac{-\sum x \sum y + n \sum xy}{n \sum x^2 - (\sum x)^2} = \frac{S_{xy}}{S_x^2} \quad \text{as before.}$$

In the numerator of b_0 add and subtract $[(\sum y)/n](\sum x)^2$ to get

$$b_0 = \frac{\dfrac{\sum y}{n}[n \sum x^2 - (\sum x)^2] - \dfrac{\sum x}{n}[-\sum y \sum x + n \sum xy]}{n \sum x^2 - (\sum x)^2}$$

$$= \bar{y} - b_1 \bar{x}.$$

Returning now to the more general case of several independent variables, if we add the assumption of constant variance for ϵ to our PRM, then the Gauss-Markov theorem says that the least-squares estimator of $\boldsymbol{\beta} = [\beta_0 \beta_1 \cdots \beta_k]'$ is BLUE. The LS criterion function is

$$\sum_{i=1}^{n} (y_i - \beta_0 - \beta_1 x_{i1} - \cdots - \beta_k x_{ik})^2,$$

to be minimized with respect to the β_j's. As before, this results in exactly the system of equations (3.4.3) solved above; however, we now know that $\mathbf{b} = (\mathbf{X'X})^{-1}\mathbf{X'y}$ is the BLUE of $\boldsymbol{\beta}$. A more formal statement of the Gauss-Markov result is this. For a PRM $\mathbf{y} = \mathbf{X\beta} + \boldsymbol{\epsilon}$ with $\mathbf{X}$ a matrix of observations on $(k + 1)$ fixed variates, $E(\boldsymbol{\epsilon}) = \mathbf{0}$ and $\boldsymbol{\Sigma} = E(\boldsymbol{\epsilon\epsilon'}) = \sigma^2\mathbf{I}$, the LS estimator $\mathbf{b} = (\mathbf{X'X})^{-1}\mathbf{X'y}$ of $\boldsymbol{\beta}$ is BLUE. The notation $\boldsymbol{\Sigma} = \sigma^2\mathbf{I}$ is for the matrix of variances and covariances of the residuals in the PRM. Its dimensions are, of course, $(n \times n)$. It appears with σ^2 down its diagonal, representing the constant variance at each observation point $(x_{i1}, \ldots, x_{ik})$, and zeros elsewhere, from the independence assumption of random sampling. If the x_j's are random variables, these same results hold, conditional on the values the x_j's assume in the sample.

To see unbiasedness, we proceed as follows:

$$(3.4.7) \qquad \mathbf{b} = (\mathbf{X'X})^{-1}\mathbf{X'y}$$
$$= (\mathbf{X'X})^{-1}\mathbf{X'}(\mathbf{X\beta} + \boldsymbol{\epsilon})$$
$$= (\mathbf{X'X})^{-1}\mathbf{X'X\beta} + (\mathbf{X'X})^{-1}\mathbf{X'\epsilon}$$
$$= \boldsymbol{\beta} + (\mathbf{X'X})^{-1}\mathbf{X'\epsilon}.$$

$E(\mathbf{b}) = \boldsymbol{\beta}$ since $E[(\mathbf{X'X})^{-1}\mathbf{X'\epsilon}] = \mathbf{0}$, because $(\mathbf{X'X})^{-1}\mathbf{X'}E(\boldsymbol{\epsilon}) = \mathbf{0}$.

The least-squares estimators can also be shown to be consistent estimators. They obviously are unbiased in large samples because the Gauss-Markov result shows them to be unbiased for *any* n. Though not so obvious, in general their individual variances are inversely related to n, so that as sample size increases, the variances of the least-squares estimators approach zero. These are the conditions required for consistency—that as sample size is increased indefinitely the expected value of the estimator converges to the parameter being estimated *and* that the variance of the estimator converges to zero.

Consistency can be argued another way, from the principle of *maximum likelihood* (ML). Maximum-likelihood estimators have consistency and large-sample efficiency as general properties. To obtain them, though, one must know (or assume) the distribution that governs the selection of items into the sample. To this point we have not had to assume anything about the form of the distribution of observations $(y_1, \ldots, y_n)$, but as we saw in the previous chapter such a distribution assumption *is* needed to do inference. We proceed to make it here only to complete the development of statistical properties for b.

If a normal distribution is assumed for each y_i, and the sample is selected under conditions of independence, then the *joint* density of the sample observations is just the product of individual densities. That is,

$f(y_1, \ldots, y_n) = f(y_1) \cdots f(y_n)$. For our problem, each of the individual distributions is a conditional normal density with mean $E(y_i | x_1, \ldots, x_k) = \beta_0 + \beta_1 x_{i1} + \cdots + \beta_k x_{ik}$ and variance σ^2—that is,

$$f(y_i) = (2\pi\sigma^2)^{-1/2} \exp\left[-\tfrac{1}{2}\sigma^{-2}(y_i - \beta_0 - \beta_1 x_{i1} - \cdots - \beta_k x_{ik})^2\right].$$

The joint density of the sample, or *likelihood function*, is therefore

$$
\begin{aligned}
L &= f(y_1, \ldots, y_n) \\
&= (2\pi\sigma^2)^{-n/2} \exp\left[-\tfrac{1}{2}\sigma^{-2} \sum_{i=1}^{n} (y_i - \beta_0 - \beta_1 x_{i1} - \cdots - \beta_k x_{ik})^2\right].
\end{aligned}
$$

The principle of maximum likelihood calls forth the estimator that will maximize the sample likelihood. In other words, we should find for each unknown parameter that function of the sample observations such that if the parameters in L were replaced by their numerical estimates for some sample the likelihood over *that* sample would be maximized. The principle of ML thus directs us to maximize L with respect to $\sigma^2, \beta_0, \beta_1, \ldots, \beta_k$ jointly. From the form of L it is apparent that whatever the value of σ^2, L will be maximized over $(\beta_0, \beta_1, \ldots, \beta_k)$ by minimizing $\sum_{i=1}^{n} (y_i - \beta_0 - \beta_1 x_{i1} - \cdots - \beta_k x_{ik})^2$, precisely the LS criterion. So in this instance the ML and LS estimators coincide.

We will not attempt here to prove minimum variance (bestness) for **b**.[†] But we will need an expression for the variances (and covariances) of the estimated coefficients. This *variance-covariance* matrix of **b** we denote by Σ_b:

(3.4.8)
$$
\Sigma_b = \begin{bmatrix}
\sigma_{b_0}^2 & \sigma_{b_0 b_1} & \cdots & \sigma_{b_0 b_k} \\
\sigma_{b_1 b_0} & \sigma_{b_1}^2 & \cdots & \sigma_{b_1 b_k} \\
\cdot & & & \\
\cdot & & & \\
\cdot & & & \\
\sigma_{b_k b_0} & & \cdots & \sigma_{b_k}^2
\end{bmatrix} = E[(\mathbf{b} - \boldsymbol{\beta})(\mathbf{b} - \boldsymbol{\beta})'].
$$

$[(k+1) \times (k+1)]$

Since $(\mathbf{b} - \boldsymbol{\beta}) = (\mathbf{X'X})^{-1}\mathbf{X'\epsilon}$ from $\mathbf{b} = \boldsymbol{\beta} + (\mathbf{X'X})^{-1}\mathbf{X'\epsilon}$ above, we have

(3.4.9)
$$
\begin{aligned}
\Sigma_b &= E[\{(\mathbf{X'X})^{-1}\mathbf{X'\epsilon}\}\{(\mathbf{X'X})^{-1}\mathbf{X'\epsilon}\}'] \\
&= E[(\mathbf{X'X})^{-1}\mathbf{X'\epsilon\epsilon'X}(\mathbf{X'X})^{-1}] \\
&= (\mathbf{X'X})^{-1}\mathbf{X'}E(\boldsymbol{\epsilon\epsilon'})\mathbf{X}(\mathbf{X'X})^{-1},
\end{aligned}
$$

[†] See, for example, A. S. Goldberger, *Econometric Theory* (New York: Wiley, 1964), pp. 163–165.

since either the columns of $\mathbf{X}$ are observation vectors on fixed variates or the expectation is taken conditional on $\mathbf{X}$.† But by the constant variance and independence in sampling specifications, $E(\epsilon_i \epsilon_j) = \sigma^2$ for $i = j$ and zero otherwise. In matrix notation these specifications are written as: $E(\epsilon\epsilon') = \sigma^2 \mathbf{I}$ with $\mathbf{I}$ an $(n \times n)$ identity matrix. Therefore,

$$
\begin{aligned}
(3.4.10) \qquad \mathbf{\Sigma}_b &= (\mathbf{X'X})^{-1}\mathbf{X'}(\sigma^2\mathbf{I})\mathbf{X}(\mathbf{X'X})^{-1} \\
&= \sigma^2(\mathbf{X'X})^{-1}\mathbf{X'X}(\mathbf{X'X})^{-1} \\
&= \sigma^2(\mathbf{X'X})^{-1}.
\end{aligned}
$$

Looking at the two-variable case again, but using expression (3.4.10),

$$
\sigma_{b_1}^2 = \frac{n\sigma^2}{n\sum x^2 - (\sum x)^2} = \frac{\sigma^2}{\sum x^{*2}}
$$

as before, and

$$
\sigma_{b_0}^2 = \frac{\sigma^2 \sum x^2}{n\sum x^2 - (\sum x)^2} = \frac{\sigma^2 \sum x^2}{n\sum x^{*2}}.
$$

If we add and subtract $\sigma^2 n\bar{x}^2$ in the numerator of this latter expression, we get

$$
\sigma_{b_0}^2 = \frac{\sigma^2}{n} + \bar{x}^2 \frac{\sigma^2}{\sum x^{*2}}
$$

as before. Finally, we consider computing the variance of a particular estimated conditional mean, $\hat{y}_0 = b_0 + b_1 x_0$. First,

$$
\begin{aligned}
\sigma_{\hat{y}_0}^2 &= \sigma_{b_0}^2 + x_0^2 \sigma_{b_1}^2 + 2x_0 \sigma_{b_0 b_1} \ddagger \\
&= \left[\frac{\sigma^2}{n} + \bar{x}^2 \frac{\sigma^2}{\sum x^{*2}}\right] + x_0^2 \left[\frac{\sigma^2}{\sum x^{*2}}\right] - 2x_0 \left[\frac{\bar{x}\sigma^2}{\sum x^{*2}}\right].
\end{aligned}
$$

The last bracketed term is $\sigma_{b_0 b_1}$, obtained as the off-diagonal element of $\mathbf{\Sigma}_b$. Since $(x_0 - \bar{x})^2 = x_0^2 - 2x_0\bar{x} + \bar{x}^2$, our final result is

$$
\sigma_{\hat{y}_0}^2 = \frac{\sigma^2}{n} + (x_0 - \bar{x})^2 \frac{\sigma^2}{\sum x^{*2}}
$$

as before.

The generalization of this formula to the multiple regression case is relatively easy, but because there are two or more conditioning variables involved, *visualizing* a prediction band around $\hat{y}_0$ is difficult. $\sigma_{\hat{y}_0}^2$ for the general case comes most readily from an inspection of the SRM in its

---

† In (3.4.9) we have used the rule for the transpose of a product of matrices, and the fact that the transpose of a symmetric matrix is the matrix itself.

‡ From the rule for the variance of a sum of random variables.

"centered" form, which also yields a useful alternative formulation of the solution equations (3.4.6), one which is a convenient vehicle for introducing the concept of multiple correlation. It develops in terms of the sample variances and covariances of y and the regressors, as follows.

From the $(k + 1)$ restrictions imposed on the SRM by analogy, we take the first one, namely $\sum (y - b_0 - b_1 x_1 - \cdots - b_k x_k) = 0$, and simplify it to

$$(3.4.11) \qquad \bar{y} = b_0 + b_1 \bar{x}_1 + \cdots + b_k \bar{x}_k$$

by dividing through by n and transposing. Now, combining (3.4.11) with the SRM by subtracting $\bar{y}$ from both sides, we get a transformed regression function where no intercept term appears and each variable is measured as a deviation from its respective mean. That is, the SRM (3.4.1) becomes

$$(3.4.12) \qquad y_i^* = b_1 x_{i1}^* + \cdots + b_k x_{ik}^* + e_i.$$

On (3.4.12) are imposed the remaining restrictions, $\sum e_i x_{ij}^* = 0$, $j = 1, \ldots, k$. This gives rise to k new normal equations:

$$(3.4.13) \qquad \sum (y^* - b_1 x_1^* - \cdots - b_k x_k^*) x_1^* = 0,$$
$$\vdots$$
$$\sum (y^* - b_1 x_1^* - \cdots - b_k x_k^*) x_k^* = 0,$$

which are to be solved for the b's in terms of y and the x_j's. The equations in (3.4.13) may be written in simplified form by defining the sums of squares and cross-products that appear there in terms of the sample variances and co-variances of y and the x_j's.†

Define

$$m_{yj} = \frac{1}{n} \sum y^* x_j^*, \qquad m_{jl} = \frac{1}{n} \sum x_j^* x_l^*, \qquad j, l = 1, \ldots, k.$$

Then (3.4.13) becomes

$$(3.4.14) \qquad m_{11} b_1 + \cdots + m_{1k} b_k = m_{y1},$$
$$\vdots$$
$$m_{k1} b_1 + \cdots + m_{kk} b_k = m_{yk}.$$

In matrix notation, let $\mathbf{b}_{)0(} = [b_1 \cdots b_k]'$, the ")0(" indicating the $\mathbf{b}$ vector

---

† Again we note the disparity between this definition and the form of a sample variance used to estimate a population variance. See footnote, p. 27.

excluding b_0. Further, let

$$\mathbf{M}_{xx} = \begin{bmatrix} m_{11} & \cdots & m_{1k} \\ \cdot & & \\ \cdot & & \\ \cdot & & \\ m_{k1} & & m_{kk} \end{bmatrix}, \qquad \mathbf{M}_{yx} = \begin{bmatrix} m_{y1} \\ \cdot \\ \cdot \\ \cdot \\ m_{yk} \end{bmatrix},$$

so the normal equations (3.4.13) appear as

(3.4.15) $\mathbf{M}_{xx}\mathbf{b}_{)0(} = \mathbf{M}_{yx}$,

with solutions

(3.4.16) $\mathbf{b}_{)0(} = \mathbf{M}_{xx}^{-1}\mathbf{M}_{yx}$.

b_0 can always be obtained once $\mathbf{b}_{)0(}$ is calculated by the identity

$$b_0 = \bar{y} - b_1\bar{x}_1 - \cdots - b_k\bar{x}_k.$$

To complete the development of this "centered" version of the SRM we shall determine the variance-covariance matrix of $\mathbf{b}_{)0(}$. The important step is to define a matrix of "deviations" for the observations on independent variables,

$$\underset{(n \times k)}{\mathbf{X}^*} = \begin{bmatrix} x_{11}^* & \cdots & x_{ik}^* \\ \cdot & & \\ \cdot & & \\ \cdot & & \\ x_{n1}^* & \cdots & x_{nk}^* \end{bmatrix},$$

from which it follows that $\mathbf{X}^{*\prime}\mathbf{X}^* = n\mathbf{M}_{xx}$ and $(\mathbf{X}^{*\prime}\mathbf{X}^*)^{-1} = (1/n)\mathbf{M}_{xx}^{-1}$. Note also that $\sum y^* x_j^* = \sum y x_j^*$ so that $n\mathbf{M}_{yx} = \mathbf{X}^{*\prime}\mathbf{y}$.

Now to parallel our previous development, $\mathbf{\Sigma}_{b_{)0(}} = E[(\mathbf{b}_{)0(} - \mathbf{\beta}_{)0(}) \cdot (\mathbf{b}_{)0(} - \mathbf{\beta}_{)0(})']$ is found to be

(3.4.17) $\mathbf{\Sigma}_{b_{)0(}} = n(\mathbf{X}^{*\prime}\mathbf{X}^*)^{-1}\left(\dfrac{1}{n}\right)\mathbf{X}^{*\prime}(\sigma^2\mathbf{I})\left(\dfrac{1}{n}\right)\mathbf{X}^* n(\mathbf{X}^{*\prime}\mathbf{X}^*)^{-1}$

$$= \sigma^2(\mathbf{X}^{*\prime}\mathbf{X}^*)^{-1}$$

$$= \dfrac{\sigma^2}{n}\mathbf{M}_{xx}^{-1}.$$

Equation (3.4.17) clearly shows the inverse dependency of the variances of the LS regression coefficients on sample size, a condition necessary for the coefficients to be consistent estimators. Although the elements of $\mathbf{M}_{xx}^{-1}$ are certainly *not* independent of sample size, they can be viewed as estimates of population variances and covariances of the x_j's. While we expect them to be more precise estimators of these parameters as sample size is increased, their numerical magnitudes will likely not change much.

In addition, $\sigma_{\hat{y}_0}^2$ is now easily written. $\hat{y}_0 = \bar{y} + b_1 x_{01}^* + \cdots + b_k x_{0k}^*$, from the "centered" form of the SRF. As in the two-variable case, the covariance of $\bar{y}$ with each of the LS regression coefficients is zero, so

$$(3.4.18) \qquad \sigma_{\hat{y}_0}^2 = \sigma_{\bar{y}}^2 + x_{01}^{*2}\sigma_{b_1}^2 + \cdots + x_{0k}^{*2}\sigma_{b_k}^2 + 2x_{01}^* x_{02}^* \sigma_{b_1 b_2} + \cdots$$
$$+ 2x_{0,k-1}^* x_{0k}^* \sigma_{b_{k-1} b_k}.$$

In writing (3.4.18) we have made use of a straightforward extension of the rule for calculating the variance of a sum of two random variables. Recognizing that $\sigma_{\bar{y}}^2 = \sigma^2/n$ and using (3.4.17), we obtain a more compact version of (3.4.18):

$$(3.4.19) \qquad \sigma_{\hat{y}_0}^2 = \frac{\sigma^2}{n}\left\{1 + (x_{01}^* \cdots x_{0k}^*)\mathbf{M}_{xx}^{-1}\begin{pmatrix} x_{01}^* \\ \cdot \\ \cdot \\ \cdot \\ x_{0k}^* \end{pmatrix}\right\}.$$

Obviously if the sample point used for predictive purposes coincides with the point of means $(\bar{x}_1, \ldots, \bar{x}_k)$, (3.4.19) reduces to $\sigma_{\hat{y}_0}^2 = \sigma^2/n$ as before. The same general observation holds here as did for the two-variable case— that $\sigma_{\hat{y}_0}^2$ increases the "further" away from $(\bar{x}_1, \ldots, \bar{x}_k)$ is $(x_{01}, \ldots, x_{0k})$.

Occasionally prediction of an "individual" value for y is of interest. For example, one might like to forecast the "actual" level of GNP from some regression model rather than the "average" level of GNP for preselected values of the independent variables appearing in the model. For this purpose $\hat{y}_0$ is still the appropriate statistic. That is, $\hat{y}_0$ is a minimum-variance un-biased estimator not only for $E(y|x_{01}, \ldots, x_{0k})$ but for $y|x_{01}, \ldots, x_{0k}$. Its computed variance in the two applications, however, is not the same.

When used to estimate $E(y|x_{01}, \ldots, x_{0k})$, the variance of $\hat{y}_0$ is given by (3.4.19), or, alternatively

$$(3.4.20) \qquad \sigma_{\hat{y}_0}^2 = \sigma^2 \mathbf{x}_0 (\mathbf{X}'\mathbf{X})^{-1}\mathbf{x}_0',$$

where $\mathbf{x}_0 = (1 \quad x_{01} \quad \cdots \quad x_{0k})$, a *row vector*. Were we to calculate the variance of $\hat{y}_0$ as an estimator for $y_0 = y|x_{01} \cdots x_{0k}$, however, it would be determined by

$$(3.4.21) \qquad E(\hat{y}_0 - y_0)^2 = E(\mathbf{x}_0 \mathbf{b} - y_0)^2$$
$$= E(\mathbf{x}_0 (\mathbf{X}'\mathbf{X})^{-1}\mathbf{X}'\mathbf{y} - y_0)^2.$$

By substituting $\mathbf{y} = \mathbf{X}\boldsymbol{\beta} + \boldsymbol{\epsilon}$ and $y_0 = \mathbf{x}_0\boldsymbol{\beta} + \epsilon_0$, we find

$$(3.4.22) \qquad E(\hat{y}_0 - y_0)^2 = \sigma^2(1 + \mathbf{x}_0(\mathbf{X}'\mathbf{X})^{-1}\mathbf{x}_0').$$

So, used as an estimator of the individual value y_0, the variance of $\hat{y}_0$ is larger than in its use as an estimator for $E(y|x_{01} \cdots x_{0k})$, being $\sigma^2 + \sigma_{\hat{y}_0}^2$.

3.5 MULTIPLE REGRESSION AND CORRELATION

From the point of view of prediction, how well does the regression equation perform as an explanator of observed variations in y? For the two-variable case it was seen that a viable concept of "goodness-of-fit" under a given form for the PRF is the ratio of explained to total variance, namely $S_{\hat{y}}^2/S_y^2$ or $1 - S_e^2/S_y^2$. This measure is also known as the squared correlation coefficient or coefficient of determination in the two-variable case. In multiple regression, however, the composite effect of several conditioning variables on y requires a restatement of the same concept, $S_{\hat{y}}^2/S_y^2$. The partitioning of S_y^2 into $S_{\hat{y}}^2$ and S_e^2, which is required in order that this definition retain its previous meaning, holds also for the multiple regression case. A rigorous statement of this fact is left to the reader.†

Rather than a simple or gross correlation coefficient we now speak of the proportion of explained variance as the (squared) *coefficient of multiple correlation*, R^2. The definition is

$$(3.5.1) \qquad R^2 = \frac{S_{\hat{y}}^2}{S_y^2} = \frac{\sum(\hat{y} - \bar{y})^2}{\sum(y - \bar{y})^2} = \frac{\sum \hat{y}^{*2}}{\sum y^{*2}} = \frac{\hat{\mathbf{y}}^{*\prime}\hat{\mathbf{y}}^*}{nm_{yy}},$$

where $\hat{\mathbf{y}}^*$ is the vector of predicted values of the y_i^*'s and $m_{yy} = S_y^2$. If we likewise use the $\mathbf{X}^*$ notation introduced in the last section, then

$$(3.5.2) \qquad \hat{\mathbf{y}}^* = \mathbf{X}^*\mathbf{b}_{)0(} = \mathbf{X}^*\mathbf{M}_{xx}^{-1}\mathbf{M}_{yx}$$

and

$$(3.5.3) \qquad \hat{\mathbf{y}}^{*\prime}\hat{\mathbf{y}}^* = \mathbf{M}_{yx}'\mathbf{M}_{xx}^{-1}\mathbf{X}^{*\prime}\mathbf{X}^*\mathbf{M}_{xx}^{-1}\mathbf{M}_{yx}$$
$$= n\mathbf{M}_{yx}'\mathbf{M}_{xx}^{-1}\mathbf{M}_{yx}.$$

† The proof might proceed along these lines: $S_y^2 = S_{\hat{y}}^2 + S_e^2$ plus a cross-product term in $\hat{y}$ and e. Now $\hat{y}_i$ depends in a linear fashion on some sample constants ($b_0, b_1, \ldots, b_k$) and $x_{i1}, \ldots, x_{ik}$. And by construction $\sum e = \sum x_1 e = \cdots = \sum x_k e = 0$. Therefore,

$$\sum \hat{y}e = b_0 \sum e + b_1 \sum x_1 e + \cdots + b_k \sum x_k e = 0.$$

Hence

(3.5.4)
$$R^2 = \frac{\mathbf{M}'_{yx}\mathbf{M}_{xx}^{-1}\mathbf{M}_{yx}}{m_{yy}} = \frac{\mathbf{M}'_{yx}\mathbf{b}_{)0(}}{m_{yy}}$$

$$= \frac{\sum_{j=1}^{k} m_{yj}b_j}{m_{yy}}.$$

Equation (3.5.4) provides a useful computational formula. The value of R^2 thus defined is generally contained in the interval $(0, 1)$.†

It should be recognized that a "high" value for R^2 need not imply a "small" prediction interval. The magnitude of the prediction interval, as we saw previously, also depends on the "distance" of the prediction point $(x_{01}, \ldots, x_{0k})$ from the point of sample means.

Another variant of the development above puts R^2 in terms of the individual simple correlation coefficients of y on the x_j's. The model to which it corresponds is of some interest also, particularly in sociology. Beginning with the transformed (centered) model,

(3.4.12)
$$y_i^* = b_1 x_{i1}^* + \cdots + b_k x_{ik}^* + e_i,$$

consider a further transformation, namely

(3.5.5)
$$\tilde{y}_i = \frac{y_i^*}{\sqrt{m_{yy}}}, \qquad \tilde{x}_{ij} = \frac{x_{ij}^*}{\sqrt{m_{jj}}}.$$

Each variable is now said to be in *standard form* (zero mean, unit variance). Rewriting the model,

(3.5.6)
$$\tilde{y}_i \sqrt{m_{yy}} = b_1 \sqrt{m_{11}}\,\tilde{x}_{i1} + \cdots + b_k \sqrt{m_{kk}}\,\tilde{x}_{ik} + e_i.$$

Now, dividing through by $\sqrt{m_{yy}}$ to "scale" the coefficients, we get

(3.5.7)
$$\tilde{y}_i = b_1 \left(\frac{\sqrt{m_{11}}}{\sqrt{m_{yy}}}\right)\tilde{x}_{i1} + \cdots + b_k \left(\frac{\sqrt{m_{kk}}}{\sqrt{m_{yy}}}\right)\tilde{x}_{ik} + e_i,$$

with the following interpretation: the effect, ceteris paribus, of a unit standard deviation change from the mean of x_j will result in a $b_j(\sqrt{m_{jj}}/\sqrt{m_{yy}})$ unit standard deviation change from the mean of y. The new coefficients, $\bar{b}_j = b_j(\sqrt{m_{jj}}/\sqrt{m_{yy}})$, $j = 1, \ldots, k$, are called *standardized regression coefficients*

---

† An exception is discussed in Section 3.8. It should also be observed that for $\mathbf{X'X}$ of full rank if $n = k + 1$, predicted and actual y *always* correspond, hence $R^2 = 1$. This occurs because a $(k + 1)$-dimensional plane (the regression line) is uniquely established by $(k + 1)$ points. For purposes of further analysis, obviously, the $n = k + 1$ case of regression is not very interesting. If $n < k + 1$, $R^2 = 1$ also, because all actual y_i's will lie on *all* calculated LS regression lines.

(or "beta" coefficients), obtained in the usual way from a regression of $\tilde{y}$ on $(\tilde{x}_1, \ldots, \tilde{x}_k)$:

$$(3.5.8) \qquad \tilde{\mathbf{b}}_{)0(} = (\tilde{\mathbf{X}}'\tilde{\mathbf{X}})^{-1}\tilde{\mathbf{X}}'\tilde{\mathbf{y}}, \qquad \text{where } \tilde{\mathbf{X}} = \mathbf{X}^* \begin{bmatrix} \dfrac{1}{\sqrt{m_{11}}} & & & 0 \\ & \cdot & & \\ & & \cdot & \\ & & & \cdot \\ 0 & & & \dfrac{1}{\sqrt{m_{kk}}} \end{bmatrix}$$

As our previous (centered) model had a representation in terms of the "moments" of the x_j's and y, so the standardized model may be represented in terms of the simple correlations between the x_j's and y.

Define the correlation matrix of independent variables, $\mathbf{\rho}_{xx}$, to be

$$(3.5.9) \qquad \mathbf{\rho}_{xx} = \begin{bmatrix} 1 & r_{12} & \cdots & r_{1k} \\ & 1 & & \\ \cdot & & \cdot & \\ \cdot & & & \cdot \\ \cdot & & & \cdot \\ r_{k1} & & & 1 \end{bmatrix}$$

$$= \begin{bmatrix} \dfrac{1}{\sqrt{m_{11}}} & & & 0 \\ & \cdot & & \\ & & \cdot & \\ 0 & & & \dfrac{1}{\sqrt{m_{kk}}} \end{bmatrix} \mathbf{M}_{xx} \begin{bmatrix} \dfrac{1}{\sqrt{m_{11}}} & & & 0 \\ & \cdot & & \\ & & \cdot & \\ 0 & & & \dfrac{1}{\sqrt{m_{kk}}} \end{bmatrix}$$

and note that $\tilde{\mathbf{X}}'\tilde{\mathbf{X}} = n\mathbf{\rho}_{xx}$, $(\tilde{\mathbf{X}}'\tilde{\mathbf{X}})^{-1} = (1/n)\mathbf{\rho}_{xx}^{-1}$. A correlation vector $\tilde{\mathbf{X}}'\tilde{\mathbf{y}} = n\mathbf{\rho}_{xx} = n[r_{y1} \cdots r_{yk}]'$ is also defined, so that

$$(3.5.10) \qquad\qquad \tilde{\mathbf{b}}_{)0(} = \mathbf{\rho}_{xx}^{-1}\mathbf{\rho}_{yx}.$$

Finally, R^2 has an interesting expansion in terms of "beta" coefficients. From before [(3.5.4)],

$$(3.5.11) \qquad R^2 = \dfrac{\sum\limits_{j=1}^{k} m_{yj}b_j}{m_{yy}} = \dfrac{\sum\limits_{j=1}^{k} m_{yj}\left(\dfrac{\sqrt{m_{yy}}}{\sqrt{m_{jj}}}\right)\tilde{b}_j}{m_{yy}}$$

$$= \sum\limits_{j=1}^{k} \tilde{b}_j\left(\dfrac{m_{yj}}{\sqrt{m_{yy}}\sqrt{m_{jj}}}\right) = \sum\limits_{j=1}^{k} \tilde{b}_j r_{yj},$$

a sum of cross-products of the standardized regression coefficients and the corresponding *simple* correlations between y and the x_j's.

Many attempts have been made to *interpret* (3.5.4) and (3.5.11) in terms of the variable or variables that make the largest contribution to explaining variations in y. But unless we have the *very* special case where the conditioning variables mutually have zero correlation in the sample, such a task can end only with an arbitrary and highly unsatisfactory result. In the next two sections we shall develop ideas leading to this conclusion.

3.6 ON THE INTERPRETATION OF REGRESSION RELATIONSHIPS[†]

Exactly how variables interact in the regression framework is the key to our understanding and using it effectively. As suggested above, it is in general fruitless to attempt a partitioning of the overall ability of a regression equation to account for variability in y into exclusive cells, each containing one of the conditioning variables. In this section we shall argue this more formally. Along the way we shall bring out several important relations that exist algebraically between *simple* and *partial* regression coefficients in the SRF. From these will come notions of interpretation for partial regression coefficients and a knowledge of what happens as independent variables are added or deleted from a regression equation.

Consider the centered form of a three-variable model,

$$(3.6.1) \qquad y_i^* = b_1 x_{i1}^* + b_2 x_{i2}^* + e_i.$$

For current purposes we will need some new notation. Let $b_{y1.2}$ be the regression coefficient for x_1 in the multiple regression of y on x_1 and x_2; let $b_{y2.1}$ stand for the regression coefficient of x_2 in the multiple regression of y on x_1 and x_2 (these then correspond to b_1 and b_2 in the equation above); finally let $e_{y.12}$ be the residual from the regression of y on x_1 and x_2.

Using $\mathbf{b}_{)0(} = \mathbf{M}_{xx}^{-1}\mathbf{M}_{yx}$, we get computational forms for these partial regression coefficients in terms of sample moments:

$$(3.6.2) \qquad b_{y1.2} = \frac{m_{y1}m_{22} - m_{12}m_{y2}}{m_{11}m_{22} - m_{12}^2},$$

$$b_{y2.1} = \frac{m_{y2}m_{11} - m_{12}m_{y1}}{m_{11}m_{22} - m_{12}^2}.$$

Now consider the regression of y^* on x_1^* alone, with *simple* regression coefficient (slope) b_{y1} and residual $e_{y.1}$:

[†] This section has been largely influenced by my colleague, Arthur S. Goldberger. His *Topics in Regression Analysis* (New York: Macmillan, 1968) contains this material plus several other unique attempts at interpretation in the regression model.

$$(3.6.3) \qquad\qquad y_i^* = b_{y1}x_{i1}^* + e_{i,y.1}.$$

The LS estimator. is, from before, $b_{y1} = m_{y1}/m_{11}$.

Finally, we need the "auxiliary" regression of x_2^* on x_1^*,

$$(3.6.4) \qquad\qquad x_{i2}^* = b_{21}x_{i1}^* + e_{i,2.1}.$$

If we were to compute b_{21}, we would do it via: $b_{21} = m_{12}/m_{11}$.

Now look at $b_{y1.2}$ again, but substitute $m_{y1} = b_{y1}m_{11}$ and $m_{12} = b_{21}m_{11}$ to get

$$b_{y1.2} = \frac{b_{y1}m_{11}m_{22} - b_{21}m_{11}m_{y2}}{m_{11}m_{22} - m_{12}^2}.$$

If we add and subtract $m_{12}^2 b_{y1}$ in the numerator,

$$b_{y1.2} = b_{y1} + \frac{m_{12}^2 b_{y1} - b_{21}m_{11}m_{y2}}{m_{11}m_{22} - m_{12}^2}.$$

The second term can be altered further by using $m_{12}^2 b_{y1} = b_{21}m_{11}m_{12}b_{y1} = b_{21}m_{12}m_{y1}$ to get

$$(3.6.5) \qquad\qquad b_{y1.2} = b_{y1} - b_{21}\left(\frac{m_{11}m_{y2} - m_{12}m_{y1}}{m_{11}m_{22} - m_{12}^2}\right)$$

$$= b_{y1} - b_{21}b_{y2.1},$$

which says, the calculated regression coefficient of y on x_1 (in the presence of x_2) equals the simple (gross) regression coefficient of y on x_1, minus the product of the coefficient from the auxiliary regression of x_2 on x_1 and the coefficient calculated from a regression of y on x_2 (in the presence of x_1).

Or, another way:

$$(3.6.6) \qquad\qquad b_{y1} = b_{y1.2} + b_{21}b_{y2.1},$$

which is analogous to the derivative

$$\frac{dy}{dx_1} = \frac{\partial y}{\partial x_1} + \frac{\partial y}{\partial x_2} \cdot \frac{dx_2}{dx_1},$$

where $y = f(x_1, x_2)$, when x_2 is itself a function of x_1. The overall effect of a change in x_1 on y derives from two sources, a direct effect $\partial y/\partial x_1$ and an indirect effect $(\partial y/\partial x_2)(dx_2/dx_1)$ that accounts for changes in x_1 acting through x_2. Through this analogy the (multiple) regression coefficients are often referred to as *partial* regression coefficients.

Next, what happens when a regressor is added or deleted?

The calculated residuals $e_{2.1}$ from the auxiliary regression of x_2 on x_1 in a very meaningful sense *measure* x_2 after allowance for x_1. If we regress

y^* on these residuals, in an SRM

(3.6.7) $$y_i^* = b_{ye_2.1}e_{i,2.1} + e_{i,y.e_2.1}$$

we would compute $b_{ye_2.1}$ by: $b_{ye_2.1} = m_{ye_2.1}/m_{e_2.1e_2.1}$. Now

(3.6.8) $$m_{ye_2.1} = \frac{1}{n}\sum y^* e_{2.1} = \frac{1}{n}\sum y^*(x_2^* - b_{21}x_1^*)$$

$$= \frac{1}{n}\sum y^* x_2^* - b_{21}\frac{1}{n}\sum y^* x_1^*$$

$$= m_{y2} - b_{21}m_{y1}$$

$$= m_{y2} - \frac{m_{12}m_{y1}}{m_{11}} \quad \left(\text{using } b_{21} = \frac{m_{12}}{m_{11}}\right)$$

and

(3.6.9) $$m_{e_2.1e_2.1} = \frac{1}{n}\sum (x_2^* - b_{21}x_1^*)^2$$

$$= m_{22} - 2b_{21}m_{12} + b_{21}^2 m_{11}$$

$$= m_{22} - \frac{m_{12}^2}{m_{11}} \quad \left(\text{again, } b_{21} = \frac{m_{12}}{m_{11}}\right).$$

Summing up,

(3.6.10) $$b_{ye_2.1} = \frac{m_{y2} - \dfrac{m_{12}m_{y1}}{m_{11}}}{m_{22} - \dfrac{m_{12}^2}{m_{11}}}$$

$$= \frac{m_{11}m_{y2} - m_{12}m_{y1}}{m_{11}m_{22} - m_{12}^2} = b_{y2.1} \quad \text{by (3.6.2).}$$

The regression of y on the calculated residuals from a regression of x_2 on x_1 yields the partial regression coefficient of y on x_2 (in the presence of x_1). Thus a partial regression coefficient measures the effect of one variable *after allowance* for the other (or others).

A further interesting step in this development is to allow for the effects of x_1 in *both* y and x_2. That is, suppose we run a regression of the residuals from y on x_1 alone ($e_{y.1}$) on the residuals from x_2 on $x_1(e_{2.1})$ in a sample regression function

(3.6.11) $$e_{y.1} = b_{e_{(y.1)}e_{(2.1)}}e_{2.1} + e_{(y.1).(2.1)},$$

ignoring the observation subscript and simplifying notation on the residual.

Then, by our well-used LS slope computation in two-variable regression,

(3.6.12) $$b_{e_{(y.1)}e_{(2.1)}} = \frac{m_{e_{(y.1)}e_{(2.1)}}}{m_{e_{(2.1)}e_{(2.1)}}}.$$

The denominator has been treated before [(3.6.9)]. As for the numerator,

$$(3.6.13) \qquad m_{e\,(y.1)\,e\,(2.1)} = \frac{1}{n} \sum (y^* - b_{y1}x_1^*)(x_2^* - b_{21}x_1^*)$$

$$= \frac{1}{n} \sum y^*(x_2^* - b_{21}x_1^*) - \frac{1}{n} \sum b_{y1}x_1^*(x_2^* - b_{21}x_1^*)$$

$$= m_{ye_{2.1}} - b_{y1}(m_{12} - b_{21}m_{11}).$$

But the trailing term is zero because $b_{21} = m_{12}/m_{11}$. Thus,

$$(3.6.14) \qquad b_{e\,(y.1)\,e\,(2.1)} = \frac{m_{e\,(y.1)\,e\,(2.1)}}{m_{e\,(2.1)\,e\,(2.1)}} = \frac{m_{ye_{2.1}}}{m_{e\,(2.1)\,e\,(2.1)}} = b_{ye_{2.1}}$$

$$= b_{y2.1}.$$

Making allowance for x_1 in *both* y and x_2 is *redundant*—fortunately, the conditioning variable x_1 cannot be "overconditioned."

What happens if we adjust y for the effects of x_1 but *not* x_2? That is, suppose we regress $e_{y.1}$ on x_2:

$$(3.6.15) \qquad e_{y.1} = b_{e\,(y.1)\,2}x_2^* + e_{(y.1).2}.$$

The slope in (3.6.15) is available from

$$(3.6.16) \qquad b_{e\,(y.1)\,2} = \frac{m_{e\,(y.1)\,2}}{m_{22}}.$$

Now,

$$(3.6.17) \qquad m_{e\,(y.1)\,2} = \frac{1}{n} \sum (y^* - b_{y1}x_1^*)x_2^*$$

$$= m_{y2} - b_{y1}m_{12}$$

$$= m_{y2} - \frac{m_{y1}m_{12}}{m_{11}} \qquad \left(\text{using } b_{y1} = \frac{m_{y1}}{m_{11}}\right),$$

so that

$$(3.6.18) \qquad b_{e\,(y.1)\,2} = \frac{m_{11}m_{y2} - m_{y1}m_{12}}{m_{11}m_{22}}$$

$$\neq b_{y2.1}.$$

This is like running a "stepwise" regression, where y is first adjusted for the effects of x_1 and then x_2 is introduced, neglecting to account for the correlation between x_2 and x_1 (and thus getting the "wrong" answer). For,

$$(3.6.19) \qquad b_{e\,(y.1)\,2} = b_{y2.1}\left(\frac{m_{11}m_{22} - m_{12}^2}{m_{11}m_{22}}\right)$$

$$= b_{y2.1}(1 - r_{12}^2).$$

Since $0 \leq r_{12}^2 \leq 1$, $|b_{e_{(y.1)}2}| \leq |b_{y2.1}|$. In absolute-value terms this "step-wise" coefficient understates the correct partial regression coefficient between y and x_2. They are *equal* if $r_{12} = 0$. Note also that if $r_{12} = 0$, $b_{21} = 0$, and from the basic relation (3.6.6) $b_{y1} = b_{y.12}$ and $b_{y2} = b_{y2.1}$. When the independent variables are uncorrelated in the sample, partial regression slopes in the multiple regression of y on x_1 and x_2 are equal to the simple regression slopes of y on x_1 and y on x_2 in two *separate* two-variable regressions. The constant term in the multiple regression equation still may be computed easily, from $b_0 = \bar{y} - b_{y1}\bar{x}_1 - b_{y2}\bar{x}_2$.

While we will not develop these ideas further here, we can easily extend all of the preceding analysis to speak of the relation between y and x_2 in the presence of a *set* of conditioning variables rather than just one. All the conclusions follow; the algebra proceeds in matrix notation.

The final "interpretation" is for R^2. Here we see that as a partial regression coefficient can be written in terms of its corresponding simple coefficient plus a "correction" term [cf. (3.6.6)], the multiple correlation coefficient R^2 for a regression of y on x_1 and x_2 can be derived as the squared simple correlation coefficient of y on x_1 (or x_2; the argument is symmetric) and a "correction" term. It is the nature of this correction term that is of primary interest to us here.

Consider the three-variable case again, and write out the predicted values for this regression:

$$(3.6.20) \qquad \hat{y}_{.12}^* = b_{y1.2}x_1^* + b_{y2.1}x_2^* = y^* - e_{y.12}.$$

$\sum \hat{y}_{.12}^* = 0$ here, so the numerator or *regression sum-of-squares* in the expression for R^2 (3.5.1) is

$$(3.6.21) \qquad \sum \hat{y}_{.12}^{*2} = n(b_{y1.2}m_{y1} + b_{y2.1}m_{y2}).$$

From before, $b_{y1.2} = b_{y1} - b_{21}b_{y2.1}$, so upon substitution (3.6.21) becomes

$$(3.6.22) \qquad \frac{1}{n}\sum \hat{y}_{.12}^{*2} = (b_{y1} - b_{21}b_{y2.1})m_{y1} + b_{y2.1}m_{y2}$$
$$= b_{y2.1}(m_{y2} - b_{21}m_{y1}) + b_{y1}m_{y1}$$
$$= b_{y2.1}m_{ye_{2.1}} + b_{y1}m_{y1} \qquad \text{[using (3.6.8)]}$$
$$= b_{ye_{2.1}}m_{ye_{2.1}} + b_{y1}m_{y1} \qquad \text{[using (3.6.10)]}.$$

Again using (3.5.1), $nb_{y1}m_{y1} = \sum \hat{y}_{.1}^{*2}$, the regression sum-of-squares when y is regressed on x_1 alone. Likewise, $nb_{ye_{2.1}}m_{ye_{2.1}}$ is the regression sum-of-squares when y is regressed on the residuals of x_2 on x_1, say $\sum \hat{y}_{.e_{(2.1)}}^{*2}$. Thus, (3.6.22) is equivalent to

$$(3.6.23) \qquad \sum \hat{y}_{.12}^{*2} = \sum \hat{y}_{.1}^{*2} + \sum \hat{y}_{.e_{(2.1)}}^{*2}.$$

Dividing (3.6.23) through by $\sum y^{*2} = nm_{yy}$,

$$(3.6.24) \qquad\qquad R^2_{y.12} = R^2_{y.1} + R^2_{y.e\,(2.1)}.$$

Adding another regressor can only *add* to R^2, since the second term (as well as the first) is always nonnegative.

The reader may verify that an alternative form for (3.6.24) is

$$(3.6.25) \qquad\qquad R^2_{y.12} = R^2_{y.1} + r^2_{y2.1}(1 - R^2_{y.1})$$

where $r^2_{y2.1} = R^2_{e\,(y.1)\cdot e\,(2.1)}$ is called the squared *partial correlation coefficient* between y and x_2. $r^2_{y2.1}$ is the squared simple correlation coefficient of y and x_2 after the effects of x_1 have been accounted for; i.e., holding x_1 constant. In our terminology it is the R^2 calculated from the regression of the residual $e_{(y.1)}$ on the residual $e_{(2.1)}$. As we saw previously, the calculated slope in this regression is just $b_{ye(2.1)}$. Likewise, $m_{ye\,(2.1)} = m_{e\,(y.1)e\,(2.1)}$. But $m_{yy} \neq m_{e\,(y.1)e\,(y.1)}$ so that $r^2_{y2.1} \neq R^2_{ye\,(2.1)}$ in general.

Note that *if* x_1 and x_2 are uncorrelated, then $b_{21} = 0$, $m_{12} = 0$, so that $m_{ye2.1} = m_{y2}$ in (3.6.24). $b_{ye2.1} = b_{y2.1}$ always, but also $b_{y2.1} = b_{y2}$ when $r_{12} = 0$, so that in the expression (3.6.22), $b_{ye2.1}m_{ye2.1} = b_{y2}m_{y2}$. Since $nb_{y2}m_{y2} = \sum \hat{y}^{*2}_{.2}$ is the regression sum-of-squares from a regression of y on x_2 alone, in this extreme case

$$(3.6.26) \qquad\qquad R^2_{y.12} = R^2_{y.1} + R^2_{y.2}.$$

When the independent variables are mutually uncorrelated, the multiple correlation coefficient is the sum of the two coefficients of determination (squared simple correlation coefficients) in the regression of y on x_1 and y on x_2. Otherwise, the second term of (3.6.24) represents the explanatory power of x_2 in the presence of x_1. Note finally that $R^2_{y.12}$ could also be put in terms of $R^2_{y.2}$ and $R^2_{y.e\,(1.2)}$, where $e_{(1.2)}$ derives from another auxiliary regression, of x_1 on x_2, and *measures* x_1 after the effects of x_2 have been accounted for. As mentioned at the outset, the argument is symmetric.

3.7 TESTING AND INFERENCE

Following the developments of Sections 2.8 and 2.9, the multiple regression model has a well-established body of inferential techniques once the appropriate distribution assumption is made on ϵ. A necessary preliminary to this development, however, is a treatment of the estimation of σ^2 for the $(k + 1)$-variable model.

As in the two-variable case, the error sum-of-squares adjusted for degrees of freedom $[(n - k - 1)$ in this case] yields an unbiased estimate of σ^2. This result we state without proof. Written out, the unbiased estimate of σ^2 is

$$(3.7.1) \qquad \mathscr{S}^2 = \frac{1}{n - k - 1} \sum_{i=1}^{n} (y_i - \hat{y}_i)^2.$$

Making a normality assumption on ϵ reproduces the distribution theory presented previously. In the multiple regression case tests of significance for individual coefficients develop as follows.

To test $H: \beta_h = \bar{\beta}_h$ versus $H_A: \beta_h \neq \bar{\beta}_h$, $\beta_h < \bar{\beta}_h$, or $\beta_h > \bar{\beta}_h$, with $\bar{\beta}_h$ a constant and $h = 0, 1, \ldots, k$, we begin by noting that $(b_h - \bar{\beta}_h) \sim N(0, \sigma_{b_h}^2)$ and $(b_h - \bar{\beta}_h)/\sigma_{b_h} \sim N(0, 1)$. Also, $(n - k - 1)\mathscr{S}^2/\sigma^2 \sim \chi_{(n-k-1)}^2$. The construction of a t-statistic follows:

$$(3.7.2) \qquad t = \frac{(b_h - \bar{\beta}_h)}{\sigma_{b_h}} \bigg/ \sqrt{\frac{\mathscr{S}^2}{\sigma^2}} \sim t_{(n-k-1)}.$$

Simplfying (3.7.2) for the calculated partial regression coefficients $b_1, \ldots, b_k$,

$$(3.7.3) \qquad t = \frac{(b_h - \bar{\beta}_h)}{\dfrac{\sigma}{\sqrt{n}} \sqrt{m^{hh}}} \bigg| \frac{\mathscr{S}}{\sigma} = \frac{b_h - \bar{\beta}_h}{\dfrac{\mathscr{S}}{\sqrt{n}} \sqrt{m^{hh}}} = \frac{b_h - \bar{\beta}_h}{\hat{\sigma}_{b_h}},$$

where again m^{hh} is the appropriate element from $\mathbf{M}_{xx}^{-1}$. A similar derivation for the test statistic for a hypothesis about β_0 leads also to this result. If the hypothesis of interest is $H: \bar{\beta}_h = 0$, the familiar "t-ratio" emerges from (3.7.3) as the test statistic of interest, for use in one- or two-sided hypothesis tests.

Unlike the two-variable case, where the test of overall significance was equivalent to a test of the significance for the slope coefficient, a test of the overall significance of the multiple regression equation is *not equivalent* to a series of tests of significance on the individual coefficients. Overall significance is, rather, a test of the *joint* hypothesis $H: \beta_1 = \cdots = \beta_k = 0$. Equivalently, it is a test of $H: R^2 = 0$, as we shall see below. The development is a straightforward application of the F-test construction presented in Section 2.9.

The specifications underlying the general multiple regression model, Ω, are

$$(3.7.4) \qquad \Omega: \begin{cases} \mathbf{y} = \mathbf{X}\boldsymbol{\beta} + \boldsymbol{\epsilon}, \\ E(\mathbf{y}) = \mathbf{X}\boldsymbol{\beta}, \\ SS_\Omega = (n - k - 1)\mathscr{S}^2, \end{cases}$$

$$E\left(\frac{SS_\Omega}{n - k - 1}\right) = \sigma^2.$$

Under $H: \beta_1 = \cdots = \beta_k = 0$ there is, in effect, no regression relation. The specifications H are, therefore, exactly those in (2.9.2):

$$(3.7.5) \qquad H: \begin{cases} y = \beta_0 + \epsilon, \\ E(y) = \beta_0, \end{cases}$$

$$\mathrm{SS}_H = \sum_{i=1}^{n} (y_i - \bar{y})^2 = nm_{yy},$$

$$E\left(\frac{\mathrm{SS}_H}{n-1}\right) = \sigma^2,$$

because $\bar{y}$ is the LS estimator for β_0 under the hypothesis. As before, SS_Ω and SS_H are not independent. However, $\mathrm{SS}_H - \mathrm{SS}_\Omega \,(\geq 0)$ *is* independent of SS_Ω. The correct F-statistic is given by

$$(3.7.6) \qquad F = \frac{\mathrm{SS}_H - \mathrm{SS}_\Omega}{\mathrm{SS}_\Omega} \cdot \frac{n-k-1}{k} \sim F_{k,\,n-k-1}.$$

Degrees of freedom are determined for the numerator as follows: SS_H/σ^2 is χ^2 with $(n-1)$ d.f.; $\mathrm{SS}_\Omega/\sigma^2$ is likewise χ^2 with $(n-k-1)$ d.f. and is contained within SS_H/σ^2. Their difference is a χ^2 with $[(n-1)-(n-k-1)] = k$ d.f.

An important simplification of (3.7.6) yields the correspondence of $H: \beta_1 = \cdots = \beta_k = 0$ with the hypothesis that the population value of R^2 is zero, $H: R^2_{\mathrm{POP}} = 0$, where the population R^2 is, by analogy to the sample R^2, determined by $R^2_{\mathrm{POP}} = 1 - \sigma^2/\sigma_y^2$. In the derivation of R^2, the "total" sum of squares of y is $\sum y^{*2}_{.12\ldots k} = nm_{yy}R^2$. Then $\mathrm{SS}_\Omega = nm_{yy} - nm_{yy}R^2 = nm_{yy}(1 - R^2)$, from the partitioning of m_{yy} into a sum of "regression" and "error" components. In this instance, the total sum-of-squares (total sample variation in y) *is* SS_H, so that

$$(3.7.7) \qquad F = \frac{nm_{yy} - nm_{yy}(1 - R^2)}{nm_{yy}(1 - R^2)} \cdot \frac{n-k-1}{k}$$

$$= \frac{R^2}{(1 - R^2)} \cdot \frac{n-k-1}{k} \sim F_{k,\,n-k-1}.$$

In looking for consistency of results in regression analysis, one should not be alarmed to see a particular regression *equation* pass this R^2 significance test at some given level while none of the *individual* regression coefficients is found to be significantly different from zero at the *same* level using the t-test (t-ratio). Almost perfect linear relations between some of the independent variables can explain such an occurrence. For when there are such dependencies in the X-matrix, the estimated variances of individual regression coefficients tend to get large, thus reducing the chances of rejecting hypotheses like $\beta_h = 0$.† However, unless the linear dependence in X is

† This point will be discussed in detail in Section 3.9.

exact (in which event no results will be forthcoming because $X'X$ is singular), the regression equation may still account for a large proportion of the observed variance in y, thus allowing the overall significance test of $H: R^2_{POP} = 0$ to result in its rejection.

On the other hand, it would be surprising to find a particular regression coefficient significantly different from zero while the $R^2_{POP} = 0$ hypothesis was *not* rejected, but it *can* happen. The explanation in this instance is on the grounds of different degrees of freedom underlying the two tests.†

Many other tests are possible within the regression model, where the restrictions imposed on β are *linear*. Some examples are given in Table 3.1.

Table 3.1

Examples of Linear Hypotheses on β

The hypothesis:	yields a test statistic distributed as:
(i) $H: \beta_1 = \beta_2 = 0$	$F_{2, n-k-1}$
(ii) $H: \begin{cases} \beta_6 + .5\beta_3 = 0 \\ 3\beta_4 - \beta_7 = 0 \end{cases}$	$F_{2, n-k-1}$
(iii) $H: \beta_2 - \beta_5 = 0$	$F_{1, n-k-1}$†

† This hypothesis can also be tested with "t", since there is one d.f. in the numerator.

New regression programs will have general linear hypothesis testing capability. Otherwise, for each test two regressions must be run, one unrestricted, the other with restrictions imposed, in order to obtain the appropriate error sums-of-squares for test purposes. Taking (ii) above as a case in point, to compute the error sum-of-squares under the hypothesis we would appropriately transform the data and consider a modified equation,

$$y = \beta_0 + \beta_1 x_1 + \beta_2 x_2 + \beta_3(x_3 - .5x_6) + \beta_4(x_4 + 3x_7) + \cdots + \epsilon.$$

The hypothesis (ii) has been used to remove β_6 and β_7 from direct consideration in the modified equation.‡

† A comprehensive treatment of these seeming inconsistencies is given in a paper by R. C. Geary and C. E. V. Leser, "Significance Tests in Multiple Regression," *The American Statistician*, Feb. 1968, pp. 20–21.

‡ Thus in testing linear hypotheses about the regression coefficients (like $H: \beta_1 - \beta_2 = 3$; or, $H: \beta_2 = \beta_3 = 0$) we build linear restrictions directly into the estimation procedure for calculating LS estimates. This is precisely what must be done to compute the relevant SS_H for testing purposes. Occasionally theory dictates that a specific linear (or equality) restriction be imposed: obviously it may be handled easily by our least-squares framework. But suppose inequality restrictions are relevant. Suppose the coefficient (or coefficients) in question must, on a priori grounds, lie between zero and one, or must be positive. These restrictions cannot be adequately handled within the LS regression framework. But such problems can be formulated for solution by mathematical programming methods. As yet little is known about the statistical properties of estimates derived in this way; however, several recent studies have appeared with at least some preliminary information on them.

The F-test statistics for use in testing such hypotheses as these have interesting interpretations in terms of a change in R^2 moving from the restricted to the unrestricted equation. Again, let the sum-of-squares under the general specifications be SS_Ω and under the hypothesis SS_H. Letting q be the number of restrictions imposed by hypothesis, the F-statistic of relevance is

$$(3.7.8) \qquad F_{q,\,n-k-1} = \frac{n-k-1}{q} \cdot \frac{SS_H - SS_\Omega}{SS_\Omega}.$$

Translating (3.7.8) into terms of explained variance before and after the hypothesis is imposed, we divide both numerator and denominator by nm_{yy} and recall that $R_\Omega^2 = 1 - SS_\Omega/nm_{yy}$, $R_H^2 = 1 - SS_H/nm_{yy}$.[†] Thus, (3.7.8) can be reframed as

$$(3.7.9) \qquad F_{q,\,n-k-1} = \frac{n-k-1}{q} \cdot \frac{R_\Omega^2 - R_H^2}{(1 - R_\Omega^2)}.$$

The numerator of (3.7.9) describes the difference in proportion of explained variance between the two models, under Ω and under H. There is one exception to the use of (3.7.9) in a testing situation, and that is for the hypothesis of zero intercept, a topic we consider in the next section. Otherwise any hypothesis test considered to this point can be accomplished using (3.7.9).

An additional test which may be of some interest considers a hypothesis of linearity in independent variables *given* linearity in parameters. It may easily be modified to consider any other specified form for the regression relation, but it depends on the existence of multiple observations at each observed point $(x_{i1}, \ldots, x_{ik})$, a luxury few bodies of economic data can boast.

For a two-variable example the nature of the test is depicted in Fig. 3.1. At each of the four observed values of the single independent variable, x, say x_h ($h = 1, \ldots, 4$), are arrays of observations on the dependent variable y_{hr} with $r = 1, \ldots, m_h$ observations at each point. The general specifications are

$$(3.7.10) \qquad \Omega: \quad y_{hr} = \theta_h + \epsilon_{hr},$$
$$E(y_{hr}) = \theta_h,$$
$$SS_\Omega = \sum_{h=1}^{l} \sum_{r=1}^{m_h} (y_{hr} - \bar{y}_h)^2,$$

---

† Note that the divisor in R_H^2 is nm_{yy}. Thus, R_H^2 may *not* be correctly calculated from a regression that takes the hypothesis into account. For instance, imposing $H: \beta_3 = 3.0$, we would calculate SS_H via the regression $y - 3x_3 = \beta_0 + \beta_1 x_1 + \beta_2 x_2 + \beta_4 x_4 + \cdots + \epsilon$. However, the R^2 calculated as part of the "normal output" for this regression equation will be based on $(y - 3x_3)$ as dependent variable rather than y.

where

$$\bar{y}_h = \frac{1}{m_h} \sum_{r=1}^{m_h} y_h,$$

the "subgroup" mean and the LS estimate of θ_h. The hypothesis specified is that the regression line is linear through the subgroup means, which is just our previous Ω specifications $\mathbf{y} = \mathbf{x}\boldsymbol{\beta} + \boldsymbol{\epsilon}$. As SS_H, therefore, we have the error sum-of-squares for the linear model.

Using the F-test construction, this hypothesis is tested with

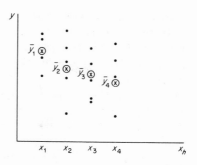

Fig. 3.1

Test of Linearity of Regression:
Two-Variable Example

$$(3.7.11) \qquad F_{(l-k-1),\,M-l} = \frac{SS_H - SS_\Omega}{SS_\Omega} \cdot \frac{M-l}{l-k-1},$$

where $M = \sum_{h=1}^{l} m_h$, the total number of obsevations. Degrees of freedom are determined for the denominator as $M - l$, where l is the number of subgroup means estimated. As before, degrees of freedom for the estimated regression model are $M - k - 1$, so that in the numerator $[(M - k - 1) - (M - l)] = l - k - 1$ degrees of freedom. Another test for nonlinearity of regression that makes fewer data demands is available, and is mentioned in Section 4.3.

To complete the development of inference theory for multiple regression we need only note that confidence intervals for individual coefficients may be constructed from the t-distribution, exactly as they were in the two-variable case. In addition we can now speak of *joint* confidence intervals for a set of coefficients or linear functions of them, analogues to the general F-tests from which they derive. These confidence *ellipsoids*, as they are known, will not be developed here; statements of the methodology can be found in books on analysis of variance under the heading of methods of multiple comparisons.

3.8 USES OF R^2 IN MODEL BUILDING AND TESTING

R^2 IN A MODEL WITH ZERO INTERCEPT

Often theoretical considerations suggest that a regression model be specified with a zero intercept. An example is the aggregate consumption model treated in the previous chapter. In addition, the classical methodology yields a statistical test for the hypothesis of zero intercept. While in the first instance it might be inappropriate to *compare* empirical results gleaned from models specified with and without intercepts precisely because *theoretical considerations* are invoked, in the second such comparisons are quite natural, simply because the statistical test of a zero intercept can be stated in terms of the residual sums-of-squares in the alternative models. One correctly expects the error sum-of-squares in the restricted model to be *larger* than in the unrestricted one; equivalently many users of the regression framework tend to think in terms of comparing R^2 for the two models. This comparison is also quite appropriate, in general, because the classical F-test for any linear restriction may be posed as a "change-in-R^2" criterion. When computations show a *larger* R^2 for the model forced through the origin than for the "free" model, one should be suspicious of his results. But not only is this disturbing outcome a real possibility when the restriction in question is $\beta_0 = 0$, R^2 may turn out to be negative or greater than one.

The difficulty that gives rise to this situation is a shared one, between computation and concept. On the one hand, there is a technical trap that causes a very well-documented calculation to produce nonsensical results in this particular instance. On the other, the *concept* of R^2 is at issue in the zero-intercept case.

To review briefly, least-squares estimation of regression coefficients in the two-variable model (I) $y_i = \beta_0 + \beta_1 x_{i1} + \epsilon_i$ $(i = 1, \ldots, n)$ under classical assumptions insures that in the sample the sum of calculated residuals $\{e_i\}$ is zero—that is, $\sum_{i=1}^{n} e_i = 0$—and also that $\sum_{i=1}^{n} e_i x_{i1} = 0$. These results in turn cause the following identities to hold, $\sum_{i=1}^{n} y_i^2 = \sum_{i=1}^{n} \hat{y}_i^2 + \sum_{i=1}^{n} e_i^2$ and $m_{yy} = m_{\hat{y}\hat{y}} + m_{ee}$, where $\hat{y}_i = b_0 + b_1 x_{i1}$, b_0 and b_1 are the LS estimates of β_0 and β_1, respectively, and $m_{yy} = (1/n) \sum_{i=1}^{n} (y_i - \bar{y})^2$, and so on. Previously we defined R^2 as the proportion of "explained" variance. Alternatively, a similar measure might be defined in terms of the "raw" moments. In either case there is internal consistency: from the raw moments, $R_r^2 = \sum \hat{y}^2 / \sum y^2$ or $R_r^2 = 1 - \sum e^2 / \sum y^2$, and with means accounted for, $R_m^2 = m_{\hat{y}\hat{y}} / m_{yy}$, $R_m^2 = 1 - m_{ee}/m_{yy}$, or, from a frequently used computational formula, $R_m^2 = b_1 m_{y1}/m_{yy}$ [see (3.5.4)]; in general $R_r^2 \neq R_m^2$. The dominant usage is "proportion of explained variance," which can be justified quite adequately from an estimation or prediction point of view.

A problem with this *concept* of R^2 (proportion of explained variance) arises when the regression equation is forced through the origin—that is, when the model is (II) $y_i = \beta_1' x_{i1} + \epsilon_i'$. Writing b_1' for the LS estimate of β_1', $\hat{y}_i' = b_1' x_{i1}$, and $e_i' = y_i - \hat{y}_i'$, applying the least-squares technique to our model results in a single normal equation, equivalent to the condition $\sum e' x_1 = 0$. Its solution is the familiar form, $b_1' = \sum y x_1 / \sum x_1^2$. Using b_1'

so calculated will insure that the computed residuals are uncorrelated with x_1, but it need not be true that $\sum e' = 0$, because in the restricted model $\sum e' = 0$ is *not* one of the normal equations. Since the sum of calculated residuals need not be zero with least-squares estimation of β'_1, the partition of m_{yy} into $m_{\hat{y}\hat{y}}$ and m_{ee} no longer holds in general: $m_{yy} \neq m_{y'y'} + m_{e'e'}$. However, the partition in terms of raw moments is still valid. This state of affairs gives rise to at least four alternative ratios that might be called "R^2" for the model with $\beta_0 = 0$.

Another (fifth) candidate appears from considering the F-statistic for testing the hypothesis of a zero intercept in model (I). On the basis of our knowledge of the construction of F-tests within the regression context, if we treat the second model as model (I) under a restriction ($\beta_0 = 0$), it is well known that the residual sum-of-squares $\sum e'^2$ for model (II) *cannot* be smaller than the like quantity for the first model, $\sum e^2$. Denoting "R^2" for model (II) by R'^2, it is unfortunately *not* always true that $R'^2 \leq R^2$. The problem is that the conclusion $R'^2 \leq R^2$ holds only for a *particular* definition of R^2.

Our purpose here is to outline briefly and contrast the several possible forms for R^2 within the context of this most simple regression framework, contrasting model (I) to model (II). That the results hold in the general multiple regression case should be clear.

First, we compare the raw-moment versions of R^2 for the two models. The raw-moment version of R^2 in the model with $\beta_0 = 0$ is easily obtained. Calculating $\sum e'^2$ results in the expression

$$(3.8.1) \qquad \sum y^2 = \sum e'^2 + b'_1 \sum yx_1.$$

But since $\hat{y}'_i = b'_1 x_{i1}$, $\sum \hat{y}'^2 = b'^2_1 \sum x^2_1 = b'_1 \sum yx_1$, so (3.8.1) becomes

$$(3.8.2) \qquad \sum y^2 = \sum e'^2 + \sum \hat{y}'^2.$$

The internal consistency of the raw-moment form obviously remains unshaken in moving from the first model to the second, since again $R'^2_r = \sum \hat{y}'^2/\sum y^2 = 1 - \sum e'^2/\sum y^2$.

Unfortunately this is not the case for the mean-corrected forms. In model (II) many alternative computations may be contemplated owing to the fact that in general $\sum e' \neq 0$. The most important relationship to be considered is

$$(3.8.3) \qquad \sum (y - \bar{y})^2 = \sum (e' - \bar{e}')^2 - \sum (\hat{y}' - \bar{\hat{y}}')^2 + 2nb'_1 m_{y1}.$$

From our previous discussion of R^2 we found that it could be calculated in three ways, namely as

$$R^2_m = 1 - \frac{\sum (e - \bar{e})^2}{\sum (y - \bar{y})^2} \quad \text{or} \quad R^2_m = \frac{\sum (\hat{y} - \bar{y})^2}{\sum (y - \bar{y})^2}$$

or $R_m^2 = b_1 m_{y1}/m_{yy}$ for this two-variable case. Of course, in model (I) $\bar{e} = 0$ and $\bar{\hat{y}} = \hat{y}$, so these expressions can be simplified. Our reason for leaving them in this form is to indicate parallel calculations for model (II) and show that in this case because $\bar{e} \neq 0$, $\bar{\hat{y}} \neq \bar{y}$, and the three ways of calculating "R^2" are generally different. To do this we use (3.8.3), which says nothing more than $\sum (y - \bar{y})^2 = \sum e^2 + \sum (\hat{y} - \bar{y})^2$ for the usual regression model, model (I), in which $\sum e = 0$.

For model (II), define:

$$R_{me}'^2 = 1 - \frac{\sum (e' - \bar{e}')^2}{\sum (y - \bar{y})^2},$$

$$R_{m\hat{y}}'^2 = \frac{\sum (\hat{y} - \bar{\hat{y}}')^2}{\sum (y - \bar{y})^2},$$

and

$$R_{mf}'^2 = \frac{b_1' m_{y1}}{m_{yy}}.$$

When divided through by $\sum (y - \bar{y})^2$, (3.8.3) becomes

(3.8.4) $1 = (1 - R_{me}'^2) - R_{m\hat{y}}'^2 + 2R_{mf}'^2.$

Another version of (3.8.4) is perhaps more interesting:

(3.8.4a) $1 = (1 - R_{me}'^2) + R_{m\hat{y}}'^2 + 2(R_{mf}'^2 - R_{m\hat{y}}'^2).$

When $R_{mf}'^2 = R_{m\hat{y}}'^2$, we get back to the relation $R_m^2 = m_{\hat{y}\hat{y}}/m_{yy} = 1 - m_{e'e'}/m_{yy}$ and the difficulties of definition disappear. It can easily be shown that a necessary and sufficient condition for the equality of $R_{mf}'^2$ and $R_{m\hat{y}}'^2$ is that the point of means $(\bar{y}, \bar{x}_1)$ lies on the regression line $\hat{y}_i = b_1' x_{i1}$, in which case the unrestricted model and the restricted model are coincident.

For purposes of further evaluation, let us suppose as an extreme case that the sample regression line with zero intercept passes through all observations. Then $R_{m\hat{y}}'^2 = 1$, $R_{mf}'^2 = 1$ and $R_{me}'^2 = 1$. It is not obvious, however, that when $R_{me}'^2 = 0$, $R_{m\hat{y}}'^2 = 0$. Nor does it follow that $R_{mf}'^2 = 1$ implies $R_{m\hat{y}}'^2 = 1$ (and hence $R_{me}'^2 = 1$). But if $R_{mf}'^2 = 1$, then $R_{m\hat{y}}'^2 = R_{me}'^2$, which is the familiar symmetry relation of the unrestricted model. Since many computer programs make use of the $R_{mf}'^2$ form, it is well to point out that neither $R_{mf}'^2$ nor $R_{m\hat{y}}'^2$ is bounded by one, and $R_{mf}'^2$ and $R_{me}'^2$ can be negative. For the former, this is because b_1' need not take the sign of m_{y1}.[†]

[†] Simple numerical examples may serve to increase further the frustration level of using any of the above measures. For the (y, x_1) observations given as $(1, 0)$, $(0, 2)$, $(1, 1)$, we get: $b_1' = \frac{1}{5}$, $R_{mf}'^2 = -\frac{3}{10}$, $R_{m\hat{y}}'^2 = \frac{3}{25}$, and $R_{me}'^2 = 1 - \frac{43}{25} = -\frac{18}{25}$. As an example where $R_{me}'^2 = 0$, consider the observations $(1, 0)$, $(1, 1)$, $(2, 2)$. Here $b_1' = 1$, $R_{mf}'^2 = \frac{3}{2}$, $R_{m\hat{y}}'^2 = 3(!)$, and $R_{me}'^2 = 0$. The reader is encouraged to draw scatter diagrams for these examples as an aid to intuition.

The comparison of restricted and unrestricted versions of a model on the basis of any of the above mean-corrected R^2's can easily produce nonsense results. Consider, for instance, the observations $(2, 1)$, $(\frac{5}{2}, 2)$, $(3, 3)$, which lie on the line $y = \frac{3}{2} + \frac{1}{2}x_1$; for these data $R_m^2 = 1$ when fitted by least squares under model (I). With the intercept set equal to zero, however, we get the following collection of results: $R_{mf}'^2 = 2.286$, $R_{m\hat{y}}'^2 = 5.224$, and $R_{me}'^2 = -.654$. $R_r'^2$, the raw-moment version of R^2 for the restricted case, in this instance is .95 and tends to capture, in at least a gross sense, the *reduction* in explanatory power due to suppression of the constant term. But there are problems of interpretation here also. They arise in reconciling the R^2 "concept" to the F-test for testing $H: \beta_0 = 0$ in model (I).

Consider the F-statistic for use in testing the hypothesis of zero intercept within the context of the unrestricted model. The proper F-ratio is, from (2.8.4):

$$(3.8.5) \qquad F_{1, n-2} = \frac{(n - 2)(\sum e'^2 - \sum e^2)}{\sum e^2}.$$

In considering (3.8.5) further it will be useful to recall the F-ratio for any test of a linear hypothesis in the regression framework in terms of R_m^2. The result of interest is (3.7.9), with a change in notation,

$$(3.8.6) \qquad F_{q, n-k-1} = \frac{n - k - 1}{q} \cdot \frac{R_m^2 - \tilde{R}_m^2}{(1 - R_m^2)},$$

with q the number of restrictions imposed, and k the number of conditioning variables. $\tilde{R}_m^2$ is, for all but the test of zero intercept, interpreted as the proportion of explained variance in the model under the linear restriction. The divisor used in the conversion from a form like (3.8.5) to (3.8.6) is nm_{yy}, so that the numerator of (3.8.6) shows the *change* in the proportion of explained variance by imposing the restriction. The difficulty in carrying these results over to the zero-intercept hypothesis is that different divisors for (3.8.5) are apparently appropriate when the restriction is imposed and when it is not.

Before the zero-intercept restriction is imposed, R_m^2 is the appropriate version of R^2. After the restriction is imposed, however, it is not clear which is the appropriate measure, nor what it is that is to be measured. Using nm_{yy} as divisor in (3.8.5) yields a new alternative for R^2 in the restricted model, namely $R_{mg}'^2 = 1 - \sum e'^2/\sum (y - \bar{y})^2$. Then (3.8.5) becomes

$$(3.8.7) \qquad F_{1, n-2} = \frac{(n - 2)(R_m^2 - R_{mg}'^2)}{(1 - R_m^2)},$$

and while we may be pressed to give an interpretation to the numerator of (3.8.7) in terms of a meaningful *change* in the "proportion of explained variance," at least this version of R^2 has an *objective* basis for its existence.

Unfortunately it suffers from the same ills as $R_{me}'^2$: as $R_{me}'^2$ can be negative, so can $R_{mg}'^2$; but as $R_{me}'^2$ is bounded by one, so is $R_{mg}'^2$. $R_{mg}'^2$ can (but need not) only equal one when $\sum e' = 0$.

Finally, changing to $\sum y^2$ as divisor in (3.8.5) casts the interpretation problem in juxtaposition, but fortunately not as an exact mirror image. In that instance, $R_r'^2 = 1 - \sum e'^2/\sum y^2$ may make "sense," but no longer can we use "proportion of (mean-corrected) variance explained" as the "concept" for R^2. $R_r^2 = 1 - \sum e^2/\sum y^2$ must be used. Then the numerator of the resulting F-statistic describes a "change" in R^2 at least with consistency of definition.

The conclusion is that the raw-moment version of R^2 is apparently superior as an index of the goodness-of-fit of a model when our primary purpose is to judge the explanatory merits of the usual regression model when compared to a regression through the origin. The justification for this point of view is that a comparison of raw-moment R^2's is consistent with a formal test of the hypothesis of zero intercept, while a comparison of mean-corrected R^2's generally is not. The usual (computer-program) calculations of R^2 are based on the R_{mf}^2 form, which when comparing models with and without the zero-intercept hypothesis imposed has no direct bearing on the formal test, and leads to rather strange and perhaps insidious results.

R^2 AS AN AID IN "MODEL-BUILDING"

Because of the relationship between R^2 and the F-test of a linear hypothesis in the regression model, the fact that in general R^2 will rise as additional explanatory variables are added to an equation is often exploited in order to go "fishing" for relations in the data with the regression framework and justify it on supposedly statistical grounds. Different models "explaining" the variation in some dependent variable are often "compared" on the basis of their R^2's. The important question is just what these comparisons mean. For as we suggested at the beginning of this section, *theoretical* considerations are all-important in model-building. Whether a particular independent variable is "important" in some regression equation can be tested formally. But of what value is a search procedure that attempts to find, for example, that subset of three—of many independent variables— which produces highest R^2? Little, if there exists a body of theory that substantiates the inclusion of variables that statistically are of minor significance. Some, perhaps, if no theory exists, or if all variables can be justified on *some* grounds and the main purpose of calculating the several statistics of interest in a regression model is to "see" which variables seem to be important explanators of variation in y. This ex post theorizing is dangerous business. The danger is that a hypothesis generated by a "fishing" expedition is then put up as being *validated* by the same data body.

Since empirical observation *is* one means by which hypotheses can be suggested, is there a firm rationale for using the regression framework to *compare* alternative models on the basis of R^2 (or, for that matter, any other statistic)? The answer is no.

Usually we speak of R^2 as it was defined previously, $R^2 = 1 - S_e^2/S_y^2$. Or, transposing terms, $(1 - R^2) = S_e^2/S_y^2$. S_e^2 is a biased estimate of σ^2; therefore if our interest is in estimating the *population* R^2, R_{POP}^2, we can expect R^2 to be a biased estimate. It has been suggested that an intuitively "better" estimator develops from

$$(3.8.8) \qquad (1 - \bar{R}^2) = \frac{\mathscr{S}^2}{\left(\dfrac{n}{n-1}\right)m_{yy}} = \frac{n-1}{n-k-1}(1 - R^2),$$

which uses $\mathscr{S}^2$, the *unbiased* estimator of σ^2, in its numerator, and $[n/(n-1)]m_{yy}$, the *unbiased* estimator for σ_y^2, in its denominator. $\bar{R}^2$ is called the "corrected" R^2. While the numerator and denominator of (3.8.8) are each unbiased estimates of their population counterparts in $(1 - R_{POP}^2)$, it unfortunately does not *follow* that $(1 - \bar{R}^2)$ is unbiased for $(1 - R_{POP}^2)$.† But it is unbiased in large samples (for that matter, so is R^2).

Any statistical basis for comparing models by $\bar{R}^2$ must rest on an ability to infer something about R_{POP}^2. Much is known about the distribution of R^2 (and thus $\bar{R}^2$) when $R_{POP}^2 = 0$. Indeed, this is the basis of the usual F-test of overall significance of the regression relationship, determined under the assumption $R_{POP}^2 = 0$. But when $R_{POP}^2 \neq 0$, the distribution of either R^2 or $\bar{R}^2$ is intractable. Thus, any comparison of models on the basis of $\bar{R}^2$ does not rest on a firm statistical theory.

On *suggestive* grounds, while the addition of an independent variable to some SRF *must* add a nonnegative quantity to R^2, its addition does not necessarily increase $\bar{R}^2$. In fact, an additional variable may not *decrease* S_e^2 enough to offset the decrease in $n - k - 1$ [and hence the *increase* in $(n-1)/(n-k-1)$] and raise $\bar{R}^2$.‡ When the competition among models

---

† This result follows because in general $E(yx) \neq E(y)E(x)$ and $E(y/x) \neq E(y)/E(x)$.

‡ The criterion for determining when the addition of a new variable will raise $\bar{R}^2$ is whether in the new equation its t-ratio is larger than one in absolute value. This result is derived from (3.8.8) and expressions that tie together R^2 before and after the variable is added and the t-ratio on the new variable, viz.,

i) $\qquad 1 - R_k^2 = (1 - R_{k-1}^2)(1 - r_{yk.1,2,\ldots,k-1}^2)$ $\qquad$ [ref. equation (3.6.25)]

ii) $\qquad 1 - R_k^2 = (1 - \bar{R}_k^2)\left(\dfrac{n-k-1}{n-1}\right)$ $\qquad$ [equation (3.8.8)]

iii) $\qquad t_k = \dfrac{r_{yk.1,2,\ldots,k-1}(n-k-1)^{1/2}}{(1 - r_{yk.1,2,\ldots,k-1}^2)^{1/2}}.$

In these formulas the notation "subscript k" refers to the (arbitrary) kth independent variable, so that R_k^2 is the R^2 in a regression of y on all independent variables, including focuses on subsets of independent variables with the *same* dependent variable, there is an ad hoc rationale for choosing the model with highest $\bar{R}^2$, however. Assuming that some specification is *the* correct one, on the average it will possess a larger sample $\bar{R}^2$ than any incorrect specification.†

To close, when the models being compared concern entirely *different* dependent variables or transformations of the same dependent variable (y vs. log y, for instance), not even these "suggestive" methods of model comparison can be used.

3.9 MULTICOLLINEARITY

Because an economist's use of regression techniques generally applies to nonexperimental data, he faces certain problems posed by the sample data. This is particularly true for time-series data, where the conditioning variables can generally be expected to be related to one another in the statistical sense of correlation. At one extreme, no difficulty is posed in a SRM by two independent variables that are perfectly linearly related: $(X'X)^{-1}$ cannot be formed and no individual estimated regression coefficients will be forthcoming.‡ Presumably, one variable is a perfect proxy for the other in this simplest example of collinearity. In practice, the source of linear dependence will

---

the kth. R_{k-1}^2 is the R^2 in a regression of y on the $k - 1$ variables excluding the kth. t_k is the t-ratio on the kth variable in the regression of y on all independent variables. $r_{yk.1,2,\ldots,k-1}$ is the partial correlation coefficient between y and x_k after accounting for the presence of the remaining $(k - 1)$ variables (recall the discussion following equation (3.6.25). Equation i) is simply an alternative form of (3.6.25); equation (iii) is readily verified for the three-variable case based on the development of Section 3.6.

When the three equations are combined, we obtain

iv) $$(1 - \bar{R}_k^2) = (1 - \bar{R}_{k-1}^2)\left(\frac{n - k}{n - k - 1 + t_k^2}\right)$$

so that if $|t_k| > 1$, $\bar{R}_k^2 > \bar{R}_{k-1}^2$ and it will "pay" to include x_k. An analogous relation obtains when a "group" of variables are considered. $\bar{R}^2$ will increase by their addition if the F-statistic for testing the *joint* hypothesis of zero coefficients for each of them is greater than one.

† This result is due to H. Theil. This particular justification for "fishing" expeditions can be extended. For example, one might ask whether there is any way in which an "optimum" subset of independent variables might be identified, a subset of variables that maximizes $\bar{R}^2$.

‡ To complete our cross-references to the "non-full-rank" case in regression, if $X'X$ is singular, the normal equations have an infinite number of solutions. But if we are interested in estimating only linear combinations of the β's (in agricultural experiments typically we may be interested only in something like $\beta_1 - \beta_2$) that are "estimable," then we can take *any solution* of the normal equations and form the corresponding linear combination (for example, $b_1 - b_2$). This estimate is *unique* and is minimum-variance unbiased.

likely be more complex. For instance, one independent variable may be a linear combination of several others; nonetheless it will be clear that the problem is suffering from linear dependence in the columns of $\mathbf{X}$.

At the other extreme, if we could control the environment responsible for generating observations on y and the x's of a given model, we should like to make each conditioning variable uncorrelated with each of the other conditioning variables for one primary reason: because the precision of each individual regression estimate will be greatest when there is no collinearity among the independent variables.

To see this, we consider again a three-variable example. For purposes of this exposition the centered model introduced in Section 3.4 will again be useful. Beginning from the transformed equation,

$$(3.9.1) \qquad y_i = \bar{y} + b_1 x_{i1}^* + \cdots + b_k x_{ik}^* + e_i,$$

we have the results $\sigma_{\bar{y}}^2 = \sigma^2/n$ and $\mathrm{Cov}\,(\bar{y}, b_j) = 0$ for $j = 1, \ldots, k$. The variance and covariance elements corresponding to $b_1, \ldots, b_k$ are given by

$$\mathbf{\Sigma}_{b_{)0(}} = \sigma^2 (\mathbf{X}^{*\prime}\mathbf{X}^*)^{-1} = \frac{\sigma^2}{n} \mathbf{M}_{xx}^{-1}.$$

So for the model in this form, the complete variance-covariance matrix of coefficient estimators looks like:

$$(3.9.2) \qquad \mathbf{\Sigma}_{\bar{y},\,b_{)0(}} = \frac{\sigma^2}{n} \begin{bmatrix} 1 & 0 & \cdots & & 0 \\ 0 & & & & \\ \cdot & & \mathbf{M}_{xx}^{-1} & & \\ \cdot & & & & \\ \cdot & & & & \\ 0 & & & & \end{bmatrix} = \frac{\sigma^2}{n} \begin{bmatrix} 1 & 0 & \cdots & & 0 \\ 0 & m^{11} & \cdots & & m^{1k} \\ \cdot & & & & \\ \cdot & & & & \\ \cdot & & & & \\ 0 & m^{k1} & \cdots & & m^{kk} \end{bmatrix}.$$

The notation is m^{jl} for the (j, l) element of $\mathbf{M}_{xx}^{-1}$. In all respects this formulation is equivalent to $\mathbf{\Sigma}_b = \sigma^2 (\mathbf{X}'\mathbf{X})^{-1}$, because $\sigma_{b_0}^2$ and the covariances between b_0 and the partial regression coefficient estimators $b_1, \ldots, b_k$ can be obtained from the elements of $\mathbf{\Sigma}_{\bar{y},\,b_{)0(}}$. But ignoring the intercept estimate makes easier the task of tracing the effects of intercorrelation among independent variables.

Using (3.9.2) in a three-variable model, we get

$$(3.9.3) \qquad \sigma_{\bar{y}}^2 = \frac{\sigma^2}{n}, \qquad \sigma_{\bar{y}b_1} = \sigma_{\bar{y}b_2} = 0,$$

$$(3.9.4) \qquad \sigma_{b_1}^2 = \frac{\sigma^2}{n} m^{11} = \frac{\sigma^2}{n} \left[\frac{1}{m_{11}(1 - r_{12}^2)} \right],$$

since

$$m^{11} = \frac{m_{22}}{m_{11}m_{22} - m_{12}^2}$$

$$= \frac{m_{22}}{m_{11}m_{22} - m_{11}m_{22}r_{12}^2}$$

$$= \frac{1}{m_{11}(1 - r_{12}^2)}.$$

Similarly,

(3.9.5) $$\sigma_{b_2}^2 = \frac{\sigma^2}{n}\left[\frac{1}{m_{22}(1 - r_{12}^2)}\right]$$

and

(3.9.6) $$\sigma_{b_1 b_2} = \frac{\sigma^2}{n}m^{12}$$

$$= \frac{\sigma^2}{n}\left[\frac{-r_{12}}{(m_{11}m_{22})^{1/2}(1 - r_{12}^2)}\right],$$

because

$$m^{12} = \frac{-m_{12}}{m_{11}m_{22}(1 - r_{12}^2)}$$

$$= \frac{(m_{11}m_{22})^{1/2}r_{12}}{m_{11}m_{22}(1 - r_{12}^2)}$$

$$= \frac{-r_{12}}{(m_{11}m_{22})^{1/2}(1 - r_{12}^2)}.$$

An analysis of the effects of collinearity between x_1 and x_2 is therefore as follows. If $r_{12} = 0$ (no correlation between x_1 and x_2), these variance formulas are exactly those for the *separate* slopes in two-variable regressions of y on x_1 and y on x_2 (with $\sigma_{b_1 b_2} = 0$), and are at a minimum. As we saw previously, when $r_{12} = 0$ the calculated slopes are identical as well.† As $r_{12} \to \pm 1$, coefficient variances (as well as the covariance term $\sigma_{b_1 b_2}$) get infinitely large. The meaning of this is that x_1 and x_2 as *separate* explanators of variability in y are difficult to tell apart statistically. Large coefficient variances make the task of model *verification* difficult.

The analysis above says nothing about the effects of multicollinearity on the predictive power of the model, as embodied in R^2. Indeed, insofar as we can say, there are none, except when $r_{12} = \pm 1$. However, even as a forecasting device one would like the estimated equation to exhibit precisely estimated coefficients as an indication of its *stability*—that is, its

† Although it is not *generally* true that if two random variables have the same variance they are identical.

(other than statistical) ability to predict for a future observation period or additional observation unit.

The "difficulty" implied by multicollinearity impedes the model-builder looking for verification of theories that suggest important variables. One can expect high standard errors on individual regression coefficients generally with high intercorrelations among two or more independent variables. In the case of just two variables that are highly correlated we expect *their* standard errors to be large; but other coefficient estimates may possess large standard errors as well, owing to the structure of correlation among these two and the remaining variables. In models that depend on aggregate time-series information high intercorrelations can be expected among a host of possible "independent" variables. Using annual per capita quantity demanded of some commodity as dependent variable with average annual price and per capita disposable income on an annual basis as independent variables is a classic case: undoubtedly there will be a high (time) correlation between the independent variables, which will result in high standard errors on each estimated partial regression coefficient. It is possible therefore for multicollinearity to cause one or both significance tests on the coefficients of price and income in the above example to fail: that is, the hypothesis $H: \beta_j = 0$ will *not* be rejected.

Owing to just such circumstances as these, where coefficient precision is of primary interest, attempts to *deal* with multicollinearity pervade the literature. An early suggestion by James Tobin[†] was first applied to the estimation of a demand function for a given commodity with time-series data, just the example we used above. A cross-section sample of households was also available for his use, and he proceeded to estimate the coefficient of income from a two-variable regression of quantity on income over the cross-section, assuming that each household faced the same commodity price. The price coefficient was estimated by first "adjusting" the per capita demand series for the effect of income, using the cross-section estimate in conjunction with the time series on per capita disposable income; this modified dependent variable was then regressed on price. Admittedly the procedure is crude, but it does have a theoretical rationale, although we do not present it here.[‡]

Without the luxury of an additional data source, multicollinearity in an empirical model may best be thought of as posing a decision problem for the investigator. On the one hand theoretical considerations suggest the inclusion of relevant variables, while in the sample one variable may be highly correlated with another (as the simplest case), leading to high standard

---

[†] "A Statistical Demand Function for Food in the USA," *J. Royal Stat. Soc.*, Series A, Vol. 113, Part 2 (1950).

[‡] It goes under the heading of estimation with *extraneous information*. Again, see Goldberger, *Econometric Theory*, pp. 255–61.

errors on the estimated coefficients of both. If one variable is *removed*, the model becomes incorrectly specified, leading to biased results. On the other, removing one of the highly intercorrelated variables would generally be expected to result in increased precision of estimation for the partial regression coefficient of the "left-in" variable. The "appropriate" trade-off between bias and greater precision for the coefficient on the "left-in" variable, is the matter in question.

One suggestion is to make the decision on the basis of a mean-square-error criterion, which directs us to compare the variance of the coefficient in question in the presence of the collinear variable to the variance plus squared bias when the collinear variable is removed. This criterion implies an equal distaste for large variance and bias (squared), which may or may not be the subjective preference of a given investigator for a particular problem. At best it is conventional. Moreover, it may be a difficult technique to use when the *source* of almost linear dependence is subtle, in that the linearly dependent variable may not be easily identifiable. High simple correlation between two variables is a sufficient but not necessary condition for the existence of multicollinearity. Nonetheless, the technique is worthy of some attention. We must first consider the important matter of specification bias in regression analysis, which is prerequisite to presenting the technique.

SPECIFICATION BIAS

The usual LS estimate of $\boldsymbol{\beta}$ in the model $\mathbf{y} = \mathbf{X}\boldsymbol{\beta} + \boldsymbol{\epsilon}$ is $\mathbf{b} = (\mathbf{X'X})^{-1}\mathbf{X'y}$. But suppose the original model was misspecified—some relevant variables were left out. Let $\mathbf{X}_1$ be the set of variables included, and $\mathbf{X}_2$ the unspecified variables. The "true" model is $\mathbf{y} = \mathbf{X}_1\boldsymbol{\beta}_1 + \mathbf{X}_2\boldsymbol{\beta}_2 + \boldsymbol{\epsilon}$, but we fit $\mathbf{y} = \mathbf{X}_1\boldsymbol{\beta}_1' + \boldsymbol{\epsilon}'$. Then for the SRM $\mathbf{y} = \mathbf{X}_1\mathbf{b}_1' + \boldsymbol{\epsilon}'$

$$(3.9.7) \qquad \mathbf{b}_1' = (\mathbf{X}_1'\mathbf{X}_1)^{-1}\mathbf{X}_1'\mathbf{y}$$
$$= (\mathbf{X}_1'\mathbf{X}_1)^{-1}\mathbf{X}_1'(\mathbf{X}_1\boldsymbol{\beta}_1 + \mathbf{X}_2\boldsymbol{\beta}_2 + \boldsymbol{\epsilon}),$$

inserting the "true" model. Thus,

$$(3.9.8) \qquad E(\mathbf{b}_1') = \boldsymbol{\beta}_1 + (\mathbf{X}_1'\mathbf{X}_1)^{-1}\mathbf{X}_1'\mathbf{X}_2\boldsymbol{\beta}_2.$$

The second term in (3.9.8) is "specification bias," a bias which will not diminish with increases in sample size. The bias term is comprised of coefficients of *separate* regressions of the left-out variables, $\mathbf{X}_2$, on the included variables, $\mathbf{X}_1$, and the model coefficients of left-out variables, $\boldsymbol{\beta}_2$. Note the similarity of (3.9.8) to our algebraic result (3.6.6), $b_{y1} = b_{y1.2} + b_{21}b_{y2.1}$, which relates the simple regression slope of y on x_1 to the partial slopes in the regression of y on x_1 and x_2, and the auxiliary slope, b_{21}. Indeed, the specification bias coefficients $(X_1'X_1)^{-1}X_1'X_2$ *are* slopes of auxiliary regressions of the X_2 variables separately on the X_1 variables. As $b_{y1.2}$ and $b_{y2.1}$ are LS estimators, they are unbiased estimates of β_1 and β_2 in $y = \beta_0 + \beta_1 x_1 + \beta_2 x_2 + \epsilon$. Therefore, $E(b_{y1}) = \beta_1 + b_{21}\beta_2$. If only the simple regression of y on x_1 is run, while $y = \beta_0 + \beta_1 x_1 + \beta_2 x_2 + \epsilon$ is the correct PRM, the bias in b_{y1} from misspecification is $b_{21}\beta_2$. Specification bias is zero if the excluded variables are each uncorrelated with the included variables (presuming the column of ones representing the constant term appears in X_1).

Other sorts of specification bias may be considered, but none so easily as the left-out variable case. Some interesting results may be obtained with the notion of specification bias, but to say much of anything requires assumptions about β_2 and the slopes of auxiliary regressions. If data on X_2 are available, then the regression should probably just be re-run. But with no data the specification-bias formula may be useful (see Problem 2 in Section 3.12).

A TEST FOR MULTICOLLINEARITY†

The "practical" matter of multicollinearity is to determine when the exclusion of some variables that appear in the PRF "pays." Excluding them causes two things to happen in the resulting SRF if multicollinearity exists to any degree. The variances of coefficients on *remaining* independent variables will generally be reduced, but the coefficients will be biased owing to specification error.

To consider the problem further, let us again use a three-variable example, writing $y_i = \beta_1 x_{i1}^* + \beta_2 x_{i2}^* + \epsilon_i$ as the PRM of interest. Adopting the notation of Section 3.6, we know that the LS estimate of β_1 in this model, $b_{y1.2}$, will be unbiased and will have a variance $\sigma_{b_{y1.2}}^2$ given by (3.9.4),

$$\sigma_{b_{y1.2}}^2 = \frac{\sigma^2}{n}\left[\frac{1}{m_{11}(1 - r_{12}^2)}\right].$$

In a model that regresses y on x_1 only, the LS slope coefficient is $b_{y1} = m_{y1}/m_{11}$. It is a biased estimate of β_1, the bias being obtained from (3.9.8):

$$(3.9.9) \qquad E(b_{y1}) = \beta_1 + \beta_2 \frac{\sum x_1^* x_2^*}{n m_{11}}.$$

The bias from misspecification is $E(b_{y1}) - \beta_1$. The variance of b_{y1} is $\sigma_{b_{y1}}^2 = \sigma^2/(nm_{11})$ [from (2.5.4), for example]. Generally, b_{y1} is biased but with

† C. Toro-Vizcarrondo and T. D. Wallace, "A Test of the Mean Square Error Criterion for Restrictions in Linear Regression," *J. Am. Stat. Assn.*, Vol. 63 (June 1968), pp. 558–72.

smaller variance then $b_{y1.2}$ (b_{y1} and $b_{y1.2}$ are numerically identical if x_1 and x_2 are uncorrelated).

A suggested technique for choosing between $b_{y1.2}$ and b_{y1} is by the mean-square-error criterion. That is, we would choose b_{y1} in favor of $b_{y1.2}$ according to whether MSE $(b_{y1}) \lessgtr$ MSE $(b_{y1.2})$. Note that MSE is only one of a myriad of possible weighting schemes for trading-off variance against bias, which may or may not correspond to an individual user's personal preferences.

In terms of our illustration,

$$(3.9.10) \qquad \text{MSE}\,(b_{y1}) = \left[\beta_2 \frac{\sum x_1^* x_2^*}{nm_{11}}\right]^2 + \frac{\sigma^2}{nm_{11}},$$

$$\text{MSE}\,(b_{y1.2}) = \frac{\sigma^2}{n}\left[\frac{1}{m_{11}(1 - r_{12}^2)}\right].$$

Through some manipulation we find that our criterion MSE $(b_{y1}) \lessgtr$ MSE $(b_{y1.2})$ reduces to $\beta_2^2/\sigma_{b_{v2.1}}^2 \lessgtr 1$. If the ratio $\beta_2^2/\sigma_{b_{v2.1}}^2$ could be observed, we would choose to use b_{y1} as our estimate of β_1 if the ratio were less than one, and $b_{y1.2}$ if it were greater than one. Of course, it cannot be observed, but it may be estimated by the squared t-ratio on $b_{y2.1}$ in the "true" model.

Indeed, if $\beta_2 = 0$, the distribution of $b_{y2.1}^2/\hat{\sigma}_{b_{v2.1}}^2$ is well known: it is the F-distribution used for testing the hypothesis $\beta_2 = 0$, with one and $n - 3$ degrees of freedom. When $\beta_2 \neq 0$, as it is for the present problem, the distribution of $b_{y2.1}^2/\hat{\sigma}_{b_{v2.1}}^2$ is a modified version of F, called *noncentral F*. It so happens that a parameter of this distribution is $\beta_2^2/\sigma_{b_{v2.1}}^2$. Thus a hypothesis test of $H: \beta_2^2/\sigma_{b_{v2.1}}^2 \leq 1$ against $H_A: \beta_2^2/\sigma_{b_{v2.1}}^2 > 1$ is possible. A table for this purpose is provided in Appendix C. For our example situation, say with $n = 25$, if the squared t-ratio $b_{y2.1}^2/\hat{\sigma}_{b_{v2.1}}^2 = 2.10$, we would not reject the hypothesis at the 5 percent level of significance and would choose to use the "restricted" estimator, b_{y1} (2.10 compared to a critical value of 7.96).

The table, of course, encompasses regression equations with any number of independent variables in them; it is not limited to the three-variable case used in our illustration. The use of this test is the same, however. We are comparing a "true" model to one that excludes *one* independent variable.

Extension of the test to cover exclusion of a combination of independent variables is also available.† It makes use of the usual F-statistic for a (linear) hypothesis, Eq. (3.7.8).

† Since *all* coefficients in the misspecified model are subject to bias, the simple comparison MSE $(b_{y1}) \lessgtr$ MSE $(b_{y1.2})$ must be modified to cover the more general case of many independent variables. The extended criterion is that the LS coefficient estimates from the misspecified SRF will be used if the MSE of *any* (all) linear combination of left-in coefficients is smaller with the particular variables excluded than with them included. Tables to cover the extended test are available in T. D. Wallace and C. Toro-Vizcarrondo, "Tables for the Mean Square Error Test for Exact Linear Restrictions in Regression," *J. Am. Stat. Assn.*, Vol. 64 (December 1969), pp. 1649–63.

This particular test is not the only one ever suggested for dealing with the multicollinearity problem, but it is the most satisfactory. Its primary limitation is that it applies to the classical regression model. When this assumption is dropped, however, even the *notion* of multicollinearity must be altered, from an essentially *sample* phenomenon to a *population* problem. Whether this change in orientation is appropriate is debatable. Even given that it is, there is some difference of opinion as to what is the relevant hypotheses to test about the *population* $X'X$ matrix, and what to *do* about multicollinearity defined in this way if it is ascertained to exist.

3.10 A BRIEF DIGRESSION ON COMPUTATION

The basic treatment of this chapter, of the problems that follow, and indeed of the entire book assumes that a digital computer is accessible with a regression program or "package" available. A few remarks on computation by digital computer are therefore in order.

First, often a "stepwise" regression program is offered. A few years ago, the word meant exactly what we used it to mean in Section 3.6—namely, a technique that *incorrectly* computed partial regression coefficients by adjusting the dependent variable for x_1, then regressing the "adjusted" variable—the residuals $e_{y.1}$—on x_2, and so on. This procedure is also occasionally suggested by so-called "graphic" methods of regression analysis. Fortunately, most "stepwise" regression programs do not make this error any longer. Rather, by a "stepwise" procedure is meant a search technique whereby the most highly correlated independent variable—most highly correlated with y—is regressed with the dependent variable. Next, a three-variable regression equation is calculated, where another of the prespecified independent variables is included: the one which, in tandem with the first, reduces the error variance by the largest margin of any of the remaining set of independent variables. The procedure continues until at the final step the full regression equation is estimated. At each step there is no computational error committed, as in the procedure characterized by our earlier use of the word "stepwise." The only criticism we might levy at the procedure is that it promotes searching for relationships in a body of data at the possible expense of good theory.

Next, a computer is fallible, both because it is inherently limited in numerical accuracy and because it depends on human beings for its instructions. Essentially the problem of numerical accuracy in regression calculations is due either to this inherent machine limitation, rounding procedures, or unsatisfactory verification techniques for finding the inverse matrix usually needed. Most regression programs base calculations on the correlation matrix ρ_{xx}, which has the advantage of possessing a determinant within a known range $(0, 1)$ no matter what the data dimensions might be. But inherent numerical accuracy varies widely and surprisingly, considering the claims of computer manufacturers. If a recent study of James Longley† is representative of the collection of machines and programs at large, we should be quick to insist on a careful review of existing programs and a large reprogramming effort to improve accuracy. It apparently is not the matrix-inversion techniques in common use that present the difficulty, but rather the inherent inaccuracy in $\mathbf{X'X}$ (or ρ_{xx}).

Multicollinearity plays a role here also. It has ramifications for numerical as well as statistical accuracy. Generally speaking, numerical accuracy in computing ρ_{xx}^{-1} deteriorates as $|\rho_{xx}| \to 0$. Thus not only do we expect poor statistical precision of estimation, but moreover the numbers that are reported can be expected to contain proportionally greater error of round-off, and so on. In other words they will contain progressively fewer *significant* digits than are reported as $|\rho_{xx}| \to 0$. And as we have no generally acceptable *measure* of multicollinearity, computer scientists as yet have no generally acceptable *measure* of the degree of singularity; they refer to the condition of "almost singularity" as *ill-conditioning*.

Presently, however, a word of warning often comes as part of the output of any given regression run, using one of several possible criteria to warn the user of the problem. The computed value of $|\rho_{xx}|$, being bounded by zero and one, is one such measure, and while it may not be reported directly, a message to the effect that the problem is ill-conditioned may be triggered if $|\rho_{xx}| < 1 \times 10^{-6}$, or some other arbitrarily small number.

Even if ill-conditioning is not a problem, numerical accuracy may be. Generally speaking, the method of cofactors‡ is an inefficient means by which to form the inverse with a computer. Other techniques are faster, but are not exact. In effect, they proceed to get the inverse by successive approximation, stopping when the inverse checks to a particular level of accuracy. Just how such "checks" are accomplished can be a source of some trepidation, and with one good example we shall rest our case.§

Suppose, for sake of illustration only, the level of accuracy for an inverse calculation is accepted at 0.1. That is, for any approximate inverse $\mathbf{B}$ of a matrix $\mathbf{A}$ we shall accept it if the elements of $\mathbf{AB}$ differ from the elements of the identity matrix by no more than 0.1. Consider the matrix

---

† "An Appraisal of Least Squares Programs for the Electronic Computer from the Point of View of the Use," *J. Am. Stat. Assn.*, Vol. 62 (September 1967), pp. 819–41.

‡ See Appendix A.

§ Given in Ben Noble, *Applied Linear Algebra* (Englewood Cliffs: Prentice-Hall, Inc., 1969), p. 258.

$$A = \begin{bmatrix} 1.0 & 1.0 \\ 1.0 & .99 \end{bmatrix}$$

and an approximate inverse

$$B = \begin{bmatrix} -89 & 100 \\ 90 & -100 \end{bmatrix}.$$

Then

$$AB = \begin{bmatrix} 1.0 & 0.0 \\ 0.1 & 1.0 \end{bmatrix},$$

which passes our accuracy criterion. Unfortunately, in the realm of numerical approximation the inverse matrix need not be unique, as it is theoretically. What makes a good "right" inverse may not be a good "left" inverse. For

$$BA = \begin{bmatrix} 11 & 10 \\ -10 & -9 \end{bmatrix},$$

rather a disturbing result.†

3.11 REGRESSION AND THE POLICY-MAKER‡

Our comments at the conclusion of Section 3.5, as amplified by the results of Section 3.6, suggest that there is no generally acceptable objective technique for ranking individual regressors in a multiple regression relationship as to the "strength" of their relationship with the dependent variable, using as a definition of "strength" the individual power to explain variation in the dependent variable. Only in the exceptional case where the independent variables are mutually uncorrelated does R^2 partition unambiguously into mutually exclusive parts.

In this section we wish not only to collect previous thoughts and evidence into a more unified presentation, but also to take up the matter of the rel-

† The actual inverse of A is

$$A^{-1} = \begin{bmatrix} -99 & 100 \\ 100 & -100 \end{bmatrix},$$

as can readily be verified.

‡ I would like to thank my colleagues Glen Cain and Harold Watts who provided the inspiration for, and several of the ideas contained in, this section.

evance of possible ranking schemes for the "strength" of individual regressors based on a variance criterion when a primary interest focuses on the magnitude of predicted mean response in the dependent variable for a given alteration in some independent variable. We will be trying to distinguish between so-called "scientific" uses of regression results and their possible "policy" uses.

If the use to which an estimated regression equation and its associated measures is put is either to estimate particular coefficients or to test hypotheses about their magnitudes, we shall say the regression is being used for "scientific" purposes, while if the equation is used to forecast the conditional mean response in y for a particular set of values for the independent variables or for an alteration in any one of them ceteris paribus, we shall call this "regression for policy purposes." Since there is a definite overlap in the procedures for both purposes, the distinction is intended to separate the two cases according to the goal of the investigator.

For the "scientific" use, it is apparent that precision of estimation is the overriding objective; the investigator would *like* small variance in an estimated coefficient, as it makes for a narrower confidence interval around the true coefficient. Similarly, because of the one-to-one correspondence between interval estimation and a formal hypothesis test about the coefficient's true value, small variance implies a greater ability to discriminate between true and false hypotheses about the population coefficient. Now, in some scientific applications of the regression framework it is necessary to pursue techniques for selectively reducing the number of independent variables—say because of multicollinearity—or it might be of general interest to rank the independent variables according to their individual contribution to the regression relationship. In the context of a scientific orientation to regression this last phrase implies a ranking according to some variance criterion, such as contribution to explained variation in y or to R^2.

Two intuitive schemes for ranking according to the "strength" of relationship under an explained variance criterion are (1) ranking based on Eqs. (3.5.11) or (3.5.4), which suggests either the term $\tilde{b}_j r_{yj}$ or $b_j m_{yj}/m_{yy}$ as a "strength" measure, and (2) ranking according to the individual t-ratios. The first method we discussed briefly in Section 3.5, concluding (in Section 3.6) that it was unsatisfactory because only under the special circumstance of mutually uncorrelated regressors would R^2 exactly partition into a sum of constituent "explained-variance" terms, each contained in the interval $(0, 1)$. In this instance there is no ambiguity in using the terms $\tilde{b}_j r_{yj}$ as relative strength indicators, since $\sum \tilde{b}_j r_{yj} = R^2$. When nonzero correlations are allowed between the independent variables, R^2 still "adds up" in terms of the $\{\tilde{b}_j r_{yj}\}$, but they need not individually be constrained to lie in a $(0, 1)$ interval. Indeed, they may be negative or positive and exceed one in absolute value. (There is nothing necessarily sacred about $(0, 1)$ boundaries, but clearly the "strength" measure should be independent of algebraic sign.) One might then consider squaring them, but the question remains just what is being measured and what relationship this newly constructed measure, $(\tilde{b}_j r_{yj})^2$ bears to the explanatory "power" of the jth regressor, defined in terms of its individual contribution to R^2.

A second possible "strength" measure is the t-ratio, or some derivative measure of it. Its use as a "strength" indicator is subject essentially to the same criticisms. This is certainly a "natural" enough measure, as it *seems* quite reasonable to consider a variable with a squared t-ratio (to eliminate the sign problem again) of 6.5 as somehow "more significant" than a variable whose squared t-ratio is 4.3. But there are dangers in making any such comparisons, because the structure of intercorrelation among observed independent variables has so much to do not only with the measured difference in "strength"—2.2 (somethings) for the above example—but with the sign and value of the t-ratio itself.

With intercorrelations present the squared t-ratios do not "add up" to any meaningful whole. Their relevance, besides being intuitive from the zero-effect hypothesis to which they correspond, derives from the following relationship, which links the t-ratios on individual regression coefficients to the F-statistic for testing the significance of the entire regression equation (3.8.7):

$$(3.11.1) \qquad F = \frac{1}{k} \sum_{j=1}^{k} \sum_{l=1}^{k} m^{jj} m^{ll} t_j t_l r_{jl},$$

where m^{jj} and m^{ll} are the (j, j) and (l, l) (diagonal) elements of $\mathbf{M}_{xx}^{-1}$, and r_{jl} is the simple correlation between the jth and lth regressors. While we will not derive this expression formally, its correspondence to our previous expression for R^2 is clear, particularly if we consider again the special case of uncorrelated regressors. Then $r_{jl} = 0$ for all j, l, $m^{jj} = 1/m_{jj}$, and we find

$$
\begin{aligned}
(3.11.2) \qquad F &= \frac{R^2}{1 - R^2} \cdot \frac{n - k - 1}{k} = \frac{1}{k} \sum_{j=1}^{k} \frac{t_j^2}{m_{jj}^2} = \frac{1}{k} \sum_{j=1}^{k} \frac{b_j^2}{\mathscr{S}^2 m^{jj} m_{jj}^2} \\
&= \frac{1}{k} \sum_{j=1}^{k} \left(\frac{b_j m_{yj}}{m_{yy}} \right) \frac{n - k - 1}{1 - R^2} \\
&= \frac{R^2}{1 - R^2} \cdot \frac{n - k - 1}{k},
\end{aligned}
$$

using the fact that when the regressors are mutually uncorrelated we may calculate each partial regression coefficient by $b_j = m_{yj}/m_{jj}$. So, in the same way the $\{\tilde{b}_j r_{yj}\}$ terms "add up" sensibly to R^2 when the regressors are mutually uncorrelated, the $\{t_j^2/m_{jj}^2\}$ terms *average* sensibly to a meaningful whole, the F-statistic for testing overall significance of regression. Otherwise, interpreting in even the loosest way the squared t-ratio as a "strength" indicator for a given regressor is without strict justification.

One final comparison is interesting, and leads us conveniently into the main matter of regression for policy purposes. As we shall note below, the beta coefficients $\{\tilde{b}_j\}$ themselves are often suggested as "strength" measures (or, more popularly, squared beta coefficients to again neutralize the algebraic sign problem). Generally speaking, squared beta coefficients do not possess even the shaky foundation for relevance as "strength" measures that either $\tilde{b}_j r_{yj}$ or t_j^2/m_{jj}^2 do. But when the regressors are mutually uncorrelated, $\tilde{b}_j r_{yj} = \tilde{b}_j^2$ and $t_j^2 = \tilde{b}_j^2(n - k - 1)/(1 - R^2)$; thus all three measures consistently measure a meaningful notion of the "strength" of relationship for an individual regressor.† When there is intercorrelation among regressors (and as a pratical matter that is *always* the case in nonexperimental situations), any of these ranking schemes suffers from being to some degree arbitrary.

While these somewhat vague notions of an individual regressor's "strength" of relationship with y in the presence of other independent variables present operational as well as conceptual difficulties unless the independent variables are mutually uncorrelated, "strength" of response in y for an alteration in some independent variable has real meaning when the regression equation in question is to be used for policy purposes. For instance, in an equation that has a student's educational achievement related to school characteristics (facilities, teacher quality, and so on) and his socioeconomic background, a relevant policy question might be: which will produce the largest change in y, a dollar invested in upgrading school facilities or a dollar invested in better housing facilities? From the population regression equation, the answer has clearly to do with the *magnitudes* of the partial regression coefficients of variables that *can* be manipulated—which, after all, are partial derivatives in a linear equational form. For comparability, however, we first should weight each of these regression coefficients by a factor that describes how much expected change in the dependent variable comes from identical unit changes in each of the manipulatable variables. That is, we should make a transformation of the relevent original regression coefficients into "policy units."

Suppose school characteristics are measured (for sake of illustration) by an index of "tutorial services" per student in the library, and socioeconomic background is proxied for by a single variable also, family income. Further, let our population regression equation be y (index of student achievement)

---

† Another suggested "strength" indicator is $\phi_j = \tilde{b}_j^2(1 - R_{j.1,\ldots,k}^2)$, a squared beta coefficient "weighted" by the proportion of variation in x_j unaccounted for by the other independent variables (that is, $R_{j.1,\ldots,k}^2$ is the R^2 found by regressing x_j on $x_1, \ldots, x_{j-1}$, $x_{j+1}, \ldots, x_k$). It is related to t_j^2 by $t_j^2 = \phi_j(n - k - 1)/(1 - R^2)$, and suffers likewise as a "strength" measure. When the regressors are mutually uncorrelated, $\phi_j = \tilde{b}_j^2$.

= constant + $.30x_1$ (tutorial services index) + $.25x_2$ (family income in \$) + ϵ.[†] Now if an additional dollar expended will buy (on the average) a 5 percent increase in tutorial services, to convert the index into dollars the relevant coefficient (.30) should be *divided* by twenty. Thus, we would get: $y =$ constant + $.015x_1$ (dollar value of tutorial services) + $.25x_2$ (family income in \$) + ϵ. From the magnitudes of these two coefficients it is apparent that a dollar invested to increase "family income" (say by a subsidy) will result in a *larger* increase in student achievement than the same dollar used to purchase 5 percent more tutorial services. On this basis the *conditional* "strength" of a regressor in affecting mean (or actual) response in y is given in terms of a weighted regression coefficient, where the weight transforms original units into comparable (across independent variables) "policy" units. Beta coefficients, for example, are weighted (and estimated) regression coefficients, but the weights that are applied ($\sqrt{m_{jj}}/\sqrt{m_{yy}}$) bear no identifiable relationship to the matter of transforming ordinary regression coefficients into comparable magnitudes for policy purposes, nor are they invariant across samples.

What is being suggested here is that the *population parameters* of interest for policy purposes should be certain weighted regression coefficients for those variables which can be manipulated for policy purposes. (Other "control" variables may still appear in the "transformed" equation with their original regression coefficients.) In this sense any of the *sample* statistics previously alluded to must necessarily yield biased estimates of these *appropriate* population parameters. So also the usual least-squares estimate of the untransformed coefficient must be a biased estimate of the transformed coefficient. The question then is how to best estimate the appropriate population parameters. The point of departure with the methodology of the so-called "scientific" use of regression is: on what grounds are we going to discuss the relative importance of individual regressors? And the point of substantive difference is that talking in terms of contribution to explained variance does not explicitly direct itself to uses of the regression results for policy purposes. Not that we are to ignore sampling variability in coming to a *sample* strength measure based on *estimated* "mean response." For sensible decision-making, *both* estimated mean response and *its* variance will generally be of some interest. To this point we now turn.

Before, we spoke of population (conditional) mean responses in y for dollar increases in each of the two independent variables for our example regression equation. If unbiased estimation of each conditional mean response is of primary importance, then (of course) least-squares estimates of both untransformed and transformed regression coefficients in the now re-

---

† This is highly simplified, of course, as many important control variables are left out, and we ignore the further complications posed when x_1 and x_2 are functionally related (for example, when a term in x_1x_2 appears).

levant population regression equation will provide them. (And, these now estimated mean responses will possess minimum variance in the class of linear unbiased estimators.)

Now let us consider the possibility of choosing among alternative policy instruments to determine which will yield the "biggest bang for the buck" on the basis of their *estimated* (transformed) coefficients. The forecasted mean response in y for an alteration in one of the independent variables, ceteris paribus, is only an estimate. The "true" mean response is known only in terms of a confidence interval based on estimated partial regression coefficients and their estimated variances and covariances. So long as the decision-maker is concerned about controlling the possibility that a forecasted response will result in an "undesirable" outcome, he must be concerned about the variance of forecasted mean response. Under a normal distribution of errors, for example, predicted y follows a normal distribution, which will be fully specified by its mean and variance. Normality is not required, however, to establish the *relevance* of a measure of the dispersion of predicted response around the true mean response.

Suppose the question is, again, on which independent variable to spend the dollar, but let both regressors have *identical* weighted (estimated) regression coefficients and *different* estimated variances.† Then according to our estimates, the relevant $(1 - \alpha)$ confidence intervals around the true mean response in y for a unit change in one independent variable holding the other constant will be centered at the same point, but one interval will be wider than the other. Saying it another way, if the weighted estimated coefficients were generated from *populations* with identical means given an interval of mean response in y that is somehow *important* to the decision-maker (say, small or negative values), a response falling into that interval is more likely to be observed in the coefficient distribution with highest variance. Exactly *how much* more likely can be determined with a normal distribution if we know the variance, or a *t*-distribution if the variance is estimated. Without the normal distribution assumed, we can at least get bounds for the probabilities in question from Tchebycheff's inequality, which relates them again to the mean and variance only.

How important is control over undesirable outcomes to the policy decision-maker? Only he can answer that. What we come to finally as a general ranking scheme for relative conditional strength or "importance" of an individual regressor is based on some sort of *utility* function. A choice rule that derives from a popular utility function in the economics literature is: $\hat{B}_j - \gamma \sigma^2_{\hat{B}_j}$, where $\hat{B}_j$ is the least-squares estimate of the (transformed) regression coefficient, B_j, $\sigma^2_{\hat{B}_j}$ is its variance, and γ is a weight describing the decision-

---

† We could easily translate things into the two forecasts of $E(y|x_1, x_2)$ and a variance for that forecast [cf. Eq. (2.6.12), extended to the three-variable case], but that conversion would only add detail and not alter the basic comparison.

maker's predilections toward uncertainty. Thus the policy instrument finally chosen would be the one with the largest estimated coefficient *discounted* for uncertainty. Though this is only an example, any utility function that is nonlinear in the estimated mean response will result in a choice rule that depends on the variance of that estimate.

Obviously, our discussion has not produced a necessarily *operational* ranking scheme. For while $\sigma_{\hat{B}_j}^2$ in the example is estimable from the sample, γ and parameters like it may not be estimable in any conventional statistical sense. The substance of the discussion is to synthesize the two "approaches" to regression analysis. On the one hand, for the policy-maker we may find a high weight on mean response and a low weight on its variance, while for the "scientific" investigator the situation may be reversed. In any event, *every* variance-oriented ranking scheme we have discussed contains subjective elements that makes its evaluation difficult if not impossible, and puts it also into the class of schemes based on the investigator's *utility function*. The main point is that these statistics do not bear a meaningful relation to *policy* questions that may be posed within the regression framework.

3.12 PROBLEMS AND ANSWERS

GENERAL PROBLEMS

1. (Sections 3.4, 3.5, 3.7) The following is proposed as a model describing growth of sunflower plants over the growing season:

$$y_i = \beta_0 + \beta_1 x_{i1} + \beta_2 x_{i2} + \epsilon_i.$$

$E(\epsilon_i) = 0$, $E(\epsilon_i^2) = \sigma^2$, $E(\epsilon_i \epsilon_j) = 0$ for $i \neq j$, where y_i is plant height (in inches) in week i, x_{i1} is week of season, and $x_{i2} = x_{i1}^2$.

From a sample of 13 weekly observations, the following measures were obtained (in the data, week of season was coded $-6, -5, \ldots, -1, 0, 1, \ldots, 6$):

$$\bar{y} = 16, \qquad m_{yy} = 70, \qquad r_{y1} = .90,$$
$$\bar{x}_1 = 0, \qquad m_{11} = 14, \qquad r_{y2} = -.20.$$
$$\bar{x}_2 = 14, \qquad m_{22} = 139.$$

a. Calculate least-squares estimates of β_0, β_1, and β_2.
b. Calculate R^2.
c. Test the hypothesis $\beta_2 = 0$ and indicate the rationale for this test.
d. Test the hypothesis $H: \beta_1 = \beta_2 = 0$.

ANSWERS:

(a) $m_{12} = 0$, either by direct calculation or by noticing the unique construction of $x_2 = x_1^2$, which makes m_{12} the third moment of x_1. Since the "distribution" of x_1 is symmetric, we expect its third moment to be zero. Since $m_{12} = 0$, calculations of b_1 and b_2 can be carried out with the two-variable formulas.

$$b_1 = r_{y1}\sqrt{\frac{m_{yy}}{m_{11}}} = (.9)\frac{8.37}{3.75} = 2.01,$$

$$b_2 = r_{y2}\sqrt{\frac{m_{yy}}{m_{22}}} = (-.2)\frac{8.37}{11.8} = -.142,$$

$$b_0 = \bar{y} - b_1\bar{x}_1 - b_2\bar{x}_2 = 16 - 0 + (.142)(14) = 18.0.$$

(b) Since $m_{12} = 0$, $r_{12} = 0$, and $R^2 = r_{y1}^2 + r_{y2}^2$,

$$R^2 = .81 + .04 = .85.$$

(c) Since $R^2 = S_{\hat{y}}^2/S_y^2$, $.85 = S_{\hat{y}}^2/70$ and $S_{\hat{y}}^2 = (.85)(70) = 59.5$.

$$S_e^2 = 70 - 59.5 = 10.5$$

because $S_y^2 = S_{\hat{y}}^2 + S_e^2$. Finally,

$$\mathscr{S}^2 = \left(\frac{n}{n-3}\right)S_e^2 = 13.7 \quad \text{and} \quad \hat{\sigma}_{b_2}^2 = \frac{13.7}{(13)(139)} = .0076,$$

again using the two-variable formula.

$$\hat{\sigma}_{b_2} = \sqrt{.0076} = .087,$$

so the t-ratio for testing $H: \beta_2 = 0$ is $t = (-.142)/(.087) = -1.63$, which is not significant at 95 percent ($t_{10,.95} = \pm 2.23$).

(d) $$F_{2,10} = \frac{.85}{.15} \cdot \frac{10}{2} = 28.3,$$

so the hypothesis $H: \beta_1 = \beta_2 = 0$ is rejected at 95 percent ($F_{2,10,.95} = 4.10$).

2. (Sections 3.6, 3.9) We are interested in estimating the marginal product of labor, $\partial Q/\partial L$, from a linear production function $Q = f(L, K)$, where $K =$ capital is the other factor. Our sample is a cross-section of firms for the industry of interest. Unfortunately, however, we do not have observations on K. We run the simple regression of Q on L and obtain the slope b_{QL}. What (if anything) can be said about $b_{QL \cdot K}$, the slope (partial regression coefficient) we *would have obtained* for Q on L in the presence of K? Present your assumptions and subsequent reasoning carefully.

ANSWER:

From theory we would expect $\partial Q/\partial L, \partial Q/\partial K > 0$. Now, unless capital is being substituted for labor over firms, $b_{KL} > 0$, and the relationship of interest,

$$b_{QL.K} = b_{QL} - b_{KL}b_{QK.L},$$

suggests that b_{QL} will generally be an *overestimate* of the partial contribution of labor in output.†

3. (Section 3.9) A good deal of literature has been devoted to the question of *why* the income coefficient of consumption (total or for a given commodity) calculated from a cross-section body of data on households differs from the income coefficient calculated from aggregate time series for the two per capita variables. Since the cross-section is taken only for one period, the relevant estimation model for the total consumption (ignoring the intercept) is

$$\text{(a)} \quad c_{it} = b_{cy}^{(c)}y_{it} + e_i, \qquad i = 1, \ldots, n$$

with the index running over households.

The model used in time-series analysis allows the inclusion of additional income lags. Suppose it is

$$\text{(b)} \quad c_t = b_{cy.y'}^{(t)}y_t + b_{cy'.y}^{(t)}y_{t-1} + e_t, \qquad t = 1, \ldots, T$$

with $y' = y_{t-1}$. In many reported cases $b_{cy}^{(c)} > b_{cy.y'}^{(t)}$.

You are to "explain" this observation, assuming version (b) is the correct model and that it may be similarly specified for the microunit—that is, the microdata may be directly aggregated (averaged) to get macrodata. Note that there are *two* relevant comparisons to consider, the relationship between $b_{cy}^{(c)}$ and $b_{cy.y'}^{(c)}$ *as if* the latter could be computed from the cross-section, and the relation between $b_{cy.y'}^{(c)}$ as computed from the cross-section versus $b_{cy.y'}^{(t)}$ computed from the time series.

ANSWER:

For the first part, if we could compute $b_{cy.y'}^{(c)}$ for the cross-section sample, we would expect $b_{cy}^{(c)} > b_{cy.y'}^{(c)}$ because of the relation that holds between the simple and partial regression coefficients, namely

$$b_{cy} = b_{cy.y'} + b_{yy'}b_{cy'.y},$$

† Problem setting and interpretation due to Z. Griliches.

and that we anticipate a positive relation to hold between current income and its lag and a positive *partial* regression coefficient for consumption on lagged income; thus, $b_{cy}^{(c)} > b_{cy.y'}^{(c)}$.

Given identical models for both samples, $b_{cy.y'}^{(c)} \neq b_{cy.y'}^{(t)}$ would be expected only because $b_{yy'}^{(c)} \neq b_{yy'}^{(t)}$. $b_{yy'}^{(t)}$ can be easily converted to a correlation coefficient, commonly referred to as a first-order lag-correlation or autocorrelation. Is there any a priori reason to expect a higher correlation of income with its first-order lag over a cross-section of individuals than over a time series of per capita disposable income on its lag? Clearly the two data bodies are "different," but so far there is no universally applicable reasoning to predict the difference. For long time series it has been observed that $b_{yy'}^{(t)} > b_{yy'}^{(c)}$; however, shorter time series, of durations like 20 years, yield the opposite result. For the latter case, then, it would appear that $b_{cy}^{(c)} > b_{cy.y'}^{(c)} > b_{cy.y'}^{(t)}$ is the correct relation.

4. (Sections 3.5, 3.6) In a sample of data available for analysis, an economic variable y is found to be related to plausible "explanatory" variables x_1 and x_2 as follows: $r_{y1} = 0$, $r_{y2} = .8$. Also, the simple correlation between x_1 and x_2 is $r_{12} = .5$. An investigator seeking to "explain" the behavior of y observes that x_1 is not related to y (that is, $r_{y1} = 0$), and on this basis proposes that x_1 be omitted from consideration. Is it true, as the proposal suggests, that R^2 for the multiple regression of y on x_1 and x_2 is the same as R^2 for the regression of y on x_2 alone? Calculate.

ANSWER:

The fallacy of the proposal is obvious from the relation

$$R^2_{y.12} = R^2_{y.2} + R^2_{y.e_2.1}.$$

Since x_1 is related to x_2 it will contribute to R^2 even though $r_{y1} = 0$.

In order to calculate R^2 we use the expansion in terms of standardized regression coefficients (3.5.11). From (3.5.8),

$$\begin{pmatrix} \tilde{b}_1 \\ \tilde{b}_2 \end{pmatrix} = \begin{pmatrix} 1 & .5 \\ .5 & 1 \end{pmatrix}^{-1} \begin{pmatrix} 0 \\ .8 \end{pmatrix}$$

$$= \begin{pmatrix} \frac{4}{3} & -\frac{2}{3} \\ -\frac{2}{3} & \frac{4}{3} \end{pmatrix} \begin{pmatrix} 0 \\ .8 \end{pmatrix} = \begin{pmatrix} -\frac{8}{15} \\ \frac{16}{15} \end{pmatrix}$$

and

$$R^2 = (-\tfrac{8}{15})(0) + (\tfrac{16}{15})(\tfrac{4}{5}) = \tfrac{64}{75} > .64.$$

5. (Sections 3.4, 3.9) In an effort to consider the ways in which personal expectations are formed, the following study was proposed. Eight "events"— indicators of the general economic climate—were arbitrarily scaled from one to eight on the basis of their historic performance as indicators of prosperity. So, for example, the event "stock market fell an average of four points" rates "one" as a prosperity indicator, while the event "new car sales up 15 percent this quarter" rates a "seven."

Three ways of presenting the eight events to sample subjects were contemplated: ordered from rating one through eight, ordered from rating eight through one, and ordered according to a given random pattern. The subjects were to respond with a "prosperity forecast" for the immediate future, on a scale of from one to five. The hypothesis under consideration is that expectations are "stronger" with the recent past reflecting a growing tendency toward better business conditions, to be analyzed by the following regression model:

$$y_i = \beta_1 x_{i1} + \cdots + \beta_8 x_{i8} + \epsilon_i,$$

where x_{ij} takes on values 1 through 8 depending on the rating of the jth event.

Upon collecting data and attempting to analyze them, it was found that $(X'X)$ was singular, hence no regression coefficients were forthcoming. Briefly evaluate the design of the study relative to its stated purpose, and explain, if you can, the outcome reported.

ANSWER:

Multicollinearity is not the problem here. There are only three observation points over the eight independent variables, hence X has row rank three no matter how large the sample.

PROBLEMS ON SPECIAL TOPICS:
THE CONSUMPTION FUNCTION REVISITED

What is permanent income? As an empirical question, this has received much attention.

The basic permanent income hypothesis of Friedman suggests that the propensity to consume out of permanent income is a constant, k. In equational form $c_t^{(p)} = k y_t^{(p)}$, with $c_t^{(p)} =$ per capita "permanent" consumption per period t and $y_t^{(p)} =$ per capita "permanent" income in t.† One widely used technique for constructing a permanent income measure is to define it as a

---

† Note: In this form k is both a marginal and an average propensity.

weighted sum of past actual values $y_t^{(p)} = \sum_{i=0}^{h} w_i y_{t-i}$ with $\sum_{i=1}^{h} w_i = 1$. Then, with permanent consumption assumed to be the sum of observed (measured) consumption and an unobservable random component (transitory consumption), interesting questions revolve around the time horizon, h, and whether or not the line passes through the origin, as the equation suggests.

1. Use your previously collected data to estimate the weights in a two-year model:

$$c_t = \alpha + k(w_0 y_t + w_1 y_{t-1}) + \epsilon_t.$$

Here ϵ_t plays the role of a random measurement error; measured consumption (c_t) equals permanent consumption $(c_t^{(p)})$ plus ϵ_t.

ANSWER:

For our data (see Section 2.9) we got the following results

$$c_t = 85.92 + .5563 y_t + .2990 y_{t-1},$$
$$\hat{k} = .5563 + .2990 = .8553, \quad SS_\Omega = 257,685.$$

2. Test the hypothesis $H: \alpha = 0$ by following the procedure outline for constructing an F-test. Specifically, (a) recalculate the regression coefficients forcing $\alpha = 0$; (b) calculate the SS under no restriction (SS_Ω) and the SS under $H: \alpha = 0$ (SS_H) as the appropriate sums of squared residuals; (c) compute

$$F_{1,n-3} = \frac{SS_H - SS_\Omega}{SS_\Omega/(n-3)}$$

and test.

ANSWERS:

For the model with zero intercept, $X'X$ is 2×2, hence easily invertible. The restricted model was estimated to be

$$c_t = .5589 y_t + .3509 y_{t-1}, \quad \hat{k} = .9098, \quad SS_H = 269,409.$$

Constructing the F-statistic,

$$F_{1,32} = \frac{SS_H - SS_\Omega}{SS_\Omega/32} = 1.456.$$

The computer run of Problem 1 above provided a t-ratio for the estimated intercept (85.92) of 1.21, which is approximately the square root of 1.456. Whichever test is used, the hypothesis of zero intercept is not rejected at a 95 percent level of significance.

3. With the aid of the computer consider an extended version of the model, introducing further income lags to y_{t-5}, and forcing $\alpha = 0$. Calculate $\hat{k}$.† Do you feel that the additional income lags are important parts of "permanent" income as empirically defined? Explain in *objective* terms, if possible.

ANSWER:

The correlation matrix for this problem is worth displaying.

$$\mathbf{\rho_{xx}} = \begin{array}{cccccc} y_t & y_{t-1} & y_{t-2} & y_{t-3} & y_{t-4} & y_{t-5} \end{array}$$

$$\mathbf{\rho_{xx}} = \begin{bmatrix} 1 & .981 & .956 & .915 & .880 & .844 \\ & 1 & .982 & .946 & .900 & .846 \\ & & 1 & .977 & .937 & .875 \\ & & & 1 & .976 & .928 \\ & & & & 1 & .972 \\ & & & & & 1 \end{bmatrix} \begin{array}{l} y_t \\ y_{t-1} \\ y_{t-2} \\ y_{t-3} \\ y_{t-4} \\ y_{t-5} \end{array}$$

As one might imagine, the results may be quite strange owing to such high intercorrelations. In fact, the determinant of this matrix is of the order of 10^{-15}.

What was obtained is as follows:

$$c_t = \underset{(2.17)}{.5092y_t} - \underset{(-.26)}{.0931y_{t-1}} + \underset{(.41)}{.1475y_{t-2}} - \underset{(-.35)}{.1175y_{t-3}}$$
$$+ \underset{(.68)}{.2246y_{t-4}} + \underset{(1.29)}{.2702y_{t-5}},$$

$\hat{k} = .9409$. The numbers in parentheses are the t-ratios for individual coefficients. At 95 percent just the coefficient on y_t is significantly different from zero ($t_{30,.95} = \pm 2.042$).

Clearly the additional income lags cause multicollinearity problems. R^2 for this equation is .9982, whereas for the zero-intercept equation calculated in the previous problem $R^2 = .9962$.‡ From a goodness-of-fit standpoint nothing much has been gained. Since the statistical significance of all but y_t is also in doubt, we have little to say in defense of this expanded version.

4. An alternative model to explain consumption says that consumption must depend on current disposable income and on past habits of consump-

---

† You obtain estimates of $kw_0, \ldots, kw_5$, and you know $\sum_{i=1}^{5} w_i = 1$.

‡ The version of R^2 used (R^2_{mf}) is the same over the two models (both of which are restricted to have zero intercepts), so comparisons between them are valid, although we would hesitate using this measure for anything else.

tion—that is, previous levels of consumption. This suggests a model of the form:

$$(1) \quad c_t = \alpha + \beta_0 y_t + \beta_1 c_{t-1} + \cdots + \beta_h c_{t-h} + \epsilon_t.$$

With our experience from the income-lag model we would expect multicollinearity to be a problem here also. So, as an operational matter (1) is often shortened to

$$(2) \quad c_t = \alpha + \beta_0 y_t + \beta_1 c_{t-1} + \epsilon_t, \qquad |\beta_1| < 1.$$

Accordingly, β_0 may be thought of as the "short-run" marginal propensity to consume. The "long-run" marginal propensity (the increase in consumption from a unit increase in *all* previous incomes) can be established to be $\beta_0/(1 - \beta_1)$, as follows.

The basic model is (2) above. Now:

$$c_1 = \alpha + \beta_0 y_1 + \beta_1 c_0 + \epsilon_1,$$
$$c_2 = \alpha + \beta_0 y_2 + \beta_1(\alpha + \beta_0 y_1 + \beta_1 c_0 + \epsilon_1) + \epsilon_2$$
$$\quad = (\alpha + \beta_1 \alpha) + \beta_0 y_2 + \beta_1 \beta_0 y_1 + \beta_1^2 c_0 + \beta_1 \epsilon_1 + \epsilon_2$$
$$\quad = \alpha(1 + \beta_1) + \beta_0(y_2 + \beta_1 y_1) + \beta_1^2 c_0 + \beta_1 \epsilon_1 + \epsilon_2,$$
$$c_3 = \alpha + \beta_0 y_3 + \beta_1 \alpha(1 + \beta_1) + \beta_1 \beta_0(y_2 + \beta_1 y_1) + \beta_1^3 c_0$$
$$\quad\quad + \beta_1^2 \epsilon_1 + \beta_1 \epsilon_2 + \epsilon_3$$
$$\quad = \alpha(1 + \beta_1 + \beta_1^2) + \beta_0(y_3 + \beta_1 y_2 + \beta_1^2 y_1) + \beta_1^3 c_0$$
$$\quad\quad + \beta_1^2 \epsilon_1 + \beta_1 \epsilon_2 + \epsilon_3,$$

so that

$$c_t = \alpha(1 + \beta_1 + \beta_1^2 + \cdots + \beta_1^{t-1})$$
$$\quad\quad + \beta_0(y_t + \beta_1 y_{t-1} + \cdots + \beta_1^{t-1} y_1)$$
$$\quad\quad + \beta_1^t c_0 + \beta_1^{t-1} \epsilon_1 + \beta_1^{t-2} \epsilon_2 + \cdots + \epsilon_t.$$

From the equation above, the effect of a unit increase in *all* past incomes is

$$\frac{\partial c_t}{\partial y_1} + \frac{\partial c_t}{\partial y_2} + \cdots + \frac{\partial c_t}{\partial y_t} = \beta_0(1 + \beta_1 + \beta_1^2 + \cdots + \beta_1^{t-1}).$$

The sum in parentheses is $1/(1 - \beta_1)$ for t large (we assume the process has been going on forever) and $|\beta_1| < 1$. So, the "long-run" marginal propensity is $\beta_0/(1 - \beta_1)$.

For your data, estimate the coefficients in (2) and compare your results to the estimates of short- and long-run marginal propensities obtained from the income-lag models.†

ANSWER:

For our data (2) is estimated as (t-ratios in parentheses):

$$c_t = -22.34 + .2087y_t + .7990c_{t-1},$$
$$\quad\quad\; (-.63) \quad (3.38) \quad\;\; (10.84)$$

$$\frac{b_0}{1 - b_1} = \frac{.2087}{.2010} = 1.033.$$

For comparison purposes, we have considered the following models:

Model I: $\quad c_t = \beta_0 y_t + \beta_1 y_{t-1} + \epsilon_t,$

Model II: $\quad c_t = \beta_0 y_t + \beta_1 y_{t-1} + \cdots + \beta_5 y_{t-5} + \epsilon'_t,$

Model III: $\quad c_t = \alpha + \beta_0 y_t + \beta_1 c_{t-1} + \epsilon''_t,$

with results shown below. Apparently the consumption-lag version does represent a substantial alternative to the income-lag models. Note also the large t-ratio on the coefficient of c_{t-1} in Model III, but that the long-run MPC for this model *exceeds* one.

	Model I	*Model II*	*Model III*
Short-run MPC	.5589	.5092	.2087
	(2.58)	(2.17)	(3.38)
Long-run MPC	$\hat{k} = .9098$	$\hat{k} = .9409$	$\dfrac{b_0}{1 - b_1} = 1.033$

While it is possible to calculate the standard error of our estimate of k in Models I and II (it involves only the sum of individual coefficient variances and two times each covariance), it is not possible to calculate the standard error of $b_0/(1 - b_1)$ for Model III exactly, since it represents a nonlinear combination of coefficients. An approximation to its standard error is available, although we do not present it here.

5. The multicollinearity problems experienced in the income-lag model with several lags included may be overcome by specifying a particular form for the lag structure, as opposed to letting the regression technique fit a "free" lag form. The most widely used specification has the coefficients on income

---

† The appearance of lagged values of c_t in (1) and c_{t-1} in (2) causes the LS estimated coefficients to be at best asymptotically unbiased, a matter we discuss in detail in the next chapter.

and its lags as a geometric progression; that is,

(3) $y_t^{(p)} = (1 - \lambda) \sum_{i=0}^{\infty} \lambda^i y_{t-i}, \qquad 0 < \lambda < 1,$

$\qquad = (1 - \lambda)y_t + (1 - \lambda)\lambda y_{t-1} + \cdots + (1 - \lambda)\lambda^h y_{t-h} + \cdots.$

This specification fits the mold suggested in the previous discussion, since

$$(1 - \lambda) \sum_{i=0}^{\infty} \lambda^i = 1, \qquad \text{for } 0 < \lambda < 1.$$

The permanent income consumption function is then given by (with constant term included)

(4) $c_t = \gamma + k y_t^{(p)} + u_t$

$\qquad = \gamma + k(1 - \lambda) \sum_{i=0}^{\infty} \lambda^i y_{t-i} + u_t.$

From an empirical standpoint this model eliminates many of the difficulties encountered previously. For instance, it has but three parameters to estimate: γ, k, and λ. However, it is not clear how one might go about estimating λ in fact—that is, using the regression framework.† The trick that solves this latter problem is to multiply (4) for c_{t-1} through by λ and subtract the resulting equation from (4) for c_t.

Perform the indicated operations and rewrite the resulting equation so that it looks like (2). Now, *without doing any new calculations*, estimate γ, k, and λ. What are the short- and long-run marginal propensities for this model, in symbols and numerically? Is there *any* difference between this model and (2)? If so, what implications follow?

ANSWER:

Writing (4) out completely,

$$c_t = \gamma + k(1 - \lambda)(y_t + \lambda y_{t-1} + \lambda^2 y_{t-2} + \cdots) + u_t$$

and

$$c_{t-1} = \gamma + k(1 - \lambda)(y_{t-1} + \lambda y_{t-2} + \cdots) + u_{t-1}.$$

Multiplying c_{t-1} by λ and subtracting from c_t leaves

$$c_t = \lambda c_{t-1} + \gamma(1 - \lambda) + k(1 - \lambda)y_t + u_t - \lambda u_{t-1},$$

† $\hat{k}$ can easily be obtained, just as before, since $\sum_{i=0}^{\infty} w_i = 1$.

which compares with the consumption-lag model of Problem 4 thus:

$$\alpha = \gamma(1 - \lambda),$$
$$\beta_0 = k(1 - \lambda),$$
$$\beta_1 = \lambda,$$
$$\epsilon_t = u_t - \lambda u_{t-1}.$$

Hence parameter estimates of γ, k, and λ are simply $\hat{\lambda} = .7990$, $\hat{k} = 1.033$, the long-run MPC, and $\hat{\gamma} = (-22.34)/(1 - \hat{\lambda}) = -111.2$. Besides the fact that this transformed income-lag model is nonlinear in its parameters, the essential and very important difference in the two models is that beginning with the classical assumptions of zero expectation, constant variance, and independence in sampling leads to different conclusions concerning the anticipated properties of LS estimates of the parameters in each. We have no reason to suspect anything in the consumption-lag model of Problem 4. However, for the income-lag model under a geometric lag structure, beginning with $E(u_t) = 0$, $E(u_t^2) = \sigma_u^2$ leads to a violation of the classical assumptions in its operational version. For since the error term is $u_t - \lambda u_{t-1}$, while $E(u_t - \lambda u_{t-1})^2 = (1 + \lambda^2)\sigma_u^2$ conditional on the y_{t-i}'s, a constant, c_{t-1} and u_t are correlated: $E(c_{t-1}[u_t - \lambda u_{t-1}]) \neq 0$. In fact, $E(c_{t-1}[u_t - \lambda u_{t-1}]) = -\lambda\sigma_u^2$. Hence we expect the LS estimates of α, β_0, and β_1 in this model to be biased. Generally, whenever a lagged value of the dependent variable appears as an "independent" variable, the LS estimates are biased. We shall have more to say on this in the next chapter.

6. From our work so far, there appear to be (at least) two plausible forms for the aggregate consumption-income relation, one function involving several income lags besides current income, and another with current income and several consumption lags. For this final exercise consider only the simplest versions of the two models, namely:

$$(5) \quad c_t = \alpha + \beta_0 y_t + \beta_1 y_{t-1} + \epsilon_t$$

and

$$(6) \quad c_t = \alpha' + \beta_0' y_t + \beta_1' c_{t-1} + \epsilon_t'.$$

In order to "choose" which version is most appropriate empirically, it is proposed to form the hybrid function

$$(7) \quad c_t = \alpha'' + \beta_0'' y_t + \beta_1'' y_{t-1} + \beta_2'' c_{t-1} + \epsilon_t''$$

and test the individual hypotheses $H_1: \beta_1'' = 0$ and $H_2: \beta_2'' = 0$. Acceptance of H_1 presumably implies version (6); acceptance of H_2 implies version (5). For your data, estimate the parameters of model (7) and perform the indicated hypothesis tests. If *both* hypotheses are either accepted or rejected, give some interpretation or explanation of this result.

ANSWER:

For the hybrid function,

$$c_t = -19.22 + .4129y_t - .2959y_{t-1} + .8941c_{t-1}.$$
$$(-.60)\quad (4.39)\quad (-2.71)\quad (11.78)$$

Both hypotheses are rejected at the 95 percent level. The explanation is probably best put in terms of multicollinearity again. Here the correlation matrix is

$$\rho_{xx} = \begin{matrix} & \begin{matrix} y_t & y_{t-1} & c_{t-1} \end{matrix} \\ \begin{bmatrix} 1 & .978 & .939 \\ & 1 & .952 \\ & & 1 \end{bmatrix} & \begin{matrix} y_t \\ y_{t-1} \\ c_{t-1} \end{matrix} \end{matrix}$$

While we can push the level of significance high enough to not reject $H_1: \beta_1'' = 0$ and at the same time reject $H_2: \beta_2'' = 0$, we will have concomitantly raised the probability of committing a type II error in the first decision to close to one.

4 Relaxation of the

Classical Assumptions

4.1 INTRODUCTION

Figure 2.2 depicted a *sample* situation where the classical assumption of common variance over the conditional distributions of y, or *homoscedasticity* as it is also called, might be questioned. In the first sections of this chapter we develop methods for dealing with this particular violation of the classical assumptions. Next, we consider the case that often arises in time-series analysis of related residuals or *serial correlation*, where the assumption $E(\epsilon_i \epsilon_j) = 0$ for $i \neq j$ is violated. This would be the case, for example, in a time-series model where structural shifts over time were not accounted for adequately by the set of conditioning variables. For this problem we can think either in terms of theoretical reasons for using a model that incorporates an assumption other than $E(\epsilon_i \epsilon_j) = 0$ for $i \neq j$ directly, or in terms of testing the *hypothesis* $E(\epsilon_i \epsilon_j) = 0$ for $i \neq j$. Again, we will be primarily concerned about effects on the properties of the usual LS estimators of a violation of this assumption.

Next, we inquire into the possibility that LS estimators have desirable properties when independent variables are themselves random variables but the conditional analysis assumption is relaxed. We find, for example, that

120

if the *assumption* of uncorrelatedness of the population residual with each independent variable is justified, many of the usual results go through.

In the introduction to Chapter 3 we suggested that in economic, sociological, and psychological models of individual or aggregate behavior there may be only a few really "independent" variables. The rest may, and perhaps should, be thought of in the context of models that contain several simultaneously determined and therefore interdependent variables. Then, to treat such complicated relationships with a technique that imposes, in effect, a line of causation from right to left in a single equation—with a single "dependent" variable—is an obvious error.

There are two issues involved here, given that we are disposed to use single-equation methods. The first concerns the effects on our usual LS estimators of "independent" variables that *really* are not independent, but are jointly dependent with y. This problem may equivalently be considered as a violation of the assumption of uncorrelatedness of the residual with the conditioning variables in the PRM. But this issue is concerned with the effects on LS estimators of a violation of $E(\epsilon x_j) = 0$ without questioning whether the single-equation model has any meaning in terms of the simultaneous system of relations that is the "correct" model. Thus, a second issue is involved—a sort of "specification" error—and to deal with it we attempt to trace the relations between coefficients in the single-equation model and their counterparts in a supposed simultaneous equation model. It is commonly referred to as the *identification* problem.

4.2 THE "GENERALIZED" REGRESSION MODEL

As a theoretical question, the extension of least-squares methods to encompass the possibility of an error variance-covariance matrix with a form other than $\sigma^2 I$ was accomplished in the 1930's by Aitken. He proved the following generalization of the Gauss-Markov theorem: with a PRM $y = X\beta + \epsilon$, X a matrix of observations on $(k + 1)$ fixed variates (or, an analysis *conditional* on X), $E(\epsilon) = 0$, but $E(\epsilon\epsilon') = \sigma^2\Lambda$, where Λ is a known nonsingular matrix of the variances and covariances of the residuals (up to the scale factor σ^2), the *generalized least-squares* estimators $b^* = (X'\Lambda^{-1}X)^{-1}X'\Lambda^{-1}y$ are BLUE and have variance-covariance matrix $\Sigma_{b^*} = \sigma^2(X'\Lambda^{-1}X)^{-1}$. The least-squares criterion function that gives rise to these particular estimators is

$$\sum_{i=1}^{n} \sum_{j=1}^{n} \Lambda^{ij} \epsilon_i \epsilon_j,$$

where Λ^{ij} is the i, j element of Λ^{-1}. Substituting $\epsilon_i = y_i - \beta_0 - \beta_1 x_{i1} - \cdots - \beta_k x_{ik}$, the LS criterion function is

$$\sum_{i=1}^{n} \sum_{j=1}^{n} \Lambda^{ij}(y_i - \beta_0 - \beta_1 x_{i1} - \cdots - \beta_k x_{ik})(y_j - \beta_0 - \beta_1 x_{j1} - \cdots - \beta_k x_{jk}).$$

For the classical case, $\Lambda = I$, therefore $\Lambda^{-1} = I$ and this criterion function reduces to the familiar

$$\sum_{i=1}^{n} (y_i - \beta_0 - \beta_1 x_{i1} - \cdots - \beta_k x_{ik})^2$$

because all terms for which $i \neq j$ in the double sum are zero.

The interpretation of these generalized least-squares estimators is that they are generated from a "weighted" LS criterion function, the weights involving reciprocals of error variances and covariances. For example, if Λ reflected the assumption that the conditional distributions each had a different variance, say σ_i^2, the criterion function would be $\sum_{i=1}^{n} \Lambda^{ii} \epsilon_i^2$. Since the Λ^{ii} terms are just the inverse conditional variances (up to a scale factor,

$1/\sigma^2$), the resulting least-squares estimators would take into account explicitly those observations with larger a priori variances by giving them less weight in the criterion function.

In the face of the $E(\epsilon\epsilon') = \sigma^2\Lambda$ specification our usual least-squares estimator $\mathbf{b} = (\mathbf{X}'\mathbf{X})^{-1}\mathbf{X}'\mathbf{y}$ still retains the "LUE" of BLUE. This is clear from

$$(4.2.1) \qquad \begin{aligned} E(\mathbf{b}) &= E(\mathbf{X}'\mathbf{X})^{-1}\mathbf{X}'\mathbf{y} \\ &= E(\mathbf{X}'\mathbf{X})^{-1}\mathbf{X}'(\mathbf{X}\boldsymbol{\beta} + \boldsymbol{\epsilon}) \\ &= \boldsymbol{\beta} + E(\mathbf{X}'\mathbf{X})^{-1}\mathbf{X}'\boldsymbol{\epsilon} \\ &= \boldsymbol{\beta}. \end{aligned}$$

The fact that $E(\epsilon\epsilon') = \sigma^2\Lambda$ therefore affects only the efficiency of $\mathbf{b}$.

So much for theory. In practice Λ is unknown. But in the face of the $E(\epsilon\epsilon') = \sigma^2\Lambda$ specification the usual LS estimators are not efficient. A logical point of inquiry is then: can Λ be estimated? If so, what are the efficiency properties of $\mathbf{b}^*$ when an *estimate* of Λ is used? Note again that no matter what *fixed* matrix is substituted for Λ the resulting $\mathbf{b}^*$ estimators will be unbiased; but if an *estimated* Λ is used, the best we can hope for generally is asymptotic unbiasedness.†

In order to consider these questions, suppose we run an ordinary LS regression of y on the x_j's and calculate residuals. Next, form

$$(4.2.2) \qquad \mathbf{ee}' = \begin{bmatrix} e_1^2 & e_1e_2 & \cdots & e_1e_n \\ \cdot & & & \\ \cdot & & & \\ \cdot & & & \\ e_ne_1 & & \cdots & e_n^2 \end{bmatrix},$$

which may be thought of as using single observations to estimate each element of Λ. But to use $\mathbf{ee}'$ as an estimate of Λ in the formation of generalized LS estimates would meet with serious difficulties. For $(\mathbf{ee}')^{-1}$ cannot be calculated because the rank of $\mathbf{ee}'$ is *one*.‡

The ordinary LS calculated residuals *do* contain some usable information. From before, using them in the form $\mathbf{e}'\mathbf{e}$ leads to an estimate of σ^2. And, as the ordinary LS estimator $\mathbf{b}$ is unbiased for $\boldsymbol{\beta}$, the LS predicted values $(\hat{y}_1, \ldots, \hat{y}_n)$ are unbiased estimates for the conditional means $E(y_i \,|\, x_{i1}, \ldots, x_{ik})$. In a real sense, therefore, we can speak of e_i being an unbiased

---

† If the estimate of Λ is *consistent*, then $\mathbf{b}^*$ attains its BLUE properties only as sample size gets very large. If an *unbiased* estimate of Λ is available we still would expect only asymptotic unbiasedness for $\mathbf{b}^*$, since the inverse of this estimate is only asymptotically unbiased for Λ^{-1}.

‡ This information comes from the theorem on the rank of a product of two matrices, which states that rank $\mathbf{AB} \leq \min$ (rank $\mathbf{A}$, rank $\mathbf{B}$); cf. Appendix A.

estimate of ϵ_i.† But because the $k + 1$ estimated regression coefficients are used in calculating the e_i's, there will be only $n - k - 1$ independent e_i's; or, the vector $\mathbf{e} = (e_1 \cdots e_n)'$ will contain only $n - k - 1$ independent pieces of "information." What is required in order to proceed is a sufficient number of restrictions on the form of $\boldsymbol{\Lambda}$ so that the information embodied in the vector of computed residuals can be utilized.

Even ignoring the singularity of $\mathbf{ee'}$, we can no longer say that the coefficients—*could* they be estimated from our proposed two-step procedure—are BLUE, but at least *some* account would be taken of the fact that $\boldsymbol{\Lambda}$ is "full," that is, $\boldsymbol{\Lambda}$ need not conform to $\sigma^2 \mathbf{I}$, but may have all non-zero elements.

A. Zellner‡ has provided the formal basis on which the proposed two-step procedure produces estimates with efficiency properties. If the elements of $\boldsymbol{\Lambda}$ can be replaced by (at least) consistent estimates of them, say as $\hat{\boldsymbol{\Lambda}}$, then the estimator $\hat{\mathbf{b}}^* = (\mathbf{X}'\hat{\boldsymbol{\Lambda}}^{-1}\mathbf{X})^{-1}\mathbf{X}\mathbf{X}'\hat{\boldsymbol{\Lambda}}^{-1}\mathbf{y}$, while being linear, is also unbiased and efficient (best) in large samples. This latter property is often referred to as *asymptotic efficiency*. If the usual normality assumption is also made, $\hat{\mathbf{b}}^*$ is unbiased for any sample size.

The uses we shall make of the generalized regression model, its implications, and their solutions appear in the following two sections, where we discuss problems that involve a specification for $E(\mathbf{ee'})$ other than $\sigma^2 \mathbf{I}$. In both sections we shall address ourselves first to the question of whether a specification other than $E(\mathbf{ee'}) = \sigma^2 \mathbf{I}$ is appropriate. There may be an a priori or theoretical reason for suspecting so; otherwise some particular forms for $\boldsymbol{\Lambda}$ may be tested. In neither section, however, will the more complicated computational formula, $\hat{\mathbf{b}}^* = (\mathbf{X}\mathbf{X}'\hat{\boldsymbol{\Lambda}}^{-1}\mathbf{X})^{-1}\mathbf{X}'\hat{\boldsymbol{\Lambda}}^{-1}\mathbf{y}$, be needed. The calculations will in all cases be performable with the usual least-squares formula $\mathbf{b} = (\mathbf{X}'\mathbf{X})^{-1}\mathbf{X}'\mathbf{y}$. The key to the ability to "make do" with the simpler formula will be to find appropriate transformations of the basic model and its data to take the $E(\mathbf{ee'}) = \sigma^2 \boldsymbol{\Lambda}$ specification *into* $E(\mathbf{ee'}) = \sigma^2 \mathbf{I}$.

4.3 HETEROSCEDASTICITY

As we saw in Fig. 2.2, the sample data may suggest that the conditional variances of y vary over the conditioning variable (or variables), a situation of *heteroscedasticity*. Later, in Section 5.2, a model will be discussed that

---

† The vector ϵ contains random variables, not parameters. So our concept of "unbiased estimation" needs some attention. What we mean by $\mathbf{e}$ being an unbiased estimator for ϵ is $E(\mathbf{e} - \epsilon) = 0$.

‡ "An Efficient Method of Estimating Seemingly Unrelated Regressions and Tests for Aggregation Bias," *J. Am. Stat. Assn.*, Vol. 57 (1962), pp. 348–68.

theoretically gives rise to this situation. Whichever the case, the problem and possible remedies for it are the same.

In general, the effect of heteroscedasticity, where each observation is assumed to have a different conditional variance but where the assumption $E(\epsilon_i \epsilon_j) = 0$ for $i \neq j$ is still in force, is on the efficiency of ordinary LS estimators of coefficients in the linear model. The unbiasedness property of ordinary LS is unaffected by the presence of interdependent disturbances in general and hence also in the special case of heteroscedasticity. This conclusion follows directly from the proof of unbiasedness (3.4.7), which uses only the property that the residual is uncorrelated with the conditioning variables [or $E(\epsilon) = 0$ in the fixed-variate case].

The intuition underlying any attempt to improve the efficiency of ordinary least-squares estimators of partial regression coefficients under heteroscedasticity follows from the idea that for a given level of precision of estimation for an estimate of the mean of a population, a larger sample will be required the more variable is the characteristic being measured in the population. If the actual collection of a sample were within our province, more observations would be required at observation points with large conditional variances to guarantee a given level of precision of estimation. Since executing a sample design is usually not possible, however, and moreover because we usually cannot estimate separate conditional variances owing to a paucity of replicated observations on y at each point $(x_1, \ldots, x_k)$, taking cognizance of heteroscedasticity in the regression framework implies somehow weighting each observation in accordance with its anticipated variability. It is "anticipated variability" that is important, because we generally do not possess data in a form to estimate the different conditional variances. And since they cannot be estimated, we must *posit* something about them to make the problem tractable, in much the same spirit as the regression model *posits* a relationship between the conditional means and the conditioning variables. Once a structural relation between the conditional variances and the conditioning variables has been established—by assumption—efficient coefficient estimates may be obtained in two equivalent ways.

The first is by appropriately transforming all variables in the regression model to achieve homoscedastic residuals in the transformed equation. For example, suppose the data in a two-variable regression equation *appear* to be heteroscedastic, as in Fig. 2.2. Model specifications are $y_i = \beta_0 + \beta_1 x_{i1} + \epsilon_i$ with $E(\epsilon_i) = 0$, $E(\epsilon_i \epsilon_j) = 0$ for $i \neq j$, but it appears that the disturbance (conditional) variance is proportional to x—that is, $E(\epsilon_i^2) = \sigma_i^2 = \lambda x_{i1}$, with λ the constant factor of proportionality. If the equation is divided through by $x_{i1}^{1/2}$ (nonzero for all i), we get

$$(4.3.1) \qquad y_i x_{i1}^{-1/2} = \beta_0 x_{i1}^{-1/2} + \beta_1 x_{i1}^{1/2} + \epsilon_i x_{i1}^{-1/2},$$

which is a three-variable regression with zero intercept. Here we have

$E(\epsilon_i x_{i1}^{-1/2}) = 0$, but now $E(\epsilon_i x_{i1}^{-1/2})^2 = \lambda$, a constant over i. Thus ordinary LS may be applied, forcing the intercept to zero in a regression of $(y_i x_{i1}^{-1/2})$ on $x_{i1}^{-1/2}$ and $x_{i1}^{1/2}$.

Note, however, that if a major interest is in the prediction of y, the regression is of a new dependent variable, $(y x_1^{-1/2})$. Besides the interpretation problems for R^2 when the intercept is forced to zero, a high R^2 for predicting $(y x_1^{-1/2})$ need not imply a high R^2 (proportion of explained variance, for instance) in predicting y alone.

The transformation procedure used above could also be used if, for example, $E(\epsilon_i^2) = \lambda x_{i1}^2$. Then

(4.3.2)
$$\frac{y_i}{x_{i1}} = \frac{\beta_0}{x_{i1}} + \beta_1 + \frac{\epsilon_i}{x_{i1}},$$

and again $E(\epsilon_i/x_{i1})^2 = \lambda$, so ordinary LS is applicable.

The second technique for dealing with the difficulties posed by heteroscedastic disturbances is usually referred to as *weighted least squares*. If $E(\epsilon_i^2) = \lambda x_{i1}$, for example, we can proceed to obtain alternative estimators for β_0 and β_1 by minimizing a "weighted" version of the LS criterion function, namely

(4.3.3)
$$\sum_{i=1}^{n} (y_i - \beta_0 - \beta_1 x_{i1})^2 (\lambda x_{i1})^{-1}.$$

Note that viewing $(y_i - \beta_0 - \beta_1 x_{i1})$ as a residual, ϵ_i, we are looking at a χ^2 statistic—almost—if the normality assumption is applied to the $\{\epsilon_i\}$. According to the theorem on formation of the χ^2 variable, each normal variable must be *standardized*. Thus *divide* each ϵ_i by its assumed standard deviation, $\sigma_i = \sqrt{\lambda x_{i1}}$. Summing and squaring gives the above criterion function. The resulting estimators, say b_0^* and b_1^*, found by minimizing this function are generalized LS estimates, and their efficiency is thus guaranteed by Aitken's generalized Gauss-Markov theorem. This correspondence was suggested earlier, when we discussed a particular case of generalized least squares where the diagonal elements of Λ differed and all off-diagonal elements were zero. The usual LS estimators for β_0 and β_1 *are* generalized LS estimators when $\sigma_i = \sigma$, a constant. Then the criterion function is $\sum e_i^2/\sigma^2$, which when minimized assuming σ^2 is a constant is equivalent to the LS criterion that minimizes $\sum e_i^2$.

Performing the required minimization for this example, we find

(4.3.4)   (a)
$$-2 \sum \left(\frac{y - b_0^* - b_1^* x_1}{\lambda x_1} \right) = 0,$$

(b)
$$-2 \sum \left(\frac{y - b_0^* - b_1^* x_1}{\lambda x_1} \right) x_1 = 0,$$

or

(a) $$\sum \left(\frac{y}{x_1}\right) = b_0^* \sum \left(\frac{1}{x_1}\right) + nb_1^*,$$

(b) $$\sum y = nb_0^* + b_1^* \sum x_1.$$

Finally,

(4.3.5) $$b_0^* = \bar{y} - b_1^* \bar{x}_1,$$

$$b_1^* = \frac{\overline{\left(\frac{y}{x_1}\right)} - y\overline{\left(\frac{1}{x_1}\right)}}{1 - \bar{x}_1\overline{\left(\frac{1}{x_1}\right)}}$$

where $\overline{(y/x_1)}$, $\overline{(1/x_1)}$ are notations for the mean ratios of (y/x_1), $(1/x_1)$. If the sample regression line goes through the origin $(b_0^* = 0)$, then $\overline{(y/x_1)} = \bar{y}/\bar{x}_1$ and $b_1^* = \bar{y}/\bar{x}_1$, which is commonly called a "ratio" estimate. This same result would occur in ordinary regression if $b_0 = 0$, since $0 = \bar{y} - b_1\bar{x}_1$, and $b_1 = \bar{y}/\bar{x}_1$. As an estimator of the ratio of population means, therefore, b_1^* is unbiased when $b_0^* = 0$ owing to the fact that $E(\epsilon) = 0$ and $E(\epsilon x_1) = 0$. If the population regression function is $E(y|x_1) = \beta_1 x_1$, then $E\{E(y|x_1)\} = \beta_1 E(x_1) = E(y)$, so $\beta_1 = E(y)/E(x_1)$. In general, of course, the sample regression line will not pass through the origin, and the usual LS slope estimate of β_1 will differ from our generalized LS estimator (4.3.5).

Finally, it should be recognized that the deflation procedure suggested at the beginning of this section also produces estimates that are identical in every sample to (4.3.5). To see this, merely calculate the *partial* LS regression coefficient as suggested by the model (4.3.1), using Eq. (3.6.2). Since (4.3.1) is to be fitted without a constant term, the moments required in (3.6.2) are in raw form, giving

(4.3.6)

$$b_1^* = b_{y2.1} = \frac{\sum \left(\frac{y}{x^{1/2}}\right)x^{1/2} \sum (x^{-1/2})^2 - \sum \left(\frac{y}{x^{1/2}}\right)x^{-1/2} \sum (x^{1/2})(x^{-1/2})}{\sum (x^{1/2})^2 \sum (x^{-1/2})^2 - [\sum (x^{1/2})(x^{-1/2})]^2}$$

$$= \frac{\sum y \sum \left(\frac{1}{x}\right) - n \sum \left(\frac{y}{x}\right)}{\sum (x) \sum \left(\frac{1}{x}\right) - n^2}.$$

Multiplying numerator and denominator by $-n^2$ gives (4.3.5).

Moving away from our illustrative case, if heteroscedasticity is present and not somehow accounted for, the ordinary LS estimator will still be unbiased but not best. And, to be sure, *dealing* with heteroscedasticity is much more difficult when more than a single conditioning variable appears in the equation. Not only is it impossible to graph data in scatters with more than three dimensions (if adequately even at three) in order to "look" at the possibility of heteroscedasticity, but no easy transformations exist either. To use the deflation method one must posit the existence of *known* factors of proportionality, say by $\sigma_i^2 = z_i\sigma^2$, with σ^2 a constant common variance component. If the $\{z_i\}$ are given, each observation may be transformed much as in Eq. (4.3.1), dividing all terms by $z_i^{1/2}$. Of course, any known function of z_i could equally well be handled.

The notion that a heteroscedastic model might be transformed into a homoscedastic one for purposes of applying ordinary LS methods is not without some further difficulty, as the following question suggests. In the deflation suggested by (4.3.1), for instance, if the ordinary LS coefficient corresponding to $x_{i1}^{1/2}$ is not zero as calculated, is that fact due to a "real" relationship between y and x_1 or is it spurious, coming from the fact that both y and x_1 are deflated by a common variable, $x_1^{1/2}$? So long as the deflator is, as we have *assumed* all along, a known constant for each observation, there is no problem. But if the deflator is the observed value of some random variable, *as it is* in many economic applications, spurious correlation will be imputed to the relation between deflated variables. This proposition was first articulated by A. Madansky in a brief and quite readable note in 1964,[†] to which the reader is referred for proof. The main point he made can also be reinterpreted constructively in light of our general remarks concerning the use of generalized LS methods, from Section 4.2. If the "true" deflator is some nonrandom quantity per observation that is unknown, and a random variable is used to estimate it, the best we can hope for is large-sample efficiency for the generalized LS estimates and hence for ordinary LS estimates derived from the transformed (deflated) equation. If the random variable does not provide even a consistent estimate of the deflator, efficiency will not be obtained at any sample size. If the deflator is random in its "true" form, we have clearly moved on to a different regression model, which involves stochastic elements in Λ, and for which there is no estimation theory.

The techniques for "dealing" with heteroscedasticity as we have described them so far are quite ad hoc. "Looking" at a sample scatter and then using a weighted regression that accounts for a conditional variance proportional to the independent variable, for instance, is quite a bootstrap operation. Unless there are strong a priori reasons for choosing a particular set of values for the conditional variances, we would rather proceed to test for the possibility of heteroscedasticity and, if it is present, attempt to get estimates with better precision than the ordinary LS regression coefficients.

[†] "Spurious Correlation Due to Deflating Variables," *Econometrica*, Vol. 32 (October 1964), pp. 652–5.

Alternatively, we may be able to build into our original statistical model the possibility of nonconstant conditional variance.

One possible test is an offshoot of our test for nonlinearity of regression presented in Chapter 2. There we assumed that at each value of some independent variable there were available repeated observations on y. It is relatively easy to construct a test of variance equality based on such data, but since it will be a rare occasion when the economic researcher has the necessary sample, we will not present it here.

A generally more usable test, but one with other limitations, takes off from the "deflation" controversy to address the problem of testing for heteroscedasticity. It is due to Goldfeld and Quandt.† The test essentially chooses between two models

(4.3.7a) $$y = X\beta + \epsilon$$

and

(4.3.7b) $$\left(\frac{y}{x_h}\right) = \left[\frac{X}{x_h}\right]\beta + \left(\frac{\epsilon}{x_h}\right).$$

Equation (4.3.7a) is the classical regression model, and (4.3.7b) is the transformed or deflated model we would use to get generalized LS estimates if heteroscedasticity were of the sort $\sigma_i^2 = \sigma^2 x_{ih}^2$. The notation $[X/x_h]$ in (4.3.7b) means that each observation (row) in X is divided by x_{ih}, a known quantity that is nonzero and may or may not be one of the variables in X or some transformation of it.

The logic underlying the Goldfeld-Quandt test is simple: if (4.3.7a) is "true," with homoscedastic errors, then (4.3.7b) will possess heteroscedastic errors and vice versa. A separate test is conducted on each equation. For (4.3.7a) observations are ordered by the "potential" deflator and subsets of outlying observations are selected. Some observations in the "middle" may be discarded—say r of them. Enough observations must be retained in each subset, however, to compute the LS regression coefficients for the model and calculate the residual variances in each. Suppose n_s is used to denote the number of observations in the "small" group, with SS_s its error sum-of-squares, and n_l is the number of observations in the "large" group with residual sum-of-squares SS_l. The test statistic is $R = [SS_l/(n_l - k - 1)]/[SS_s/(n_s - k - 1)]$ and has an F-distribution with $(n_l - k - 1)$ and $(n_s - k - 1)$ degrees of freedom. The null hypothesis is of homoscedasticity. Therefore on the assumption that (4.3.7a) is homoscedastic we would expect R to be "large" if homoscedasticity is violated. An identical test is then run on (4.3.7b), where the observations are ordered according to $(1/x_{ih})$.

† "Some Tests for Homoscedasticity," *J. Am. Stat. Assn.*, Vol. 60 (June 1965), pp. 593–9.

The possible outcomes of our tests obviously number three: rejection in both cases, nonrejection in both cases, and rejection in one case with nonrejection in another. The first two results are therefore inconclusive in choosing between (4.3.7a) and (4.3.7b), but the third is taken as evidence in favor of one model (whose test ended in nonrejection) and against the other (whose test resulted in rejection).

The test has some problems. The omitted observations obviously play a crucial role in the final outcome in several ways. Degrees of freedom are lost by discarding observations, and the power of the test is related inversely to r, although apparently not monotonically. The aura of throwing off observations is also disturbing. Again, as in the case of deflation, the hypothesis test of homoscedasticity rests on a specific hypothesis about the *form* of heteroscedasticity. But at least the form is *tested* before being applied.[†]

The possibility for estimating a *conditional variance regression function* has only recently received much attention. The main motivation for exploring this line of approach to the problem of detecting and correcting for heteroscedasticity is to eliminate any dependence on restricted a priori forms for the conditional variances.

The most successful attempt to deal with the matter of estimating a conditional variance function has been made by Rutemiller and Bower.[‡] But it does not have the virtue of easy application. In fact, it requires a heavy computational effort. The idea is, nonetheless, simple and elegant.

Instead of a single regression model, a two-equation PRM is specified:

(4.3.8)
$$y_i = \beta_0 + \beta_1 x_{i1} + \cdots + \beta_k x_{ik} + \epsilon_i,$$
$$\sigma_i = \gamma_0 + \gamma_1 x_{i1} + \cdots + \gamma_k x_{ik} + u_i.$$

The maximum-likelihood method is used, with the resulting objective to minimize the function

$$\sum_{i=1}^{n} \frac{(y_i - \beta_0 - \beta_1 x_{i1} - \cdots - \beta_k x_{ik})^2}{\sigma_i^2}.$$

The correspondence to generalized least squares is obvious. The number of normal equations derived by the minimization is $(2k + 2)$ and they are complicated functions of the data points. They are solvable by numerical methods, however, and the resulting estimators of the β_j's and γ_j's have large-sample normality, consistency, and efficiency properties. Tests of homoscedasticity can also be obtained. For example, in a two-variable conditional variance

---

† Goldfeld and Quandt also offer a nonparametric test, which we do not discuss here. A competing test that rests on the assumption of normality for population disturbances has quite recently been proposed by H. Glejser ["A New Test for Heteroskedasticity," *J. Am. Stat. Assn.*, Vol. 64 (March 1969), pp. 316–23].

‡ "Estimation in a Heteroscedastic Regression Model," *J. Am. Stat. Assn.*, Vol. 63 (June 1968), pp. 552–7.

function, $E(\sigma_i) = \gamma_0 + \gamma_1 x_{i1}$, the hypothesis $\gamma_1 = 0$ corresponds to homoscedasticity.

4.4 AUTOREGRESSIVE DISTURBANCES

A restriction on the form of Λ that makes the efficient estimation problem tractable and arises often in economics concerns so-called *autoregressive disturbances*. In time-series data, for instance, it is often reasonable to expect the residuals $\{\epsilon_i\}$ in $y = X\beta + \epsilon$ to be identically distributed (normal, same mean and variance) but not to be independent. This would be the case were the model structure shifting over time but not in such a way that the shifts could adequately be captured in terms of the set of independent variables. As is often observed empirically, the disturbances in such cases may be taken to follow a *first-order autoregressive process*,

$$(4.4.1) \qquad \epsilon_i = \rho\epsilon_{i-1} + u_i,$$

where it is assumed that $|\rho| < 1$, $E(u) = 0$, $E(u_i^2) = \sigma_u^2$, $E(u_i u_j) = 0$ for $i \neq j$. Thus the error process is thought of as being made up of a systematic component, $\rho\epsilon_{i-1}$, to capture a structural shift, and a random component, u_i, representing such things as measurement error in the dependent variable. The "effects" of past disturbances are greatest in the immediate future, and become negligible due to the assumption $|\rho| < 1$. This assumption assures the "stationarity" of the process, meaning that the essential characteristics of the random variables $\{\epsilon_i\}$, such as their means, variances, and covariances, remain the same no matter when observations are taken.

By repeated substitution we find that the general term ϵ_i may be written in terms of some initial value ϵ_0 and $u_1, \ldots, u_i$, as

$$(4.4.2) \qquad \epsilon_i = \rho^i\epsilon_0 + \rho^{i-1}u_1 + \cdots + \rho u_{i-1} + u_i.$$

Since the selection of ϵ_0 is arbitrary, we choose it to be in the distant past, so that the term $\rho^i\epsilon_0$ is negligible. Therefore $E(\epsilon_i) = 0$, because $E(u_1) = \cdots = E(u_i) = 0$.

We also find that $E(\epsilon_i^2) = \sigma_u^2/(1 - \rho^2) = \sigma^2$ and $E(\epsilon_i\epsilon_j) = \sigma^2\rho^{|i-j|}$. Or,

$$(4.4.3) \qquad \sigma^2\Lambda = \sigma^2 \begin{bmatrix} 1 & \rho & \rho^2 & \cdots & \rho^{n-1} \\ \rho & 1 & & & \\ \rho^2 & & \cdot & & \\ \cdot & & & \cdot & \\ \cdot & & & & \cdot \\ \rho^{n-1} & & & & 1 \end{bmatrix}.$$

Presumably we do not know ρ, but if ordinary LS is first applied to obtain the calculated residuals, $\{e_i\}$, they can be used to obtain a sample coefficient of auto- or serial correlation, $\hat{\rho}$, given by

$$(4.4.4) \qquad \hat{\rho} = \frac{\sum e_i e_{i-1}}{\sqrt{\sum e_i^2}\sqrt{\sum e_{i-1}^2}}.$$

which is almost the LS estimate of ρ in a PRM $e_i = \rho e_{i-1} + u_i$. This value $\hat{\rho}$ may then be used to form an estimate of Λ, say $\hat{\Lambda}$, and to get an estimate of β from $(X'\hat{\Lambda}^{-1}X)^{-1}X'\hat{\Lambda}^{-1}y$. These "two-step" estimates will have desirable large-sample properties, because $\hat{\rho}$ consistently estimates ρ. $\hat{\Lambda}$ can be inverted, whereas ee' is singular.

As with the heteroscedasticity case, it is possible to incorporate the autoregressive scheme directly into our usual regression framework by a suitable data transformation. For, consider the following well-used transformation. Begin with

$$(4.4.5) \qquad y_i = \beta_0 + \beta_1 x_{i1} + \cdots + \beta_k x_{ik} + \epsilon_i$$

and

$$(4.4.6) \qquad \epsilon_i = \rho \epsilon_{i-1} + u_i,$$

with the same assumptions as before. Lagging (4.4.5) one period and multiplying by ρ gives

$$(4.4.7) \qquad \rho y_{i-1} = \rho \beta_0 + \beta_1 \rho x_{i-1,1} + \cdots + \beta_k \rho x_{i-1,k} + \rho \epsilon_{i-1}.$$

Subtracting from y_i,

$$(4.4.8) \qquad y_i - \rho y_{i-1} = (1 - \rho)\beta_0 + \beta_1(x_{i1} - \rho x_{i-1,1}) + \cdots$$
$$+ \beta_k(x_{ik} - \rho x_{i-1,k}) + \epsilon_i - \rho \epsilon_{i-1}.$$

The residual in (4.4.8) is just $u_i = \epsilon_i - \rho \epsilon_{i-1}$ and has the appropriate properties for a proper application of LS to this equation. (Compare this to the result of Problem 5 in the special-topics section at the end of Chapter 3.) The rationale for the use of first differences in time-series regression is seen to rest on the belief that $|\rho|$ is *close* to one. ρ can never *be* one, else $\sigma^2 = \sigma_u^2/(1 - \rho^2)$ is infinite.

Several iterative methods are available for dealing with this model within the ordinary LS framework (rather than going to the generalized LS method), by first obtaining a consistent estimate of ρ, next suitably adjusting the dependent and independent variables, and finally recalculating the estimates.

One method for obtaining a consistent $\hat{\rho}$ is from (4.4.4), above. This suggestion was originally due to Cochrane and Orcutt.[†] Another is by a procedure due to Durbin.[‡] He suggests finding the LS estimates of the coefficients in our (4.4.8) with y_{i-1} transposed to the right-hand side of the equation and treated as an additional independent variable. The calculated coefficient on y_{i-1} is taken as the estimate of ρ. Although $\hat{\rho}$ determined in this manner is consistent, that fact should not, at this point, be obvious to the reader. Indeed, Durbin's suggested regression equation does violate one of the important Gauss-Markov assumptions, because y_{i-1} and ϵ_{i-1} are not independent. Accordingly, $\hat{\rho}$ derived in this manner will be biased. That the bias approaches zero for large samples will be argued in the next section.

Once a consistent $\hat{\rho}$ is found, it remains to "appropriately" transform the data. This is accomplished by forming series $y_i - \hat{\rho}y_{i-1}$, $x_{i1} - \hat{\rho}x_{i-1,1}$, and so on, as suggested by (4.4.8). This transformation effectively reduces the number of observations by one. Recently it has been found that the Cochrane-Orcutt $\hat{\rho}$ used this way does not guarantee large-sample efficiency and, in fact, can make things worse than using ordinary LS on the original model.[§] A similar conclusion undoubtedly holds in the case of Durbin's $\hat{\rho}$. The key to obtaining a desirable result whichever $\hat{\rho}$ is used is to utilize a transformation of the first observation, $y_1\sqrt{(1 - \hat{\rho}^2)}$, in addition to the transformed series previously generated.

We present these two methods as apparent equals because there seems to be little evidence to suggest the contrary. For "large" samples they are equally good, and clearly superior to ordinary LS applied to the original model.[||] In particular, if the independent variables also exhibit marked autocorrelation, ordinary LS will compare poorly in general. But, of course, the two-step procedure involves more computations.

Rao and Griliches[*] provide some information about the relative merits of these methods in small samples, concluding that the two-step methods offer a definite improvement in efficiency over ordinary LS when $|\hat{\rho}| > .3$.[#] As among the Cochrane-Orcutt and Durbin $\hat{\rho}$'s they single out

---

[†] "Application of Least Squares to Relationships Containing Auto-Correlated Error Terms," *J. Am. Stat. Assn.*, Vol. 44 (March 1949), pp. 32–61.

[‡] "The Fitting of Time Series Models," *Review Int. Stat. Inst.*, Vol. 28 (1960), pp. 233–43.

[§] K. Kadiyala, "A Transformation Used to Circumvent the Problem of Autocorrelation," *Econometrica*, Vol. 36 (January 1968), pp. 93–6.

[||] Were there not independent variables involved in specifying the mean of y, and our model was $y = \mu + \epsilon$ with ϵ an autocorrelated error term, the ordinary LS estimate of μ (the sample mean) would be relatively efficient even in large samples. Chipman *et al.* in "Efficiency of the Sample Mean when Residuals Follow a First-Order Stationary Markoff Process," *J. Am. Stat. Assn.*, Vol. 63 (December 1968), pp. 1237–46, found that its relative efficiency as compared to generalized LS (variance $\hat{\mu}$ GLS/variance $\hat{\mu}$ OLS) was at *worst* .87.

[*] "Small-Sample Properties of Several Two-Stage Regression Methods in the Context of Autocorrelated Errors," *J. Am. Stat. Assn.*, Vol. 64 (March 1969), pp. 253–72.

[#] Theoretically, and ignoring autocorrelation in independent variables, the relative efficiency of ordinary LS is found to be $(1 - \rho^2)/(1 + \rho^2)$. A little arithmetic will show that for values $|\rho| < \frac{1}{3}$ ordinary LS is relatively efficient ($> .8$).

Durbin's estimate as "better," but the evidence is not conclusive. Either $\hat{\rho}$ should provide satisfactory results.

Up to this point we have been speaking as if there were some a priori reason for suspecting serial correlation in the residuals. It may be, however, that first-differencing or other alternatives for specifically accounting for serial correlation are called for on the basis of empirical observation. In this regard a first-order scheme may be tested via the Durbin-Watson test, one of a set of three related statistical tests for serial correlation.

The test statistic used in the D-W test is

$$(4.4.9) \qquad d = \frac{\sum\limits_{i=2}^{n} (e_i - e_{i-1})^2}{\sum\limits_{i=1}^{n} e_i^2},$$

also referred to as the Von Neumann ratio.† d relates directly to the sample coefficient of serial correlation, $\hat{\rho}$ (4.4.4), using the following approximations:

$$(4.4.10) \qquad \sum_{i=1}^{n} e_i^2 \doteq \sum_{i=2}^{n} e_{i-1}^2 \doteq \sum_{i=2}^{n} e_i^2.$$

Therefore,

$$(4.4.11) \qquad d \doteq \frac{2\sum\limits_{i=1}^{n} e_i^2 - 2\sum\limits_{i=2}^{n} e_i e_{i-1}}{\sum\limits_{i=1}^{n} e_i^2} = 2 - 2\hat{\rho} = 2(1 - \hat{\rho}).$$

If $\hat{\rho} \to 1$ (positive serial correlation), $d \to 0$; as $\hat{\rho} \to -1$ (negative serial correlation), $d \to 4$; if $\hat{\rho} = 0$ (no serial correlation), $d = 2$.

The distribution of d, assuming that the residuals e_i follow a $N(0, \sigma^2)$ distribution, lies between the distributions of two other statistics, called d_L and d_U, as depicted in Fig. 4.1. The test is one-sided, of the hypothesis of no negative (positive) serial correlation, the hypothesis being rejected as d is greater than $4 - d_L^*$ (less than d_L^*). For economic time-series data, which almost invariably exhibit positive serial correlation, the positive alternative will be appropriate.

In the diagram, d_L^* and d_U^* are the critical values for a given significance level, α, and parameters n and k. Note that there is an inconclusive region in each case, where no decision can be made. This is because the distribution of d is not known exactly, but is bounded by two other known distributions. A 95 percent level table for the test is available in Appendix C for n in (15, 100) and k in (1, 5).

Other tests for serial correlation are worth mentioning, although

† Although it differs slightly from the original Von Neumann statistic.

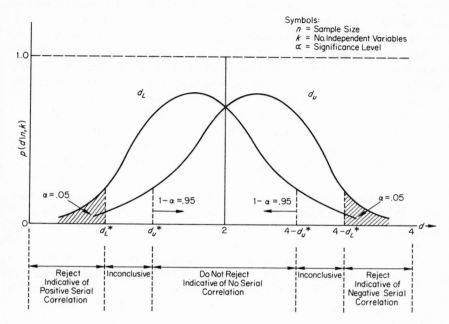

Fig. 4.1

Bounds for the Distribution of the Durbin-Watson Statistic, *d.* (This particular figure was suggested by K. O. Kymn in the *American Statistician,* April 1968, p. 35.)

the D-W test appears to be the most generally usable. It is not without its shortcomings, however.

Durbin and Watson's test builds on an earlier development by Von Neumann and B. I. Hart.† The "improvement" in the Von Neumann test is that it is specifically adapted for use in regression analysis by Durbin and Watson, thus taking direct account of the fact that the calculated residuals are dependent on both the number of observations and the number of independent variables in a regression model. As a result, the power of the D-W test is quite good. As a matter of practical application, however, the D-W test does possess the "inconclusive" region, which is large for few observations and more than a few independent variables. To alleviate the potential misuses of the inconclusive region as an area of nonrejection rather than an area of nondecision, as it is, Theil-Nagar‡ have produced an approximate distri-

---

† B. I. Hart and J. Von Neumann, "Tabulation of the Probabilities for the Ratio of the Mean Square Successive Difference to the Variance," *Annals Math. Stat.*, Vol. 13 (1942), pp. 207–14.

‡ H. Theil and A. L. Nagar, "Testing the Independence of Regression Disturbances," *J. Am. Stat. Assn.*, Vol. 56 (1961), pp. 793–806.

bution for d. It amounts essentially to the use of $P(d_U)$ as an approximation for $P(d)$, and can be expected to be adequate in some special situations only. More recently, Henshaw[†] improved upon the T-N work, obtaining a more accurate approximation to $P(d)$. The computations required to use the Henshaw test are many compared to D-W. For this reason and because the D-W test is powerful, it is still recommended, although with a reminder to heed the caution expressed by Theil-Nagar about the inconclusive region. It really is *inconclusive*. It is possible to compute the exact distribution of the D-W statistic for any *given* application; the exact distribution depends on the X-matrix. In the near future computer programs will undoubtedly include this computation as one of the "standard" pieces of output.

The assumptions underlying all these tests call for truly exogenous independent variables, *not* including lagged values of the dependent variable. When lagged values of the dependent variable do appear, the D-W statistic is *biased* toward two—that is, biased *against* finding serial correlation.[‡]

Theil and Nagar are worried about a relevant problem. For, the existence of serial correlation (or, more generally, related disturbances) violates an underlying assumption of the classical model. The ramifications of using ordinary LS estimates when serial correlation is present are that $\mathscr{S}^2$ no longer provides an unbiased estimate of σ^2 and the formula $\Sigma_b = \sigma^2(X'X)^{-1}$ is wrong. These two points can be seen by referring to Eqs. (2.6.1)–(2.6.4) and (3.4.8)–(3.4.10), where explicit use of the assumption $E(\epsilon_i \epsilon_j) = 0$ for $i \neq j$ is made. Thus the associated measures that come along with LS coefficient estimates cannot be used for purposes of testing, and so on. For instance, since the usual estimated variances of partial regression coefficients are incorrect when serial correlation is present, so are the t-ratios used for testing the significance of each coefficient. An autocorrelated error generally causes an *upward* bias in R^2.

We should also add that while we have concentrated on a first-order autocorrelated error, higher-order schemes may be tested for and estimated, leading to improved efficiency in estimation.

The D-W test may also provide a means for judging the nonlinearity hypothesis. The idea is that nonlinearity may be characterized by adjacent residuals which tend to be of the same sign when arranged by order of increasing magnitude of some independent variable. Thus, in Fig. 4.2 the scatter of y on x suggests a nonlinear relationship. For such an example we would expect the sample serial correlation coefficient for the residuals *arranged in this way* to be large and positive, indicating, in this instance,

† "Testing Single Equation Least Squares Regression Models for Autocorrelated Disturbances," *Econometrica*, Vol. 34 (July 1966), pp. 646–60.

‡ Marc Nerlove and Kenneth F. Wallis, "Use of the Durbin-Watson Statistic in Inappropriate Situations," *Econometrica*, Vol. 34 (1966), pp. 235–38.

nonlinearity rather than serial correlation. Since there is a one-to-one correspondence between $\hat{\rho}$ and d, the
Durbin-Watson statistic, the test (for
positive serial correlation) may be
carried out with d for the "arranged"
series of residuals.

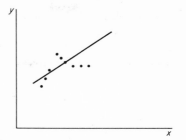

Fig. 4.2

To close our treatment of *interdependent disturbances*, as we might
refer to this section, we mention some
work that has been done and is being
done on the general matter of analyzing least-squares residuals. From a general dissatisfaction with the Durbin-Watson test, its inconclusive region and
limited view of interrelated disturbances (as a first-order autoregressive
process), and a desire to develop a simple test for the nonnormality of least-
squares residuals, Theil has suggested modified least-squares residuals—called
BLUS residuals—as the proper objects of attention for analysis. In particular,
ordinary LS residuals do not satisfy the $\sigma^2\mathbf{I}$ covariance matrix specifications
supposed for the population residuals on the average. That is, $E(\mathbf{ee}') \neq \sigma^2\mathbf{I}$.
Whereas, a very general test for noninterrelated disturbances would be to
test $\sigma^2\mathbf{I}$ as a hypothesis. The Theil BLUS residuals do have $\sigma^2\mathbf{I}$ as their
expected covariance matrix under the hypothesis, and thus are good statistics
for the test. Again, there are computational and other limitations to the
procedures involved, but they will likely be refined and in more general use
in the near future.

Heteroscedastic disturbances are not, of course, the only interesting
complication to be introduced into the classical model. Another important
case to consider is the violation of the uncorrelatedness condition of the
population residual, ϵ, with the conditioning variables. This *contemporaneous
uncorrelatedness* property *is* a characteristic of the PRF specified as a conditional mean function when independent variables are themselves stochastic.
Yet there may be other model specifications that give rise to a regression
model with PRF characteristics, and vice versa: there may be interesting
translations of a PRM into a regression model that violates the uncorrelatedness property.

In the following three sections we consider relevant models that fit this
latter mold, where specifications lead to regression-type models that do not
possess the contemporaneous uncorrelatedness characteristic $E(\epsilon x) = 0$
necessary to make LS estimation even consistent. In all three sections the discussion focuses on just what properties *are* possessed by the LS estimators,
and whether more desirable alternative estimators are available. The discussion initially considers the possibilities for unconditional analysis of a PRM
specified with stochastic independent variables, the case of *stochastic regres-*

sion. The phraseology *classical regression* is reserved for the model specifications heretofore adhered to: either the fixed-X case or a conditional analysis on sto´chastic **X**. Section 4.8 completes our treatment of the classical regression model and the viability of its underlying assumptions.

4.5 CONDITIONAL ANALYSIS, UNCONDITIONAL ANALYSIS, AND THE AUTOREGRESSIVE MODEL

Throughout, it has been assumed that samples can be generated at will for *given* **X**. If **X** is a matrix of observations on fixed variates, we have the classical case; otherwise, the concept of conditional expectation is used to promote the same idea for **X** random. Obviously there are many situations where this statistical basis for the regression model breaks down. The assumption of "laboratory conditions" is clearly unrealistic for most economic applications of the regression method, and in particular for time-series analysis. The precise implications of this fact are not known, but it forms the basis for a different school of thought about statistical modeling in situations where samples cannot be replicated according to the requirements of the Gauss-Markov theorem or conditional expectations. This is the *Bayesian* view of statistics, and it has—at least conceptually—much to recommend it. We consider Bayesian regression in Section 4.8, finding that under certain circumstances it also leads to LS estimates of the regression parameters.

The inability to replicate samples is not the only difficulty in *using* LS regression methods without being conservative in interpreting their results. There is also the problem of the stability of the observation matrix of independent variables, **X**, if other than a *conditional analysis* is desired.

Extending our discussion to cover an analysis that is *not* conditioned on **X**, the previous results go through with but a few alterations when strong limitations are imposed on *how* the **X**-matrix of random variables can behave. Briefly, if the variables in **X** and $\boldsymbol{\epsilon}$ are independently distributed, we can use the product rule for expectations to find that the unbiasedness property holds, since

$$E(\mathbf{b}) = \boldsymbol{\beta} + E[(\mathbf{X}'\mathbf{X})^{-1}\mathbf{X}'\boldsymbol{\epsilon}] = \boldsymbol{\beta} + E[(\mathbf{X}'\mathbf{X})^{-1}\mathbf{X}']E(\boldsymbol{\epsilon}) = \boldsymbol{\beta}$$

because $E(\boldsymbol{\epsilon}) = 0$. No longer does the Gauss-Markov theorem apply, so "bestness" is not guaranteed for small samples. Owing to the correspondence of least squares to maximum likelihood if $\boldsymbol{\epsilon}$ is normally distributed, however, asymptotic efficiency will hold. If the independence assumption is relaxed, least-squares estimates *may* still possess large-sample properties of consistency and asymptotic efficiency. LS estimates will be consistent if $E(\epsilon X) = 0$. Actually, X and ϵ *can* be correlated in a sample so long as *asymptotically* they are uncorrelated. Then

$$\bar{E}(\mathbf{b}) = \boldsymbol{\beta} + \bar{E}\left(\frac{1}{n}\mathbf{X}'\mathbf{X}\right)^{-1}\bar{E}\left(\frac{1}{n}\mathbf{X}'\boldsymbol{\epsilon}\right) = \boldsymbol{\beta} \qquad \text{if } \bar{E}\left(\frac{1}{n}\mathbf{X}'\boldsymbol{\epsilon}\right) = \mathbf{0},$$

where bars over the E-operator mean asymptotic expectation. Here again the use of $1/n$ in each term is necessary to guarantee that these sample variances and covariances (sums-of-squares and cross-products) converge to their population (assumed finite) values. Otherwise, as $n \longrightarrow \infty$, $\sum_{i=1}^{n} x_{ih}^2 \longrightarrow \infty$, for example.

An important thing to recall at this point is that consistency requires more than just asymptotic unbiasedness. While we do not prove it, we take as generally true that sample variances and covariances in our problem consistently estimate their population counterparts. Then $\mathbf{b}$ is not only asymptotically unbiased, it is consistent. $E(\epsilon) = 0$ is *not enough* to get consistency of LS estimates in the unconditional analysis of "stochastic regression" —that is, it is a necessary but not sufficient condition.†

Finally, if we are interested in the "conditional" regression model (PRM) and a *conditional distribution theory* for the LS coefficients, the presence of stochastic regressors causes no problems. If, in addition, $\mathbf{y}$ (alternatively, ϵ) and X share a multivariate normal distribution, the conditional distribution theory is also an unconditional distribution theory.

Now we move to consider a frequently occurring model in economics that illustrates the *need* for unconditional analysis as well as its application.

A model that is of some interest in the analysis of consumption arises when consumption is specified as dependent on a geometric scheme of past income levels—that is, the PRM is

$$(4.5.1) \qquad c_t = \gamma + k(1 - \lambda) \sum_{i=0}^{\infty} \lambda^i y_{t-i} + \epsilon_t.$$

The classical assumptions are made on ϵ_t. For this equation t is the observation subscript, denoting "time."

Even with a finite number of terms, (4.5.1) has some obvious operational drawbacks. Specified for time-series data we can expect y_t and its lags to be highly collinear. Thus multicollinearity is expected; as a result the parameter estimates will likely have high variances. Written for a cross-section sample, data demands are impossible to fulfill. Rarely is more than a single time observation available on a given cross-section sample.

The observation that this PRM can be "reduced" to another regression

---

† See also the discussion of Section 5.2.

model without these operational difficulties through the use of the lag transformation of the previous section is due to Koyck. It is applied as follows:

(4.5.2) $c_t - \lambda c_{t-1} = \gamma(1 - \lambda) + k(1 - \lambda)y_t + \epsilon_t - \lambda\epsilon_{t-1}$

and, therefore,

(4.5.3) $c_t = \gamma(1 - \lambda) + k(1 - \lambda)y_t + \lambda c_{t-1} + w_t,$

where $w_t = \epsilon_t - \lambda\epsilon_{t-1}$, a *moving average* of ϵ_t and ϵ_{t-1}. Conditional on the
y_t's if $E(\epsilon_t) = 0$, then $E(w_t) = 0$. If $E(\epsilon_t^2) = E(\epsilon_{t-1}^2) = \sigma^2$, then $E(w_t^2) =$
$\sigma^2 + \lambda^2\sigma^2 = \sigma^2(1 + \lambda^2)$, a constant. Even if $E(\epsilon_t\epsilon_{t-1}) = 0$, $E(w_tw_{t-1}) \neq 0$.
And most important, $E(\epsilon_ty_t) = 0$, $E(w_ty_t) = 0$ *but* $E(w_tc_{t-1}) \neq 0$. So, since
there is interdependence in the disturbances of this transformed model,
ordinary LS will not produce minimum variance estimates. Since $E(w_tc_{t-1}) \neq$
0, LS will produce conditionally *and unconditionally* biased estimates (of *all*
parameters; not just of λ). This is easily seen, because

(4.5.4) $\mathbf{b} = \boldsymbol{\beta} + (\mathbf{X'X})^{-1}\mathbf{X'}w,$

so that conditional on y_t:

(4.5.5) $\bar{E}(\mathbf{b}) = \boldsymbol{\beta} + \underbrace{(\mathbf{X'X})^{-1}\bar{E}(\mathbf{X'}w)}_{\text{Bias}}$

LS estimates of $\gamma(1 - \lambda)$, $k(1 - \lambda)$, and λ are biased and inconsistent. Note
also that even if we had unbiased estimates of $\gamma(1 - \lambda)$, $k(1 - \lambda)$, and λ,
unbiased estimates of nonlinear functions of parameters generally do not
yield unbiased estimates of the parameters themselves—in this instance γ
and k. They will, however, be consistent.

Generally speaking, whenever a lagged value of the dependent variable
appears as an "independent" variable, this particular bias will arise. In the
example used here, (4.5.1), the problem of bias elimination is even more
severe—that is, when the model has lagged values of the dependent variable
acting as independent variables *and* a moving-average error term.

Each difficulty taken alone is tractable. As we saw previously, the matter
of a first-order autocorrelated or *autoregressive* error scheme can be resolved
by estimating the relevant coefficient of autocorrelation and then, in a second
step, applying least-squares methods on a suitably transformed model. Treatment of the moving-average error by approximation to the autoregressive
case is often satisfactory. While ML methods are available to handle a moving-
average error directly, they are not so easily implemented as our two-step
procedure of the previous section, and (for this reason) we do not discuss
them here in any detail.

The appearance of lagged values of the dependent variable as independent variables in an otherwise classical PRM is referred to as an autoregressive model, and will now be analysed.

To take the simplest case, consider the model

$$(4.5.6) \qquad y_t = \beta_0 + \beta_1 y_{t-1} + \epsilon_t,$$

$|\beta_1| < 1$. Quite obviously the independent variable is no longer a "fixed variate" in the classical sense. Instead, y_{t-1} is a random variable, generated itself through a model like (4.5.6) but written for the previous period. For this reason a conditional analysis is not very interesting. Indeed, conditional on y_{t-1}, "different" samples of size T can differ only by one observation: the residual vector $\epsilon = (\epsilon_1 \cdots \epsilon_T)'$ must contain *constants* in $T - 1$ positions. Thus, conditional on y_{t-1}, $E(\epsilon | y_{t-1}) \neq \mathbf{0}$.

If we move to an unconditional analysis, and assume $E(\epsilon_t) = 0$,

$$E(\epsilon_t \epsilon_{t'}) = \begin{cases} \sigma^2, & t = t', \\ 0, & t \neq t', \end{cases}$$

and $E(y_t \epsilon_t) = 0$, the problem is more appealing. While y_{t-1} is not dependent on ϵ_t, *it is dependent* on all past disturbances, $\epsilon_{t-1}, \ldots$. Therefore we might expect least-squares estimates of β_0 and β_1 in (4.5.6) to be biased, which they are. What is not so clear is the fact that this bias disappears as sample size increases. This result is due to the fact that while dependent on past disturbances, y_{t-1} can be taken to be independent of all "future" disturbances, $\epsilon_t, \epsilon_{t+1}, \ldots, \epsilon_T$.

The derivation of the expected value of the LS slope estimator b_1 for β_1 is not easy. It is given approximately by

$$(4.5.7) \qquad E(b_1) \doteq \beta_1 - \frac{1 + 3\beta_1}{T - 1},$$

showing that for β_1 in the range $\beta_1 > -.33$ the least-squares estimate is expected to contain *negative* bias—that is, to underestimate β_1. The bias obviously disappears for $T \rightarrow \infty$, and has been shown to be small for $T > 20$.

For this simple first-order model there are alternatives to least squares. One possibility exploits (4.5.7), by substituting b_1 for $E(b_1)$ and solving for β_1, giving a new estimator

$$(4.5.8) \qquad \hat{\beta}_1 = \frac{T-1}{T-4} b_1 + \frac{1}{T-4}.$$

In a simulation experiment recently reported, Orcutt and Winokur† confirm

---

† "First Order Autoregression: Inference, Estimation and Prediction," *Econometrica*, Vol. 37 (January 1969), pp. 1–14.

the general superiority of this "modified" LS estimator as compared to b_1. Of course, with β_1 near zero the bias in b_1 will be small.

While our discussion has centered on a two-variable or first-order autoregressive scheme, a similar analysis applies to the more general autoregressive model

$$(4.5.9) \qquad y_t = \beta_0 + \beta_1 y_{t-1} + \cdots + \beta_k y_{t-k} + \epsilon_t,$$

although the exact nature of the small-sample bias in least-squares estimates of $\beta_0, \beta_1, \ldots, \beta_k$ has not been worked out.

When a moving average-error term is combined with the autoregressive model, least-squares estimates of the partial regression coefficients are not consistent. And while several estimators are available for this model,† we shall concentrate on only one, the *instrumental variables* approach.

The model we adopt for investigation is

$$(4.5.10) \qquad y_t = \alpha x_t + \beta y_{t-1} + w_t,$$

where $w_t = u_t - \rho u_{t-1}$, $|\beta|$, $|\rho| < 1$, $E(u_t) = 0$, $E(u_t u_{t'}) = 0$ for $t \neq t'$, $E(u_t^2) = \sigma_u^2$ and x_t is an "independent" variable, uncorrelated with w_t. There is no intercept term in (4.5.10) for convenience only; or, (4.5.10) may be viewed as in deviation or centered form. Equation (4.5.10) is recognized as a slightly more general version of our reduced consumption function (4.5.3); there (in this notation) $\beta = \rho$, a special case of obvious interest.

For the model (4.5.10) the (unconditional) large-sample bias in the least-squares estimators of α, β is easy to derive. Ordinary least-squares estimates a and b of α and β relate to them by the familiar equation

$$(4.5.11) \qquad \begin{pmatrix} a \\ b \end{pmatrix} = \begin{pmatrix} \alpha \\ \beta \end{pmatrix} + (\mathbf{X'X})^{-1}\mathbf{X'w}$$

$$= \begin{pmatrix} \alpha \\ \beta \end{pmatrix} + (\mathbf{X'X})^{-1}\left[\begin{array}{c} \sum x_t(u_t - \rho u_{t-1}) \\ \sum y_{t-1}(u_t - \rho u_{t-1}) \end{array} \right].$$

Now we know that $E[x_t(u_t - \rho u_{t-1}] = 0$ and $E[y_{t-1}(u_t - \rho u_{t-1})] = -\rho E(u_{t-1}^2) = -\rho \sigma_u^2$. But unfortunately we cannot casually break up $E(\mathbf{X'X})^{-1}\mathbf{X'w}$ into the product of two expectations, because at least one of the variables in $\mathbf{X}$ is random (y_{t-1}) and *not* independent of w. There is a calculus of large-sample or *asymptotic* expectations, however, that allows us to write

$$\bar{E}\left(\frac{1}{T}\mathbf{X'X}\right)^{-1}\left(\frac{1}{T}\mathbf{X'w}\right) = \bar{E}\left(\frac{1}{T}\mathbf{X'X}\right)\bar{E}\left(\frac{1}{T}\mathbf{X'w}\right).$$

† The best current reference on this model is G. E. P. Box and Gwilym Jenkins, *Time Series Analysis, Forecasting, and Control* (San Francisco: Holden-Day, 1970).

The division by $1/T$ in each term is required by the theorem utilized. Note that

$$\left(\frac{1}{T}\mathbf{X}'\mathbf{X}\right)^{-1}\left(\frac{1}{T}\mathbf{X}'w\right) = (\mathbf{X}'\mathbf{X})^{-1}\mathbf{X}'w.$$

Using this result,

$$(4.5.12) \quad \bar{E}\begin{pmatrix} a \\ b \end{pmatrix} = \begin{pmatrix} \alpha \\ \beta \end{pmatrix} + \bar{E}\left(\frac{1}{T}\mathbf{X}'\mathbf{X}\right)^{-1}\begin{bmatrix} \bar{E}\frac{1}{T}\sum x_t(u_t - \rho u_{t-1}) \\ \bar{E}\frac{1}{T}\sum y_{t-1}(u_t - \rho u_{t-1}) \end{bmatrix}$$

$$= \begin{pmatrix} \alpha \\ \beta \end{pmatrix} + \bar{E}\left(\frac{1}{T}\mathbf{X}'\mathbf{X}\right)^{-1}\begin{pmatrix} 0 \\ -\rho\sigma_u^2 \end{pmatrix}.$$

Since the expected values of $x_t(u_t - \rho u_{t-1})$ and $y_{t-1}(u_t - \rho u_{t-1})$ do not depend on T, they are also the corresponding asymptotic expectations.

Interpreting (4.5.12), it is useful to think of the matrix $\bar{E}[(1/T)\mathbf{X}'\mathbf{X}]^{-1}$ as the population matrix that is estimated by $[(1/T)\mathbf{X}'\mathbf{X}]^{-1}$. As such, it is the inverse of a matrix of variances and covariances. The bias in b, then, is seen to be the $(2, 2)$ element of $\bar{E}[(1/T)\mathbf{X}'\mathbf{X}]^{-1}$, which is generally positive, times $-\rho\sigma_u^2$, leading to a *negative* bias if $\rho > 0$. The ordinary LS estimate is therefore expected to underestimate β if there is positive autocorrelation in the residuals, the usual case in time-series economic models.†

In the special case where $\beta = \rho$—that is, the autoregressive model and moving average error have identical parameters—"corrected" LS estimates are possible. For then (4.5.12) becomes

$$(4.5.13) \quad \bar{E}\begin{pmatrix} a \\ b \end{pmatrix} = \begin{pmatrix} \alpha \\ \beta \end{pmatrix} + \bar{E}\left(\frac{1}{T}\mathbf{X}'\mathbf{X}\right)^{-1}\begin{pmatrix} 0 \\ -\beta\sigma_u^2 \end{pmatrix}.$$

This suggests that if a consistent estimate for σ_u^2 is available, (4.5.13) might be used in a two-step procedure. The consistent estimators $\hat{\alpha}, \hat{\beta}$ are determined by solving the equations

$$(4.5.14) \quad (\mathbf{X}'\mathbf{X})\begin{pmatrix} \hat{\alpha} \\ \hat{\beta} \end{pmatrix} = \begin{pmatrix} \sum x_t y_t \\ \sum y_{t-1} y_t + \dfrac{\hat{\beta}\sum \hat{w}_t^2}{1 + \hat{\beta}b} \end{pmatrix},$$

† With β underestimated by least squares, the "mean lag" or average adjustment per period of y_t to changes in past levels of y is also underestimated. The concept of mean lag is useful in interpreting habit persistence or adjustment models of the (4.5.3) form. It is defined to be the average number of time periods required for the effects of a change in y_t to be completely dissipated through the autoregressive mechanism. Or, $\partial y_t/\partial y_{t-1} + \ldots + \partial y_t/\partial y_1$ as if past values of y, once realized, were kept at their same levels forever. By writing out the solved version of y_t and recognizing that $\partial y_t/\partial y_{t-1} \equiv \partial y_t/\partial w_{t-1}$, the mean lag for the autoregressive model without a moving average error is $\beta/(1 - \beta)$.

where b is the ordinary LS estimator for β in (4.5.10) and $\hat{w}_t$ is the LS calculated residual from this same SRM. $\hat{\alpha}, \hat{\beta}$ so determined clearly require the solution of a nonlinear equation. The estimates which satisfy (4.5.14) are consistent, but are not (even asymptotically) efficient.

Alternatively, estimators for the parameters of (4.5.10) can be obtained by the method of *instrumental variables*, which not only guarantees consistency but is easier to apply than is the previous technique. It is not limited to the $\beta = \rho$ case, but it also is not a simple matter to verify that the assumptions it rests on are met in practice.

The general technique applies to an unconditional analysis of our usual model $\mathbf{y} = \mathbf{X\beta} + \boldsymbol{\epsilon}$, where the set of "independent" variables contains random variables for which $E(\epsilon x) \neq 0$. The instrumental variables estimator is formed with a matrix $\mathbf{Z}$ of observations on $k + 1$ "instruments"—other variables—with the properties that each instrumental variable is at least asymptotically uncorrelated with $\boldsymbol{\epsilon}$, and *is* correlated with a member of $\mathbf{X}$. The estimator suggested is

$$(4.5.15) \qquad\qquad \hat{\boldsymbol{\beta}} = (\mathbf{Z'X})^{-1}\mathbf{Z'y}$$

Note, then, that

$$(4.5.16) \qquad\qquad \hat{\boldsymbol{\beta}} = \boldsymbol{\beta} + (\mathbf{Z'X})^{-1}\mathbf{Z'}\boldsymbol{\epsilon}$$

by substituting $\mathbf{y} = \mathbf{X\beta} + \boldsymbol{\epsilon}$ in (4.5.15), and

$$(4.5.17) \qquad\qquad \bar{E}(\hat{\boldsymbol{\beta}}) = \boldsymbol{\beta},$$

because the elements of $\mathbf{Z}$ are uncorrelated (by assumption) with $\boldsymbol{\epsilon}$, causing the second term in (4.5.16) to be zero.† The consistency of $\hat{\boldsymbol{\beta}}$ comes with the additional conclusion that its variance-covariance matrix depends on $1/T$. Therefore with T allowed to increase indefinitely, the estimators cluster around $\boldsymbol{\beta}$, which is the property of consistency.

The variance-covariance matrix of $\hat{\boldsymbol{\beta}}$ is estimated by

$$(4.5.18) \qquad \hat{\boldsymbol{\Sigma}}_{\beta} = \left(\frac{\hat{\mathbf{e}}'\hat{\mathbf{e}}}{T - k - 1}\right)(\mathbf{Z'X})^{-1}(\mathbf{Z'Z})(\mathbf{Z'X})^{-1},$$

which clearly shows the dependency of $\hat{\boldsymbol{\beta}}$ on the choice of instruments for precision as well as consistency. Not a great deal is known about testing and interval estimation for the instrumental variables estimator, although

† More formally,

$$\bar{E}(\mathbf{Z'X})^{-1}\mathbf{Z'}\boldsymbol{\epsilon} = \bar{E}\left(\frac{1}{T}\mathbf{Z'X}\right)^{-1}\left(\frac{1}{T}\mathbf{Z'}\boldsymbol{\epsilon}\right) = \bar{E}\left(\frac{1}{T}\mathbf{Z'X}\right)^{-1}\bar{E}\left(\frac{1}{T}\mathbf{Z'}\boldsymbol{\epsilon}\right) = 0,$$

using the rule for asymptotic expectations introduced previously.

it generally possesses a normal distribution in large samples if ϵ has a normal distribution. The use of the estimated variances given by (4.5.18) in forming confidence intervals, for example, should be regarded as an approximation only. In the case of a model where the instruments do not contain a lagged value of the dependent variable and the error ϵ is not autocorrelated, these confidence intervals will generally be *larger* as estimated than they are in truth at any given confidence level. At least the error is in a conservative direction for this example.

Applied to the autoregressive model (4.5.10) with moving average error, it has been suggested by Liviatan to use the instrumental variables technique with x_{t-1} as the instrument for x_t and x_t for y_{t-1}. Thus we have

$$(4.5.19) \qquad \mathbf{X} = \begin{bmatrix} x_1 & y_0 \\ \cdot & \cdot \\ \cdot & \cdot \\ \cdot & \cdot \\ x_T & y_{T-1} \end{bmatrix}, \qquad \mathbf{Z} = \begin{bmatrix} x_0 & x_1 \\ \cdot & \cdot \\ \cdot & \cdot \\ \cdot & \cdot \\ x_{T-1} & x_T \end{bmatrix},$$

and

$$\mathbf{Z'X} = \begin{bmatrix} \sum_{t=1}^{T} x_t x_{t-1} & \sum_{t=1}^{T} y_{t-1} x_{t-1} \\ \sum_{t=1}^{T} x_t^2 & \sum_{t=1}^{T} y_{t-1} x_t \end{bmatrix},$$

yielding an estimator

$$\binom{\hat{\alpha}}{\hat{\beta}} = (\mathbf{Z'X})^{-1} \mathbf{Z'y}.$$

With x_t and y_t both economic time series, the required nonzero (in fact, high) correlations between x_t and x_{t-1}, y_t and x_t seem sure. Whether in fact $E(x_t w_t) = E(x_{t-1} w_t) = 0$, the requirement for consistency, is not so clear, and cannot be checked. It is not known how seriously deviations in these assumptions affect the properties of the estimates. This estimator applied to the $\beta = \rho$ case provides another consistent but asymptotically inefficient estimator. The ML estimator for (4.5.10) and its special case (when $\beta = \rho$) is complicated and will not be developed here.†

What about "large-sample properties," which seem in the end to be what almost everything comes to? Economists using time-series data do not have "large" samples. Indeed, only a little is known about the behavior of LS in situations where the assumptions guaranteeing its small-sample excellence are violated. But the general conclusion from empirical (simulation)

† Again, see Box-Jenkins, *ibid.*

studies to date is that ordinary least-squares techniques are relatively impervious to applications where assumptions guaranteeing their desirable small-sample behavior are violated. Moreover, the accompanying testing and inference theory is apparently quite insensitive to departures from the underlying normality assumption, given the evidence from available studies. Least squares appears to be a quite "robust" technique of estimation.†

4.6 SIMULTANEOUS DETERMINATION AND THE IDENTIFICATION PROBLEM

In earlier sections we have dealt with problems and solutions to them arising out of violations of the classical assumptions that make LS estimates BLUE. But in economics and other social sciences that use single-equation models to treat phenomena and relationships that in reality exhibit a multiplicity of causations, simultaneity, or feedbacks, there is a more fundamental question: given that a more complicated model is called for, what relation, if any, holds between a single PRM and the parameters of this "correct" model? In this sense the single equation may play the role of a solution or *reduced-form* equation, in much the same way that a theoretical demand equation is one of a set of solutions to the first-order or *structural* system of equations derived from a maximization of the consumer's utility function. Quite intuitively, if one of the independent variables in regression and the dependent variable are somehow *mutually determined*, the single equation PRM will clearly be incorrect. In the parlance of our regression assumptions, we will then have described a situation where the assumption $E(\epsilon x) = 0$ is violated on a priori grounds, leading to biased LS results.‡

Once the "correct" structure has been specified, the sample observations *may* have been generated by more than one underlying structure—that is, by a model that *looks* like ours but with different parameters. In that sense our specified structure is said not to be *identified* in terms of any regression equation that purports to be one of its solution or reduced-form equations.

In this section we consider these ideas in a very intuitive way; a more formal presentation is contained in Chapter 6. They are appropriately discussed at this point in our development as another instance in which LS estimation will be (unconditionally) inconsistent due to $E(\epsilon x) \neq 0$.

To elaborate, consider the problem of estimating the parameters in a demand function with time-series data, by the elementary model

---

† This is not to suggest that LS should generally be used though it is known not to possess desireable properties and some alternative is available which is superior at least asymptotically. But asymptotic properties may not provide an adequate criterion upon which to judge the relative merits of an estimator when only small samples are available.

‡ Usually referred to in this instance as *simultaneous-equation bias*.

$$(4.6.1) \qquad\qquad q_t = \alpha + \beta p_t + u_t,$$

where q_t is quantity demanded at time t and p_t is the market price at t. In writing (4.6.1) we have, to simplify things for the moment, ignored other appropriate conditioning variables such as income and prices of other goods. Observations on q and p presumably represent equilibrium points. The identification question is: if we fit a line to (q, p) points over time, can we be sure that a demand curve is being traced out?

In fact, the observations could have been generated by a variety of situations, as depicted in the cases (a), (b), and (c) of Fig. 4.3. If supply shifts while demand remains stable [case (a)], we clearly trace out a demand curve, and vice versa [case (b)]. In the third picture [case (c)] it is quite obvious that the single-equation regression of q on p produces neither a demand nor a supply schedule. There will probably be no prior basis for determining which of the above pictures applies to any given situation.

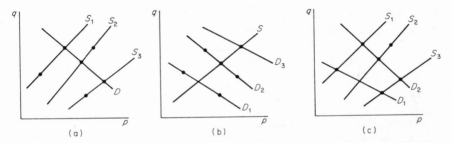

Fig. 4.3

To consider the matter further we require a more elaborate model specification. Indeed, a single equation cannot, by definition, properly represent the simultaneous determination implied by "equilibrium." As one such specification, observations might better be taken to have been generated by a "structure" such as

$$(4.6.2) \qquad
\begin{aligned}
q_t^d &= \alpha + \beta p_t + u_t && \text{(demand),}\\
q_t^s &= \gamma + \delta p_t + v_t && \text{(supply),}\\
q_t^d &= q_t^s = q_t^e && \text{(market clearance),}
\end{aligned}$$

with statistical specifications: $E(u_t) = E(v_t) = 0$; $E(u_t^2) = \sigma_u^2$, $E(v_t^2) = \sigma_v^2$; $E(u_t v_t) = \sigma_{uv} \neq 0$; $E(u_t u_{t'}) = E(v_t v_{t'}) = 0$ for $t \neq t'$. Equation (4.6.2) is a simple mathematical model of "how" market price and equilibrium quantity are established. It is our *structure*. Equations relating the *equilibrium* quantity, q_t^e, and price are obtained by *solving* (4.6.2). These equations are the focal point for further discussion.

Equating q_t^s and q_t^d for market "clearance,"

(4.6.3) $\alpha + \beta p_t + u_t = \gamma + \delta p_t + v_t$

in equilibrium; therefore,

(4.6.4) $p_t = \dfrac{\gamma - \alpha}{\beta - \delta} + \dfrac{v_t - u_t}{\beta - \delta},$

$$q_t^e = \frac{\beta\gamma - \alpha\delta}{\beta - \delta} + \frac{\beta v_t - \delta u_t}{\beta - \delta},$$

the so-called *reduced form* of the original system. Both of the equations in (4.6.4) involve a constant term and *no* explanatory or conditioning variables other than unobservable random elements; hence operationally we seemingly cannot do anything about estimating the coefficients that appear in (4.6.2) from them. That is, the structural coefficients are not "identified" in the reduced form, in the sense that the sample observations cannot be said to have been uniquely generated by our structure. In fact, they may be generated randomly, according to the reduced form.

We could, however, go ahead and regress q_t on p_t. What *will* we get? Consider the sample regression model

(4.6.5) $q_t = a + bp_t + e_t$

and, rather than the *sample* LS estimate for b, look at its *population* analogue. We would *like* to look at the expected value of $b = m_{pq}/m_{pp}$, but clearly since q_t and p_t are structurally related (the simultaneity problem), p_t will not be uncorrelated with e_t, so b will be biased at least in small samples. In large samples we make use of a theorem that says that if $\hat{\theta}_1$ and $\hat{\theta}_2$ are *consistent* estimators of θ_1 and θ_2, then $\hat{\theta}_1/\hat{\theta}_2$ will be a consistent estimator of θ_1/θ_2.[†] The sample moments m_{pq} and m_{pp} are generally consistent estimators of their population counterparts σ_{pq} and σ_p^2. Therefore, we consider the ratio σ_{pq}/σ_p^2 as the large-sample value of b.

σ_{pq} and σ_p^2 are easily obtained from the equations in (4.6.4):

(4.6.6) $\sigma_p^2 = \dfrac{\sigma_v^2 + \sigma_u^2 - 2\sigma_{vu}}{(\beta - \delta)^2}$

and

(4.6.7) $\sigma_{pq} = \dfrac{(\beta\sigma_v^2 + \delta\sigma_u^2 - [\beta + \delta]\sigma_{vu})}{(\beta - \delta)^2},$

---

† Recall the use of a similar theorem in the previous section.

so the population analogue of b is

(4.6.8)
$$\frac{\sigma_{pq}}{\sigma_p^2} = \frac{(\beta\sigma_v^2 + \delta\sigma_u^2 - [\beta + \delta]\sigma_{vu})}{(\sigma_v^2 + \sigma_u^2 - 2\sigma_{vu})}.$$

Upon analyzing (4.6.8), we see first that in general σ_{pq}/σ_p^2 is *not* equal to either β or δ. If, however, $\beta = \delta$, then it is, although one would be hard-pressed to give this result a sensible economic interpretation. If $\sigma_u^2 = 0$, then u_t is a constant over t, and $\sigma_{vu} = 0$ also. Then $\sigma_{pq}/\sigma_p^2 = \beta$. This says the supply curve is doing all the jumping around; hence we trace out the demand function. If $\sigma_v^2 = 0$, we get a like conclusion for the supply function: $\sigma_{pq}/\sigma_p^2 = \delta$. While the analysis formalizes our intuitive interpretation of the problem, it is of limited operational value, as it remains a matter of economic judgment whether in some given body of data $\sigma_u^2 = 0$, or $\sigma_v^2 = 0$, and so on.

As an alternate set of specifications, suppose we posit that there is a one period supply lag in the system. This gives rise to a *recursive* model (a cobweb),

(4.6.9)
$$q_t^d = \alpha + \beta p_t + u_t \qquad \text{(demand)},$$
$$q_t^s = \gamma + \delta p_{t-1} + v_t \qquad \text{(supply)},$$
$$q_t^d = q_t^s = q_t^e \qquad \text{(market clearance)}.$$

From this system we get the following reduced form:

(4.6.10)
$$p_t = \frac{\gamma - \alpha}{\beta} + \frac{\delta}{\beta}p_{t-1} + \frac{v_t - u_t}{\beta},$$
$$q_t^e = \gamma + \delta p_{t-1} + u_t.$$

With the same statistical specifications on this model as were invoked for the "simultaneous" model, it is clear that each of the reduced-form equations may be estimated separately by least squares to get consistent estimates of (δ/β) and δ—then to estimate β. For in the quantity relation, p_{t-1} is independent of u_t; and the price equation is a first-order autoregression for which the least-squares estimate of δ/β is consistent. The structure is *identified* in the sense that reduced-form parameters are known functions of the original parameters, which in turn we can estimate by going backward. It turns out that given identification, LS estimates of reduced-form coefficients, once "solved," generally provide estimates of structural parameters with desirable large-sample properties, although they are not necessarily unbiased for small samples. This is the method of *indirect least squares*.

To summarize, if more than one structure can give rise to the same reduced-form system (or set of observations), then there is no identification. There are, however, cases of *overidentification*, where the reduced form provides more than one path back to a particular structural parameter. Techniques of estimation other than indirect LS exist for such cases. And there are certain simple conditions to be checked for any given equation to insure identification. These matters we reserve for general discussion in Chapter 6. But we can serve our intuition by considering a few examples at this point.

Suppose we slightly alter our simultaneous market-clearance model (4.6.2) by modifying the supply equation to include the influence of "rainfall" on supply, as if the appropriate a priori supply equation were

$$(4.6.11) \qquad q_t^s = \gamma + \delta p_t + \theta r_t + v_t,$$

while retaining the demand equation and market-clearance identity as previously written. The reduced form for this model still consists of two equations,

$$(4.6.12) \qquad p_t = \frac{\gamma - \alpha}{\beta - \delta} + \frac{\theta}{\beta - \delta} r_t + \frac{v_t - u_t}{\beta - \delta},$$

$$q_t^e = \frac{\gamma\beta - \delta\alpha}{\beta - \delta} + \frac{\beta\theta}{\beta - \delta} r_t + \frac{\beta v_t - \delta u_t}{\beta - \delta}.$$

Least squares applied individually to the two reduced-form equations yields estimates of $\pi_{10} = (\gamma - \alpha)/(\beta - \delta)$, $\pi_{11} = \theta/(\beta - \delta)$, $\pi_{20} = (\gamma\beta - \delta\alpha)/(\beta - \delta)$, and $\pi_{21} = \beta\theta/(\beta - \delta)$. Clearly, we can get unique estimates of β and α from $\hat{\beta} = \hat{\pi}_{21}/\hat{\pi}_{11}$ and $\hat{\alpha} = \hat{\pi}_{20} - \hat{\beta}\hat{\pi}_{10}$. These estimators are not generally unbiased, but being obtained as functions of (unbiased) least-squares estimators they will be consistent. However, no unique functions of reduced-form parameters exist to "identify" θ, γ, and δ. So, in this example the demand-function parameters are "identified" while the parameters of the supply function are not.

To conclude this illustration, suppose the supply function were specified to contain an additional exogenous variable beyond "rainfall," say an index of composite input prices, I. Thus, consider as the supply equation of interest

$$(4.6.13) \qquad q_t^s = \gamma + \delta p_t + \theta r_t + \eta I_t + v_t,$$

in conjunction with the demand equation and market-clearance identity of (4.6.2). For this case we find

$$(4.6.14a) \qquad p_t = \frac{\gamma - \alpha}{\beta - \delta} + \frac{\theta}{\beta - \delta} r_t + \frac{\eta}{\beta - \delta} I_t + \frac{v_t - u_t}{\beta - \delta}$$

or

$$p_t = \pi_{10} + \pi_{12} r_t + \pi_{13} I_t + \frac{v_t - u_t}{\beta - \delta}$$

and

(4.6.14b) $\qquad q_t^e = \dfrac{\gamma\beta - \delta\alpha}{\beta - \delta} + \dfrac{\beta\theta}{\beta - \delta}r_t + \dfrac{\beta\eta}{\beta - \delta}I_t + \dfrac{\beta v_t - \delta u_t}{\beta - \delta}$

or

$$q_t^e = \pi_{20} + \pi_{21}r_t + \pi_{22}I_t + \dfrac{\beta v_t - \delta u_t}{\beta - \delta}.$$

As before, we can determine some of the original parameters from the reduced form and hence find consistent estimates for them from least-squares estimates of the π's. Specifically, it is the demand equation for which parameter estimates are available. $\hat{\alpha} = \hat{\pi}_{20} - \hat{\beta}\hat{\pi}_{10}$ again, and $\hat{\beta} = \hat{\pi}_{21}/\hat{\pi}_{11}$. But also $\hat{\beta} = \hat{\pi}_{22}/\hat{\pi}_{12}$; that is, *another* estimate of β is available from the reduced form, with no guarantee that these numbers must coincide in any particular application. This is the case of *overidentification*, where more than one path back to original parameters exists in the reduced form.

Are there ways to identify an unidentified equation? Yes. Merely *know* the values of enough of the parameters in question, thereby limiting the number of paths needed from the reduced form back into the structure. In our first example, if γ and δ were "known," that knowledge would be sufficient to identify α and β, being equivalent to Fig. 4.3(b). More often the "identifying restrictions" placed on a model take the form of zero coefficients. But just as useful, though perhaps less obvious, are restrictions concerning the relevant variances and covariances of the structural equations. In the model (4.6.2) we found that if either $\sigma_u^2 = 0$ or $\sigma_v^2 = 0$, the model was identified. Another example of a case of underidentification with the symptom $E(\epsilon x) \neq 0$ giving rise to biased least-squares estimates is the errors-of-observation model introduced in Chapter 2. In the next section we consider it more fully.

4.7 ERRORS OF OBSERVATION

For most economic models the observations should be treated as if they contained measurement error, which undoubtedly is the case. One might expect that if the effect of errors in measurement were about the same on all variables, it would somehow "cancel" out and not affect our analysis. To the extent that measurement error is systematic, this expectation is essentially justified. For if an independent variable in a regression model were always subject to an error of observation of $-\$5$, it would not affect the regression relationship between y and this variable; it would only affect the intercept term. But if errors of observation are random, this expectation is most certainly unfulfilled.

A brief introduction to the problems encountered when both the dependent and independent variables in a two-variable model are subject to measurement error was presented at the conclusion of Chapter 2. There the scheme considered was

$$(4.7.1) \qquad\qquad Y_i = \alpha + \beta X_i,$$
$$y_i = Y_i + v_i,$$
$$x_i = X_i + u_i,$$

a deterministic model (for convenience only), where the "true" variables are subject to random observation errors u_i and v_i. The assumptions made are that the "true" random variables Y_i and X_i each are independent of u_i and v_i and u_i is independent of v_i. We also assume $E(u_i) = E(v_i) = 0$, $E(u_i^2) = \sigma_u^2$, $E(v_i^2) = \sigma_v^2$, and $E(u_i u_j) = E(v_i v_j) = 0$ for $i \neq j$.

Substituting the observed values y_i and x_i into the main model equation of (4.7.1),

$$(4.7.2) \qquad\qquad y_i = \alpha + \beta x_i + (v_i - \beta u_i).$$

LS methods can easily be applied to (4.7.2), but since x_i is correlated with $(v_i - \beta u_i)$, least-squares estimates will be biased and inconsistent. This can be seen as follows. The LS slope estimate, b, is

$$(4.7.3) \qquad b = \frac{\dfrac{1}{n} \sum (x_i - \bar{x}) y_i}{\dfrac{1}{n} \sum (x_i - \bar{x})^2}$$

$$= \frac{\dfrac{1}{n} \sum [(X_i - \bar{X}) + (u_i - \bar{u})][\alpha + \beta(X_i + u_i) + (v_i - \beta u_i)]}{\dfrac{1}{n} \sum [(X_i - \bar{X}) + (u_i - \bar{u})]^2}$$

$$= \frac{\dfrac{1}{n}[\beta \sum \{(X_i - \bar{X})X_i + (X_i - \bar{X})u_i + (u_i - \bar{u})X_i + (u_i - \bar{u})u_i\}}{\dfrac{1}{n}[\sum (X_i - \bar{X})^2 + 2\sum (X_i - \bar{X})(u_i - \bar{u}) + \sum (u_i - \bar{u})^2]}$$

$$\frac{+ \sum (X_i - \bar{X})v_i + \sum (u_i - \bar{u})v_i - \beta \sum \{(X_i - \bar{X})u_i + (u_i - \bar{u})u_i\}]}{\dfrac{1}{n}[\sum (X_i - \bar{X})^2 + 2\sum (X_i - \bar{X})(u_i - \bar{u}) + \sum (u_i - \bar{u})^2]}$$

Upon taking the expectation of b, terms in $(X_i - \bar{X})(u_i - \bar{u})$, $(X_i - \bar{X})v_i$,

$(u_i - \bar{u})v_i$ will vanish owing to our independence assumptions, which leads to

$$(4.7.4) \qquad E(b) = E\left[\frac{\beta\left(\frac{1}{n}\sum(X_i - \bar{X})X_i\right)}{\frac{1}{n}\sum(X_i - \bar{X})^2 + \frac{1}{n}\sum(u_i - \bar{u})^2}\right].$$

While the expected value of a ratio of random variables is not generally the ratio of their expected values, it is for asymptotic expectations. What we *can* say about b is

$$(4.7.5) \qquad \bar{E}(b) = \frac{\beta\bar{E}\left[\frac{1}{n}\sum(X_i - \bar{X})X_i\right]}{\bar{E}\left[\frac{1}{n}\sum(X_i - \bar{X})^2\right] + \bar{E}\left[\frac{1}{n}\sum(u_i - \bar{u})^2\right]} = \frac{\beta}{1 + \sigma_u^2/\sigma_X^2},$$

where σ_X^2 is the population variance of X. From (4.7.5) we see that the LS slope estimate, b, is biased downward, unless $\sigma_u^2 = 0$, in which case there is no measurement error in X_i and we revert to a regression situation where b will be conditionally *and* unconditionally unbiased (recall v_i is independent of X_i). With a population residual specified in $Y_i = \alpha + \beta x_i + \epsilon_i$, an identical analysis follows, assuming ϵ_i is independent of everything else. The only effect is that the error variance σ_v^2 is replaced by $\sigma_v^2 + \sigma_\epsilon^2$.

Another fruitful way to consider *why* LS might be expected to produce biased estimates of the parameters in (4.7.2) is as follows. A least-squares regression of y_i on x_i *does* provide an unbiased estimate of *some* conditional mean function. The question is whether that function is $\alpha + \beta x_i$.

Taking the conditional expectation of (4.7.2), we have

$$(4.7.6) \qquad E(y_i|x_i) = \alpha + \beta x_i + E(v_i|x_i) - \beta E(u_i|x_i).$$

Since v_i is assumed at the outset to be independently distributed from X_i and u_i, it will be independently distributed from x_i. Hence, $E(v_i|x_i) = 0$. But $E(u_i|x_i)$ will generally *not* be zero and *will* be a function of x because of the statistical relationship between u_i and $x_i = X_i + u_i$. The conditional mean function unbiasedly estimated by a LS regression of y_i on x_i is $\alpha + \beta[x_i - E(u_i|x_i)]$ and *not* $\alpha + \beta x_i$.

This is enough to establish the anticipation that LS estimates of α and β will generally be biased. To see exactly the form of $\alpha + \beta[x_i - E(u_i|x_i)]$ and say anything more requires that a distribution assumption be made so that $E(u_i|x_i)$ can be evaluated.

This most simple errors-in-variable model can be interpreted in very much the same way as the simultaneous market-clearance model of the previous section. There it was quite clear that the reduced form provided no way to identify model slope parameters. The cause of the problem is more subtle here. It is that least squares minimizes deviations of actual observations around the SRF in a vertical direction only, while in the errors-in-variables model some account must be taken of random error in a horizontal direction as well. But it is not clear how much "weight" should be given to each. What is required to identify the model is knowledge of this "direction," the ratio σ_u^2/σ_v^2. Without this information neither least squares nor maximum likelihood can provide an estimator for β that is consistent.†

With knowledge of $\lambda = \sigma_u^2/\sigma_v^2$ in the simple model (4.7.1) the ML estimators for α and β are as follows, from maximizing a likelihood function based on independent normal distributions for u_i and v_i.‡ $\hat{\beta}$ is found by solving the quadratic equation

(4.7.7) $$\lambda\hat{\beta}^2 m_{xy} - \hat{\beta}(\lambda m_{yy} - m_{xx}) - m_{xy} = 0,$$

taking the positive root when $m_{xy} > 0$ and vice versa. $\hat{\alpha}$ is determined by

(4.7.8) $$\hat{\alpha} = \bar{y} - \hat{\beta}\bar{x},$$

the familiar LS formula. When $\sigma_u^2 = 0$, $\lambda = 0$, and (4.7.7) becomes $\hat{\beta}m_{xx} = m_{xy}$, or $\hat{\beta} = m_{xy}/m_{xx}$, the LS result. With $\sigma_v^2 = 0$, $\lambda \rightarrow \infty$, and (though not quite so obvious) $\hat{\beta} = m_{yy}/m_{xy}$, the reciprocal of the LS slope in a regression of x on y.

Is the required knowledge readily available? In general, the answer is no. On the assumption that both Y_i and X_i are subject to the same "sort" of measurement error one would put $\sigma_u^2/\sigma_v^2 = 1$ and proceed. Or, if it can be ascertained that the variance of the error in X_i is no more, say, than 5 percent of the variance of X_i, the LS estimate can be corrected accordingly. An example of the $\sigma_u^2/\sigma_v^2 = 1$ case is the autoregressive model of Section 4.5 with a moving average-error term and equal autoregressive parameters:

(4.7.9) $$y_t = \alpha x_t + \beta y_{t-1} + u_t - \beta u_{t-1}.$$

Regrouping terms, $(y_t - u_t) = \beta(y_{t-1} - u_{t-1}) + \alpha x_t$, which is in the form of a two-variable errors-in-variables model where $\sigma_{u_t}^2/\sigma_{u_{t-1}}^2 = 1$ because $\sigma_{u_t}^2 = \sigma_{u_{t-1}}^2$. Another example of the simple errors-in-variables model (4.7.1) is the permanent-income hypothesis, which talks in terms of permanent and transitory components of income and consumption in attempting to explain why

---

† That this conclusion holds for the ML method is not obvious because the two methods do not coincide in this case. Assuming independent normal distributions for u_i and v_i leads to the likelihood function. See J. Johnston, *Econometric Methods* (New York: McGraw-Hill, 1963), pp. 150–52, for the development.

‡ Johnston, *ibid.*, p. 152.

a least-squares regression of measured consumption on measured income produces a downward-biased estimate of the average propensity to consume.

As we have seen, even with the required information—which is substantial once we move out of the realm of two-variable regression—actual estimation is not a simple two-step procedure or a correction of biased LS coefficients. A more tractable procedure uses simple modifications of the LS normal equations. For more information, the reader is again referred to Johnston.†

Are there other methods that can be employed without the additional knowledge required by LS or ML? Instrumental variables is one, but again there are practical limitations to its use. For estimating (4.7.2) the instrument should be chosen so as to have high correlation with x_i and no correlation with v_i and u_i. A related technique suggests grouping the observations by a criterion related to x_i but not related to u_i. Drawing on the consumption-function literature again, in order to reduce the bias in the LS estimate gleaned from a regression of measured consumption on measured income one should like to group observations on the basis of their "permanent" income.

The instrumental variable technique applied to the errors-in-variables model has an interesting interpretation as a way of identifying the model (4.7.2) with information *other* than σ_u^2/σ_v^2. For, suggesting that an "instrument" z_i exists that satisfies the conditions $E(xz) \neq 0$ but $E(vz) = E(uz) = 0$ might well be interpreted as saying that besides (4.7.2) there is *another* structural equation relating x_i to some truly exogenous variable z_i, in a relation like

$$(4.7.10) \qquad x_i = \gamma + \delta z_i + \epsilon_i,$$

where $E(\epsilon_i z_i) = 0$, $E(\epsilon_i) = 0$. There is no reason *not* to allow ϵ_i to be correlated with the composite error term in (4.7.2), $(v_i - \beta u_i)$.

Treating (4.7.2) and (4.7.10) as our "structure" and solving for its reduced form, we have

$$(4.7.11a) \qquad y_i = (\alpha + \beta\gamma) + \beta\delta z_i + (v_i - \beta u_i + \beta\epsilon_i),$$
$$(4.7.11b) \qquad x_i = \gamma + \delta z_i + \epsilon_i.$$

Now, LS applied to (4.7.11b) will consistently estimate γ and δ. Also, LS will consistently estimate the parameters $(\alpha + \beta\gamma)$ and $\beta\delta$ of (4.7.11a) because *it* meets the necessary requirements—z_i is uncorrelated with $(v_i - \beta u_i + \beta\epsilon_i)$ and $E(v_i - \beta u_i + \beta\epsilon_i) = 0$. From $(\widehat{\beta\delta})$ and $\hat{\delta}$ can be obtained a consistent estimate of β; from $(\widehat{\alpha + \beta\gamma})$, $\hat{\beta}$ and $\hat{\gamma}$ comes $\hat{\alpha}$.

Exactly the same results will be obtained by using LS in (4.7.10), *predicting* x_i from the indicated regression and *then* regressing y_i on $\hat{x}_i$. This pro-

† *Econometric Methods,* Chap. 6.

cedure is an example of the *two-stage least squares* (2SLS) method used in simultaneous-equation econometric models. It also is the technique one would use generally on models of *recursive structure*, an example of which is the structure consisting of Eqs. (4.7.2) and (4.7.10), as will be described more fully in Chapter 6.

As we have seen in the preceding several examples, when $E(\epsilon x) \neq 0$, sometimes ordinary LS estimators provide asymptotic unbiasedness, consistency, and efficiency, while in most cases they do not have desirable properties. But also we find that occasionally the method of least squares is not at fault. Rather, in some instances no technique can provide estimators with desirable properties. These are the instances when the single-equation model is underidentified. Being part of a system of equations need not cause difficulty in using least squares, however. For as we saw in the cobweb model, certain recursive structures can also be satisfactorily approached with the least-squares technique.

4.8   BAYESIAN REGRESSION†

Probably the most biting criticism of the classical regression framework is that it assumes replication of samples on a given set of x's for its fundamental results, because (particularly in time-series analysis) replication is impossible as a practical matter for many situations in economics. The "Bayesian" suggestion is to proceed with inference *conditional* on the sample. Replication, therefore, is not assumed.

It is not appropriate for us to join this issue at any length here, primarily because there are both philosophical and operational questions to be treated, in a much more general context. As a decision-making tool, however, the Bayesian outlook captures the essence of how individuals forecast the future: by assessing the probabilities attached to future events, based on an evaluation of the past. Classical inference purports to do the same, but requires sample information as a prerequisite to any decision-making. The underlying classical concept is of a well-defined population with fixed characteristics or parameters to estimate or to make inferences about. The Bayesian framework, on the other hand, admits subjective as well as objective information, by first arguing that parameters, per se, are to be treated as variables, not constants. The appeal of this interpretation is manifold: for example, in the matter of sampling from human populations for any biological, demographic, or economic variables, the "population" is dynamic. It is changing instanta-

† We assume the reader has at least an introductory knowledge of the Bayesian approach. A classic introduction to the subject is R. Schlaifer, *Introduction to Statistics for Business Decisions* (New York: McGraw-Hill, 1961), although several very readable newer books are available. A brief description is also included in Appendix B.

neously. Hence it is impossible to have a "well-defined" population as classical statistics supposes. This dynamic aspect of many populations provides support for the notion of a variable parameter.

For Bayesian analysis the key input vehicle is the so-called *prior distribution*, a frequency distribution for the unknown parameter or parameters, to be assessed by the decision-maker on the basis of his experience, past information, and so on. If purely subjective evaluations are to be collected in the prior distribution, the decision-maker is forced to be quite definite about his experience, to the extent that he must form a frequency distribution for the parameter or parameters of interest. This may be accomplished by "fitting" a known distribution to correspond to his crude notions, or he may reflect "no information" by assigning equal probability weights to each possible value of the parameter.

The operational advantage of the Bayesian analysis is substantial. It allows the resolution of impasses encountered in choosing optimal classical tests (critical regions), by taking the "best" test for each hypothetical parameter value and combining this information with the prior distribution. In effect, the prior distribution is used to do an expected-value calculation for the best of the "best" tests using the prior probabilities as weights. This step, under very general conditions, and according to reasonable definitions of "best," gets rid of the parameter entirely as a condition on which the decision is made. For, recall that in classical hypothesis testing the design of critical regions is based on conditions—whether the hypothesis is true or false. The Bayesian approach puts "likelihoods" on these classical conditions— the events "true" and "false"—allowing the expected-value calculation mentioned previously to be made.

Objective sample information plays an important role in Bayesian analysis. The inference procedure is conditional on sample results, if there are any. In the classical technique, whether the sample has been drawn or not at the time the test is designed is a moot point: the test is designed as if no sample had been taken. In Bayesian analysis no information is ignored. If sample information is available, it is used to revise the prior distribution according to Bayes' theorem. The analysis then proceeds using this revised or *posterior distribution* of the variable parameter or parameters.

Bayesian analysis in regression requires an assumption about (and belief in) a prior distribution of the regression coefficients $\boldsymbol{\beta}$ in $\mathbf{y} = \mathbf{X}\boldsymbol{\beta} + \boldsymbol{\epsilon}$, say $f(\boldsymbol{\beta})$. The coefficients are taken to be random variables with a distribution $f(\boldsymbol{\beta})$, a mean vector $\bar{\boldsymbol{\beta}}$, and higher-order moments. We consider also the posterior distribution of $\boldsymbol{\beta}$ given the sample observations, $\mathbf{y}$, namely, $f(\boldsymbol{\beta}\,|\,\mathbf{y})$. The Bayesian result of importance uses the symmetry property

(4.8.1)
$$f(\mathbf{y}, \boldsymbol{\beta}) = f(\mathbf{y}\,|\,\boldsymbol{\beta})f(\boldsymbol{\beta})$$
$$= f(\boldsymbol{\beta}\,|\,\mathbf{y})f(\mathbf{y})$$

for the joint distribution of coefficients and the sample, so that

(4.8.2) $f(\mathbf{y}|\boldsymbol{\beta})f(\boldsymbol{\beta}) = f(\boldsymbol{\beta}|\mathbf{y})f(\mathbf{y})$

or

$$f(\boldsymbol{\beta}|\mathbf{y}) = \frac{f(\mathbf{y}|\boldsymbol{\beta})\,f(\boldsymbol{\beta})}{f(\mathbf{y})}$$
$$: f(\mathbf{y}|\boldsymbol{\beta})f(\boldsymbol{\beta})^{\dagger}$$

if the sample is fixed—that is, regarded as a datum. Sometimes $f(\mathbf{y}|\boldsymbol{\beta})$ is called the "likelihood" function, and rewritten $l(\boldsymbol{\beta}|\mathbf{y})$.

The two most complete formulations of Bayesian regression are with uniform (rectangular) and normal prior distributions. Sketched briefly, they compare to the classical framework as follows.

In the uniform or "noninformative" prior case, the sample is assumed to be normally distributed—that is, $f(\mathbf{y}|\boldsymbol{\beta}) \sim N(\mathbf{X}\boldsymbol{\beta}, \sigma^2\mathbf{I})$, and to depend on $k + 2$ parameters, the β_j's and σ^2. Prior distributions are assumed for $\boldsymbol{\beta}$ and σ, say $f(\boldsymbol{\beta}), f(\sigma)$. Specifically, both are assumed independently uniform, and $f(\sigma)$: $1/\sigma$.

Under these specific assumptions the posterior distribution of $\boldsymbol{\beta}$ is *multivariate t* (a t-distribution in the $k + 1$ regression parameters). The marginal distribution of any particular β_j is *univariate t* (usual t-distribution in one variable). One obtains point estimates of each β_j by taking the expected value of its marginal distribution. Ordinary least-squares estimators *are* the means of the posterior distribution in the case of a uniform prior and multivariate-t posterior, though in general Bayesian estimates are not equivalent to ordinary LS estimates.

In the normal prior case, the specification $\boldsymbol{\beta} \sim N(\bar{\boldsymbol{\beta}}, \Sigma_\beta)$ in conjunction with a normal sample (as in the previous case) produces a normal posterior distribution for $\boldsymbol{\beta}$. Estimates for the β_j's may be obtained as the expected value of $\boldsymbol{\beta}$ in the *conditional* posterior distribution assuming Σ_β and σ^2 are *known*. Given these assumptions, the indicated estimates and their variances are formed very much as generalized LS estimates would be, but they are not equivalent to either ordinary LS estimates or generalized LS estimates in the model with interdependent disturbances. To obtain such estimators from the *marginal* posterior distribution of $\boldsymbol{\beta}$ is more difficult.

The reason for including at least a brief outline of the Bayesian approach to regression is that the underlying philosophy of that method of analysis is very appealing, and one may expect a good deal from it. We do not offer it here in usable form, but only hope to introduce the user of classical regression to its basic ideas. Like the classical approach, Bayesian analysis goes

---

† ":" means "proportional to."

on within the context and confines of an assumed distribution, and we can expect both techniques to depend heavily on the virility of the underlying distribution assumption. But even here the Bayesian approach offers the advantage (if conceptual only) of explicit modification in light of new information, and the possibility of investigating the sensitivity of results to prior specification, which is not easy in classical inference. The appeal of an analysis conditioned on the sample is clear. Often the results of applying the classical model appear as a special case within the Bayesian approach.

4.9 PROBLEMS AND ANSWERS

GENERAL PROBLEMS

1. A simple regression of aggregate consumption on aggregate income over the period 1929–65 revealed the following information:

$$c_t = .030 + .91y_t, \qquad R^2 = .95, \qquad \text{D-W} = 1.02.$$
$$(.10)$$

The parenthesized number is the standard error of the coefficient on income, and D-W is the Durbin-Watson statistic.

Using the same data, a student proposes to run aggregate savings, s_t, on aggregate income in order to generate an estimate of the marginal propensity to save. Since $y_t = s_t + c_t$ in the data, you reason, there is no need to do so because almost all the information that would come out of that regression analysis is available from the equation above.

Fill in the blanks below, and explain how you arrived at each number or why you cannot fill in a particular blank.

$$s_t = \underline{\hspace{1cm}} + \underline{\hspace{1cm}} y_t, \qquad R^2 = \underline{\hspace{1cm}}, \qquad \text{D-W} = \underline{\hspace{1cm}}.$$
$$(\underline{\hspace{1cm}})$$

ANSWER:

$$s_t = -.030 + .09y_t, \qquad R^2 = ?, \qquad \text{D-W} = 1.02.$$
$$(.10)$$

Simply substituting the data indentity $c_t = y_t - s_t$ into the equation given, we find that $s_t = -.030 + (1 - .91)y_t$. The coefficient on y_t in this equation can be viewed as a constant (one) minus the variable coefficient whose value happens to be .91 for this sample. Thus the variances of the LS slope estimates [$(1 - .91)$ and .91 for *this* sample] are the same. R^2 cannot be calculated from the information given because the sample variance of savings is not available. Lastly, because $y_t = c_t + s_t$ in the data, the residuals at every observation in the savings function must be the negatives of the residuals in the consumption function. The numerator and denominator of the D-W statistic, therefore, are unchanged.

2. A researcher proposes to fit a linear demand function for tomato products,

$$q_t = \beta_0 + \beta_1 y_t + \beta_2 p_t + \beta_3 I_t + \epsilon_t,$$

over a twenty-five year period. He has observations for aggregate quantity, q_t (in millions of tomato equivalents per year), aggregate money income, y_t, average price, p_t, and a price index for a composite of other vegetable items, I_t. A colleague suggests that population shifts ought to be accounted for, so he then puts the quantity and income variables on a per capita basis. This same colleague suggests also that the price and income variables ought to be deflated, say by the consumer's price index, but the researcher counters by saying that microtheory has demand a function of prices and money income, so no deflation is necessary. Ignoring identification or aggregation problems, with whom do you agree and why?

ANSWER:

Deflation *is* necessary because another part of the theory says that proportional changes in prices and money income leave the optimal allocation unchanged: that is, the demand function is zero homogeneous in money income and prices. A linear equation is *not* homogeneous of degree zero. So either prices and income must be purged of changes in the general level of prices over time or an alternative functional form that is zero homogeneous must be used.

PROBLEMS ON SPECIAL TOPICS:
THE CONSUMPTION FUNCTION—CRITIQUE

Briefly present and critically evaluate the empirical work on the consumption function. Be sure to test for serial correlation in the residuals of your chosen model and report on that result as it affects your findings. Would you suggest first differencing all variables to eliminate serial correlation effects in your model?

ANSWER:

Although our attempt at objectively choosing between Models I and III was not altogether successful, Model III presents the most acceptable version on several counts. First, some additional data on the three versions under consideration are relevant.

	Model I	Model II	Model III
R^2	.9175 (.9962)	(.9982)	.9814
d	.3300	.3929	1.344

In parentheses are R^2's calculated by the R^2_{mf} formula in Models I and II without intercept terms. While they are mutually comparable, they are not comparable to the other two R^2's reported, for Models I and III with intercepts.

Only in Model III do the partial regression coefficients all pass the simple t-test for significance. Serial correlation is an obvious problem in Models I and II, where the null hypothesis is rejected in favor of positive serial correlation. In Model III the calculated value for d falls in the inconclusive region, but since c_{t-1} appears as an independent variable, we can expect d to be biased against finding positive serial correlation. Perhaps the best that can be said in this instance is that the possibility of its existence should not be overlooked. First differencing is already built into Model III, at least in an implicit sense, with the appearance of c_{t-1}. Indeed, the hybrid version of Problem 6 of the previous chapter is a completely first-differenced model; in both instances while the dependent variable differs (c_t versus $c_t - c_{t-1}$), what is being accomplished does not. For these to be effective ways of isolating and controlling serial correlation $\hat{\rho}$ will have to be close to one, which it is not. In fact, $\hat{\rho} \doteq 1 - d/2$, which is .33 for Model III. The next step in improving these results would be to use $\hat{\rho}$ to appropriately adjust the data and to reestimate Model III.

While we have looked at the consumption function from the point of view of Friedman's permanent-income hypothesis, it can equally well be considered as one equation in a system of equations that determine aggregate income, consumption, and so on. This raises the possibility of an identification problem *and* the probability that the error term in the consumption function is related to income. The first problem can presumably be checked with a complete specification of the system. The second difficulty is a familiar one by now; a possible alternative estimation procedure to (biased) least squares is instrumental variables, but other, better techniques exist. All these matters are introduced and discussed in Chapter 6.

5 Functional Forms Including

Dummy Variables

5.1 INTRODUCTION

It may not be at all clear that the *linear* regression model is suitable for representing a particular causal relationship. For it necessarily imposes a specific functional form to the relationship, which may or may not restrict the ensuing analysis of the model. Statistical inference is dependent on a statistical model: in this case, the conditional mean function and a normality assumption comprise the model. Occasionally convenience or a priori reasoning intervene to suggest a model that is *not* linear in parameters. At other times equations may contain nonlinearities in the independent variables. In this chapter we investigate the flexibility of our regression framework to accommodate other functional forms and still produce parameter estimates with desirable properties.

Recall that linear in the sense of the Gauss-Markov theorem means linear in parameters, not necessarily variables. If the regression equation is linear in both parameters *and* variables, we have a *special* case of what may be thought of as "additivity"—namely when the separate effects of conditioning variables may be "added up" to get the total effect on y. For example,

$$y = \beta_0 + \beta_1 x_1^2 + \beta_2 x_2 + \epsilon$$

is (1) linear in parameters, hence "linear"; (2) nonlinear in x_1, but (3) additive since the partial effects of x_1 and x_2 do not depend on the other variable; that is, $\partial y/\partial x_1$ does not depend on x_2.

$$y = \beta_0 + \beta_1 x_1 x_2 + \epsilon$$

is (1) "linear," (2) nonlinear in variables, (3) nonadditive. Both examples are nonlinear in variables, but for purposes of estimation or forecasting we have simply to treat the nonlinear variable forms as "new" variables. In terms of new variables both examples are linear and additive. So long as we can produce a linear function in *known* functions of the conditioning variables the LS method will produce BLUE estimates of the coefficients in a multiple regression equation that otherwise meets the classical conditions. The general polynomial—for instance,

$$y = \beta_0 + \beta_1 + \beta_2 x^2 + \cdots + \beta_k x^k + \epsilon$$

—fits this description, since the transformed variables are known functions of x and can be calculated exactly from the sample points (y, x). $y = \beta_0 + \beta_1 x^\alpha + \epsilon$ clearly does not fit the description unless α is known.

163

5.2 TRANSFORMATIONS INVOLVING THE DEPENDENT VARIABLE

It still may be possible to fit a nonlinear equation using our available LS methods by suitably transforming *both* sides of the equation. A frequently occurring form in economics that allows this is the so-called Cobb-Douglas function,

$$(5.2.1) \qquad y = \beta_0 x_1^{\beta_1} x_2^{\beta_2} \cdots x_k^{\beta_k},$$

which has desirable properties as an empirical law of production and perhaps as a utility function. For instance,

$$\frac{\partial y}{\partial x_j} = \frac{y}{x_j} \beta_j, \quad \text{so that} \quad \beta_j = \frac{\partial y}{\partial x_j} \cdot \frac{x_j}{y}.$$

The function exhibits constant elasticities, the $\{\beta_j\}$. This multiplicative model may easily be transformed by logarithms into what looks like a usual PRF, linear in its parameters:

$$(5.2.2) \qquad \log y = \log \beta_0 + \beta_1 \log x_1 + \cdots + \beta_k \log x_k.$$

But how should the random term enter?

Usually we begin by stating $E(y \mid x_1, \ldots, x_k)$ equals some function of $(x_1, \ldots, x_k)$. In this instance, if the PRF is $E(y \mid \{x_j\}) = \beta_0 x_1^{\beta_1} \cdots x_k^{\beta_k}$, then it is *not* true that

$$E(\log y \mid x_1, \ldots, x_k) = \log \beta_0 + \beta_1 \log x_1 + \cdots + \beta_k \log x_k.$$

That is to say, the conditional *mean* of $\log y$ is *not* the function $\log \beta_0 + \cdots + \beta_k \log x_k$. In fact, since the log function is concave in y (that is, has a negative second derivative), we can demonstrate that

$$(5.2.3) \qquad E(\log y \mid x_1, \ldots, x_k) \leq \log E(y \mid \{x_j\}).$$

This is equivalent to saying that the geometric mean of y is less than or equal to its arithmetic mean.

Suppose we then specify the population regression model to be of the form

$$(5.2.4) \qquad \checkmark \quad y = \beta_0 x_1^{\beta_1} \cdots x_k^{\beta_k} \epsilon,$$

with $E(x_j \epsilon) = 0$ for all j, $E(\epsilon) = 1$, and $\text{Var}(\epsilon) = E(\epsilon - 1)^2 = \sigma^2$. Then

$$E(y \mid \{x_j\}) = \beta_0 x_1^{\beta_1} \cdots x_k^{\beta_k},$$

and

$$(5.2.5) \qquad \log y = \log \beta_0 + \beta_1 \log x_1 + \cdots + \beta_k \log x_k + \log \epsilon.$$

The conditional expectation of log y is

$$(5.2.6) \qquad E(\log y \,|\, x_1, \ldots, x_k) = \log \beta_0 + \beta_1 \log x_1 + \cdots + \beta_k \log x_k$$
$$+ E(\log \epsilon \,|\, x_1, \ldots, x_k).$$

As before, the conditional mean of the disturbance equals its unconditional mean, but $E(\log \epsilon) \neq 0$, since by the same rule as above, $E(\log \epsilon) \leq \log E(\epsilon) = 0$.

If, however, we define $\epsilon^* = \log \epsilon - E(\log \epsilon)$, the difference between the logarithm of the residual and its expected value, then $E(\epsilon^*) = 0$. So use

$$(5.2.7) \qquad \log y = [\log \dot{\beta}_0 + E(\log \epsilon)] + \beta_1 \log x_1 + \cdots$$
$$+ \beta_k \log x_k + \epsilon^*$$

as the operational model in order to get BLUE estimates of the slope coefficients (not β_0). This example leads us to observe that whenever $E(\epsilon) \neq 0$ in the classical model, all we need do is define $\epsilon^* = \epsilon - E(\epsilon)$ and $\beta'_0 = \beta_0 + E(\epsilon)$ to get to the classical assumptions. Therefore, with **X** fixed, if $E(\epsilon) \neq 0$, the bias effect is on the constant term only. A similar conclusion follows for stochastic regression so long as the residual is uncorrelated with conditioning variables. [$E(\epsilon x)$ is trivially zero for the "x" representing the constant term, which is one for every observation.]

That $E(\epsilon) \neq 0$ affects the unbiasedness property only of the constant term so long as $E(\epsilon x) = 0$ holds for other conditioning variables is seen clearly by example. For the two-variable case, we have [from (2.5.2)]

$$(5.2.8) \qquad b - \beta = \frac{\sum x^* \epsilon}{\sum x^{*2}} = \frac{\sum (x - \bar{x})(\epsilon - \bar{\epsilon})}{\sum (x - \bar{x})^2}$$

and, by a similar substitution,

$$(5.2.9) \qquad a - \alpha = \bar{\epsilon} - (b - \beta)\bar{x}.$$

Because $\sum x^* \epsilon$ equals $\sum x^*(\epsilon - \bar{\epsilon})$, as can readily be verified, $E(b - \beta) = 0$ *whatever* is $E(\bar{\epsilon}) = E(\epsilon)$, so long as $E(x^* \epsilon) = 0$, whereas $E(a - \alpha) \neq 0$ if $E(\bar{\epsilon}) = E(\epsilon) \neq 0$. Note that the uncorrelatedness property is stated $E(x^* \epsilon) = 0$, whereas we have previously written it $E(x\epsilon) = 0$. These two expressions are equivalent only when $E(\epsilon) = 0$.

A further aspect to the multiplicative disturbance formulation is of some interest: that the conditional variance of y *varies* over observations (heteroscedasticity). This is easy to see, for write

$$(5.2.10) \qquad y - E(y \,|\, \{x_j\}) = \beta_0 x_1^{\beta_1} \cdots x_k^{\beta_k}(\epsilon - 1)$$
$$= [E(y \,|\, \{x_j\})](\epsilon - 1).$$

Therefore,

$$(5.2.11) \qquad E[y - E(y \,|\, \{x_j\})]^2 = [E(y \,|\, \{x_j\})]^2 E(\epsilon - 1)^2$$
$$= [E(y \,|\, \{x_j\})]^2 \sigma^2.$$

Variation in y (conditional on $x_1, \ldots, x_k$) is proportional to the squared conditional expectation of y. It has been suggested that this situation may sometimes be a blessing in disguise—when the log-log form for a PRF is appropriate *and* systematic changes in the variance of y are (or should be) in evidence. For example, if an expenditure function with constant elasticity with respect to income were hypothesized, one might expect higher variation in expenditures on a good with higher income as well as higher expenditures on the average.

Although the conditional variance of y is not constant, the logarithmic transformation does the additional service of forcing homoscedasticity. Thus, while in original units LS estimates, could they be obtained, would be inefficient, in the linearized version LS estimators will possess the usual properties, except for the intercept estimator. By (5.2.6) we find

$$(5.2.12) \qquad \log y = E(\log y) + \epsilon^*,$$

so that the conditional variance of $\log y$ is just the conditional variance of ϵ^*, $E(\epsilon^{*2})$, a constant over $\{x_j\}$.

Other sorts of essentially exponential models can be transformed suitably to make them linear models in transformed variables. The log-log model just considered is one. Another is the simple growth curve $y_t = y_0(1 + r)^t \epsilon_t$, and a model that is semilogarithmic upon transformation is covered in the problems section of this chapter. Yet all such examples either presume prior knowledge of the "true" model or, in the case of the semilog problem, take a primarily empirical or ad hoc point of view, allowing the data to determine the model insofar as that is possible. As we have seen, choosing between models on some objective basis is not possible in general. But choosing between models that are members of a particular *class* of models *is* possible under certain conditions. Again, the data will ultimately do the choosing, but only in the same sense that the data "choose" a value for some unknown parameter through an estimation procedure.

The analysis of a class of models that is characterized by a "transformation" index is due to Box and Cox.† Their idea is to specify the conditional mean function more generally by the model

$$(5.2.13) \qquad E[\mathbf{y}^{(\lambda)}] = \mathbf{X}\boldsymbol{\beta}$$

with all the classical assumptions imposed. That is, they seek the transformation (λ) of $\mathbf{y}$ that makes (5.2.13) hold under the classical assumptions. (λ) is to be regarded as a transformation "index," which may be multidimensional. In the example we consider, however, λ will be a scalar. Equation (5.2.13) has an obvious usefulness in that it allows rather complicated models to become tractable in terms of the linear regression theory. Alternatively, it may be viewed as a way to find a transformation from a heteroscedastic model into a homoscedastic one, or from a nonnormal one into one where the normal distribution assumption on ϵ is appropriate.

The actual methodology necessary to estimate β, σ^2, *and* (λ) is based on maximum likelihood. But to understand its logic is not difficult. The joint density function of $y_1^{(\lambda)}, \ldots, y_n^{(\lambda)}$ is normal by assumption. *Given* (λ), the maximum-likelihood estimators of β and σ^2 are just the LS estimators of multiple regression. The *maximized* likelihood function (joint density function) is obtained merely by plugging the LS estimates $\mathbf{b}$ and $\mathscr{S}^2$ in for $\boldsymbol{\beta}$ and σ^2. The maximum-likelihood estimate of (λ) is that (λ) for which the likelihood function (now with $\mathbf{b}$ and $\mathscr{S}^2$ inserted) is maximized.

A particularly interesting class of such models for economics is the class of "power transformations" on y, which includes the semilog function $\log \mathbf{y} = \mathbf{X}\boldsymbol{\beta} + \boldsymbol{\epsilon}$. For this class we require $y > 0$ and define the one parameter transformation index (λ) by

$$(5.2.14) \qquad y^{(\lambda)} = \begin{cases} \log y & \text{if } \lambda = 0, \\ \dfrac{y^{\lambda} - 1}{\lambda} & \text{if } \lambda \neq 0. \end{cases}$$

That this functional specification is complete can be verified by checking that

$$\lim_{\lambda \to 0} \left(\frac{y^{\lambda} - 1}{\lambda} \right) = \log y.$$

The appropriate formula to consider then is an abbreviated log-likelihood function

$$(5.2.15) \qquad \log L_{\max}(\lambda) = -\frac{n}{2} \log \mathscr{S}^2 + (\lambda - 1) \sum \log y_i,$$

† "An Analysis of Transformations," *J. Roy. Stat. Soc.*, Ser. B, Vol. 26 (1964), pp. 211–43.

the notation $\log L_{\max}(\lambda)$ meaning that the log-likelihood function is already conditionally maximized for given λ by utilizing the least squares quantities, **b** and $\mathscr{S}^2$. The procedure used to find the ML estimate $\hat{\lambda}$ is to let λ attain various values, for each computing LS estimates **b** and $\mathscr{S}^2$, and inserting $\mathscr{S}^2$ into (5.2.15). The value for λ which maximizes (5.2.15) is its ML estimate $\hat{\lambda}$.

A confidence interval and test theory for $\hat{\lambda}$ so determined rests on the χ^2 distribution, for large samples. The result of interest is:

$$(5.2.16) \qquad \Pr\{\log L_{\max}(\hat{\lambda}) - \tfrac{1}{2}\chi^2_{1,\alpha} \leq \log L_{\max}(\lambda)\} = 1 - \alpha$$

where $\chi^2_{1,\alpha}$ is the upper α-point of a chi-square distribution with one degree of freedom, corresponding to the single parameter being estimated, λ.

This confidence interval (5.2.16) on $\log L_{\max}(\lambda)$ can be used to determine a confidence interval for λ as we illustrate in Figure 5.1. Here the graph of (5.2.15) is shown for a regression model with dependent variable given by (5.2.14). The conditionally maximized log-likelihood function reaches its

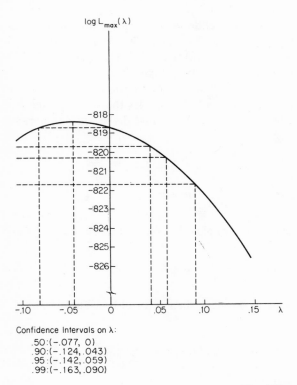

Confidence Intervals on λ:
```
.50:(-.077, 0)
.90:(-.124,.043)
.95:(-.142,.059)
.99:(-.163,.090)
```

Fig. 5.1

Illustration of Confidence Interval Determination for
Box-Cox Transformation

maximum over the range of λ at $\hat{\lambda} = .039$, at which point its value is -818.4. Consulting a table of χ^2, we find that for one degree of freedom the upper α-points are .455, 2.71, 3.84, and 6.63, corresponding to $(1 - \alpha)$ of .50, .90, .95, and .99 respectively. Subtracting one-half of each of these numbers from -818.4 gives the corresponding one-sided confidence intervals, as indicated by (5.2.16). We locate the four intervals on λ specified at the bottom of the figure graphically, as the drawing suggests. For this example, the hypothesis $H: \lambda = 0$ is not rejected at even moderately large levels of significance, supporting log y as the "appropriate" transformation of y in this model.

Of additional interest is the same power transformation applied simultaneously to the set of conditioning variables, in a PRM

$$(5.2.17) \qquad \frac{y_i^\lambda - 1}{\lambda} = \frac{\beta_0^\lambda - 1}{\lambda} + \beta_1\left(\frac{x_{i1}^\lambda - 1}{\lambda}\right) + \cdots + \beta_k\left(\frac{x_{ik}^\lambda - 1}{\lambda}\right) + \epsilon_i.$$

As $\lambda \rightarrow 0$, (5.2.17) becomes

$$(5.2.18) \qquad \log y_i = \log \beta_0 + \beta_1 \log x_{i1} + \cdots + \beta_k \log x_{ik} + \epsilon_i$$

—just (5.2.5), the transformed Cobb-Douglas model. Equation (5.2.17) itself is very similar to certain formulations of the *constant elasticity of substitution* (CES) production function,[†] and obviously allows a convenient test of the Cobb-Douglas hypothesis (corresponding to $\lambda = 0$). Computationally, one proceeds to find the ML estimator for λ in (5.2.17) as before, calculating $\mathscr{S}^2$ from many different regression models—each with different λ—and choosing as $\hat{\lambda}$ the one that makes (5.2.15) a maximum.

5.3 USES OF DUMMY (OR BINARY) VARIABLES

Often qualitative factors may be important as conditioning variables, to be considered jointly with what to this point have been assumed to be continuous independent variables. For instance, a regression analysis of monthly sales should include an allowance for "seasonality," which can be accomplished using a series of binary (0, 1) variables, as we shall see below. Regression analysis is sometimes thought of as the classical linear model under Ω when all conditioning variables are quantitative. A linear model that mixes qualitative and quantitative information is usually referred to as an *analysis of covariance*, and while regression and covariance analysis

† As in R. G. D. Allen, *Macroeconomic Theory* (New York: Macmillan, 1968), p. 52.

are formally special cases of the so-called *analysis of variance* (where all independent variables represent qualitative factors), things can conveniently be juxtaposed so that the analysis of variance can be considered within a regression context. This is the approach we adopt in this section.

We begin by setting out the essential ideas of an analysis-of-variance on a single qualitative factor—a one-way analysis. Then these same concepts are articulated within the multiple regression framework. The section concludes with some relevant observations on the general use of binary variables in regression.

Consider the following set of specifications for a PRF:

(5.3.1)
$$E(y \mid x) = \begin{cases} \beta_1 & \text{if } x = X_1, \\ \beta_2 & \text{if } x = X_2, \\ \cdot \\ \cdot \\ \cdot \\ \beta_k & \text{if } x = X_k. \end{cases}$$

x is a "variable" or "factor" that takes on the discrete "values" $X_1, \ldots, X_k$. For example, suppose y = yield/acre and x represents various fertilizer "treatments." The $\{\beta_j\}$ are called *main effects* in analysis-of-variance parlance, but they should be viewed as the $\beta_1, \ldots, \beta_k$ of the usual regression model as well. A sample of n observations on the dependent variable, y, might conveniently be displayed in the following matrix:

(5.3.2)

Obs. \ Treatment	1	2	$\cdots$	k
1	y_{11}	y_{12}	$\cdots$	y_{1k}
2	y_{21}	y_{22}	$\cdots$	y_{2k}
3	y_{31}	y_{32}	$\cdots$	y_{3k}
$\cdot$	$\cdot$	$\cdot$		$\cdot$
$\cdot$	$\cdot$	$\cdot$		$\cdot$
$\cdot$	$\cdot$	$\cdot$		$\cdot$
n_j	$y_{n_1, 1}$	$y_{n_2, 2}$		$y_{n_k, k}$

The number of observations in each column is denoted by n_j, so that

$$\sum_{j=1}^{k} n_j = n.$$

The overall mean of these sample observations, the *grand mean*, is just

$$\bar{y} = \frac{1}{n} \sum_{i=1}^{n_j} \sum_{j=1}^{k} y_{ij},$$

and the total variation of the $\{y_{ij}\}$ from the grand mean $\bar{y}$, SS_T, is

(5.3.3)
$$SS_T = \sum_{i=1}^{n_j} \sum_{j=1}^{k} (y_{ij} - \bar{y})^2.$$

Note that without explicitly breaking y down by "treatment" levels SS_T is equivalent to $\sum_{i=1}^{n} (y_i - \bar{y})^2$ in the more familiar regression model. Now define the column mean

$$\bar{y}_j = \frac{1}{n_j} \sum_{i=1}^{n_j} y_{ij}$$

and add it and subtract it in SS_T to get

(5.3.4)
$$SS_T = \sum_i \sum_j (y_{ij} - \bar{y}_j + \bar{y}_j - \bar{y})^2$$
$$= \sum_i \sum_j (y_{ij} - \bar{y}_j)^2 + \sum_j n_j(\bar{y}_j - \bar{y})^2$$
$$+ 2\sum_i \sum_j (y_{ij} - \bar{y}_j)(\bar{y}_j - \bar{y}).$$

The last term may be rewritten

$$2 \sum_{j=1}^{k} (\bar{y}_j - \bar{y}) \sum_{i=1}^{n_j} (y_{ij} - \bar{y}_j).$$

Since

$$\bar{y}_j = \frac{1}{n_j} \sum_{i=1}^{n_j} y_{ij},$$

this term is zero. Thus SS_T partitions into two other sums-of-squares, say SS_e and SS_R, and the entire business may conveniently be summarized in an ANalysis Of VAriance table:

ANOVA Table

Source of variation	SS	d.f.	"Corrected" SS
Within treatments (residual)	SS_e	$n - k$	$SS_e/(n - k)$
Among column means (regression)	SS_R	$k - 1$	
Total	SS_T	$n - 1$	

In the last column, $SS_e/(n - k)$ is the unbiased estimator for the residual variance, σ^2. Degrees of freedom for SS_R are computed as the difference between degrees of freedom for SS_T and SS_e.

Assuming the y_{ij} are normally distributed, an analysis of variance of this simplest sort may be performed with the appropriate F-test, namely

(5.3.5) $$\frac{\text{SS}_R}{\text{SS}_e} \cdot \frac{n-k}{k-1} \sim F_{k-1,n-k}.$$

The hypothesis under consideration is that the qualitative factor is of *no* significance in explaining variation in y.

This F-statistic is exactly the F-statistic for testing significance of regression (that is, $\beta_1 = \cdots = \beta_k = 0$) in a model

(5.3.6) $$y_i = \beta_1 x_{i1} + \cdots + \beta_k x_{ik} + \epsilon_i,$$

where the conditioning variables are "dummies" proxying for the qualitative treatments—that is, where

$$x_j = \begin{cases} 0 & \text{if } x \neq X_j, \\ 1 & \text{if } x = X_j. \end{cases}$$

This may be seen as follows.

Note first that the observation matrix $\mathbf{X}$ for the model (5.3.6) looks like

(5.3.7)

$$\mathbf{X} = \begin{bmatrix} 1 & 0 & 0 & \cdots & 0 \\ \cdot & & \cdot & & \cdot \\ \cdot & & \cdot & & \cdot \\ \cdot & & \cdot & & \cdot \\ 1 & 0 & 0 & \cdots & 0 \\ 0 & 1 & 0 & \cdots & 0 \\ \cdot & & \cdot & & \cdot \\ \cdot & & \cdot & & \cdot \\ \cdot & & \cdot & & \cdot \\ 0 & 1 & 0 & \cdots & 0 \\ & & \text{and so on} & & \end{bmatrix} \begin{array}{l} \left.\vphantom{\begin{matrix}1\\1\\1\\1\end{matrix}}\right\} n_1 \\ \left.\vphantom{\begin{matrix}1\\1\\1\\1\end{matrix}}\right\} n_2 \end{array}$$

Its columns are therefore *linearly independent*, with zero correlation between all "independent" variables. As a result, LS estimation in (5.3.6) can be accomplished by k separate regressions. (It should be noted that when other conditioning variables are present, this will not be generally true.)

By simple regression (no intercept) our estimate of any β_j, say b_j, is $b_j = \sum yx_j / \sum x_j^2$. But

$$\sum_{i=1}^{n} x_{ij}^2 = \sum_{i=1}^{n} x_{ij} = n_j$$

because x_j takes on only $(0, 1)$ values and its sum "counts" the number of times the jth "treatment" occurs in the sample. Also, since if $x_j = 1$ on a given observation, all other x's are zero,

$$\sum_{i=1}^{n} x_j x_{j'} = 0 \quad (j \neq j') \quad \text{and} \quad \sum_{i=1}^{n} y_i x_{ij} = \sum_{i=1}^{n_j} y_{ij} = n_j \bar{y}_j$$

by definition. Thus,

(5.3.8)
$$b_j = \frac{n_j \bar{y}_j}{n_j} = \bar{y}_j.$$

Equation (5.3.8) shows that the LS estimates of the $\{\beta_j\}$ are the column means of the data matrix $[y_{ij}]$. Since $\hat{y}_i = b_1 x_{i1} + \cdots + b_k x_{ik}$ and only one x_j can equal one on any observation, we have $\hat{y}_i = b_j$ for $x = X_j$. So $\hat{y}_i$ will be $b_1 (= \bar{y}_1) \, n_1$ times, b_2, n_2 times, and so on. Constructing the "explained" variance or regression SS, we have

(5.3.9)
$$SS_R = \sum_{j=1}^{k} n_j (b_j - \bar{y})^2 = \sum_{j=1}^{k} n_j (\bar{y}_j - \bar{y})^2$$

and since

$$SS_T = \sum_{i=1}^{n} (y_i - \bar{y})^2 = \sum_{i=1}^{n_j} \sum_{j=1}^{k} (y_{ij} - \bar{y})^2,$$

(5.3.10)
$$SS_e = \sum_i \sum_j (y_{ij} - \bar{y}_j)^2.$$

The correspondence between a regression model in dummy variables and the one-way analysis of variance is complete. Similar correspondences can be established between regression with dummy variables and more complex analysis-of-variance problems.

To see the above relationships compactly, the multiple regression framework yields

(5.3.11)
$$X'X = \begin{bmatrix} n_1 & & 0 \\ & \cdot & \\ & \cdot & \\ 0 & & n_k \end{bmatrix}$$

$$X'y = \begin{bmatrix} n_1 \bar{y}_1 \\ \cdot \\ \cdot \\ n_k \bar{y}_k \end{bmatrix}, \qquad (X'X)^{-1} = \begin{bmatrix} \dfrac{1}{n_1} & & 0 \\ & \cdot & \\ & & \cdot \\ 0 & & \dfrac{1}{n_k} \end{bmatrix},$$

so that

(5.3.12)
$$\begin{bmatrix} b_1 \\ \cdot \\ \cdot \\ \cdot \\ b_k \end{bmatrix} = (\mathbf{X'X})^{-1}\mathbf{X'y} = \begin{bmatrix} \bar{y}_1 \\ \cdot \\ \cdot \\ \cdot \\ \bar{y}_k \end{bmatrix}.$$

Also, since $\boldsymbol{\Sigma}_b = \sigma^2(\mathbf{X'X})^{-1}$,

(5.3.13)
$$\boldsymbol{\Sigma}_b = \sigma^2 \begin{bmatrix} \dfrac{1}{n_1} & & & 0 \\ & \cdot & & \\ & & \cdot & \\ & & & \cdot \\ 0 & & & \dfrac{1}{n_k} \end{bmatrix}.$$

Precision of estimation varies directly with the number of observations at each "value" of x. Note that this result is no more than the usual relation that the variance of the sample mean is σ^2/n for samples drawn with replacement or from large populations without replacement.

Other uses for the binary representation in regression make it clearly an adaptable tool of analysis. For example, to represent a seasonal influence $E(y|x) = \beta_j$ for season (j) [or, $E(y|x, z) = \beta_j + \gamma z$ for season (j) and z another conditioning variable], we would construct dummy variables x_1, x_2, x_3, x_4 as follows:

Quarter	x_1	x_2	x_3	x_4
1	1	0	0	0
2	0	1	0	0
3	0	0	1	0
4	0	0	0	1

corresponding to the model $y = \beta_1 x_1 + \beta_2 x_2 + \beta_3 x_3 + \beta_4 x_4 + \gamma z + \epsilon$.

"Discretizing" a continuous variable to proxy for an unspecified non-linear form can also be a useful device. Consider the model:

(5.3.14)
$$E(y|x) = \begin{cases} \beta_1 & \text{if } X_1 \leq x < X_2, \\ \beta_2 & \text{if } X_2 \leq x < X_3, \\ \cdot \\ \cdot \\ \cdot \\ \beta_k & \text{if } X_k \leq x. \end{cases}$$

Again, this PRF is amenable to the dummy-variable technique in a regression framework, and produces a "step" function in x. Similarly, a "floating-slope" version of (5.3.14) would be

(5.3.15)
$$E(y \mid x) = \begin{cases} \beta_1 x & \text{if } X_1 \leq x \leq X_2 \\ \cdot & \cdot \\ \cdot & \cdot \\ \cdot & \cdot \\ \beta_k x & \text{if } X_k \leq x. \end{cases}$$

Some cautions should be noted in using the dummy-variable technique in any of these variations. The first has to do with the appropriate specification of dummy variables when a general constant term, β_0, appears in the PRF. In the previous development the PRF had *no* general constant term. Instead, the main effects were essentially constant terms defined over the levels of application of the qualitative factor. But when other independent variables appear in conjunction with the qualitative factor, specification of a general constant term may be desired.

The difficulty alluded to is easily seen from considering our seasonality example used in a model that includes a constant term. The X matrix will not be of full rank, and $X'X$ will thus be singular. Ignoring the specifics of other variables, the observation matrix for a regression problem with constant term, the four seasonal dummies, and other quantitative conditioning variables has the form

(5.3.16)
$$X = \begin{bmatrix} 1 & 1 & 0 & 0 & 0 & \cdot & \\ 1 & 0 & 1 & 0 & 0 & \cdot & \\ \cdot & 0 & 0 & 1 & 0 & \cdot & \text{other} \\ \cdot & & & & & \cdot & \text{variables} \\ \cdot & & & & & \cdot & \\ \cdot & & & & & & \\ 1 & & \text{and so on} & & & \cdot & \end{bmatrix}$$

Since column one can be produced by summing over the next four columns, X cannot be of full column rank.

If a bona fide constant is to appear, the dummy representation of x must be modified. For the seasonality example, the following respecification will do:

Season	x_1	x_2	x_3
1	0	0	0
2	1	0	0
3	0	1	0
4	0	0	1

This is to say that the models

(5.3.17) $y = \beta_0 + \beta_1 x_1 + \beta_2 x_2 + \beta_3 x_3 + \gamma z + \epsilon$

and

(5.3.18) $y = \beta_1' x_1 + \beta_2' x_2 + \beta_3' x_3 + \beta_4' x_4 + \gamma z + \epsilon$

are equivalent. Noting that for every observation i, $x_1 + x_2 + x_3 + x_4 = 1$, we may add and subtract B_4' in the model (5.3.18) to get

(5.3.18a) $y = \beta_4' + (\beta_1' - \beta_4')x_1 + (\beta_2' - \beta_4')x_2$
$$+ (\beta_3' - \beta_4')x_3 + \gamma z + \epsilon$$

with the following equivalences,

(5.3.19) $\beta_0 = \beta_4',$
$$\beta_1 = (\beta_1' - \beta_4'),$$
$$\beta_2 = (\beta_2' - \beta_4'),$$
$$\beta_3 = (\beta_3' - \beta_4').$$

We therefore can easily move back and forth between these models. Either representation embodies the nature of the dummy-variable model, which is to allow a shifting intercept over the qualitative factor with a simultaneous estimation of partial regression coefficients for other quantitative variables.

Tests of significance using dummy variables carry through as usual. Normally, however, a *set* of dummies is of interest, as they jointly represent some qualitative variable. Thus in model (5.3.18) the interesting hypothesis is of no seasonal effect; that is, $H: \beta_1' = \beta_2' = \beta_3' = \beta_4' = 0$. This hypothesis can be tested by constructing the appropriate F-test, in the spirit of Section 2.8.

Binary dependent variables are sometimes of interest, and may be characterized in the regression context, but not without some difficulty. The specification of such a model is simple enough. For, letting $y = 1$ if the event of interest occurs and $y = 0$ otherwise, $E(y \mid x_1, \ldots, x_k) = \beta_0 + \beta_1 x_1 + \cdots + \beta_k x_k$ is still a proper PRF. Owing to the $(0, 1)$ nature of y, however, the PRF now describes as the conditional expectation of y the conditional probability of occurrence for the event in question. Thus a predicted value for y from the SRF is an estimate of the conditional probability of the event's occurence given the x_j's.

One problem with the regression specification above is that there must be heteroscedasticity. For by interpreting $E(y \mid \{x_j\})$ as a probability of occurence for a simple Bernoulli variable, y, we know the variance of such a variable to be $E(y \mid \{x_j\})[1 - E(y \mid \{x_j\})]$, corresponding to the more familiar $p(1 - p)$ or pq formula. Thus, LS methods applied to this model can be expected to be inefficient. Moreover, nothing in the specifications guarantees that for all sets of values for the x_j's the predicted probability will be bounded by zero and one, which on a priori grounds it must be. The heteroscedasticity problem can be overcome easily because $E(y|\{x_j\})$ is directly estimated by the regression procedure. Its estimate is just $\mathbf{Xb}$. Therefore $\hat{\mathbf{\Lambda}}$ for the model is available, and generalized LS may be used to get asymptotically efficient estimates. The $(0, 1)$ bound on predicted y is not so easy to circumvent or to solve. Some attempts create an "index" value for $\mathbf{X\beta}$ that *must* be bounded by $(0, 1)$. Such is the case in the so-called probit or logit models. Otherwise, mathematical programming techniques can be used to estimate $\mathbf{\beta}$ while insuring that predicted y falls in $(0, 1)$.

5.4 NONLINEAR REGRESSION

The virtues of a linear model under classical assumptions are, aside from its basic simplicity, the BLUE properties guaranteed by the Gauss-Markov theorem. These properties do not generally hold for estimators derived from nonlinear PRF's under an application of the LS criterion. But with a normality assumption the least-squares and maximum-likelihood estimators correspond again, leading to the establishment of at least large-sample unbiasedness, consistency, and efficiency properties for the nonlinear LS estimators. This said, we shall attempt to outline the general developments of calculation and inference methods for the nonlinear estimators.

To differentiate the nonlinear and linear models slightly, our notation will give the conditional expectation of y given conditioning variables $(x_{i0}, x_{i1}, \ldots, x_{ik})$ as a function, h, of these variables and a vector of parameters $\mathbf{\theta} = (\theta_1 \cdots \theta_p)'$:

$$(5.4.1) \qquad E(y|x_0, \ldots, x_k) = h(x_0, \ldots, x_k; \theta_1, \ldots, \theta_p)$$

or

$$\mathbf{y} = h(\mathbf{X}; \mathbf{\theta}) + \mathbf{\epsilon}.$$

We have kept the correspondence of the previous model to $(k + 1)$ independent variables (where previously $x_{i0} = 1$ for all i), but now there are $p \leq n$ parameters to be estimated. The least-squares criterion function remains unchanged, being

$$(5.4.2) \qquad \sum_{i=1}^{n} [y_i - h(x_{i0}, \ldots, x_{ik}; \theta_1, \ldots, \theta_p)]^2.$$

Its minimization also maximizes the likelihood function of the sample observations, as was observed in Section 3.4.

There are two main methods for finding the $\hat{\boldsymbol{\theta}}$ that minimizes (5.4.2). One is to proceed directly to the establishment of normal equations. These will generally be complicated, nonlinear equations. Even in apparently simple cases the normal equations may turn out to be quite difficult, solvable only through numerical procedures. For example, the equation $y = e^{-\theta_1 t} + \epsilon$ ($t \geq 0$) has as its least-squares normal equation for θ_1 the following:

$$\sum (y - e^{-\theta_1 t})(-te^{-\theta_1 t}) = \sum te^{-2\theta_1 t} - \sum yte^{-\theta_1 t} = 0,$$

which is a transcendental equation.

The technique we shall concentrate on for present purposes successively approximates $\hat{\boldsymbol{\theta}}$ through a linearization of h. Any function under very general conditions can be approximated to an arbitrary degree of accuracy by a polynomial equation; this is known as the Taylor series expansion. For a function of a single argument, say $g(\theta)$, we have

$$(5.4.3) \qquad g(\theta) \doteq g(\theta_0) + (\theta - \theta_0)g^1(\theta_0) + \cdots + \frac{(\theta - \theta_0)^k}{k!}g^k(\theta_0),$$

where θ_0 is an expansion constant that is arbitrarily chosen, and $g^i(\theta_0)$, $i = 1, \ldots, k$, stands for the ith derivative of g evaluated at $\theta = \theta_0$. The more terms included, the better is the approximation. The "linear" approximation to $g(\theta)$, meaning linear in θ, consists of the first two terms in (5.4.3), $g(\theta) \doteq g(\theta_0) + (\theta - \theta_0)g^1(\theta_0)$.

The extension of the single-argument (parameter) case is straightforward. Applied to the function $h(\mathbf{X}; \boldsymbol{\theta})$, the linear Taylor series approximation is given by

$$(5.4.4) \qquad h(\mathbf{X}; \boldsymbol{\theta}) \doteq h(\mathbf{X}; \boldsymbol{\theta}_0) + \sum_{j=1}^{p} \left[\frac{\partial h}{\partial \theta_j} \bigg|_{\theta_j = \theta_j^{(0)}} \right] (\theta_j - \theta_j^{(0)}).$$

$\boldsymbol{\theta}_0 = (\theta_1^{(0)} \cdots \theta_p^{(0)})'$ is the vector of chosen expansion constants; the notation $[\partial h/\partial \theta_j | \theta_j = \theta_j^{(0)}]$ represents the *partial* derivative of h with respect to θ_j evaluated at $\theta_j^{(0)}$. Equation (5.4.4) has the form of a linear conditional mean regression function when written

$$(5.4.5) \qquad y - h(\mathbf{X}; \boldsymbol{\theta}_0) \doteq \sum_{j=1}^{p} \beta_j^{(0)} z_j^{(0)} + \epsilon,$$

where $\beta_j^{(0)} = (\theta_j - \theta_j^{(0)})$ and $z_j^{(0)} = [\partial h/\partial \theta_j | \theta_j = \theta_j^{(0)}]$. The approximation of $\hat{\boldsymbol{\theta}}$ then is accomplished by assigning starting values $\theta_1^{(0)}, \ldots, \theta_p^{(0)}$, transforming y, and regressing $y - h(\mathbf{X}; \boldsymbol{\theta}_0)$ on the $z_j^{(0)}$'s. This first step yields LS estimates of the $\beta_j^{(0)}$'s, $b_1^{(0)}, \ldots, b_p^{(0)}$, from which first-round estimates of the θ_j's are obtained by $\theta_j^{(1)} = \theta_j^{(0)} + b_j^{(0)}$. The process is continued, using revised values for $\boldsymbol{\theta}$, until two adjacent iterations produce values that do not differ by an amount larger than some prespecified small number.

For purposes of illustration, suppose the nonlinear model of interest is again $y = e^{-\theta_1 t} + \epsilon$ with the sample of observations shown in the table below.†

y	t
0.80	1
0.45	4
0.04	16

Then $h(t; \theta_1) = e^{-\theta_1 t}$ and $\partial h/\partial \theta_1 = dh/d\theta_1 = -te^{-\theta_1 t}$. In outline fashion below are reproduced the five iterations needed to compute $\hat{\theta}_1$ within .01 accuracy, from a starting value $\theta_1^{(0)} = .5$.

Iteration 1 : $\theta_1^{(0)} = .5$

$h(t; \theta_1^{(0)}) = e^{-\theta_1^{(0)} t}$	$y - h(t; \theta_1^{(0)})$	$z_1^{(0)} = -te^{-\theta_1^{(0)} t}$
.6065	.19	−.61
.1353	.31	−.54
.0002	.04	−.00

$$\sum [y - h(t; \theta_1^{(0)})]z_1^{(0)} = -.28 \quad \sum (z_1^{(0)})^2 = .66 \quad b_1^{(1)} = \frac{-.28}{.66} = -.43$$

Result: $\theta_1^{(1)} = \theta_1^{(0)} + b_1^{(1)} = .5 - .43 = .07$.

Iteration 2 : $\theta_1^{(1)} = .07$

$h(t; \theta_1^{(1)}) = e^{-\theta_1^{(1)} t}$	$y - h(t; \theta_1^{(1)})$	$z_1^{(1)} = -te^{-\theta_1^{(1)} t}$
.9324	−.13	− .93
.7558	−.31	−3.0
.3263	−.29	−5.2

$$\sum [y - h(t; \theta_1^{(1)})]z_1^{(1)} = 2.6 \quad \sum (z_1^{(1)})^2 = 37. \quad b_1^{(2)} = \frac{2.6}{37} = .070$$

Result: $\theta_1^{(2)} = \theta_1^{(1)} + b_1^{(2)} = .07 + .07 = 0.14$.

Iteration 3 : $\theta_1^{(2)} = .14$

$h(t; \theta_1^{(2)}) = e^{-\theta_1^{(2)} t}$	$y - h(t; \theta_1^{(2)})$	$z_1^{(2)} = -te^{-\theta_1^{(2)} t}$
.8693	−.07	− .87
.5712	−.12	−2.3
.1164	−.08	−1.8

$$\sum [y - h(t; \theta_1^{(2)})]z_1^{(2)} = .48 \quad \sum (z_1^{(2)})^2 = 9.3 \quad b_1^{(3)} = \frac{.48}{9.3} = .052$$

Result: $\theta_1^{(3)} = \theta_1^{(2)} + b_1^{(3)} = .14 + .05 = .19$.

† From N. R. Draper and H. Smith, *Applied Regression Analysis* (New York: Wiley, 1966), Chap. 10, Exercise A, p. 299.

Iteration 4: $\theta_1^{(3)} = .19$

$h(t; \theta_1^{(3)}) = e^{-\theta_1^{(3)}t}$	$y - h(t; \theta_1^{(3)})$	$z_1^{(3)} = -te^{-\theta_1^{(3)}t}$
.8269	−.03	− .83
.4677	−.02	−1.9
.0478	−.01	− .76

$$\sum [y - h(t; \theta_1^{(3)})]z_1^{(3)} = .070 \quad \sum (z_1^{(3)})^2 = 4.9 \quad b_1^{(4)} = \frac{.07}{4.9} = .014$$

Result: $\theta_1^{(4)} = \theta_1^{(3)} + b_1^{(4)} = .19 + .014 = .20.$

Iteration 5: $\theta_1^{(4)} = .20$

$h(t; \theta_1^{(4)}) = e^{-\theta_1^{(4)}t}$	$y - h(t; \theta_1^{(4)})$	$z_1^{(4)} = -te^{-\theta_1^{(4)}t}$
.8187	−.02	− .82
.4493	.00	−1.8
.0408	.00	− .65

$$\sum [y - h(t; \theta_1^{(4)})]z_1^{(4)} = .02 \quad \sum (z_1^{(4)})^2 = 4.3 \quad b_1^{(5)} = \frac{.02}{4.3} = .0046$$

Result: $\theta_1^{(5)} = \theta_1^{(4)} + b_1^{(5)} = .20 + .00 = .20.$

Since iterations (4) and (5) result in the same value for $\hat{\theta}_1$ according to our tolerance, $\hat{\theta}_1 = .20$.

While in actuality the computation of an estimated standard error for $\hat{\theta}_1$ is difficult, it too may be approximated by the "linear" formulas. $\mathscr{S}^2$ is computed no differently in the nonlinear case, which for the example has a value

$$\mathscr{S}^2 = \left(\frac{1}{3-1}\right) \sum_{i=1}^{3} \hat{\epsilon}_i^2 = \frac{1}{2}(.0004) = .0002,$$

using $\hat{\epsilon}_i = y_i - h(t_i; \theta_i^{(5)})$. Since $\hat{\theta}_1 = \theta_1^{(5)} = \theta_1^{(4)} + b_1^{(5)}$, and $\theta_1^{(4)}$ is a *known* quantity,

$$\hat{\sigma}_{\hat{\theta}_1}^2 \doteq \hat{\sigma}_{b_1^{(5)}}^2 = \frac{\mathscr{S}^2}{\sum (z_1^{(5)})^2} = \frac{.0002}{4.3} = .000046$$

so that $\hat{\sigma}_{\theta_1} \doteq .007$. For the multiparameter case, $\Sigma_\theta \doteq \sigma^2(\mathbf{Z}'\mathbf{Z})^{-1}$ and $\hat{\Sigma}_\theta \doteq \mathscr{S}^2(\mathbf{Z}'\mathbf{Z})^{-1}$, with the $\mathbf{Z}$ matrix constructed on the basis of the final values for $\hat{\theta}$. Finally, approximate confidence intervals (and the basis for hypothesis tests) come directly from the distribution theory established for the linear model. For the example case, $t_{.95,2} = \pm 4.303$, hence $\Pr\{.17 \leq \hat{\theta}_1 \leq .23\} \doteq .95$.

In closing we should remark that as a matter of computational efficiency the linearization procedure may not always be the best way to proceed. It is offered here primarily for its expository value. Nor can solution methods be expected to find $\hat{\theta}$ to an arbitrarily chosen tolerance *always*. Often the LS criterion function for a complex nonlinear function in θ will possess numerous "flat" portions, each of which can, to the satisfaction of many numerical methods, be interpreted as "the" maximum.

5.5 AN EXAMPLE OF REGRESSION WITH DUMMY VARIABLES

In this section we take the liberty of reproducing the results of an article† in which the regression technique is used to test various "intuitive" hypotheses. The models include dummy variables to represent such non-quantitative factors as political outlook. Tests revolve around these dummies taken in tandem, since they represent as *groups* certain qualitative influences on the dependent variable, which in turn is *supposed* to measure equality in the distribution of income on a statewide basis. Whether it in fact *is* income equality that is being "measured" by y is debatable. This points to the occasional difficulty of establishing a perfect relationship between *concept* and measured variable.

The measurement used, for those unfamiliar with the terminology, derives from a plot of cumulative percentage income earned versus cumulative relative frequency in some population divided into income classes. So, a perfectly "equal" distribution is one where the top 5 percent of the population earns 5 percent of total income, the top 10 percent earns 10 percent, and so on—a 45° line in such a diagram. The equality measure is the area under the actual (Lorenz) curve divided by the area encompassed by the 45° line.

Simon Kuznets has offered for consideration the hypothesis that income is more equally divided in mature than in developing economies. One approach to determining the tenability of this hypothesis is merely to *observe* such differences if they exist. This is not as easy as it sounds, for to frame a good test of the hypothesis depends on many things, including the concept of income employed, the construction of an appropriate sample, and the measure of equality used.

Also of great significance is an understanding of the development process and reasons for such apparent distributional differences in income: is there anything about the process of capital accumulation and hence economic development that tends to make the personal distribution of income become more equal? Only introductory work on the subject exists at present.

† D. J. Aigner and A. J. Heins, "On the Determinants of Income Equality," *Am. Econ. Rev.*, Vol. 57 (March 1967), pp. 175–84. Reprinted with the permission of the American Economic Association.

Soltow's[†] work indicates that educational level plays an important role in support of the Kuznets relationship, as shown by the existence of greater equality among more highly skilled or educated groups of people. And in an effort to explain the parallel movement of equality of the overall distribution of income and per capita income differences between the states, Smolensky[‡] conjectures that increased mobility, particularly the movement from rural to urban areas during the period 1880–1950 in the United States, is the primary factor tending to reduce dispersion in incomes. While decreased regional dispersion is not necessarily coincidental with decreased dispersion within regions, one would expect that mobility tends to diminish both interregional and intraregional inequality in incomes if it is a significant factor at all.

Despite these efforts there is no formal theory available that satisfactorily concerns itself with the relationship between development and the inequality of incomes. So the matter has generally rested on observations of the income distributions in a variety of countries, where the data bases used for such observations are rather different and thus lead to debatable conclusions concerning consistency or inconsistency with the Kuznets generalization. The question just raised cannot be broached with such observations.

Recognizing that development inexorably brings many noneconomic changes, to approach the problem we pose it would be appropriate to hold social, cultural, and political factors constant in order to identify changes in the equality of income derived from the economic development process per se. And, certainly, comparability of the data used is a necessary ingredient in the observation process. The 1960 Census provides us with detailed data on the distribution of family income in the fifty states of the United States and, since data were similarly constructed in all cases and the political and economic structure is rather homogeneous at least across the continental United States, these data should yield some interesting insights into the impact of regional development on the personal distribution of income.

One would expect that social and cultural attributes have their impact on the distribution of income. Kravis[§] suggests the following attributes which, aside from the state of development, could be expected to impinge on the income distribution: (1) human characteristics, (2) barriers to mobility, such as legal and social barriers involved in racial discrimination, (3) economic structure, and (4) social and political organizations.

Using the development hypothesis as a base, we have formulated a linear regression model for the states (excluding Alaska and Hawaii) in an attempt to explain variations in equality of the income distribution, as measured by

† Lee Soltow, "The Distribution of Income Related to Changes in the Distribution of Education, Age, and Occupation," *Rev. Econ. Stat.*, Vol. 42 (November 1960), pp. 450–53.

‡ E. Smolensky, "Industrialization and Income Inequality: Recent United States Experience," *Papers and Proceedings*, The Regional Science Association, Vol. 7 (1961).

§ Irving B. Kravis, "International Differences in the Distribution of Income," *Rev. Econ. Stat.*, Vol. 42 (November 1960), pp. 408–16.

the equality ratio,† by mean family income of the population as development indicator, and a variety of control variables that substantially implement the factors outlined by Kravis, as follows:

QUANTITATIVE FACTORS:

Y: Area under Lorenz curve as a percentage of maximum possible area (measure of equality)

X_1: Percentage of population white

X_2: Percentage of population urban

X_3: Median school years completed

X_4: Percentage unemployment

X_5: Median age of population

X_6: Percentage of population employed in mining and manufacturing

X_{13}: Mean family income

QUALITATIVE FACTORS:

X_7: 1 if consistently Republican; 0 if not

X_8: 1 if consistently Democratic; 0 if not
(X_7 and X_8 both 0 if no voting consistency)

X_9: 1 if using sales tax; 0 if not

X_{10}: 1 if using income tax; 0 if not
(X_9 and X_{10} may be both 0 or both 1)

X_{11}: 1 if conservative state; 0 if not

X_{12}: 1 if liberal state; 0 if not
(X_{11} and X_{12} both 0 if rated middle-of-the-road)

The dummy variables X_7 and X_8 are based on state voting records during the period 1940–60 in presidential elections, both variables assuming zero values if the given state was split 3-3 as between Republican-Democrat over the six elections considered. Obviously strict party affiliation is not a sufficient indicator of adherence to given social policies, particularly for some Southern states. Thus an additional set of dummy variables, X_{11} and X_{12}, is included to offset whatever biases may be inherent in X_7 and X_8. These variables are assigned values on a purely judgmental basis and hence may be questioned on subjective grounds.‡

† The area under the Lorenz curve as a percentage of maximum possible area. This measure is the complement of Gini's concentration ratio in percentage terms.

‡ Here we use the terms "liberal" and "conservative" to denote, on a state basis, commitment to large redistribution and welfare programs or a basic laissez faire philosophy, respectively.

Since we have little more than judgment to rely upon in anticipating the partial relationships of income equality and these variables, any speculating we do as regards these relationships cannot be derived from more than a naive theory except for the case of mean income, where the Kuznets thesis suggests a positive relationship. Without launching into a lengthy harangue concerning the remaining variables, for all of which some a priori case can be made, our interest centers more toward an evaluation of their relevance than testing any hypotheses about them.

Table 5.1 contains the results of six alternative configurations of variables, with partial regression coefficients, t-ratios,† and R^2's (unadjusted) noted. It is significant to the reliability of these results that there is an overwhelming lack of intercorrelation in the independent variables, as seen in Table 5.2.

Throughout the six variants, if a 99 percent confidence level is used, the significant variables are (1) mean family income and (2) the percentage of population that is white. In variant (6) the percentage of the population employed in mining and manufacturing is also significant at the 99 percent level. With respect to the behavior of net regression coefficients for X_1 and X_{13} it is interesting to note that they are very stable over five of six variants, with b_1 ranging between .17 and .21 in all but variant (4) and the estimated coefficient for mean income taking on values between .0018 and .0022 except in variant (5).

Thus it would seem that the Kuznets hypothesis is supported in a situation where a high degree of control is exercised over other population attributes, implicitly by the basic similarity of political and economic structure throughout the United States and explicitly by the other variables employed. The significance of X_1 as an explanator of variations in income equality would seem to enforce already prominent evidence on the effect of racial differences on income and its distribution.

Of the "traditional" variables other than X_6, median age of the population is significant at the 95 percent level in both variants (5) and (6). This variable could be expected to exhibit a negative partial regression coefficient for a variety of reasons but primarily because an older population would likely have a high degree of rigidity of skills and hence cause enforcement and proliferation of already established equality barriers. Variable X_3, median school years completed, was chosen to describe the basic skill level of each state population and is significant in variant (6) at the 90 percent level.

The significance of X_2 at the 80 percent level is interesting also in light of Kuznets' views on income equality in developed versus underdeveloped economies. If we adopt the urban center as a focal point for capital formation, then through Kuznets' eyes we should expect a tendency toward greater

---

† Critical values for "t" are approximately ± 2.70 for 99 percent, ± 2.02 for 95 percent, ± 1.68 for 90 percent, and ± 1.30 for 80 percent.

Table 5.1

Regression Coefficients (*t*-ratios in parentheses)

Regression Variant	Variables Included													R^2 (d.f. in parentheses)
	X_1	X_2	X_3	X_4	X_5	X_6	X_7	X_8	X_9	X_{10}	X_{11}	X_{12}	X_{13}	
1	.198 (6.39)			−.005 (−.020)		.034 (1.24)							.00180 (5.68)	.78 (43)
2	.204 (6.04)			−.061 (−.025)		.035 (1.25)			.623 (0.95)	−.355 (−0.55)			.00176 (5.49)	.79 (41)
3	.210 (6.93)			.181 (0.76)		.030 (1.11)					1.690 (2.42)	.378 (0.49)	.00216 (6.36)	.81 (41)
4	.155 (4.82)			.131 (0.59)		.027 (1.03)	1.44 (2.12)	−.722 (−1.06)					.00183 (5.67)	.82 (41)
5	.211 (6.52)	−.057 (−1.92)		−.096 (−0.45)	−.293 (−2.18)	.069 (2.45)							.00265 (5.85)	.83 (41)
6	.172 (4.18)	−.041 (−1.33)	1.020 (1.83)	.149 (0.64)	−.333 (−2.53)	.096 (3.16)	.440 (0.63)	−.074 (−1.02)	.430 (0.77)	−.344 (0.60)	.970 (1.27)	.761 (1.01)	.00204 (3.88)	.89 (34)

Table 5.2

Correlation Matrix

	Y	X_1	X_2	X_3	X_4	X_5	X_6	X_7	X_8	X_9	X_{10}	X_{11}	X_{12}	X_{13}
Y	1.00	.75	.43	.73	−.01	.38	.20	.41	−.57	−.14	−.35	−.35	.30	.76
X_1		1.00	.23	.68	.05	.45	−.03	.39	−.44	−.28	−.28	−.40	.27	.48
X_2			1.00	.48	−.13	.49	.29	−.18	−.15	.02	−.24	−.47	.36	.79
X_3				1.00	−.18	.26	−.23	.22	−.47	−.14	−.23	−.37	.28	.68
X_4					1.00	−.08	−.04	−.13	.16	.13	−.13	−.26	.15	−.06
X_5						1.00	.44	.16	−.32	−.22	−.30	−.21	.34	.49
X_6							1.00	.07	−.04	−.08	−.13	−.08	.20	.25
X_7								1.00	−.48	−.06	−.20	.28	.04	.08
X_8									1.00	.12	.09	−.04	.09	−.45
X_9										1.00	−.22	.22	−.25	−.14
X_{10}											1.00	−.04	−.09	−.27
X_{11}												1.00	−.48	−.53
X_{12}													1.00	.33
X_{13}														1.00

inequality of income for those states with large urban population concentrations. While this conjecture is partially borne out by the data, the evidence is undoubtedly clouded by interactions with racial barriers in the urban center and the occupational mix variable, X_6. Such interactions, while expected in general, would appear inconsequential for these data as inferred from the values for the appropriate correlation coefficients.

For the qualitative variables, in variants (3) and (4) a particular political affiliation and "philosophy" are of significance (95 percent level) in explaining variations in income equality, X_7 appearing in variant (4) with a positive sign (corresponding to a consistently Republican voting record), and X_{11} in variant (3) with a like sign (corresponding to a conservative political and social attitude). Both variables fall to significance levels below 80 percent in the main equation, variant (6).

It is, however, inappropriate to use the individual t-ratios in Table 5.1 for assessing the importance of the sets of dummy variables, such as political affiliation as a structural variable, since the dummy variables in question were constructed in tandem. Thus to inquire after the statistical significance of political party affiliation requires that the joint hypothesis $\beta_7 = \beta_8 = 0$ be tested. A similar remark applies in the case of tax structure (X_9 and X_{10}) and political philosophy (X_{11} and X_{12}).

Table 5.3

Statistics for Testing Qualitative Variables

Basic Variant	Hypothesis	F-statistic	d.f. (f_1, f_2)	Selected F-levels for rejection
2	$\beta_9 = \beta_{10} = 0$	0.87	2,41	$F_{.99,2,41} = 5.17$
3	$\beta_{11} = \beta_{12} = 0$	2.99	2,41	$F_{.95,2,41} = 3.23$
4	$\beta_7 = \beta_8 = 0$	4.55	2,41	$F_{.90,2,41} = 2.44$
6	$\beta_7 = \beta_8 = \beta_{11} = \beta_{12} = 0$	4.13	4,34	$F_{.99,4,34} = 3.93$
	$\beta_9 = \beta_{10} = 0$	6.77	2,34	
	$\beta_7 = \beta_8 = 0$	8.03	2,34	$F_{.995,2,34} = 6.22$
	$\beta_{11} = \beta_{12} = 0$	6.77	2,34	

Table 5.3 presents the relevant F-statistics, using variants (2), (3), and (4) and variant (6) as bases for the testing of coefficients taking on zero values simultaneously. Seven hypotheses are considered, with primary interest centering on those within variant (6). For this case, each individual qualitative attribute of the states as well as the composite political factor (political party and/or philosophy) is significant at a 99 percent level or above.

The Kuznets observation is interesting primarily because it suggests that economic development per se may be a harbinger of social justice. The

	Equality Ratio (percent)[a] Y	Percentage of Population White[a] X_1	Percentage of Population Urban[a] X_2	Median School Years Completed[b] X_3	Percentage Unemployment[c] X_4
Alabama	56.79	69.9	55.0	9.5	5.6
Alaska	65.03	77.2	37.9	12.0	14.4
Arizona	61.70	89.8	74.5	10.9	5.3
Arkansas	55.74	78.1	42.8	9.2	5.6
California	64.93	92.0	86.4	11.9	5.8
Colorado	64.75	89.4	80.7	10.6	4.3
Connecticut	66.08	95.6	78.3	10.8	3.9
Delaware	62.58	86.1	65.6	10.9	4.7
D.C.	59.46	45.2	100.0	11.6	4.4
Florida	59.13	82.1	74.0	10.7	4.9
Georgia	57.98	71.4	55.3	9.5	3.9
Hawaii	64.08	32.0	76.5	11.2	3.3
Idaho	66.08	98.5	47.5	11.3	5.4
Illinois	64.74	97.0	73.7	11.9	3.9
Indiana	65.69	94.1	62.4	10.7	3.9
Iowa	62.34	99.0	53.1	11.2	3.3
Kansas	63.07	95.4	61.0	11.5	3.6
Kentucky	56.92	92.8	44.5	8.9	6.3
Louisiana	57.20	67.9	63.3	9.3	6.3
Maine	66.73	99.4	51.3	10.7	6.2
Maryland	64.61	83.0	72.7	10.5	4.7
Massachusetts	59.42	97.6	83.6	11.3	4.3
Michigan	66.13	90.6	73.4	10.8	6.8
Minnesota	63.69	98.8	62.1	10.9	5.4
Mississippi	52.98	57.7	37.7	9.1	5.0
Missouri	60.53	90.8	66.6	10.1	5.0
Montana	65.54	96.4	50.2	11.3	6.6
Nebraska	62.51	97.4	54.3	11.5	3.0
Nevada	66.07	92.3	70.4	12.0	5.8
New Hampshire	67.98	99.6	58.3	10.7	3.9
New Jersey	66.41	91.3	88.6	10.6	3.9
New Mexico	61.34	92.1	65.7	10.9	6.0
New York	64.05	91.1	85.4	10.8	4.9
No. Carolina	57.98	74.6	39.5	9.5	3.6
No. Dakota	63.15	98.0	35.2	10.0	5.9
Ohio	66.15	91.8	73.4	10.8	5.4
Oklahoma	59.24	90.5	62.9	10.6	4.4
Oregon	65.94	97.9	62.2	11.5	6.0
Pennsylvania	65.56	92.4	71.6	10.4	6.5
Rhode Island	66.53	97.6	86.4	10.1	4.7
So. Carolina	57.42	65.1	41.2	9.2	3.6
So. Dakota	60.99	96.0	39.3	10.5	4.1
Tennessee	56.73	83.5	52.3	9.2	5.1
Texas	58.82	87.4	75.0	10.4	4.4
Utah	68.04	98.1	74.9	12.1	3.9
Vermont	65.26	99.8	38.5	10.7	4.5
Virginia	59.51	79.2	55.8	10.1	4.0
Washington	66.85	96.4	68.1	11.8	6.2
W. Virginia	60.08	95.1	38.2	9.1	9.3
Wisconsin	65.84	97.6	63.8	10.6	3.8
Wyoming	66.23	97.8	56.8	11.8	5.0

a Calculated from data or data taken from *1960 Census of Population*, Vol. I, Parts 2–52, (hereafter referred to as *Census*), Table 65. Equality ratio is area under the Lorenz curve as a proportion of maximum possible area, namely, one minus the concentration ratio.

b *Census*, Table 47.

c *Census*, Table 52.

Median Age of Population[d] (years) X_5	Percentage Employed in Mining and Manufacturing[e] X_6	Political Affiliation[f]		Tax Base[g]		Political Philosophy[f]		Mean Family Income[a] (dollars) X_{13}
		Rep. X_7	Dem. X_8	Sales X_9	In-come X_{10}	Cons. X_{11}	Lib. X_{12}	
25.9	26.5	0	1	1	1	1	0	4816.47
23.3	7.1	0	1	0	1	0	1	8197.05
25.6	12.8	0	0	1	1	0	0	6573.85
28.8	20.1	0	0	1	1	0	0	4131.41
30.0	24.2	1	0	1	1	0	0	7789.70
31.2	31.9	1	0	1	1	0	0	7573.79
31.8	40.2	0	0	1	0	0	0	8212.22
28.8	32.8	0	0	0	1	0	0	7493.84
32.2	6.2	0	1	0	0	0	1	7723.47
31.1	13.1	0	0	1	0	1	0	5847.65
25.9	26.3	0	1	1	1	1	0	5167.43
24.3	16.0	1	0	1	1	0	1	7645.55
25.9	13.5	0	0	0	1	0	0	5935.70
27.8	15.7	0	1	1	0	0	0	6684.67
28.9	35.4	1	0	1	0	1	0	6557.53
30.3	18.6	0	0	1	1	1	0	5826.94
29.9	16.6	1	0	1	1	1	0	6165.20
27.6	21.2	0	1	0	1	0	0	4914.82
25.3	15.6	0	1	1	1	1	0	5303.10
29.3	33.1	1	0	1	0	1	0	5474.50
28.6	24.5	0	0	1	1	1	0	7366.72
32.1	35.5	0	1	0	1	0	1	6113.88
28.2	38.0	1	0	1	0	0	1	7104.92
28.5	19.5	0	1	0	1	0	1	6342.03
24.1	19.1	0	1	1	1	1	0	3886.70
31.6	24.7	0	1	1	1	0	0	5979.07
27.4	10.2	0	0	0	1	0	0	6100.73
30.2	12.2	1	0	0	0	1	0	5692.67
29.4	6.3	0	1	1	0	0	1	7770.51
30.9	39.8	1	0	0	1	1	0	6376.09
32.3	36.1	0	0	0	0	0	0	7910.12
22.7	7.6	0	1	1	1	0	0	6238.57
33.0	28.6	0	0	0	1	0	1	7625.27
25.5	31.7	0	1	1	1	1	0	4817.37
26.0	3.7	1	0	1	1	1	0	5229.42
29.4	37.0	1	0	1	0	1	0	7006.17
30.0	13.2	0	0	1	1	0	0	5542.32
30.7	25.4	1	0	0	1	0	1	6699.01
32.0	36.4	0	0	1	0	1	0	6612.76
31.9	39.3	0	1	1	0	0	1	6348.72
23.4	32.1	0	1	1	1	1	0	4618.46
27.6	6.6	1	0	1	0	1	0	4936.89
27.9	26.0	0	0	1	1	1	0	4878.87
26.9	16.2	0	1	0	0	1	0	5897.28
22.9	16.0	0	0	1	1	0	0	6658.19
29.2	24.9	1	0	0	1	1	0	5618.82
27.1	22.4	0	0	0	1	1	0	5940.37
29.5	24.7	0	0	1	0	0	1	7032.00
28.4	33.3	0	1	1	0	0	0	5177.91
29.3	32.9	1	0	0	1	0	1	6696.73
27.1	7.7	1	0	1	0	1	0	6680.70

d *Census*, Table 16.

e *Census*, Table 62.

f See text.

g *Retail Sales and Individual Income Taxes in State Tax Structures*, Tax Foundation, Inc., Project Note No. 48 (1962).

results above support such a hypothesis, and that is a rather comforting thought. This is not to suggest that social and economic policies designed to redistribute resources are useless, but, instead, that time and wealth accumulation are on the side of equality.

That the evidence indicates racial makeup as an important determinant of income inequality is not surprising. And, if the distribution of resources is an important aspect of overall social justice, then it would seem that recent public policies designed to remove racial barriers in the social and economic market places of the United States are not misconceived, at least on the basis of their intent.

5.6 PROBLEMS AND ANSWERS

GENERAL PROBLEMS

1. (Section 5.3) A researcher has a body of monthly data on bank balance sheets for a five-year period, with which he hopes to estimate a number of regression equations, having dependent variables such as purchases of treasury bills, loans to other banks, and so on. In each such equation "season" of the year (that is, month) is to be controlled along with several other independent variables. As an alternative to a dummy-variable formulation, however, he proposes merely to code month of the year appropriately, say by the series $1, 2, \ldots, 12$.

    a. Critically evaluate this scheme for handling the qualitative variable, "month-of-the-year," in contrast to the dummy-variable technique. Mention points on the estimation of relevant coefficients, testing the significance of "month-of-the-year," and so on.

    b. Since he obviously has "control" over the coding scheme for this seasonal variable, he reasons, a "better" coding would *spread* the values out, the objective being to make the variance of the seasonal variable as *large* as possible, in deference to the notion that as a matter of experimental design a large variance for any independent variable reduces the variance of its estimated regression coefficient, ceteris paribus. Discuss the merits (or demerits) of this proposal.

Answers:

    (a) Given that we are concerned with the operational or empirical specification of a qualitative variable, there can be no a priori theoretical difference between the two ways of characterizing "season." As a practical matter, however, there are two main contrasts between them. On the one hand, the single variable implies but a single coefficient to estimate as opposed to eleven with the dummy-variable approach. A difference of ten degrees of freedom cannot be ignored generally, and probably should not be ignored with sixty observations. The "price" paid in adopting the single variable with its fixed coding scheme is hard to determine precisely. One must compare the potential costs of a fixed sequence representing "season," in terms of some sort of specification error, to the "free" specification embodied in a shifting intercept for each season.

(b) Nonsense. So long as the coding is kept uniform, with equal differences between seasons, the suggestion is simply to multiply the series coded $(1, 2, \ldots, 12)$ by a constant. Clearly, multiplying any variable in a regression model by a constant (that is, a change in units) does not affect the t-ratio for testing its significance. In regressions contrasting the variables x_4 and $\tilde{x}_4 = 10x_4$, for example, we find $\tilde{b}_4 = .10b_4$ and $\sigma^2_{\tilde{b}_4} = .01\sigma^2_{b_4}$. Thus, $t = b_4/\sigma_{b_4} = \tilde{b}_4/\sigma_{\tilde{b}_4}$.

2. (Section 5.2) The rate of unemployment obviously impinges on the longevity of persons on the unemployment-compensation roles. It is of interest to forecast the "survival rate," s, the proportion of persons who continue receiving unemployment compensation from one week to the next, on the basis of the proportion of the labor force unemployed, u.

You are to propose and defend a plausible model for forecasting s on the basis of knowledge about u, suggest how its parameters might be estimated, and say something about the statistical properties of those estimates, using whatever a priori information you have, the fact that in the data only "small" values of u appear, and the observation that scatters of s and u show up as straight lines on semilogarithmic paper as in Fig. 5.2. Note that the scaling of s is "backwards" along the logarithmic scale.

ANSWER:

Were the scaling of the logarithmic axis not "backwards," we would consider $\log s = \beta u + \epsilon'$ as a possible (transformed) model. The backwards scaling suggests, rather, the model $\log (1 - s) = \beta u + \epsilon'$, which, when exponentiated, gives $(1 - s) = e^{\beta u}\epsilon$ or $s = 1 - e^{\beta u}\epsilon$. There are some a priori restrictions to enforce on our chosen model, and some empirical information. A priori, we know two points on the function we seek—namely, $(0, 0)$ and $(1, 1)$. There can be no survival if there is no unemployment, and if there is 100 percent unemployment, everyone survives. Lastly, our current experience suggests that an ability to predict s for "large" values of u is not important.

The function above has $s = 0$ when $u = 0$, but $s \rightarrow -\infty$ when $u \rightarrow \infty$. An alternative version is $\log (1 - s) = (\log \beta)u + \epsilon'$, which in exponential form is $s = 1 - \beta^u \epsilon$. Here $s = 0$ when $u = 0$ and $s = 1$

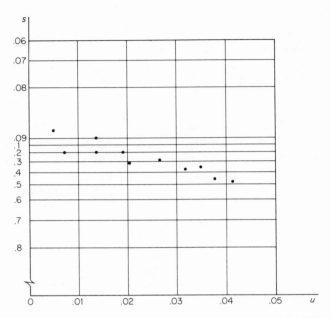

Fig. 5.2

as $u \longrightarrow \infty$ so long as $0 < \beta < 1$. So, while all the a priori restrictions are not satisfied, this model seems to incorporate the most of the available and relevant information.

PROBLEMS ON SPECIAL TOPICS:
THE PRODUCTION FUNCTION†

Beginning from a deterministic production function of the Cobb-Douglas form $q = AL^{\alpha}K^{\beta}$, with q = output, L = labor, K = capital, and A, α, and β unknown coefficients, derive the system of equations that determines the optimal levels of K and L for an individual firm operating in perfect competition. Next, make the structure operational by appropriately specifying its stochastic elements. Justify whatever specifications you make.

Viewed in terms of *your* structure, if the production function were considered alone for purposes of estimation, would least-squares estimates of parameters have desirable properties, both statistical and economic? More specifically, point out carefully the effects of your error specification on

---

† Consideration of this topic at this point, besides being apropos the discussion of functional form, is a good preliminary to Chapter 6, and provides another example of the relationships between structure, their reduced forms, and the applicability of LS estimation in cases like those considered in Section 4.6.

the statistical properties of these estimates, including a consideration of the simultaneous nature of the system. Also, consider the economic implications of the model (as they are embodied in the estimated parameters), touching on such questions as whether this model is to be preferred to one under the constraint $\alpha + \beta = 1$, and so on.

ANSWER:

Beginning with the profit function $\Pi = pq - p_L L - p_K K$, with the p's fixed prices, we substitute the production function for q and maximize Π with respect to L and K. This yields the first-order system:

$$\frac{\partial \Pi}{\partial L} = \left(\frac{\alpha}{L}\right) qp - p_L = 0; \qquad \frac{\partial \Pi}{\partial K} = \left(\frac{\beta}{K}\right) qp - p_K = 0.$$

When rewritten and combined with the production function, our structure becomes

$$q = AL^\alpha K^\beta, \qquad \frac{q}{L} = \frac{p_L}{\alpha p}, \qquad \frac{q}{K} = \frac{p_K}{\beta p}.$$

Our unit of observation is the firm; thus "appropriate" stochastic specifications will relate to questions of how firms differ in their ability to achieve an "optimal" configuration of inputs *and* output. Without some stochastic element in the system, *all* firms in the industry would operate at exactly the same (q, K, L) point.

A convenient specification for the way the random terms enter is to use a multiplicative error on each of the equations above, in the spirit of Eq. (5.2.4). This gives the structure

$$q = AL^\alpha K^\beta \epsilon_1, \qquad \frac{q}{L} = \left(\frac{p_L}{\alpha p}\right) \epsilon_2, \qquad \frac{q}{K} = \left(\frac{p_K}{\beta p}\right) \epsilon_3.$$

The "sense" of this stochastic specification is as follows. ϵ_1 is to be regarded as a "technical" disturbance, differentiating firms on the basis of their technical abilities (and luck). ϵ_2 and ϵ_3, on the other hand, represent differences among firms in their ability to attain optimal input levels for any given output level (and luck).

Writing the structure in logarithmic form, we have

$$\log q - \alpha \log L - \beta \log K = \log A + \log \epsilon_1,$$

$$\log q - \log L = \log \left(\frac{p_L}{\alpha p}\right) + \log \epsilon_2,$$

$$\log q - \log K = \log \left(\frac{p_K}{\beta p}\right) + \log \epsilon_3,$$

a linear simultaneous system in three mutually "dependent" variables. Each of *these* random terms is assumed to have mean zero and constant variance [in deference to the problems raised in the error specification of equations such as (5.2.4)]. Also, owing to the simultaneous nature of the system, we will allow the error terms to be mutually correlated across equations while retaining the classical assumptions *within* each equation. Specifically, we assume (for example)

$$E(\log \epsilon_1) = 0, \qquad E(\log \epsilon_{1i} \log \epsilon_{1j}) = \begin{cases} \sigma_1^2, & i = j, \\ 0, & i \neq j, \end{cases}$$

but also

$$E(\log \epsilon_{1i}\epsilon_{2j}) = \begin{cases} \sigma_{12}, & i = j, \\ 0, & i \neq j. \end{cases}$$

The cross-equation assumptions have nothing to do with the main point made below, and are included for completeness only.

Without writing out the actual solution, it should be apparent that the *solution* to this linear system, its reduced form, will show that the input variables are directly related to the disturbance term in the production function. Therefore, LS applied to the (transformed) production function alone can be expected to produce biased estimates (it can also be argued that the bias in the estimates of α and β is positive). The reader should also note the similarity of this reduced form to the reduced form of the simultaneous market-equilibrium model of Section 4.6. In both cases the reduced-form equations have dependent variables each related *only* to a constant term and unobservable stochastic elements (prices are assumed constant *over* firms in perfect competition), a situation indicating the existence of an identification problem.

The implications of $\alpha + \beta = 1$ are twofold. First, if $\alpha + \beta = 1$, then a proportional increase in both the labor and capital inputs produces exactly that proportional increase in output. The production function is linear homogeneous (that is, of degree one) and there are constant returns to scale. Secondly, we find that labor's "share" in the value of output is $p_L L/pq = \alpha$ in this model, and capital's "share" is β, if prices are fixed. Thus, if $\alpha + \beta = 1$, the shares "add up." If $\alpha + \beta \neq 1$, they do not. With cross-section data this result can be interpreted as leaving something (positive, hopefully) for short-run entrepreneurial profit. With time-series data, where firms might be expected to be in long-run equilibrium, the $\alpha + \beta \neq 1$ condition is not so easily disposed of.

Without the $\alpha + \beta = 1$ constraint imposed beforehand, of course, one may use the regression model and its attendant testing methods to test for decreasing or increasing returns to scale by testing $H: \alpha + \beta = 1$ against the appropriate alternative. Usually this test is affected greatly by high collinearity between the L and K series in addition to being biased, as argued above.

One further problem in this model has to do with the homogeneity of the production function and the restriction $\alpha + \beta = 1$. The fact that returns to scale can only be *always* increasing, decreasing, or constant in a homogeneous production function presents the theoretical problem of firms' getting infinitely large or infinitesimally small in the first two instances, and there being no optimal level of output (size) in the latter. The first point should be obvious. The second comes from the observation that to insure a unique solution to the set of equations in $\log q$, $\log L$, and $\log K$ the condition $1 - \alpha - \beta \neq 0$ becomes necessary. If $\alpha + \beta = 1$, no reduced form exists.

With all this said, there are obviously *other* production functions than the exponential Cobb-Douglas form that will not be subject to these *particular* problems (but will present others). But no matter which function is chosen for empirical analysis, there still will be rather substantial difficulties involved in ascertaining just what sort of function is being fit *aside* from the potential identification problem at the firm level. If the data are a cross-section of firms, what is the sense of a conditional mean function for them? Do they in reality share the *same* production function? If considered for aggregate time-series data, what meaning does the aggregate function have? Is it an aggregate of firm or industry production functions, or just some macro construct relating aggregate output and input levels?[†]

There are, of course, other stochastic specifications available. One that is worthy of mention here *justifies* the application of LS techniques on the production function in isolation. It is due to Zellner, Kmenta, and Drèze,[‡] to whose article the reader is referred for details.

[†] For answers to many of these questions for the Cobb-Douglas model, the reader is referred to M. Nerlove, *Estimation and Identification of Cobb-Douglas Production Functions* (Skokie, Ill.: Rand-McNally, 1965).

[‡] "Specification and Estimation of Cobb-Douglas Production Function Models," *Econometrica*, Vol. 33 (October 1966), pp. 784–95.

6 An Introduction to

System Methods

6.1 INTRODUCTION

The main emphasis of the preceding chapters has been on single-equation models and methods for their estimation. But for many applications in economics single-equation methods like least squares will suffer because the true structure of the model is more complicated. In this sense LS might be expected to produce biased estimates owing to a sort of specification bias, but a specification bias different in nature from that discussed in Section 3.9. An introduction to this *simultaneous-equation bias* problem for LS estimation was provided by Section 4.6. Its symptom is the violation of $E(\epsilon x) = 0$ in the single-equation regression model of interest, so in this sense simultaneous-equation bias cannot be differentiated from other complications that give rise to the same symptom, like the autoregressive model. It takes a priori reasoning to conclude that modeling a particular economic phenomenon calls for a system of equations rather than a single one.

As we saw in Section 4.6, least squares need not produce biased estimates of the parameters of a single equation extracted from a system of equations. The "structure" of the structure must be analyzed to tell. Part of the analysis required is to ascertain whether the single equation of interest is *identified* in the structure. If it is not identified, then *no* estimation technique will consistently estimate its parameters. If the equation is identified, then LS techniques can be used effectively to consistently estimate its coefficients. A further relevant case is that of *overidentification*. Here again LS techniques can be applied, but in both situations—identification and overidentification— more complicated procedures than LS on the given equation are generally required. We refer to them as "LS techniques" because the final estimates are built up from LS procedures.

System models that do not have multiple dependent variables appearing in their equations are also of some interest. These systems are characterized by a set of "related regressions"—classical PRM's with related disturbance terms. While LS applied to each such equation gives unbiased estimates, a gain in efficiency of estimation is often obtained by exploiting the related disturbances. This model is known as the *multivariate regression* model, and we consider it first. Then we turn to a more detailed discussion of simultaneous-equation models than was contained in Section 4.6.

6.2 MULTIVARIATE REGRESSION

Any single regression equation might well be viewed as being "related" to various other regression equations that describe similar behavior, but for "different" dependent variables. For instance, a single demand equation is really taken out of context: it "belongs" to a *set* of demand functions, defined over the behavioral unit whose decisions are being observed. In a real sense the observed values of quantities purchased or expenditures on different categories of household consumption goods are related through the optimization of utility. They appear first as the *jointly* dependent variables of the first-order conditions and then are separated in the *reduced form* or *solution* system of demand equations, which relates each such optimal consumption level to the same set of given prices and money income.

With a disturbance term appended and linear in parameters, each equation is a regression equation in a system of regression equations; these equations are related, if only after the fact, because the observed values of their dependent variables were derived from an underlying joint determination. To capture this fact we assume that while no "dependent" variables appear as regressors in any equation, the equation disturbance terms *are* statistically related. Another example of such a system describes profit related to several independent variables for various firms in the same industry. Here the prior simultaneous determination of profit levels is due to the market mechanism. What the assumed intercorrelatedness among equation disturbances says is that one firm's profits depends on some unknown factor influencing the profits of other firms in the industry.

Given that our interest still centers on estimation of the coefficients in *one* such equation, what does the multivariate framework offer that our single-equation method does not?† In general, the answer is: efficiency. To see this, let us write any individual equation, the *m*th, as

(6.2.1) $$\mathbf{y}_m = \mathbf{X}_m\boldsymbol{\beta}_m + \boldsymbol{\epsilon}_m,$$

one of M such equations in a system of regression equations or *multivariate regression system*

(6.2.2)

$$
\begin{bmatrix} \mathbf{y}_1 \\ \cdot \\ \cdot \\ \cdot \\ \mathbf{y}_M \end{bmatrix} = \begin{bmatrix} \mathbf{X}_1 & \mathbf{0} & \cdots & \mathbf{0} \\ \mathbf{0} & \mathbf{X}_2 & & \\ \cdot & & \cdot & \\ \cdot & & & \\ \mathbf{0} & & & \mathbf{X}_M \end{bmatrix} \begin{bmatrix} \boldsymbol{\beta}_1 \\ \cdot \\ \cdot \\ \cdot \\ \boldsymbol{\beta}_M \end{bmatrix} + \begin{bmatrix} \boldsymbol{\epsilon}_1 \\ \cdot \\ \cdot \\ \cdot \\ \boldsymbol{\epsilon}_M \end{bmatrix}
$$

$\quad\quad\quad\quad\quad$ y $\quad\quad\quad\quad\quad$ Z $\quad\quad\quad$ β $\quad\quad$ ε

In (6.2.2), $\mathbf{y}$ is an $(Mn \times 1)$ vector, $\mathbf{Z}$ is the $\left[Mn \times \sum_{m=1}^{M} (k_m + 1) \right]$ block-

† We abstract from an interest in the *system* per se. Obviously if our interest is in the estimation of symmetric cross-price elasticities for a set of demand equations, the *system* will be all-important.

diagonal matrix of observations on independent variables, $\boldsymbol{\beta}$ is the $\left[\sum\limits_{m=1}^{M}(k_m + 1) \times 1\right]$ vector of parameters, and $\boldsymbol{\epsilon}$ is the $(Mn \times 1)$ vector of population disturbances. In its compact form, $\mathbf{y} = \mathbf{Z}\boldsymbol{\beta} + \boldsymbol{\epsilon}$, the system is just one big regression equation. Classical assumptions are made on each of the $\{\boldsymbol{\epsilon}_m\}$, but allowance is made for the equations to exhibit intercorrelation. The variance-covariance matrix of $\boldsymbol{\epsilon}$ is thereby specified to be of the form

(6.2.3)

$$\underset{(Mn \times Mn)}{\boldsymbol{\Sigma}} = E(\boldsymbol{\epsilon}\boldsymbol{\epsilon}') = \begin{bmatrix} \sigma_{11}\mathbf{I} & \sigma_{12}\mathbf{I} & \cdots & \sigma_{1M}\mathbf{I} \\ \sigma_{21}\mathbf{I} & \sigma_{22}\mathbf{I} & & \\ \cdot & & \cdot & \\ \cdot & & & \cdot \\ \cdot & & & \\ \sigma_{M1}\mathbf{I} & & & \sigma_{MM}\mathbf{I} \end{bmatrix},$$

where the identity matrices are each of dimension $(n \times n)$ and $E(\epsilon_{mi}\epsilon_{m'j}) = \sigma_{mm'}$ if $i = j$ and zero otherwise.

If $\boldsymbol{\Sigma}$ is *known*, Aitken's generalized LS will yield BLUE estimators b^* computed as

(6.2.4) $$\mathbf{b}^* = (\mathbf{Z}'\boldsymbol{\Sigma}^{-1}\mathbf{Z})^{-1}\mathbf{Z}'\boldsymbol{\Sigma}^{-1}\mathbf{y}.$$

If there are zero covariances specified between equations, then (6.2.4) reduces to ordinary LS on each equation taken separately, as can readily be verified. Similarly, but not so obviously, (6.2.4) reduces to ordinary LS on each equation also if the $\mathbf{X}_m$ matrices are all identical. The first result is quite intuitive; the second we state without proof. It is that the efficiency feature of the multivariate regression framework is dependent on the sharing of *some* independent variables by the individual equations but not *all* independent variables. No efficiency gains from an application of generalized LS would thus be anticipated for a set of demand equations over households with identical series of prices and money income as the independent variables in every equation.

The implementation of the multivariate regression framework when $\boldsymbol{\Sigma}$ must be *estimated* follows exactly the development of Section 4.2. A consistent estimator for $\boldsymbol{\Sigma}$ is obtained with estimates $\hat{\sigma}_{mm'} = (1/n)[\mathbf{e}_m'\mathbf{e}_{m'}]$ from ordinary LS fits of each equation. The second step forms consistent and asymptotically efficient generalized LS estimators from (6.2.4) with $\hat{\boldsymbol{\Sigma}}^{-1}$ inserted for $\boldsymbol{\Sigma}^{-1}$.†

---

† An iterative procedure can be contemplated, using the second-step residuals for a revised $\hat{\boldsymbol{\Sigma}}$, and so on until the generalized LS estimators cease to change. These "final" estimators have been shown to be maximum-likelihood estimators; they possess asymptotic properties identical to those of the two-step estimators.

Many hypothesis tests may be of interest within this "system" framework. One in particular is the hypothesis of coefficient vector equality $H: \boldsymbol{\beta}_1 = \cdots = \boldsymbol{\beta}_M$. For such a test $X_1, \ldots, X_M$ would be of identical dimensions. While we will not discuss test procedure for the multivariate regression framework, our classical F-test forms its basis.

If equations are *not* related, in the sense $\sigma_{mm'} = 0$, a test of coefficient vector equality can easily be carried out with single-equation methods (recall that in this instance the multivariate generalized LS estimator reduces to ordinary LS on each separate equation). It supposes that equations have identical error variances, and amounts to testing that different samples of observations were drawn from populations that share the same PRF. For example, in a two-equation comparison with $(k + 1)$ independent variables and n_1, n_2 observations on y in two samples, the F-statistic for testing $H: \boldsymbol{\beta}_1 = \boldsymbol{\beta}_2 = \boldsymbol{\beta}$ (vector notation) is

$$(6.2.5) \qquad F = \frac{(\text{SS}_H - \text{SS}_\Omega)/(k + 1)}{\text{SS}_\Omega/[n_1 + n_2 - 2(k + 1)]},$$

where SS_H is the sum of squared residuals computed from a regression $\mathbf{y} = \mathbf{X}\boldsymbol{\beta} + \boldsymbol{\epsilon}$ with the two samples pooled, and SS_Ω is the sum of squared residuals from each separate equation. Equivalently, all observations could be used in estimating a PRF where a $(0, 1)$ dummy variable is specified, taking on the value zero if the observation was drawn from population 1 and one if drawn from population 2. A t-test of the significance of the coefficient on this dummy variable will yield results identical to the F-test using (6.2.5). H would be rejected for F larger than the appropriate critical value chosen from an F-distribution with $(k + 1)$ and $[n_1 + n_2 - 2(k + 1)]$ degrees of freedom. This particular test can be adapted to cover the case where either n_1 or n_2 (but not both) is *less* than $(k + 1)$.† The example test given above extends directly to the case of more than two independent samples.

The multivariate regression model accommodates stochastic independent variables for conditional analysis in exactly the same manner as the single-equation model. Likewise, the special methods available for coping with autoregressive disturbances carry over to the multivariate regression system. Using first-round ordinary LS on each equation to consistently estimate ρ_m for the error process $\epsilon_{mi} = \rho_m \epsilon_{m,i-1} + u_{mi}$ in the mth equation, and the formulas

$$(6.2.6) \qquad \sigma^2_{\epsilon_m} = (1 - \rho^2_m)^{-1}\sigma_{mm},$$

$$\sigma_{\epsilon_m \epsilon_{m'}} = (1 - \rho_m \rho_{m'})\sigma_{mm'},$$

---

† See, for example, J. Johnston, *Econometric Methods* (New York: McGraw-Hill, Inc., 1963), pp. 137–8.

we can consistently estimate Σ, which is of the form

$$
\Sigma = \begin{bmatrix}
\dfrac{\sigma_{11}}{1-\rho_1^2}
\begin{bmatrix}
1 & \rho_1 & \cdots & \rho_1^{n-1}\\
\rho_1 & & & \\
\cdot & & \cdot & \\
\cdot & & & \cdot \\
\cdot & & & \\
\rho_1^{n-1} & & & 1
\end{bmatrix}
&
\dfrac{\sigma_{12}}{1-\rho_1\rho_2}
\begin{bmatrix}
1 & \rho_1 & \cdots & \rho_1^{n-1}\\
\rho_2 & & & \\
\cdot & & \cdot & \\
\cdot & & & \cdot \\
\cdot & & & \\
\rho_2^{n-1} & & & 1
\end{bmatrix}
& \cdots \\
\dfrac{\sigma_{21}}{1-\rho_2\rho_1}
\begin{bmatrix}
1 & \rho_1 & \cdots & \rho_2^{n-1}\\
\rho_1 & & & \\
\cdot & & \cdot & \\
\cdot & & & \cdot \\
\cdot & & & \\
\rho_1^{n-1} & & & 1
\end{bmatrix}
& \cdots & \\
\cdot & &
\end{bmatrix}.
$$

Operationally, each equation is first transformed appropriately by $\hat{\rho}_m$ (recall Section 4.4); the two-step procedure for multivariate regression just considered is then used on the transformed data, first to estimate the $\{\sigma_{mm'}\}$ and finally to generate the promised asymptotically efficient and consistent estimates by generalized LS.

As an example of the potential for gains in efficiency with the multivariate regression framework, we present numerical results for a two-equation model of gross investment abstracted from the article by A. Zellner that established most of the theoretical results so far described.[†] Two firms, General Electric and Westinghouse, are presumed to behave according to the investment function

(6.2.7) $y_m = \beta_{0m} + \beta_{1m}x_{1m} + \beta_{2m}x_{2m} + \epsilon_m, \qquad m = 1, 2,$

where the usual assumptions are imposed on ϵ_m. y_m is current gross investment for firm m, x_{1m} is beginning-of-the-year capital stock, and x_{2m} is the value of the firm's outstanding shares at the beginning of the year. The observation subscript has been suppressed in (6.2.7); twenty annual observations are available for each firm (1935–54).

Following the notation of (6.2.2), we present the relevant sums-of-squares and cross-products:

(6.2.8) $\begin{bmatrix} \mathbf{y}_1'\mathbf{y}_1 \\ \mathbf{y}_1'\mathbf{y}_2 \\ \mathbf{y}_2'\mathbf{y}_2 \end{bmatrix} = \begin{bmatrix} 254{,}113.50 \\ 103{,}869.607 \\ 43{,}732.4023 \end{bmatrix},$

† "An Efficient Method of Estimating Seemingly Unrelated Regressions and Tests for Aggregation Bias," *J. Am. Stat. Assn.*, Vol. 57 (June 1962), pp. 348–68.

$$\begin{bmatrix} \mathbf{y}_1'\mathbf{X}_1 \\ \mathbf{y}_1'\mathbf{X}_2 \\ \mathbf{y}_2'\mathbf{X}_1 \\ \mathbf{y}_2'\mathbf{X}_2 \end{bmatrix} = \begin{bmatrix} 2045.8 & 1{,}005{,}863.46 & 4{,}093{,}308.29 \\ 2045.8 & 221{,}467.99 & 1{,}531{,}586.94 \\ 857.83 & 413{,}156.104 & 1{,}719{,}503.680 \\ 857.83 & 90{,}592.412 & 643{,}262.570 \end{bmatrix},$$

$$\mathbf{X}_1'\mathbf{X}_1 = \begin{bmatrix} 20 & 8003.2 & 38{,}826.5 \\ & 4{,}395{,}946.84 & 15{,}769{,}824.07 \\ & & 78{,}628{,}914.21 \end{bmatrix},$$

$$\mathbf{X}_1'\mathbf{X}_2 = \begin{bmatrix} 20 & 8003.2 & 38{,}826.5 \\ 1712.8 & 974{,}281.31 & 6{,}153{,}588.29 \\ 13{,}418.2 & 3{,}369{,}944.27 & 27{,}247{,}303.72 \end{bmatrix},$$

$$\mathbf{X}_2'\mathbf{X}_2 = \begin{bmatrix} 20 & 1712.8 & 13{,}418.2 \\ & 220{,}345.72 & 1{,}344{,}261.18 \\ & & 9{,}942{,}109.78 \end{bmatrix}.$$

In the case of symmetric matrices ($\mathbf{X}_1'\mathbf{X}_1$ and $\mathbf{X}_2'\mathbf{X}_2$) just the upper parts are given.

Single-equation least-squares results are calculated from the familiar formulas $\mathbf{b}_1 = (\mathbf{X}_1'\mathbf{X}_1)^{-1}\mathbf{X}_1'\mathbf{y}_1$ and $\mathbf{b}_2 = (\mathbf{X}_2'\mathbf{X}_2)^{-1}\mathbf{X}_2'\mathbf{y}_2$, giving

(6.2.9)
$$\mathbf{b}_1 = \begin{bmatrix} -9.9563 \\ .1517 \\ .0266 \end{bmatrix}, \qquad \mathbf{b}_2 = \begin{bmatrix} -.5094 \\ .0924 \\ .0529 \end{bmatrix}.$$

Step two in the computational procedure requires that these coefficient estimates be used to get vectors of calculated residuals for each equation, from which are estimated $\hat{\sigma}_{11}$, $\hat{\sigma}_{12}$, and $\hat{\sigma}_{22}$. These intermediate results need not be computed. For, writing

(6.2.10)
$$[\mathbf{y}_1 \mathbf{y}_2] = [\mathbf{X}_1 \mathbf{X}_2]\begin{bmatrix} \mathbf{b}_1 & 0 \\ 0 & \mathbf{b}_2 \end{bmatrix} + [\mathbf{e}_1 \mathbf{e}_2],$$

or $\mathbf{Y} = \mathbf{XB} + \mathbf{E}$, we find

(6.2.11) $\mathbf{E}'\mathbf{E} = (\mathbf{Y} - \mathbf{XB})'(\mathbf{Y} - \mathbf{XB}) = \mathbf{Y}'\mathbf{Y} - \mathbf{B}'\mathbf{X}'\mathbf{XB}$

$$= \begin{bmatrix} \mathbf{y}_1'\mathbf{y}_1 & \mathbf{y}_1'\mathbf{y}_2 \\ \mathbf{y}_2'\mathbf{y}_1 & \mathbf{y}_2'\mathbf{y}_2 \end{bmatrix} - \begin{bmatrix} \mathbf{b}_1\mathbf{X}_1'\mathbf{X}_1\mathbf{b}_1 & \mathbf{b}_1\mathbf{X}_1'\mathbf{X}_2\mathbf{b}_2 \\ \mathbf{b}_2\mathbf{X}_2'\mathbf{X}_1\mathbf{b}_1 & \mathbf{b}_2\mathbf{X}_2'\mathbf{X}_2\mathbf{b}_2 \end{bmatrix}$$

$$= \begin{bmatrix} 13{,}216.5899 & 3988.0118 \\ 3988.0118 & 1821.2808 \end{bmatrix}.$$

In the text we spoke of consistently estimating $\sigma_{mm'}$ by $(1/n)[\mathbf{e}_m'\mathbf{e}_{m'}]$, mainly to eliminate any confusion when different numbers of independent variables appear in the equations. Since in this instance the two equations are identical in this respect, we shall divide by degrees of freedom instead. Thus, (6.2.11) is equal to $(20 - 3)[\hat{\sigma}_{mm'}]$.

As can readily be verified from (6.2.3),

(6.2.12)
$$\Sigma^{-1} = \begin{bmatrix} \sigma^{11}\mathbf{I} & \cdots & \sigma^{1M}\mathbf{I} \\ \cdot & & \cdot \\ \cdot & & \cdot \\ \cdot & & \cdot \\ \sigma^{M1}\mathbf{I} & \cdots & \sigma^{MM}\mathbf{I} \end{bmatrix},$$

where the $\{\sigma^{mm'}\}$ are inverse elements for the $M \times M$ matrix $[\sigma_{mm'}]$. This fact represents a substantial saving in computational effort. It allows us to *construct* $\hat{\Sigma}^{-1}$ by inverting the $M \times M$ matrix $[\hat{\sigma}_{mm'}]$ rather than directly inverting $\hat{\Sigma}$, an $Mn \times Mn$ matrix. For this example it means inverting a 2×2 matrix as opposed to a 40×40.

We find for $[\hat{\sigma}_{mm'}]^{-1}$:

(6.2.13)
$$(17)^{-1}[\hat{\sigma}_{mm'}]^{-1} = \begin{bmatrix} .000223009584 & -.000488319216 \\ -.000488319216 & .00161832608 \end{bmatrix}.$$

From the structure of $\mathbf{Z}$,

(6.2.14)
$$\mathbf{Z}'\Sigma^{-1}\mathbf{Z} = \begin{bmatrix} \sigma^{11}\mathbf{X}_1'\mathbf{X}_1 & \cdots & \sigma^{1M}\mathbf{X}_1'\mathbf{X}_M \\ \cdot & & \cdot \\ \cdot & & \cdot \\ \cdot & & \cdot \\ \sigma^{M1}\mathbf{X}_M'\mathbf{X}_1 & \cdots & \sigma^{MM}\mathbf{X}_M'\mathbf{X}_M \end{bmatrix},$$

so that the first part of the Aitken generalized LS estimator based on our *estimate* of Σ is found by inverting

$$\mathbf{Z}'\hat{\Sigma}^{-1}\mathbf{Z} = \begin{bmatrix} \hat{\sigma}^{11}\mathbf{X}_1'\mathbf{X}_1 & \hat{\sigma}^{12}\mathbf{X}_1'\mathbf{X}_2 \\ \hat{\sigma}^{21}\mathbf{X}_2'\mathbf{X}_1 & \hat{\sigma}^{22}\mathbf{X}_2'\mathbf{X}_2 \end{bmatrix},$$

where $\hat{\sigma}^{21} = \hat{\sigma}^{12}$. Of course, this inverse matrix is also the matrix of estimated variances and covariance of the generalized LS estimators,

(6.2.15) $(\mathbf{Z}'\hat{\Sigma}^{-1}\mathbf{Z})^{-1} =$

$$\begin{bmatrix} 789.6028 & -.1704 & -.3516 & 155.8156 & .4573140 & -.2731373 \\ & .0006006 & -.0000360 & -.0515761 & .0007562 & -.0000197 \\ & & .0001885 & -.0635894 & -.0003914 & .0001447 \\ & & & 54.2149 & .1177480 & -.0878539 \\ & & & & .0026914 & -.0005191 \\ & & & & & .0001972 \end{bmatrix}.$$

The remaining matrix required is

(6.2.16)

$$\mathbf{Z}'\hat{\boldsymbol{\Sigma}}^{-1}\mathbf{y} = \begin{bmatrix} \hat{\sigma}^{11}\mathbf{X}_1'\mathbf{y}_1 + \hat{\sigma}^{12}\mathbf{X}_1'\mathbf{y}_2 \\ \hat{\sigma}^{21}\mathbf{X}_2'\mathbf{y}_1 + \hat{\sigma}^{22}\mathbf{X}_2'\mathbf{y}_2 \end{bmatrix} = (17) \begin{bmatrix} 0.037338 \\ 22.565127 \\ 73.180290 \\ 0.38925 \\ 38.460988 \\ 293.105260 \end{bmatrix},$$

which when used in the computation indicated in (6.2.4) gives the comparative results reported in Table 6.1. The *apparent* gain in efficiency (these are still estimates, after all) is substantial. The reduction in estimated variance in the estimator for β_{12}, for example, is 22 percent.

Table 6.1

Comparative Results of Single-Equation LS
and the Two-Stage Aitken Estimator

Firm	Coefficient	SINGLE-EQUATION LS		TWO-STAGE GENERALIZED LS	
		Estimate	Estimated Variance	Estimate	Estimated Variance
G.E.	β_{10}	−9.9563	984.1	−32.4807	789.6
	β_{11}	.1517	.0006605	.1326	.0006006
	β_{12}	.0266	.0002423	.0421	.0001885
Westinghouse	β_{20}	−.5094	64.24	−2.0113	54.21
	β_{21}	.0924	.003147	.0459	.002691
	β_{22}	.0529	.0002468	.0611	.0001972

6.3 INTERDEPENDENT LINEAR SYSTEMS

A linear multivariate regression system viewed as the *reduced form* of some *structural* system of equations that links $\mathbf{y}_1, \ldots, \mathbf{y}_M$ can obviously be used quite adequately to *predict* $\mathbf{y}_1, \ldots, \mathbf{y}_M$ for any given $\mathbf{Z}$. But if the investigator is interested in attributes of the structure itself, the reduced-form system may not provide enough information to allow deducing structural coefficients from estimated reduced-form coefficients. As we discussed it earlier, the notion of an incomplete backward linkage between reduced form and structure is the identification problem in econometrics.

A linear reduced-form system is companion to a linear structural system. The word "linear" refers now to how both the parameters *and* the variables enter. Structural systems in which nonlinear variables appear are more difficult to deal with, and systems with nonlinearities in how the parameters enter can be treated only in terms of linear systems that "approximate" them. We will limit ourselves here to linear systems.

Following standard notation, at an observation point t the linear structural system appears as

(6.3.1) $$\mathbf{BY}_t + \mathbf{\Gamma Z}_t = \mathbf{U}_t,$$

where $\mathbf{B}$ is an $(M \times M)$ nonsingular matrix of unknown coefficients on the M jointly dependent or *endogenous* variables in $\mathbf{Y}_t (M \times 1)$. Likewise, $\mathbf{\Gamma}$ is an $(M \times K)$ matrix of unknown coefficients on variables $\mathbf{Z}_t (K \times 1)$. The variables in $\mathbf{Z}_t$ may be either fixed variates or random variables and may consist of variables truly *exogenous* to the system and/or lagged values of the dependent variables, referred to as *predetermined* variables. As in the regression case, if only fixed variates appear in $\mathbf{Z}_t$, the analysis is on the unconditional distribution of $\mathbf{Y}_t$; otherwise we will be working with $\mathbf{Y}_t$ conditional on $\mathbf{Z}_t$. Alluding to our example system (4.6.2), with (4.6.11) as the supply equation, we have, for example,

$$\begin{array}{cc} \mathbf{B} \\ (2 \times 2) \end{array} = \begin{bmatrix} 1 & -\beta \\ 1 & -\delta \end{bmatrix}, \qquad \begin{array}{cc} \mathbf{Y}_t \\ (2 \times 1) \end{array} = \begin{bmatrix} q_t^e \\ p_t \end{bmatrix},$$

$$\begin{array}{cc} \mathbf{\Gamma} \\ (2 \times 2) \end{array} = \begin{bmatrix} -\alpha & 0 \\ -\gamma & -\theta \end{bmatrix}, \qquad \begin{array}{cc} \mathbf{Z}_t \\ (2 \times 1) \end{array} = \begin{bmatrix} 1 \\ r_t \end{bmatrix}, \qquad \mathbf{U}_t = \begin{bmatrix} u_t \\ v_t \end{bmatrix}.$$

$\mathbf{U}_t$ is the random disturbance vector of dimension $(M \times 1)$, which at the outset will be assumed to possess a multivariate normal distribution with zero mean vector and variance-covariance matrix $\mathbf{\Sigma}$. We need the multivariate distribution assumption in order to fully discuss the identification problem. It is different from the joint distribution that describes the density for some sample point as it might be established by the assumption of random sampling, where each sample random variable has an independent normal distribution. In that situation the joint or multivariate density is just the product of individual densities, whereas allowing $\mathbf{\Sigma}$ to be non-diagonal implies cross-correlation between equations. The density functions for $\mathbf{U}_t$ and $\mathbf{Y}_t$ in this latter case are slightly more complicated.

Given the density function for $\mathbf{U}_t$, a density for $\mathbf{Y}_t$ can easily be derived. For, multiplying (6.3.1) through by $\mathbf{B}^{-1}$ and transposing terms,

(6.3.2) $$\mathbf{Y}_t = -\mathbf{B}^{-1}\mathbf{\Gamma Z}_t + \mathbf{B}^{-1}\mathbf{U}_t$$
$$= \mathbf{\Pi Z}_t + \mathbf{V}_t,$$

which is a multivariate regression model written at the single observation point t, with $E(\mathbf{Y}_t) = -\mathbf{B}^{-1}\mathbf{\Gamma}\mathbf{Z}_t$ [because $E(\mathbf{V}_t) = 0$] and variance-covariance matrix $\mathbf{\Lambda} = (\mathbf{B}^{-1})\mathbf{\Sigma}(\mathbf{B}^{-1})'$. It is also the reduced form of (6.3.1).

For our particular illustrative system,

$$\mathbf{B}^{-1} = \frac{1}{\beta - \delta}\begin{bmatrix} -\delta & \beta \\ -1 & 1 \end{bmatrix};$$

hence,

$$\mathbf{\Pi} = -\mathbf{B}^{-1}\mathbf{\Gamma} = \frac{-1}{\beta - \delta}\begin{bmatrix} (\delta\alpha - \gamma\beta) & -\beta\theta \\ (\alpha - \gamma) & -\theta \end{bmatrix}.$$

Since $\mathbf{U}_t$ has a multivariate normal distribution and $\mathbf{Y}_t$ is a linear transformation of $\mathbf{U}_t$, $\mathbf{Y}_t$ also has the multivariate normal distribution. This result, which we do not prove, is an extension of Theorem 1, Section 2.5. With random sampling now assumed over the observation points $t = 1, \ldots, T$, these individual densities are multiplied together to get the density function for the sample $(\mathbf{Y}_1, \ldots, \mathbf{Y}_T)$, which forms the basis for maximum-likelihood estimation of $\mathbf{B}$ and $\mathbf{\Gamma}$ or $\mathbf{\Pi}$.

By way of introduction to the estimation problems posed by either (6.3.1) or (6.3.2), for the reduced-form system maximum likelihood and generalized LS correspond, since they share the same criterion function,

$$\sum_{t=1}^{T} (\mathbf{Y}_t - \mathbf{\Pi}\mathbf{Z}_t)'\mathbf{\Lambda}^{-1}(\mathbf{Y}_t - \mathbf{\Pi}\mathbf{Z}_t),$$

assuming $\mathbf{\Lambda}$ is known. We already *know* that there is enough information in the sample to consistently estimate $\mathbf{\Lambda}$ and $\mathbf{\Pi}$. With $\mathbf{\Lambda}$ estimated, however, generalized LS applied to (6.3.2) is *not* equivalent to ML estimation.

For the structural system as well, the two methods do not correspond. The maximum-likelihood method applied to $f(\mathbf{Y}_1, \ldots, \mathbf{Y}_T)$ written in terms of $\mathbf{B}$ and $\mathbf{\Gamma}$ is called *full-information maximum-likelihood* (FIML), and is computationally quite difficult, but promises estimators with desirable asymptotic properties. The least-squares method applied to the structure will generally produce biased and inconsistent estimates because the equations contain jointly dependent variables as "independent" variables, which will be correlated with the equation disturbance terms. A consistent "variant" of least-squares methods, called *two-stage least squares*, will receive primary attention in our treatment here.

What guarantees that FIML or any other method *will* be able to generate estimators with desirable properties for $\mathbf{B}$, $\mathbf{\Gamma}$, and $\mathbf{\Sigma}$? This is the essential question of identification, whether the distribution of endogenous variables given the exogenous variables and the distributional form of the sample can be shown to be *uniquely* generated by a structure. If so, the structure is identified. Put another way, a structure is not identified if there exists another structure within the class of linear structures being considered that—given the form of the sample density function—can produce the same sample.

To establish general conditions that guarantee identification if met is not easy even for the linear system. Particularly subtle are the identification relationships on Σ, as we saw in the errors-in-variables model. But insofar as identification of coefficients is concerned, some basic identification conditions can be derived. If it is possible to go backwards from reduced-form coefficients, which *are* identified, to structural coefficients, clearly that is sufficient to guarantee identification for the structural coefficients $\mathbf{B}, \mathbf{\Gamma}$. But generally it will not be possible to do so. Under what conditions will it be possible? The answer is, when there are enough side conditions or linear restrictions on the matrices $\mathbf{B}$ and $\mathbf{\Gamma}$. For example, if every equation contained *all* endogenous, exogenous, and predetermined variables specified in the system, we could not possibly identify the coefficients in any particular equation—for econometrically all equations would be the same. If some variables that do not appear in one equation *do* appear in others, *its* coefficients may be identified. These "zero restrictions" on coefficients are the easiest to discuss, although much more general restrictions may appear in the system and aid in identification, such as identitites between variables (national income equals total consumption plus savings plus government expenditures in a Keynesian macromodel, for instance).

For a structural system to be identified, each equation in it must be identified. So for purposes of exposition let us consider the identification problem for the coefficients of one of the M equations. Of the M endogenous variables that appear in the system, let M_Δ of them appear in the equation of interest. Then $M_{\Delta\Delta} = M - M_\Delta$ do not appear in this equation. Similarly, of the total of K exogeneous and predetermined variables let K_* appear in the equation. $K_{**} = K - K_*$ therefore are excluded from this equation but appear elsewhere in the system. In terms of this equation, we partition the reduced form according to the endogenous variables that appear in it, $\mathbf{Y}_{\Delta t}$, and its exogenous and predetermined variables $\mathbf{Z}_{*t}$,

$$(6.3.3) \qquad \begin{pmatrix} \mathbf{Y}_\Delta \\ \hline \mathbf{Y}_{\Delta\Delta} \end{pmatrix}_t = \begin{pmatrix} \mathbf{\Pi}_{\Delta *} & \vdots & \mathbf{\Pi}_{\Delta **} \\ \hline \mathbf{\Pi}_{\Delta\Delta *} & \vdots & \mathbf{\Pi}_{\Delta\Delta **} \end{pmatrix} \begin{pmatrix} \mathbf{Z}_* \\ \hline \mathbf{Z}_{**} \end{pmatrix}_t + \begin{pmatrix} \mathbf{V}_\Delta \\ \hline \mathbf{V}_{\Delta\Delta} \end{pmatrix}_t,$$

with obvious dimensional equivalences to M_Δ, $M_{\Delta\Delta}$, K_*, and K_{**}.

Now from the reduced form, $\mathbf{\Pi} = -\mathbf{B}^{-1}\mathbf{\Gamma}$ and $\mathbf{B}\mathbf{\Pi} = -\mathbf{\Gamma}$. Suppose we let our particular equation be the first equation of the system, and let the first row of $\mathbf{B}$ be $[\boldsymbol{\beta}_\Delta | \boldsymbol{\beta}_{\Delta\Delta}]$ with the first row of $\mathbf{\Gamma}$ written $[\boldsymbol{\gamma}_* | \boldsymbol{\gamma}_{**}]$. The first relation in $\mathbf{B}\mathbf{\Pi} = -\mathbf{\Gamma}$—for our equation—is

$$(6.3.4) \qquad [\boldsymbol{\beta}_\Delta | \boldsymbol{\beta}_{\Delta\Delta}] \begin{pmatrix} \mathbf{\Pi}_{\Delta *} & \vdots & \mathbf{\Pi}_{\Delta **} \\ \hline \mathbf{\Pi}_{\Delta\Delta *} & \vdots & \mathbf{\Pi}_{\Delta\Delta **} \end{pmatrix} = -[\boldsymbol{\gamma}_* | \boldsymbol{\gamma}_{**}].$$

As can readily be verified, the rules for matrix multiplication generalize to the case of partitioned matrices. So (6.3.4) contains two equations,

(6.3.5)
$$\boldsymbol{\beta}_\Delta \boldsymbol{\Pi}_{\Delta *} + \boldsymbol{\beta}_{\Delta\Delta} \boldsymbol{\Pi}_{\Delta\Delta *} = -\boldsymbol{\gamma}_*,$$
$$\boldsymbol{\beta}_\Delta \boldsymbol{\Pi}_{\Delta **} + \boldsymbol{\beta}_{\Delta\Delta} \boldsymbol{\Pi}_{\Delta\Delta **} = -\boldsymbol{\gamma}_{**}.$$

According to our original specifications both $\boldsymbol{\beta}_{\Delta\Delta}$ and $\boldsymbol{\gamma}_{**}$ are vectors of zeros. Therefore,

(6.3.6)
$$\boldsymbol{\beta}_\Delta \boldsymbol{\Pi}_{\Delta *} = -\boldsymbol{\gamma}_*, \qquad \boldsymbol{\beta}_\Delta \boldsymbol{\Pi}_{\Delta **} = 0$$

are the relations that tie the reduced coefficients and the structural coefficients together. If $\boldsymbol{\beta}_\Delta$ can be established from $\boldsymbol{\beta}_\Delta \boldsymbol{\Pi}_{\Delta **} = 0$, it then can be used to calculate $\boldsymbol{\gamma}_*$ in the other equation.

For there to be a unique nontrivial solution to the homogeneous equations $\boldsymbol{\beta}_\Delta \boldsymbol{\Pi}_{\Delta **} = 0$, the rank of $\boldsymbol{\Pi}_{\Delta **}$ must be exactly $M_\Delta - 1$. Of course, $\boldsymbol{\Pi}_{\Delta **}$ need not be square, in which event an additional necessary condition obtains, $K_{**} \geq M_\Delta - 1$. This latter condition is usually referred to as the *order* condition for identifiability: the number of exogenous and predetermined variables *excluded* from the equation must at least be as great as the number of endogenous variables *included* minus one. Adding K_* to both sides of the order condition, $K \geq M_\Delta + K_* - 1$; the total number of exogenous and predetermined variables in the system must exceed the *total* number of variables in the equation minus one. If $K_{**} = M_\Delta - 1$, the rank of $\boldsymbol{\Pi}_{\Delta **}$ can at most be $M_\Delta - 1$. The rank condition is both necessary and sufficient for identification, while the order condition is only necessary, but in the case $K_{**} = M_\Delta - 1$ we would *expect* unique solutions to $\boldsymbol{\beta}_\Delta \boldsymbol{\Pi}_{\Delta **} = 0$ and hence identification.[†] If $K_{**} < M_\Delta - 1$, there can be no solutions to $\boldsymbol{\beta}_\Delta \boldsymbol{\Pi}_{\Delta **} = 0$, the case of *underidentification*. If $K_{**} > M_\Delta - 1$ and the rank of $\boldsymbol{\Pi}_{\Delta **} = M_\Delta$, only a trivial solution to $\boldsymbol{\beta}_\Delta \boldsymbol{\Pi}_{\Delta **} = 0$ exists: that is, $\boldsymbol{\beta}_\Delta = 0$. This is usually referred to as the case of *overidentification*, because innumerable solutions can be obtained by discarding as many columns of $\boldsymbol{\Pi}_{\Delta **}$ as are necessary to force the rank of $\boldsymbol{\Pi}_{\Delta **}$ to be $M_\Delta - 1$. Obviously the choice of columns to be discarded will affect the solution of $\boldsymbol{\beta}_\Delta \boldsymbol{\Pi}_{\Delta **} = 0$.

To illustrate the use of the order condition, we refer to the illustrative systems of Section 4.6. In (4.6.2), for *both* the demand and supply equations $K_{**} = 0$, while $M_\Delta - 1 = 1$. Hence, *both* equations are *underidentified*. When (4.6.11) is the supply equation, *it* is underidentified (again, $K_{**} = 0$

---

† Note that only the *ratios* of coefficients can be uniquely determined in a system of homogeneous linear equations. But since we have treated the "dependent" variable in the equation along with the other jointly determined variables appearing in it, we need only divide by the coefficient on the dependent variable to get things in the usual form.

and $M_\Delta - 1 = 1$), while the demand equation is *identified* since $K_{**} = 1$ and $M_\Delta - 1 = 1$. In the last example, the supply equation (4.6.13) remains underidentified, while the demand equation is *overidentified* ($K_{**} = 2$; $M_\Delta - 1 = 1$).

The case of overidentification is the point of departure for discussing the different estimation schemes proposed for interdependent linear systems. For when an equation is just-identified, identical parameter estimates are obtained from virtually all the methods designed for single-equation estimation. When it is overidentified, the methods generally will result in different estimates, owing to the fact that each has implicit in it a separate scheme for choosing among the multitude of estimates possible by discarding columns of $\Pi_{\Delta**}$. When the equation is underidentified, generally no method can produce consistent estimators save the method of instrumental variables, whose proper implementation is almost impossible as a practical matter, and even if possible amounts to specifying additional equations that *will* identify the equation in question, as we saw in Section 4.7.

The main single-equation methods for estimating the coefficients of an equation extracted from a system such as (6.3.1) are (i) indirect LS, meaning least squares applied to the equations of the reduced form, with structural coefficients coming from the solutions to (6.3.6); (ii) instrumental variables; (iii) two-stage least-squares; and (iv) limited-information maximum-likelihood. These latter two techniques are consistent, belonging to the so-called "k-class" of estimators. Neither is in general asymptotically efficient, there being FIML and *three-stage least-squares* techniques that exploit more fully the relationship between the particular equation in question and the other equations in the system. Small-sample properties of all these techniques are known almost entirely from simulation experiments.

Of the single-equation methods we shall concentrate on two-stage least squares (abbreviated 2SLS), which has been shown to be quite robust in a variety of applications. The 2SLS estimator itself is quite simple, and may be computed (as its name suggests) by two successive applications of ordinary least-squares methods. An intuitive development of the 2SLS estimator is as follows.

Consider estimating by least squares the reduced form (6.3.2) written out for the sample of T observations. Instead of $\mathbf{Y}_t$ ($M \times 1$), we shall reorganize things slightly to correspond to our past regression notation, with one of the jointly dependent variables treated as "the" dependent variable for the equation of interest, say $\mathbf{y}$ ($T \times 1$), with the remaining endogenous variables appearing in the equation written $\mathbf{Y}_{(\Delta-1)}$ a matrix of dimension $T \times (M_\Delta - 1)$. Likewise, $\boldsymbol{\beta}_{(\Delta-1)}$ will stand for the $[(M_\Delta - 1) \times 1]$ vector of coefficients on the $\mathbf{Y}_{(\Delta-1)}$ variables, with $\boldsymbol{\gamma}_*$ the ($K_* \times 1$) coefficient vector for $\mathbf{Z}_*$, the ($T \times K_*$) matrix of observations on the exogenous and predetermined variables appearing in the equation. The single, identified *or* overidentified equation of interest is, in this notation,

$$(6.3.7) \qquad \mathbf{y} = \mathbf{Y}_{(\Delta-1)}\boldsymbol{\beta}_{(\Delta-1)} + \mathbf{Z}_*\boldsymbol{\gamma}_* + \mathbf{u},$$

with $\mathbf{u}$ the $(T \times 1)$ population residual vector for the equation.

Now, from the reduced form, least squares applied equation by equation results in a set of fitted regression equations for the $\mathbf{Y}_{(\Delta-1)}$ variables,

$$(6.3.8) \qquad \mathbf{Y}_{(\Delta-1)} = \mathbf{Z}[(\mathbf{Z}'\mathbf{Z})^{-1}\mathbf{Z}'\mathbf{Y}_{(\Delta-1)}] + \hat{\mathbf{V}}_{(\Delta-1)},$$

where $\hat{\boldsymbol{\Pi}}_{(\Delta-1)} = (\mathbf{Z}'\mathbf{Z})^{-1}\mathbf{Z}'\mathbf{Y}_{(\Delta-1)}$, $\mathbf{Z}$ is the entire $(T \times K)$ matrix of exogenous and predetermined variables appearing in the system, and $\hat{\mathbf{V}}_{(\Delta-1)}$ is the $[T \times (M_\Delta - 1)]$ matrix of calculated residuals. In (6.3.8) also the notation has been slightly altered from (6.3.2), the original statement of the population reduced form for a single observation point.†

Suppose we add and subtract $\hat{\mathbf{V}}_{(\Delta-1)}\boldsymbol{\beta}_{(\Delta-1)}$ in (6.3.7), which yields

$$(6.3.9) \qquad \begin{aligned} \mathbf{y} &= \mathbf{Y}_{(\Delta-1)}\boldsymbol{\beta}_{(\Delta-1)} - \hat{\mathbf{V}}_{(\Delta-1)}\boldsymbol{\beta}_{(\Delta-1)} + \mathbf{Z}_*\boldsymbol{\gamma}_* + \mathbf{u} + \hat{\mathbf{V}}_{(\Delta-1)}\boldsymbol{\beta}_{(\Delta-1)} \\ &= (\mathbf{Y}_{(\Delta-1)} - \hat{\mathbf{V}}_{(\Delta-1)})\boldsymbol{\beta}_{(\Delta-1)} + \mathbf{Z}_*\boldsymbol{\gamma}_* + (\mathbf{u} + \hat{\mathbf{V}}_{(\Delta-1)}\boldsymbol{\beta}_{(\Delta-1)}), \end{aligned}$$

and consider applying least squares again to this equation. The rationale for this suggestion is that if we *knew* the population residuals $\mathbf{V}_{(\Delta-1)}$ and used least squares on the equation

$$(6.3.10) \qquad \mathbf{y} = [\mathbf{Y}_{(\Delta-1)} - \mathbf{V}_{(\Delta-1)}]\boldsymbol{\beta}_{(\Delta-1)} + \mathbf{Z}_*\boldsymbol{\gamma}_* + (\mathbf{u} + \mathbf{V}_{(\Delta-1)}\boldsymbol{\beta}_{(\Delta-1)}),$$

we would get unbiasede stimators for $\boldsymbol{\beta}_{(\Delta-1)}$ and $\boldsymbol{\gamma}_*$, because $[\mathbf{Y}_{(\Delta-1)} - \mathbf{V}_{(\Delta-1)}]$ is an *exact* linear function of $\mathbf{Z}$; $[\mathbf{Y}_{(\Delta-1)} - \mathbf{V}_{(\Delta-1)}] = \mathbf{Z}\boldsymbol{\Pi}_{(\Delta-1)}$. Since the reduced form meets multivariate regression specifications, the ordinary least-squares estimate of $\boldsymbol{\Pi}_{(\Delta-1)}$ is conditionally unbiased, and so then $\hat{\mathbf{V}}_{(\Delta-1)} = \mathbf{Y}_{(\Delta-1)} - \mathbf{Z}\hat{\boldsymbol{\Pi}}_{(\Delta-1)}$ in the sense that $E(\hat{\mathbf{V}}_{(\Delta-1)} - \mathbf{V}_{(\Delta-1)}) = 0.‡$ $\hat{\boldsymbol{\Pi}}_{(\Delta-1)}$ is not efficient so long as there is correlation among residuals across reduced-form equations. Nonetheless, using the *predicted* values for $\mathbf{Y}_{(\Delta-1)}$ in (6.3.9)— that is,

$$(\mathbf{Y}_{(\Delta-1)} - \hat{\mathbf{V}}_{(\Delta-1)}) = \hat{\mathbf{Y}}_{(\Delta-1)} = \mathbf{Z}[(\mathbf{Z}'\mathbf{Z})^{-1}\mathbf{Z}'\mathbf{Y}_{(\Delta-1)}]$$

from (6.3.8), ordinary least squares can be expected to produce at least asymptotically unbiased estimators for $\boldsymbol{\beta}_{(\Delta-1)}$ and $\boldsymbol{\gamma}_*$. It turns out that they

† Here the population reduced form is $\mathbf{Y} = \mathbf{Z}\boldsymbol{\Pi} + \mathbf{V}$ rather than $\mathbf{Y} = \boldsymbol{\Pi}\mathbf{Z} + \mathbf{V}$ as in (6.3.2), with appropriate modifications on the dimensions of $\mathbf{Y}$, $\mathbf{Z}$, $\boldsymbol{\Pi}$, and $\mathbf{V}$ as originally stated.

‡ Recall our previous remark on an "extended" definition of unbiasedness in the footnote on p. 124.

are also consistent, having variance-covariance matrix

$$(6.3.11) \quad \Sigma_{\binom{\beta_{(\Delta-1)}}{\gamma_*}} = \sigma_u^2 \begin{bmatrix} (\mathbf{Y}'_{(\Delta-1)} & \mathbf{Y}_{(\Delta-1)} & -\mathbf{V}'_{(\Delta-1)} & \mathbf{V}_{(\Delta-1)}) & \mathbf{Y}'_{(\Delta-1)}\mathbf{Z}_* \\ \mathbf{Z}'_*\mathbf{Y}_{(\Delta-1)} & & & \mathbf{Z}'_*\mathbf{Z}_* \end{bmatrix}^{-1}.$$

$\Sigma_{\binom{\beta_{(\Delta-1)}}{\gamma_*}}$ can be estimated using $\hat{\mathbf{V}}_{(\Delta-1)}$ for $\mathbf{V}_{(\Delta-1)}$ and the usual estimator for σ_u^2 formed from the fitted equation disturbances.

That 2SLS estimators are generally consistent can be argued formally by noting that 2SLS is, in effect, an application of the instrumental-variables technique, for which consistency was previously established. The "instruments" used are the members of $\hat{\mathbf{Y}}_{(\Delta-1)}$ for $\mathbf{Y}_{(\Delta-1)}$ and $\mathbf{Z}_*$ for itself. That is, we will show that the instrumental-variables estimator [recall (4.5.15)] for $[\boldsymbol{\beta}_{(\Delta-1)} \ \boldsymbol{\gamma}_*]'$ given by

$$(6.3.12) \quad \begin{bmatrix} \tilde{\boldsymbol{\beta}}_{(\Delta-1)} \\ \tilde{\boldsymbol{\gamma}}_* \end{bmatrix} = \left(\begin{bmatrix} \hat{\mathbf{Y}}'_{(\Delta-1)} \\ \mathbf{Z}'_* \end{bmatrix} [\mathbf{Y}_{(\Delta-1)} \ \mathbf{Z}_*] \right)^{-1} \begin{bmatrix} \hat{\mathbf{Y}}'_{(\Delta-1)} \\ \mathbf{Z}'_* \end{bmatrix} \mathbf{y}$$

is identical to the 2SLS estimator,

$$(6.3.13) \quad \begin{bmatrix} \hat{\boldsymbol{\beta}}_{(\Delta-1)} \\ \hat{\boldsymbol{\gamma}}_* \end{bmatrix} = \left(\begin{bmatrix} \hat{\mathbf{Y}}'_{(\Delta-1)} \\ \mathbf{Z}'_* \end{bmatrix} [\hat{\mathbf{Y}}_{(\Delta-1)} \ \mathbf{Z}_*] \right)^{-1} \begin{bmatrix} \hat{\mathbf{Y}}'_{(\Delta-1)} \\ \mathbf{Z}'_* \end{bmatrix} \mathbf{y}.$$

Their coincidence obviously occurs if $\hat{\mathbf{Y}}'_{(\Delta-1)}\hat{\mathbf{Y}}_{(\Delta-1)} = \hat{\mathbf{Y}}'_{(\Delta-1)}\mathbf{Y}_{(\Delta-1)}$ and $\mathbf{Z}'_*\mathbf{Y}_{(\Delta-1)} = \mathbf{Z}'_*\hat{\mathbf{Y}}_{(\Delta-1)}$.

These latter identities are easily confirmed, since

$$(6.3.14) \quad \begin{aligned} \hat{\mathbf{Y}}'_{(\Delta-1)}\hat{\mathbf{Y}}_{(\Delta-1)} &= \mathbf{Y}'_{(\Delta-1)}\mathbf{Z}(\mathbf{Z}'\mathbf{Z})^{-1}\mathbf{Z}'\mathbf{Z}(\mathbf{Z}'\mathbf{Z})^{-1}\mathbf{Z}'\mathbf{Y}_{(\Delta-1)} \\ &= \mathbf{Y}'_{(\Delta-1)}\mathbf{Z}(\mathbf{Z}'\mathbf{Z})^{-1}\mathbf{Z}'\mathbf{Y}_{(\Delta-1)} \\ &= \hat{\mathbf{Y}}'_{(\Delta-1)}\mathbf{Y}_{(\Delta-1)} \end{aligned}$$

and

$$(6.3.15) \quad \begin{aligned} \mathbf{Z}'_*\hat{\mathbf{Y}}_{(\Delta-1)} &= \mathbf{Z}'_*\mathbf{Z}(\mathbf{Z}'\mathbf{Z})^{-1}\mathbf{Z}'\mathbf{Y}_{(\Delta-1)} \\ &= [\mathbf{Z}'_*\mathbf{Z}_* \ \vdots \ \mathbf{Z}'_*\mathbf{Z}_{**}] \begin{bmatrix} \mathbf{Z}'_*\mathbf{Z}_* & \vdots & \mathbf{Z}'_*\mathbf{Z}_{**} \\ \hdashline \mathbf{Z}'_{**}\mathbf{Z}_* & \vdots & \mathbf{Z}'_{**}\mathbf{Z}_{**} \end{bmatrix}^{-1} \mathbf{Z}'\mathbf{Y}_{(\Delta-1)} \\ &= [\mathbf{I} \ \vdots \ \mathbf{0}]\mathbf{Z}'\mathbf{Y}_{(\Delta-1)} \\ &= [\mathbf{I} \ \vdots \ \mathbf{0}] \begin{bmatrix} \mathbf{Z}'_* \\ \hdashline \mathbf{Z}'_{**} \end{bmatrix} \mathbf{Y}_{(\Delta-1)} \\ &= \mathbf{Z}'_*\mathbf{Y}_{(\Delta-1)}. \end{aligned}$$

When the equation in question is just identified, $M_\Delta - 1 = K_{**}$ and

2SLS, limited-information maximum likelihood and "indirect" least squares (LS on the reduced form) give *identical* estimates in every sample. When $K_{**} > M_\Delta - 1$, the indirect method is infeasible, and while the remaining two techniques then differ, they share the property of consistency and have the same asymptotic variance-covariance matrix (6.3.11). Three-stage LS (3SLS) develops from applying 2SLS to every equation in the structure, which results in a multivariate regression framework for the 2SLS *estimated* structure; efficient estimation is obtained using generalized LS on the entire system where the $\sigma_{mm'}$ elements are estimated by 2SLS. Each equation must be at least just-identified to use 3SLS. 3SLS generally shares with FIML the same asymptotic variance-covariance matrix for its estimators.

2SLS applied to the demand equation of (4.6.2) with (4.6.11) as the relevant supply equation would proceed by first regressing p_t on r_t, to obtain a series of "predicted" values $\{\hat{p}_t\}$. Then the just-identified demand equation would be estimated by least squares in the regression of q_t^e on $\hat{p}_t$. Since the supply equation itself is underidentified, neither of the full "system" methods, 3SLS or FIML, is applicable. As our preceding discussion has indicated, *in every sample* the estimates of coefficients of the demand equation obtained in this way will be *identical* to the estimates produced by indirect LS. This would not be the case were (4.6.13) the supply equation. For then the demand equation would be overidentified.

Distributional properties for either of the ML techniques follow directly from the ML theory. The estimators follow the normal distribution asymptotically, thus forming the basis for tests of hypotheses and confidence interval calculations. 2SLS and 3SLS are, by virtue of their interpretation as instrumental variables methods, also generally distributed normally in large samples.

Occasionally interdependent systems exhibit subsets of equations that are structured *recursively*, and for these subsets the more elaborate estimation techniques may not be required. Moreover, recursive models also insure identification. The simple cobweb model introduced in Section 4.6 is one example of a recursive scheme.

The essential characteristic of *recursive* structure is a triangular **B**-matrix with otherwise identical specifications to the basic structure (6.3.1). That is,

$$(6.3.16) \qquad \mathbf{B} = \begin{bmatrix} \beta_{11} & 0 & \cdots & & 0 \\ \beta_{21} & \beta_{22} & 0 & \cdots & 0 \\ \cdot & & \cdot & & \\ \cdot & & & \cdot & \cdot \\ \cdot & & & & \beta_{MM} \end{bmatrix}.$$

So long as $\beta_{mm} \neq 0$ for $m = 1, \ldots, M$, **B** will be nonsingular. The *strictly* *recursive* scheme has Σ a diagonal matrix, and LS applied equation-by-equation will result in consistent estimates, as we shall now verify.

From the reduced form of the recursive model we know that $\mathbf{Y}_t = \mathbf{\Pi Z}_t + \mathbf{B}^{-1}\mathbf{U}_t$, so that $E(\mathbf{Y}_t\mathbf{U}_t') = \mathbf{B}^{-1}\Sigma$. Moreover, a triangular matrix has a triangular inverse; hence, denoting the elements of $\mathbf{B}^{-1}$ by $\beta^{mm'}$,

(6.3.17)
$$\mathbf{B}^{-1}\Sigma = \begin{bmatrix} \beta^{11}\sigma_{11} & 0 & \cdots & & 0 \\ \beta^{21}\sigma_{21} & \beta^{22}\sigma_{22} & 0 & \cdots & 0 \\ \cdot & & \cdot & & \\ \cdot & & & \cdot & \\ \cdot & & & & \beta^{MM}\sigma_{MM} \end{bmatrix},$$

because Σ is diagonal.

In the corresponding equation system, the first equation can be consistently estimated by LS, since it involves but one endogenous variable. Equation two has both y_1 and y_2 appearing, but by (6.3.17) $E(v_1u_2) = 0$, so that LS applied *directly* will also yield consistent estimates of its coefficients. The cascading specification of endogenous variables with a coincident cascading of appropriate zero correlations gives rise to an identical conclusion for LS applied directly to the remaining equations. Without such stringent restrictions on the form of Σ, 2SLS will yield consistent estimators for parameters of the recursive model.

The advantages of the recursive structure are hard to ignore. Its most vocal proponent, H. Wold, in fact argues persuasively for the recursive structure *ab initio*, as if it were a recursive world. Recursive structuring seems most appropriate in time-series models when the period of observation is *short*. As the data become more aggregated over *time*, simultaneous models will generally better suit the a priori notions one has about the economic phenomena being modeled.

Appendixes

A Elementary

Matrix Operations

Obtaining least-squares coefficients in the linear multiple regression model involves solving a simultaneous system of linear equations that can conveniently be written in shorthand fashion—so-called *matrix notation*. Manipulating matrices in a way analogous to the elementary algebraic operations with real numbers then becomes important. And there is, thankfully, an algebra of matrices.

For our purposes the most important algebraic operation to be carried over to matrix operations is division. As a single equation $ax = b$ can easily be solved for x in terms of a and b as $x = b/a$ or $x = a^{-1}b$, a system of linear equations $\mathbf{A}\mathbf{x} = \mathbf{y}$, with $\mathbf{A}$, $\mathbf{x}$, and $\mathbf{y}$ all matrices, can be solved symbolically as $\mathbf{x} = \mathbf{A}^{-1}\mathbf{y}$. But the notion and formation of $\mathbf{A}^{-1}$ is not quite so simple as the reciprocal of a number.

The following list outlines the fundamentals leading up to and including the formulation of the so-called inverse matrix, $\mathbf{A}^{-1}$.

1. *Matrix.* An array of nm numbers arranged in n rows and m columns is called a *matrix* of order $(n \times m)$.

$$\mathbf{A} = [a_{ij}] = \begin{bmatrix} a_{11} & a_{12} & \cdots & a_{1m} \\ a_{21} & & & \cdot \\ \cdot & & & \cdot \\ \cdot & & & \cdot \\ a_{n1} & \cdots & & a_{nm} \end{bmatrix}, \quad \begin{matrix} i = 1, \ldots, n, \\ j = 1, \ldots, m. \end{matrix}$$

Where $n = m$, the matrix is *square*. For square matrices where $a_{ij} = a_{ji}$ $(i \neq j)$, the matrix is *symmetric*. An $(n \times 1)$ matrix will be termed a *vector* of n dimensions.

2. *Transpose.* Given a matrix $\mathbf{A} = [a_{ij}]$ of order $(n \times m)$ we define the *transpose* of $\mathbf{A}$, called $\mathbf{A}'$, to be the matrix $\mathbf{A}' = [a_{ji}]$ of order $(m \times n)$.

3. *Addition.* The sum of two matrices $\mathbf{A}$ and $\mathbf{B}$ is defined only when $\mathbf{A}$ and $\mathbf{B}$ are of the same order. Then $\mathbf{A} + \mathbf{B} = [a_{ij} + b_{ij}]$.

4. *Scalar multiplication.* A scalar (number) is a (1×1) matrix. The multiplication of a matrix $\mathbf{A}$ by a scalar k is achieved by: $k\mathbf{A} = [ka_{ij}]$.

5. *Subtraction.* The difference between two matrices is the sum $\mathbf{A} + (-1)\mathbf{B} = \mathbf{A} - \mathbf{B}$.

6. *The null matrix.* A matrix in which every element is zero is a *null* matrix. Notation: $\mathbf{A} = \odot$, or $\mathbf{A} = \mathbf{0}$.

7. *Equality of matrices.* Two matrices $\mathbf{A}$ and $\mathbf{B}$ are equal if $\mathbf{A}$ and $\mathbf{B}$ are *conformable* for addition (of the same order) and $a_{ij} = b_{ij}$ for all i and j.

8. Matrix addition is

    (a)   Associative: $(\mathbf{A} + \mathbf{B}) + \mathbf{C} = \mathbf{A} + (\mathbf{B} + \mathbf{C})$.

    (b)   Distributive: $k(\mathbf{A} + \mathbf{B}) = k\mathbf{A} + k\mathbf{B}$.

    (c)   Commutative: $\mathbf{A} + \mathbf{B} = \mathbf{B} + \mathbf{A}$.

9. *Vector inner product.* The inner product of two vectors $\mathbf{X} = [x_i]$ and $\mathbf{Y} = [y_i]$ of the same dimension, n, is defined as

$$(\mathbf{X}, \mathbf{Y}) = \sum_{i=1}^{n} x_i y_i.$$

In matrix form we are led to consider:

10. *Matrix multiplication*. The matrix product **AB** is defined only when the number of columns in **A** equals the number of rows of **B**. **A** and **B** are then said to be *conformable* for multiplication. Considering the vectors that are rows of **A** and the vectors that are columns of **B**, the matrix product **AB** = **C** is defined as the indexed array of inner products of these vectors. With **A** = $[a_{ij}]$ of order $(n \times m)$ and **B** = $[b_{jk}]$ of order $(m \times p)$, we have

$$\mathbf{C} = \mathbf{AB} = [c_{ik}] = \left[\sum_{j=1}^{m} a_{ij} b_{jk} \right].$$

A is called the "premultiplier" and **B** is called the "postmultiplier." As a special case of matrix multiplication, the inner product of the n-dimensional column vectors **X** = $[x_i]$ and **Y** = $[y_i]$, namely (**X**, **Y**), may be represented by

$$\mathbf{X'Y} = \left[\sum_{i=1}^{n} x_i y_i \right],$$

a scalar.

Notes:

(a) In general, **AB** $\neq$ **BA**. Matrix multiplication is generally not commutative. In fact, even if **AB** is defined, **BA** may not be defined.
(b) Distributive and associative laws hold: (**A** + **B**)**C** = **AC** + **BC**; **A**(**BC**) = (**AB**)**C**.
(c) In general, **AB** = $\odot$ does not require either **A** = $\odot$ or **B** = $\odot$.

11. *Transpose of a product*. The transpose of a product of matrices is the product of the transposes, taken in reverse order. Thus, (**AB**)' = **B'A'**.

12. *The identity matrix*. Define a square matrix of order $(n \times n)$ that has ones down its diagonal and zeros elsewhere as the *identity* matrix, **I**. Then for **A** a square matrix of order $(n \times n)$, **AI** = **IA** = **A** (commutative).

Note: **BI** = **B** and **IC** = **C**, where **B** and **C** are not square, but **B** and **I**, **I** and **C** are conformable for multiplication.

13. *Linear dependence*. For a matrix **A** of order $(n \times m)$, denote the columns of **A** as the set of n-dimensional vectors $\{\mathbf{A}_j\}$. The set $\{\mathbf{A}_j\}$ is said to be *linearly dependent* if there exist scalars c_j, not all zero, such that

$$\sum_{j=1}^{m} \mathbf{A}_j c_j = \odot,$$

where $\odot$ is an n-dimensional vector of zeros. Another way of stating the condition of linear dependence is to say that one of the columns, say $\mathbf{A}_r$, can be formed as a linear combination of the remaining $(m - 1)$ columns of **A**. That is,

$$\mathbf{A}_r = \sum_{\substack{j=1 \\ j \neq r}}^{m} \mathbf{A}_j d_j.$$

From the definitional equation, choose $\mathbf{A}_r$ to be a vector with $c_r \neq 0$. Then

$$\sum_{\substack{j=1 \\ j\neq r}}^{m} \mathbf{A}_j c_j = -c_r \mathbf{A}_r \quad \text{and} \quad \mathbf{A}_r = \sum_{\substack{j=1 \\ j\neq r}}^{m} \mathbf{A}_j d_j$$

with $d_j = -c_j/c_r$. If scalars c_j, not all zero, *cannot* be found to satisfy the above condition, the set $\{\mathbf{A}_j\}$ is said to be *linearly independent*.

14. *Rank of a matrix.* For a matrix $\mathbf{A}$ of order $(n \times m)$ *with* $n \geq m$, the *rank* of $\mathbf{A}$ is the number of linearly independent columns of $\mathbf{A}$, say $r \leq m$. In general, the rank of a matrix cannot exceed its smallest dimension.

15. *Rank of a product.* The rank of a product of two matrices, say $\mathbf{C} = \mathbf{AB}$, is no greater than the smallest rank of the factors, $\mathbf{A}$ and $\mathbf{B}$.

16. *Matrix "division."* (a) *Determinants.* There is associated with the square matrix $\mathbf{A}$ of order $(n \times n)$ a number $|\mathbf{A}|$, called the *determinant* of $\mathbf{A}$, defined as follows: For the (2×2) matrix

$$\mathbf{A} = \begin{bmatrix} a_{11} & a_{12} \\ a_{21} & a_{22} \end{bmatrix}, \quad |\mathbf{A}| = \begin{vmatrix} a_{11} & a_{12} \\ a_{21} & a_{22} \end{vmatrix} = a_{11}a_{22} - a_{12}a_{21}.$$

For larger-order determinants, define D_{ij} as the determinant of the $[(n-1) \times (n-1)]$ matrix formed by striking out the ith row and jth column of $\mathbf{A}$. D_{ij} is called the (i, j) "minor" of $\mathbf{A}$. For example:

$$|\mathbf{A}| = \begin{vmatrix} a_{11} & a_{12} & a_{13} \\ a_{21} & a_{22} & a_{23} \\ a_{31} & a_{32} & a_{33} \end{vmatrix}, \quad D_{11} = \begin{vmatrix} a_{22} & a_{23} \\ a_{32} & a_{33} \end{vmatrix}.$$

Next, define the (i, j) *cofactor* of $\mathbf{A}$ to be $\Delta_{ij} = (-1)^{i+j} D_{ij}$—that is, the (i, j) minor with a negative sign attached if the sum of subscripts is odd, and a positive sign if the sum is even. [Examples: $\Delta_{11} = D_{11}$, $\Delta_{12} = (-1)D_{12}$.] Now,

$$|\mathbf{A}| = \sum_{i=1}^{n} a_{ij}\Delta_{ij} = \sum_{j=1}^{n} a_{ij}\Delta_{ij}.$$

So,

$$|\mathbf{A}| = \begin{vmatrix} a_{11} & a_{12} & a_{13} \\ a_{21} & a_{22} & a_{23} \\ a_{31} & a_{32} & a_{33} \end{vmatrix}$$

$$= a_{11}\begin{vmatrix} a_{22} & a_{23} \\ a_{32} & a_{33} \end{vmatrix} - a_{21}\begin{vmatrix} a_{12} & a_{13} \\ a_{32} & a_{33} \end{vmatrix} + a_{31}\begin{vmatrix} a_{12} & a_{13} \\ a_{22} & a_{23} \end{vmatrix}.$$

(b) *Inverse.* The *inverse* of a matrix $\mathbf{A}$ of order $(n \times n)$ is the matrix $\mathbf{A}^{-1}$ such that $\mathbf{AA}^{-1} = \mathbf{I}$, $\mathbf{A}^{-1}\mathbf{A} = \mathbf{I}$. Only square matrices have inverses; if the inverse exists, $\mathbf{A}$ is of full rank (n) (and vice versa) and is called *nonsingular*. If the inverse does not exist, $\mathbf{A}$ is *singular*. Alternatively, $\mathbf{A}$ is nonsingular if and only if $|A| \neq 0$. Equivalently, A is singular if and only if $|A| = 0$.

(c) Forming the inverse.

(1) Evaluate $|A|$.
(2) Form the matrix of cofactors, $[\Delta_{ij}]$.
(3) Form the *adjoint* matrix, which is the transpose of $[\Delta_{ij}]$. That is, $[\Delta_{ij}]' = [\Delta_{ji}]$.
(4) Then, $A^{-1} = (1/|A|)[\Delta_{ji}]$. The inverse is formed by dividing each element in $[\Delta_{ji}]$ by $|A|$.

While we have defined $|A|$ to be

$$\sum_{i=1}^{n} a_{ij}\Delta_{ij} \quad \text{or} \quad \sum_{j=1}^{n} a_{ij}\Delta_{ij},$$

it can be shown that

$$\sum_{\substack{i=1 \\ j \neq k}}^{n} a_{ij}\Delta_{ik} = 0 \quad \text{and} \quad \sum_{\substack{j=1 \\ i \neq r}}^{n} a_{ij}\Delta_{rj} = 0.$$

That is, the inner product of any row or column of A with an "alien" row or column of the matrix of cofactors is zero (see Problem 1 that follows). Thus,

$$A[\Delta_{ji}] = \begin{bmatrix} |A| & 0 & \cdots & 0 \\ 0 & |A| & & \vdots \\ \vdots & & \ddots & 0 \\ 0 & \cdots & 0 & |A| \end{bmatrix} \quad \text{and} \quad AA^{-1} = A\left[\frac{\Delta_{ji}}{|A|}\right] = I.$$

17. *Product form of the inverse.* Consider the following system of simultaneous linear equations:

$$a_{11}x_1 + a_{12}x_2 + \cdots + a_{1n}x_n = y_1$$
$$\vdots \qquad\qquad\qquad\qquad \vdots$$
$$a_{n1}x_1 + a_{n2}x_2 + \cdots + a_{nn}x_n = y_n$$

or, in matrix notation, $Ax = y$. A is an $(n \times n)$ matrix of known coefficients, y is an $(n \times 1)$ vector of known quantities and x is an $(n \times 1)$ vector of unknowns. Doing "row operations" on the equations of the linear system above does not alter its properties—that is, does not change the unique solution (if it exists) to them.

By row operations we mean:

(1) Multiply a row by a constant.
(2) Add (subtract) one row to (from) another.
(3) Combination of (1) and (2).

The result of row operations can be represented by the product of each matrix, A, x, or y, with a matrix of zeros and ones unique to that particular operation. For instance, multiply row 2 by six to get a new coefficient matrix

$$A_1 = \begin{bmatrix} a_{11} & \cdots & a_{1n} \\ 6a_{21} & & 6a_{2n} \\ \cdot & & \cdot \\ \cdot & & \cdot \\ \cdot & & \cdot \\ a_{n1} & \cdots & a_{nn} \end{bmatrix}.$$

Define the matrix

$$E_1 = \begin{bmatrix} 1 & 0 & \cdots & & 0 \\ 0 & 6 & 0 & \cdots & 0 \\ \cdot & & 1 & & \\ \cdot & & & \cdot & \cdot \\ \cdot & & & \cdot & \cdot \\ 0 & & \cdots & & 1 \end{bmatrix},$$

an $(n \times n)$ identity matrix except for a 6 in the (2, 2) position. Then $A_1 = E_1 A$. Or, add row 2 to row 1 (leave row 2 unchanged), to get

$$A_2 = \begin{bmatrix} (a_{11} + a_{21}) & \cdots & (a_{1n} + a_{2n}) \\ a_{21} & \cdots & a_{2n} \\ \cdot & & \cdot \\ \cdot & & \cdot \\ \cdot & & \cdot \\ a_{n1} & \cdots & a_{nn} \end{bmatrix}.$$

For this operation,

$$E_2 = \begin{bmatrix} 1 & 1 & 0 & \cdots & 0 \\ 0 & 1 & 0 & \cdots & 0 \\ \cdot & 0 & & & \cdot \\ \cdot & \cdot & & & \cdot \\ \cdot & \cdot & & & 0 \\ 0 & 0 & \cdots & 0 & 1 \end{bmatrix} \quad \text{and} \quad A_2 = E_2 A.$$

Finally, consider a combination of these two, where six times row 2 is added to row 1, with row 2 left unchanged:

$$\mathbf{A}_3 = \begin{bmatrix} (a_{11} + 6a_{21}) & \cdots & (a_{1n} + 6a_{2n}) \\ a_{21} & \cdots & a_{2n} \\ \vdots & & \vdots \\ a_{n1} & \cdots & a_{nn} \end{bmatrix},$$

$$\mathbf{E}_3 = \begin{bmatrix} 1 & 6 & 0 & \cdots & 0 \\ 0 & 1 & 0 & \cdots & 0 \\ \vdots & & & & \vdots \\ & & & & 0 \\ 0 & \cdots & & 0 & 1 \end{bmatrix} \quad \text{and} \quad \mathbf{A}_3 = \mathbf{E}_3 \mathbf{A}.$$

Suppose, then, we proceed to do row operations on $\mathbf{A}$ and $\mathbf{y}$ until we have transformed $\mathbf{A}$ into an identity matrix. Note that the same operations are to be performed on $\mathbf{y}$, so that the essential character of the system remains unchanged. Thus,

$$\mathbf{E}_1 \mathbf{A} \mathbf{x} = \mathbf{E}_1 \mathbf{y},$$

$$\mathbf{E}_2 \mathbf{E}_1 \mathbf{A} = \mathbf{E}_2 \mathbf{E}_1 \mathbf{y},$$

until

$$\underbrace{[\mathbf{E}_k \cdots \mathbf{E}_1]\mathbf{A}}_{\mathbf{I}} \mathbf{x} = \underbrace{[\mathbf{E}_k \cdots \mathbf{E}_1]}_{\mathbf{E}} \mathbf{y}.$$

Now we have the form: $\mathbf{x} = \mathbf{E}\mathbf{y}$, and since $\mathbf{E}\mathbf{A} = \mathbf{I}$, $\mathbf{E} = \mathbf{A}^{-1}$. If we begin with an augmented matrix $[\mathbf{A} : \mathbf{I}]$ and perform row operations until $\mathbf{A}$ is transformed into an identity matrix, $\mathbf{A}^{-1}$ will be generated in place of the original identity matrix; that is, we will end up with $[\mathbf{I} : \mathbf{A}^{-1}]$.

PROBLEMS

1. Give as rigorous a proof as possible of the fact that the inner product of the ith row of a matrix with the kth $(i \neq k)$ row of its corresponding matrix of cofactors is zero.

ANSWER:

By definition, the determinant of a matrix, $\mathbf{A}$, is $|\mathbf{A}| = \sum_i a_{ij}\Delta_{ij} = \sum_j a_{ij}\Delta_{ij}$. But $\sum_j a_{ij}\Delta_{kj} = 0$ for $i \neq k$ because this sum may be viewed as an expansion of the determinant of a matrix, say $\mathbf{B}$, where the ith and kth rows of $\mathbf{B}$ are the *same*. Thus it vanishes.

2. Find solutions to the following systems of linear equations $\mathbf{Ax} = \mathbf{y}$ by direct matrix inversion and by row operations.

a.
$$\mathbf{A} = \begin{bmatrix} \frac{1}{2} & -1 & 0 \\ 3 & 1 & -2 \\ \frac{3}{2} & 2 & 1 \end{bmatrix}, \qquad \mathbf{y} = \begin{bmatrix} 1 \\ 2 \\ 3 \end{bmatrix}.$$

ANSWER:
$$\mathbf{A}^{-1} = \begin{bmatrix} \frac{10}{17} & \frac{2}{17} & \frac{4}{17} \\ -\frac{12}{17} & \frac{1}{17} & \frac{2}{17} \\ \frac{9}{17} & -\frac{5}{17} & \frac{7}{17} \end{bmatrix}, \qquad \mathbf{x} = \begin{bmatrix} \frac{26}{17} \\ -\frac{4}{17} \\ \frac{20}{17} \end{bmatrix}.$$

b.
$$\mathbf{A} = \begin{bmatrix} 1 & 0 & \frac{1}{2} & 0 \\ 3 & -2 & -1 & 3 \\ \frac{5}{2} & -\frac{1}{2} & 2 & 0 \\ -1 & 2 & 2 & -3 \end{bmatrix}, \qquad \mathbf{y} = \begin{bmatrix} 1 \\ 2 \\ 3 \\ 4 \end{bmatrix}.$$

ANSWER:
No solution.

c.
$$\mathbf{A} = \begin{bmatrix} 1 & -2 & -1 \\ \frac{1}{2} & 0 & 2 \\ -1 & -2 & 3 \end{bmatrix}, \qquad \mathbf{y} = \begin{bmatrix} 0 \\ 0 \\ 0 \end{bmatrix}.$$

ANSWER:
$$\mathbf{A}^{-1} = \begin{bmatrix} \frac{1}{3} & \frac{2}{3} & -\frac{1}{3} \\ \frac{7}{24} & \frac{1}{6} & -\frac{5}{24} \\ -\frac{1}{12} & \frac{1}{3} & \frac{1}{12} \end{bmatrix}, \qquad \mathbf{x} = ?$$

B A Review

of Classical and Modern

Statistical Inference†

B.1 INTRODUCTION

The orientation of the main body of the text is a "probability orientation." Because some readers may require additional work before they fully understand the material, and in order that the book may be almost completely self-contained, this review chapter on the methodology of statistical inference or decision-making is included. The emphasis here is on *principles*, with the goal of integrating the classical and modern or "Bayesian" schools of thought about how decision problems involving uncertain outcomes ought to be approached. An important class of real-world decision problems not treated here requires *sequential analysis*—as might be the case, for instance, in controlling quality on some continuous production line. This type of inference problem is of definite interest in industry, but it occurs infrequently in economics and so is ignored in the present treatment.

In what follows we assume that the reader is familiar generally with statistical methods and probability theory, and in particular has a working

† This review summarizes Chapters 5, 6, and 7 of the author's *Principles of Statistical Decision Making* (New York: Macmillan, 1968).

224

knowledge of the most often used probability distributions and the calculus of mathematical expectation concerning the moments of such distributions.

B.2 SAMPLING AND ESTIMATION —CLASSICAL APPROACH

We can discuss the subject of statistical inference in two ways—by analyzing (1) the relation between a parameter and an estimate of it or (2) rules of decision formation (hereafter *decision rules*). The five subsections that follow take the first approach, discussing statistical inference about parameters from sample information, in the form of estimates of these parameters. The method of making *inferences* uses probability statements about the unknown parameters derived from their sample estimates. Thus we require knowledge of the frequency distribution of an estimator to make inferential statements about the parameter in question.

To introduce the fundamental ideas underlying statistical inference, let us consider the following situation. A probability sample is taken of a well-defined group of doctors in order to discover the smoking habits of the whole group. Doctors are selected into the sample of n by a procedure that assigns an equal probability to the selection of any given doctor into the sample at any stage of the sampling procedure. Let us assume that a doctor is selected, answers yes or no to a question designed to register him either as a "smoker" or a "nonsmoker," and then is returned to the group. The same process is repeated until the entire sample has been gathered.

In the main group of doctors, the *population* for sampling purposes, there must be an actual proportion of "smokers" by the adopted definition, whatever it is. Call this proportion $\tilde{P}$. Now suppose we use the sample proportion, p, as an estimate of this unknown, $\tilde{P}$. That is, if of 20 doctors sampled we find 5 smokers, we estimate $\tilde{P}$ as $\frac{5}{20} = .25$. Of course $\tilde{P}$ either is or is not .25, in fact. But viewing the comparison *ex ante* we can never know the true relation between $\tilde{P}$ and any p. We can only discuss this relation in probability terms, expressing, for example, our "confidence" in p as an estimate of $\tilde{P}$.

When will we be more confident of p and when will we not? One way of using the term confidence is to relate it to a probability measure of p compared to $\tilde{P}$. For example, since any *given* sample is a result of a random experiment, and a *given* sample yields a particular value of p, we may conceptually generate a frequency distribution for p merely by considering all possible samples of a given size, n, as a sample space. The selection procedure assigns probabilities to their occurrence, and by the definition of the random variable p over this sample space we can construct its distribution $f(p)$. Presumably $\tilde{P}$ will be contained in the range of p; thus we may consider the probabilities that a sample p will fall in various intervals from information about $f(p)$, such as $P(p \geq \tilde{P})$, or $P(p \leq \tilde{P})$, or whatever, the notation $P(p \geq \tilde{P})$ meaning the probability that p equals or exceeds $\tilde{P}$. Of course, as a practical matter we must know whatever parameters are involved in $f(p)$ in order to make any such probability statements.

Precision may also be defined simply as how "close" p is to $\tilde{P}$, the most conventional measure being the second moment of p around $\tilde{P}$, called the mean-square-error of p: $\mathrm{MSE}_p = E[p - \tilde{P}]^2$, where E is the expectation operator. If it so happens that p has as its expected value $\tilde{P}$, then the formula above is just the variance of p. Again, we apparently cannot know this variance since it involves $\tilde{P}$, the parameter we are attempting to estimate. Apparently we must also *estimate* σ_p^2 before we can say much about p as an estimate of $\tilde{P}$. So, for example, we might devise a way to obtain an estimate of σ_p^2 and be able to quote as follows, that our estimate p of $\tilde{P}$ is .25 with a (estimated) standard deviation from $\tilde{P}$ of .05. This use of σ_p as the indicator of precision is, to reiterate, based on $E(p) = \tilde{P}$ holding. We may be more "confident" of this result than, for example $p = .23$ with a standard deviation of .10.

Quite clearly we require the development of concepts of "confidence," "precision," and so on, into a formal framework of analysis. We begin by treating the topic of random sampling as it pertains to the generation of frequency distributions for sample estimators of population characteristics.

B.2.1 SIMPLE RANDOM SAMPLING —FINITE POPULATION MEAN AND VARIANCE

We broadly dichotomize sampling procedures into probability methods and nonprobability or judgment methods. A *probability sample* guarantees that each member of a population of interest has a nonzero, known probability of selection into the sample, while a judgment method does not. Statistical inference of the sort we are herein concerned with requires probability sampling, and so we shall limit our discussion to those methods. In particular we consider simple random sampling.

There exist many probability methods for sample selection, each of which may be "best" for some application. Of these the most basic is *simple random sampling* (SRS), where the probability that any sample of size n is selected is equal over all such samples. For example, for a population of size N and a sample of size n, the total number of different samples is just

$$\binom{N}{n}$$

if each time an element of the population is selected it is *not* returned to the population prior to the next such selection.† Then SRS is defined to be a technique of selection of the individual elements that gives

$$1\bigg/\binom{N}{n}$$

as the probability that a particular sample of n is drawn.

If individual elements are replaced into the population (that is, there exists some chance that the *same* element will be drawn n times), then there are N^n possible size-n samples, each of which must be guaranteed a probability $1/N^n$ under SRS.

The selection method that insures these conditions are met in the two cases outlined is called an *EPSEM*, Equal Probability SElection Method. In the first case, where sampling is done *without* replacement, at *each stage* in the selection procedure the *remaining* population elements are assigned

† The notation $\binom{N}{n}$ is for the number of combinations of N items taken n at a time.

equal chances of being selected on the next draw.† Without elaborating, it is easy to argue that each possible sample of size n must be equally likely to obtain. For sampling with replacement any particular element has an equal chance of being selected at any stage of the drawing process—and, indeed, this probability remains constant throughout the drawings. Again, it is quite clear that each possible n-sample will be equally likely, with probability $1/N^n$. Other probability-oriented techniques are available, and in many instances they are more efficient than SRS in collecting sample information, where efficiency is defined as yielding information of a given precision at lowest cost. But to examine *principles* of inference an in-depth excursion into sampling theory is unnecessary, so we shall confine ourselves to the two SRS techniques.

The objective of sampling is to gain information about certain characteristics of the population $\{A_i\}$. What characteristics? For the population of doctors in a previous example the "characteristic" was a population proportion. We might be concerned with other quantitative insights into the population, such as its mean value for some other measurement taken on the $\{A_i\}$, a variance of this measured attribute, and so on.

The simplest general way to consider attributes of a population is to view the population elements as elementary events in a sample space $\{A_i\}$. Suppose we assign equal probability weights to these A_i's and define the measured (or qualitative) attribute of interest as a random variable, say $\bar{X}$. By this contrived set of conditions we must be able to produce $f(\bar{X})$, a frequency function for the attribute, defined via the population. This $f(\bar{X})$ by definition merely collects A_i's with equal values of $\bar{X}$ and adds their probabilities. So, for example, $f(\bar{X})$ might contain five elements that have the value $\bar{X} = k$. By the assignment of equal weights to each A_i, $f(\bar{X} = k) = 5/N$.‡

Now $f(\bar{X})$ may be used to define the population mean μ simply as its expected value—that is,

$$(\text{B.2.1.1}) \qquad \mu = E(\bar{X}) = \sum_{\text{all } \bar{X}} \bar{X} f(\bar{X}) = \frac{1}{N} \sum_{i=1}^{N} X_i,$$

where X_i is the measured attribute on A_i. Similarly, a population variance σ^2 may be obtained as

$$(\text{B.2.1.2}) \qquad \sigma^2 = E[\bar{X} - \mu]^2$$
$$= \frac{1}{N} \sum_{i=1}^{N} (X_i - \mu)^2$$
$$= \frac{1}{N} \sum_{i=1}^{N} X_i^2 - \mu^2.$$

† Through a random-numbers table or other suitable device.
‡ Here we are dealing with finite populations, as we have implicitly from the beginning. We will extend our results to the infinite-population case later.

If a qualitative, dichotomous attribute is of interest, then let $X_i = 1$ if A_i possesses the attribute of interest and $X_i = 0$ if not. Then (B.2.1.1) counts the number of $\{A_i\}$ that possess the attribute, and μ defines the population proportion $\tilde{P}$.

For present purposes we shall concern ourselves only with sample inferences about these two population characteristics, its mean (or a proportion) and variance. Of course there are many other characteristics that might be of interest, but in principle the methodology we shall propose may be extended to cover any such problem.

B.2.2. ESTIMATES AND THEIR PROPERTIES

Suppose we have a simple random sample of size n. The "information" contained in the sample takes the form, obviously, of measurements $\{X_j\}$ on the sample subset of $\{A_j\}$. If we wished to say something—infer something—about μ, for instance, how should we utilize these sample observations? One very intuitive "estimator"† of μ is the sample arithmetic average, say $\bar{x}_n$, where

$$(\text{B.2.2.1}) \qquad \bar{x}_n = \frac{1}{n} \sum_{j=1}^{n} X_j.$$

The problem, then, is to evaluate the relationship of $\bar{x}_n$ and μ in probability terms. For there is, from the definition of the SRS method, a definite probability attached to the obtention of this sample. Therefore, looking at all possible samples of this same size, $\bar{x}_n$ is a random variable with a frequency function $f(\bar{x}_n)$. A sample of size 20 from a population of 500 that yields $\bar{x}_{20} = 5$ (units) *may* have been generated by $\mu = 5$, $\mu = 16$, $\mu = 103$, and so on. Can we provide an objective judgment as to which μ is the true one? Perhaps this goal may be accomplished by a statement of the likely interval in which μ is contained. In any case the objective judgment we refer to cannot be a judgment with certainty, since samples are, in general, smaller than the entire population.‡

One such evaluation that appears useful a priori is the *position* of μ in $f(\bar{x}_n)$. Specifically, is $E(\bar{x}_n) = \mu$? We already (by definition) know that μ is the mean of the population; is it also the mean of the *sampling distribution* of $\bar{x}_n$? Given that we can specify $f(\bar{x}_n)$, we may answer the question directly by merely finding $E(\bar{x}_n)$.

For the case at hand, $\bar{x}_n$ is a linear combination of the $\{X_j\}$. *Ex ante* we cannot predict which A_j will be selected to fill the next vacant slot in the

† An *estimator* is the functional form in which sample observations are utilized; an *estimate* is the value the estimator takes on for a particular set of observations.

‡ It may not even be possible to identify parameters exactly—or, in different words, make certain judgments about them *given* the entire population. Some elaboration on this point is given in Section B.4.

sample, and hence we cannot predict the *value* X_j. In fact, the value that does (*ex post*) fill any given slot is the result of a random selection. Let us first consider the initial sample value, X_1. The frequency distribution that governs the actual value X_1 is $f(\bar{X})$. So, if we had selected a sample of size $n = 1$ only, it is easy to see that $E(\bar{x}_1) = \mu$.

For notational purposes, let us define x_j as the *random variable* corresponding to the jth selection into the sample, with frequency distribution $f(x_j)$, and consider the extension of the analysis above to $n = 2$ under the assumption that sampling is done *with replacement*. Then x_1 and x_2 are independent random variables because of SRS methods being utilized, and also $f(x_1) = f(x_2) = f(\bar{X})$. Clearly,

(B.2.2.2)
$$
\begin{aligned}
E(\bar{x}_2) &= \tfrac{1}{2}E(x_1 + x_2) \\
&= \tfrac{1}{2}[E(x_1) + E(x_2)] \\
&= \tfrac{1}{2}(2\mu) \\
&= \mu.
\end{aligned}
$$

Under these assumptions, the mean of the sample means for 2-samples is μ, the population mean. The extension of (B.2.2.2) to n-samples should be obvious. In that case also we find that $E(\bar{x}_n) = \mu$.

What if sampling is done without replacement? Clearly the $\{x_j\}$ are *not* independent.† Theoretically the $\{x_j\}$ do not possess identical frequency functions, as before they did. If N is quite large in relation to n, however, the fact of nonindependence will not bear materially on the previous results, as the $f(x_j)$ may be considered identical empirically.

In general terms the property that an estimator have the parameter of interest as its expected value in each sampling distribution (that is, whatever is actual sample size) is called *unbiasedness*. If b_n is an estimator of the population value B for an n-sample, unbiasedness implies, for example, the graphs of Fig. B.1. The definition is: for b_n an estimator of B, if $E(b_n) = B$, then b_n is said to be an *unbiased* estimator of B.

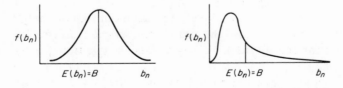

Fig. B.1

Examples of Unbiased Estimation

---

† Because their joint frequency function $f(x_1, \ldots, x_n)$ is *not* the product of their respective individual functions $f(x_1), \ldots, f(x_n)$.

If this is the definition of unbiased estimation, what is *biased* estimation? Very simply it is the opposite of unbiased estimation—that is, when $E(b_n) \neq B$. Figure B.2 depicts a situation of biased estimation. The quantity $E(b_n) - B$ is called the *bias*. So if, for example, we were attempting to estimate the *mode* of a population with a sample mean, $\bar{x}_n$, that has $E(\bar{x}_n) = \mu$, $\bar{x}_n$ would be a biased estimate of the mode so long as it did not correspond with μ.

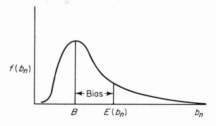

Fig. B.2

An Example of Biased Estimation

To illustrate these concepts let us elaborate on the opening example of this section, which concerned the estimation of the proportion of smoking doctors, $\tilde{P}$. Again, an intuitive estimator of $\tilde{P}$ is p_n, the sample proportion for n observations. If we put $x_j = 1$ when the *observed* element A_j is a smoker and $x_j = 0$ if not, then the sample proportion, p_n, takes the general form of an arithmetic mean—that is,

(B.2.2.3)
$$p_n = \frac{1}{n} \sum_{j=1}^{n} x_j.$$

From our discussion of Section B.2.1, if sampling is done with replacement so that $f(x_1) = f(x_2) = \cdots = f(x_n)$, then the expected value of p_n is

(B.2.2.4)
$$E(p_n) = \frac{1}{n} \sum_{j=1}^{n} E(x_j)$$
$$= \tilde{P},$$

since each x_j has the same expectation, $\tilde{P}$.

Note that $y = np_n = \sum_{j=1}^{n} x_j$ has the form of a *binomial* random variable. Indeed, we may deduce that sampling for dichotomous attributes with replacement must theoretically produce a binomial sampling distribution for np_n, since each slot to be filled in the sample is the analogue for a Bernoulli trial, where the probability of success is just the probability that the chosen element possesses the attribute of interest. This probability is $\tilde{P}$. Thus the expected value of np_n, a binomial random variable, is $n\tilde{P}$ as before; the expected value of p_n is obviously $\tilde{P}$, and p_n is *also* governed by a binomial distribution, since when $np_n = k$, $p_n = k/n$, and so on. The only difference, then, between the distribution of np_n and p_n is that the abscissa values of the distribution of np_n are divided by n.

If sampling is accomplished without replacement, the probability of "success" is *not* constant over the n drawings (trials); the trials are *not* independent. The probability that the first element selected (at random) possesses the attribute is $\tilde{P} = Y/N$, where Y is the number of elements possessing the attribute in the population. But the probability of success on the second draw clearly depends on what happens on the first. If an element with the attribute is selected first, then $(Y - 1)/(N - 1)$ is the probability that a similar occurrence applies to the second draw. But if no attribute was observed on draw one, then this probability is $Y/(N - 1)$, and so on. If we generalize this process, we find the distribution of np_n to be

$$(\text{B.2.2.5}) \qquad P(np_n = k \,|\, N, Y, n) = \frac{\binom{Y}{k}\binom{N - Y}{n - k}}{\binom{N}{n}},$$

which is the general term of the *hypergeometric* distribution, and bears a close resemblance to calculation techniques for obtaining probabilities that card hands will contain certain configurations of cards.

What can be said about p_n as an unbiased estimate of $\tilde{P}$ when sampling is done without replacement—that is, when the hypergeometric distribution is the sampling distribution? Theoretically, for any $n < N$ we cannot say much unless we assume the size of N, Y, and n are such that the differences between, for example, $Y/(N - 1)$, $(Y - 1)/(N - 1)$, and so on are very small and may therefore be ignored empirically. Such an assumption is tantamount to assuming that the probability of success on each trial is a constant, $\tilde{P}$. Then the previous binomial case holds, for which unbiasedness has already been shown. It is *not necessary* to make such an assumption for purposes of inference about Y, the number of population elements that possess the attribute, or $\tilde{P}$. We only use it here to give some intuitive feeling for the relationship between the hypergeometric and binomial distributions and to provide a simple (though restrictive) empirical indication of the unbiasedness of a sample proportion in the case of sampling without replacement.†

Obviously there are many ways of combining sample observations for the purpose of estimating μ, only one of which is as an arithmetic mean, $\bar{x}_n$. $\bar{x}_n$ does possess the desirable property of unbiasedness as an estimator

---

† As a practical matter the binomial often provides a useful approximation to the hypergeometric, and we will assume throughout that this approximation is a satisfactory one.

of μ, but that may not be a sufficient criterion to use in deciding which estimator among many to use as an estimator of μ or, in general, of any given population characteristic.

Consider, for example, $x_n^* = \bar{x}_n + (1/n)$ as an estimator of μ. Upon taking its expectation, we see that

$$E\left(\bar{x}_n + \frac{1}{n}\right) = \mu + \frac{1}{n},$$

so that x_n^* is a biased estimator of μ, the bias being $1/n$. Now if n is "large" it is apparent that $x_n^* \doteq \bar{x}_n$, and under sampling with replacement $x_n^* \longrightarrow \bar{x}_n$ as $n \longrightarrow \infty$, which by our previous work implies $E(x_n^*) \longrightarrow \mu$ as $n \longrightarrow \infty$. This *asymptotic unbiasedness* is moreover called the property of *consistency* if in conjunction with $E(x_n^*) \longrightarrow \mu$ there is an accompanying clustering of values x_n^* around μ. This provides a "loose" definition of consistency. A more formal treatment is given in the next subsection. If this latter condition did not hold, then the bias would not *progressively* move toward zero; that is, there would not necessarily be better inference from taking larger samples—a relationship we perhaps take for granted a priori.

Under what circumstances might a biased estimator be preferred to an unbiased one? Also, how might we reasonably choose between two unbiased estimators? Dealing with the latter question first, we find its answer in a comparison of the precision of alternative estimators as measured by their respective second moments around the population constant. Clearly an estimator that has its possible values (possible over attainable samples of a given size) clustered around the population parameter is more desirable than one whose values (for the same sample size) are more widely dispersed, simply because the probability that any given n-sample will produce an estimate in some arbitrary range is larger in the former case. This probability is some measure of our "confidence" in the estimate we actually obtain, but is obtained by *ex ante* considerations.

Consider the comparison indicated in Fig. B.3, where the distributions of two estimators $b_n^{(1)}$ and $b_n^{(2)}$ of B are shown. While both estimators have B as their expected value, $b_n^{(1)}$ appears to be superior, since the probability

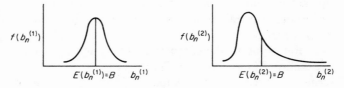

Fig. B.3

Comparison of Precision for Two Unbiased Estimators

that any actual $b_n^{(1)}$ falls within some small interval to either side of B is larger than if $b_n^{(2)}$ were used.

A general criterion for making such comparisons is the Mean Square Error concept. We define the MSE for any estimator as follows:

$$\text{(B.2.2.6)} \qquad \text{MSE}_{b_n} = E[b_n - B]^2,$$

an indicator of how the actual values of an estimator are, on the average, distributed around the constant B.

Some manipulation of (B.2.2.6) gives MSE in terms of the variance of b_n, $\sigma_{b_n}^2$, and the bias $[E(b_n) - B]$: adding and subtracting $E(b_n)$ in (B.2.2.6),

$$\text{(B.2.2.7)} \qquad \text{MSE}_{b_n} = E[b_n - E(b_n) + E(b_n) - B]^2$$
$$= \sigma_{b_n}^2 + [E(b_n) - B]^2 + 2E[b_n - E(b_n)][E(b_n) - B].$$

Now the last term may be rewritten as $2[E(b_n) - B]E[b_n - E(b_n)]$, since $E(b_n) - B (= \text{Bias})$ is a constant. But $E[b_n - E(b_n)] = 0$, so

$$\text{(B.2.2.8)} \qquad \text{MSE}_{b_n} = \sigma_{b_n}^2 + [E(b_n) - B]^2.$$

For a statement of the MSE criterion we shall say that an estimator $b_n^{(1)}$ of B is superior in MSE to $b_n^{(2)}$ if $\text{MSE}_{b_n}^{(1)} < \text{MSE}_{b_n}^{(2)}$. The use of MSE in this way implies a subjective evaluation of the relative evils of large variance (*inefficiency*) and bias, which has variance and squared bias traded off against one another. Its use is mainly conventional, and the reader should note that for some uses it may be desirable to place different weights on these two terms. A theoretical justification for the MSE criterion follows in the next section, tying it to an arbitrary sampling distribution. Note that if b_n is an unbiased estimator, (B.2.2.8) becomes

$$\text{(B.2.2.9)} \qquad \text{MSE}_{b_n} = \sigma_{b_n}^2 \qquad \text{if } E(b_n) = B.$$

Then for purposes of selecting a "best" estimator from among several *unbiased* alternatives, the MSE criterion—in this case, a *variance* criterion—provides a simple rule. Likewise, if the alternatives under consideration are all biased estimators with *equal* biases for a given sample size, a variance criterion will again select a "best" estimator. If, however, the choice is to be made from among a set of estimators with varying attributes a method that incorporates certain weights on variance and bias, such as the MSE criterion, must be used.

Returning to the comparison of $\bar{x}_n$ and $\bar{x}_n + (1/n)$ as estimators of μ, we know $E(\bar{x}_n) = \mu$ but $E[\bar{x}_n + (1/n)] = \mu + (1/n)$. Applying the MSE criterion directs us to compare $\text{MSE}_{\bar{x}_n} = \sigma_{\bar{x}_n}^2$ with $\text{MSE}_{[\bar{x}_n + (1/n)]} = \sigma_{\bar{x}_n}^2 + (1/n^2)$. In this case the unbiased estimate also possesses smallest MSE and so is judged superior. Based on a variance (only) criterion the two estimators would be judged equally good.

As a further hypothetical illustration of these ideas suppose another competitor to $\bar{x}_n$ as an estimator of μ is given by

(B.2.2.10) $$\tilde{x}_n = \sum_{j=1}^{n} w_j x_j, \qquad \sum_{j=1}^{n} w_j = 1,$$

where the x_j's are random variables as defined previously. It is easy to see that

(B.2.2.11) $$E(\tilde{x}_n) = \sum_{j=1}^{n} w_j E(x_j) = \mu \sum_{j=1}^{n} w_j = \mu.$$

Thus, if we specify any set of w_j so that $\sum w_j = 1$ and combine the sample observations by (B.2.2.10), we will produce an estimate with an expected value of μ. Suppose for $n = 3$ we specify $w_1 = \frac{1}{2}$, $w_2 = \frac{1}{4}$, $w_3 = \frac{1}{4}$ and observe $x_1 = 5$ (units), $x_2 = 3$, and $x_3 = 10$. Then $\bar{x}_3 = \frac{18}{3} = 6$, and $\tilde{x}_3 = 5\frac{3}{4}$. Both estimators are unbiased: if we selected all possible samples of size 3, for each calculated $\bar{x}_3$ and $\tilde{x}_3$, and then averaged these values over all samples, we would find that *both* averages equaled μ. Upon calculating the variances for each (since they are unbiased), however, we would find that $\bar{x}_3$ is the more efficient estimator.

In general, if the sample-draw random variables are independent, and have the same $f(x_j)$, with $E(x_j) = \mu$ and $\sigma^2_{x_j} = \sigma^2$ (the population variance), then

(B.2.2.12) $$\sigma^2_{\bar{x}_n} = \frac{1}{n^2} \sum_{j=1}^{n} \sigma^2_{x_j} = \frac{n}{n^2} \sigma^2 = \frac{\sigma^2}{n},$$

using familiar rules for calculating variances. This formula applies under sampling with replacement. Using the same assumptions for $\tilde{x}_n$, we find

(B.2.2.13) $$\sigma^2_{\tilde{x}_n} = \sum_{j=1}^{n} w_j^2 \sigma^2_{x_j} = \sigma^2 \sum_{j=1}^{n} w_j^2.$$

Whether $\bar{x}_n$ is a better (more efficient) estimator depends on

$$\frac{1}{n} < \sum_{j=1}^{n} w_j^2,$$

which holds except when all $w_j = 1/n$—that is, when $\tilde{x}_n = \bar{x}_n$.† Thus the

---

† This inequality is easy to demonstrate with the aid of calculus. We wish to find the set of w_j that minimizes $\sum_{j=1}^{n} w_j^2$ subject to the restriction that $\sum_{j=1}^{n} w_j = 1$. The solutions are available using the Lagrangean multiplier technique from the equations:

$$2w_j + \lambda = 0, \qquad j = 1, \ldots, n,$$
$$\sum w_j - 1 = 0.$$

Every w_j must equal $-\lambda/2$ and $-n\lambda/2 = 1$, so $\lambda = -2/n$ and $w_j = 1/n$ ($j = 1, \ldots, n$). This minimization is an example of the method of least-squares estimation, where we attempt to deduce the estimator (a function of sample observations) that provides minimum variance (MSE) over the n-sample.

sample mean and, therefore, the sample proportion are "best" estimators of μ and $\tilde{P}$ among all linear estimators, those estimators which appear as linear functions of the sample observations.

As pointed out previously, in actuality choice among alternative estimators in some cases will involve unbiased versus biased estimators when the biased estimator possesses a smaller MSE. Thus, while for a given sample size the unbiased estimator has the population parameter as its average value, it may be relatively imprecise compared to the biased estimator.

As a final note in this discussion of properties of estimators, one need not rely on intuition (or analogy) in order to produce alternative estimators to be evaluated by the suggested criteria. Techniques are available for generating estimators that will possess certain properties, notably the methods of *least squares* (LS) and *maximum likelihood* (ML). LS, to be applicable, depends on certain assumptions being met but produces unbiased linear estimates of minimum variance (and hence MSE). The ML method requires and utilizes the joint frequency distribution of sample observations and generally produces consistent estimators. The techniques rest on different assumptions. But in some cases both may be applicable and they may yield identical estimators. LS is often the superior method owing to the efficiency of the estimator produced and the lack of required knowledge of the form of the distribution of sample observations.

The preceding problem of finding an "appropriate" estimator for the population mean provides a good basis for illustrating the two techniques. First we must *articulate* the statistical model under which observations are presumably generated. For the random-sampling-with-replacement situation, we have assumed that an *observation*, x_j, is related to the population mean as follows: $E(x_j) = \mu$. Alternatively, we may write

(B.2.2.14)
$$x_j = \mu + \epsilon_j, \qquad j = 1, \ldots, n,$$

where ϵ_j is an unobservable random variable with zero mean. Observations on the $\{x_j\}$ and therefore the $\{\epsilon_j\}$ are independent, and the variance of each ϵ_j is σ^2, a constant (the population variance of x_j).

To utilize the LS method requires no further assumptions. It directs us to minimize the sum

(B.2.2.15)
$$\sum_{j=1}^{n} \epsilon_j^2 = \sum_{j=1}^{n} (x_j - \mu)^2$$

with respect to μ, which in this case gives as the LS estimator $\hat{\mu} = \bar{x}_n$, as can readily be verified. The least-squares estimators in general are found by minimizing the sum of squared "residuals" in the model with respect to the unknown parameters. They possess the properties of unbiasedness and minimum variance among alternative linear unbiased estimators (as we have shown for $\bar{x}_n$), but only when applied to so-called *linear* models—that is, models that are linear in parameters.†

In order to apply the maximum likelihood technique to this same model it is additionally required that the probability distribution of each x_j be specified. For sake of illustration, suppose that the $\{x_j\}$ are normally distributed with identical means (μ) and variances (σ^2). Then the joint distribution of sample observations is just

$$(B.2.2.16) \qquad L(\mu, \sigma^2) = f(x_1, \ldots, x_n | \mu, \sigma^2) = \prod_{j=1}^{n} \left(\frac{1}{\sqrt{2\pi}\,\sigma} \right) e^{-(1/2\sigma^2)(x_j - \mu)^2},$$

more commonly referred to in this context as the *likelihood function* for the sample. The reader should note that it has been constructed utilizing the assumption of independence of the x_j's. The principle of maximum likelihood suggests that we use as estimates of μ and σ^2 those *numbers* which *maximize* (B.2.2.16) for *our* sample. The procedure utilized to do this is again an application of the calculus.

Taking first partial derivatives of (B.2.2.16) and equating them to zero would be the direct approach. But we may simplify matters in this case by first noting that a maximum of (B.2.2.16) occurs at the same point $(\hat{\mu}, \hat{\sigma}^2)$ for which $\log L(\mu, \sigma^2)$ is maximized, because $\log (.)$ is an increasing function of its argument. And $\log L(\mu, \sigma^2)$ is just

$$(B.2.2.17) \qquad \log L(\mu, \sigma^2) = -\frac{n}{2} \log (2\pi) - \frac{n}{2} \log \sigma^2$$

$$-\frac{1}{2}\left(\frac{1}{\sigma^2}\right) \sum_{j=1}^{n} (x_j - \mu)^2.$$

Without actually writing out the appropriate partial derivatives we can see that *whatever* is σ^2, $\log L(\mu, \sigma^2)$ will be maximized over μ when $\sum_{j=1}^{n} (x_j - \mu)^2$ is a *minimum*—exactly the LS criterion. Thus for known or unknown σ^2, $\bar{x}_n$ provides the ML estimator for μ.

In general, maximum likelihood estimators are consistent, and they have minimum variance and possess normal distributions in very large samples even if the $\{x_j\}$ themselves are not normally distributed. The ML estimators, and hence their properties, are not limited to the class of linear estimators, as are LS estimators. Of course, in this example the maximum likelihood estimator of μ *coincides* (is identical in every sample) to the LS estimator; therefore it is also unbiased and has minimum variance for every sample size among alternative linear unbiased estimators. It so happens that weighted

---

† The model $x_j = \mu^2 + \epsilon_j$, for example, is a nonlinear model. While the method of LS provides an unbiased, minimum-variance estimator for μ^2, namely $\overline{(\mu^2)}$, the estimator $\hat{\mu} = \sqrt{\overline{(\mu^2)}}$ does *not* possess these attributes.

sums of independent, normally distributed random variables are also normally distributed, so that $\bar{x}_n$ possesses a normal distribution for any sample size, since the underlying population distribution is assumed normal.

Generally we require knowledge of the sampling distribution of any estimator to make inferential statements about its relation to the population parameter of interest. So, to *use* the LS estimator of μ in this way we would have to invoke some distribution assumption (or prior knowledge). The central limit theorem says that for large enough sample size, $(\bar{x}_n - \mu)/(\sigma/\sqrt{n})$ will be approximately normally distributed with mean zero and variance one. How good the approximation might be in any given situation, or how large the sample size must be, are not easily answered questions. Yet use of the maximum likelihood method likewise requires a distributional specification, which may not be so obvious as in the case of a binomial problem. Fortunately, we may avert some of these difficulties by appealing to a famous theorem of statistics, *Tchebycheff's inequality*.

B.2.3 TCHEBYCHEFF'S INEQUALITY—CONFIDENCE INTERVALS

Tchebycheff's inequality allows us to make probability statements about an estimator and how it is distributed around a population constant *without* knowledge of the form of this distribution. Thus, it provides a theoretical basis for such statements when no particular distribution is assumed or justified and is of great generality.

The theorem may be easily stated and proved:

Let x be a random variable and k a constant. Then for *any $e > 0$*

(B.2.3.1) (a) $$P(|x - k| > e) < \frac{\sigma_x^2 + [E(x) - k]^2}{e^2},$$

and since $P(|x - k| > e) + P(|x - k| \leq e) = 1$,

(b) $$P(|x - k| \leq e) \geq 1 - \frac{\sigma_x^2 + [E(x) - k]^2}{e^2}.$$

The numerator of the fraction is simply MSE_x, and e is any positive number, representing a preset bound on the absolute difference between x and k.

If x is an unbiased estimator of k, then $E(x) = k$, and a special case arises:

(B.2.3.2) (a) $$P(|x - k| > e) < \frac{\sigma_x^2}{e^2},$$

(b) $$P(|x - k| \leq e) \geq 1 - \frac{\sigma_x^2}{e^2}.$$

We shall proceed to prove (B.2.3.1a), which implies (B.2.3.1b). The proof is in terms of a discrete random variable for convenience only. The result applies equally well to continuous random variables.

Let x have possible values $x_1, \ldots, x_n$ with probabilities $p_1, \ldots, p_n$. Suppose that of n differences $(x_i - k)$, exactly m of them are such that $|x_i - k| > e$, and, therefore, $n - m$ of them have $|x_i - k| \leq e$. We may easily speak of the probability $P(|x - k| > e)$ in terms of the m possible values of x that have $|x_i - k| > e$. That is,

$$P(|x - k| > e) = \sum_{i=1}^{m} p_i.$$

Consider the expected value of $(x - k)^2$, given by

$$E(x - k)^2 = \sum_{i=1}^{n} (x_i - k)^2 p_i.$$

It follows directly that

$$E(x - k)^2 \geq \sum_{i=1}^{m} (x_i - k)^2 p_i.$$

Now if $|x_i - k| > e$, then $(x_i - k)^2 > e^2$, so that

$$E(x - k)^2 > \sum_{i=1}^{m} e^2 p_i = e^2 \sum_{i=1}^{m} p_i$$

and

$$\frac{E(x - k)^2}{e^2} > \sum_{i=1}^{m} p_i.$$

But from our initial specification,

$$\sum_{i=1}^{m} p_i = P(|x - k| > e),$$

which leads to the final result,

$$P(|x - k| > e) < \frac{E(x - k)^2}{e^2}.$$

The above probability statement may, of course, be rewritten without absolute-value notation. Form (b) is more commonly used, however, and when the absolute-value signs are removed appears as

(B.2.3.3) $P[x - e \leq k \leq x + e] \geq 1 - \dfrac{E(x - k)^2}{e^2}.$

Equation (B.2.3.3) is a classical statement of the *confidence interval*: if x is an estimator of k, then the "probability that the interval $(x - e, x + e)$ contains k is . . . ." Clearly from (B.2.3.3) the smaller the MSE of x the closer to one is the probability that the interval contains k.

The formal definition of consistency is quite closely related to this last statement. For e chosen arbitrarily small (but positive), if as sample size increases indefinitely the probability in (B.2.3.3) approaches one, we say that x is a consistent estimator for k. According to Tchebycheff's in-equality, for this to happen x must be asymptotically unbiased (the bias must become infinitesimally small for large n) and its variance must also approach zero for large n. For, these two terms make up the mean square error of x, which appears in (B.2.3.3) and which must be zero for the prob-ability that the interval $(x - e, x + e)$ contains k to be one.

To relate the confidence interval to our previous notions of the pre-cision of an estimate, note that the value of e may be arbitrarily set, say as so many mean-square-error units, and so on.† Suppose, for example, x is an unbiased estimator of k. Then the special case of the theorem applies, and $E(x - k)^2 = \sigma_x^2$. Also, let $e = 3\sigma_x$. That is, we are requesting the probability that $x \pm 3\sigma_x$ will contain the parameter k. The probability is

$$(B.2.3.4) \qquad P[x - 3\sigma_x \leq k \leq x + 3\sigma_x] \geq 1 - \frac{\sigma_x^2}{9\sigma_x^2} = 1 - \frac{1}{9}$$

$$\geq \frac{8}{9}.$$

How does this probability statement relate to the problem of interpre-tation for one sample? Suppose 90 samples are taken at random, each of a given size, n. For each sample the estimate x (an actual, calculated value) is combined with the arbitrary constant $e = 3\sigma_x$ to form 90 intervals. The interpretation is that were these 90 intervals to be plotted as in Fig. B.4, they would enclose k with a relative frequency at least equal to $\frac{8}{9}$—or, we would expect 80 of the 90 sample intervals to cover k.

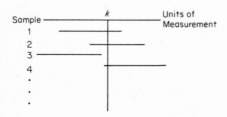

Fig. B.4

† Although the bounds produced for, e.g., $e \leq 1\text{MSE}_x$ are not very informative.

Since the inequality operates without a specific distribution assumption, we should expect it to provide only the most general boundaries on actual probabilities, "actual" as determined for any particular distribution.

For a binomial problem with $n = 30$, $\tilde{P} = .5$ and, using the sample proportion, $p_n = y/n$, as an (unbiased) estimator of $\tilde{P}$, we find $\sigma_p = (1/n^2) \cdot$ $\sigma_y^2 = (n\tilde{P}\tilde{Q})/n^2 = (\tilde{P}\tilde{Q})/n = .25/30 = .008$. $\sigma_p = \sqrt{.008} \doteq .09$ and $3\sigma_p = .27$, corresponding to Fig. B.5, where a continuous function is drawn for visual ease only. The calculated 3-sigma limits are .23 and .77 with $\frac{7}{30}$ and $\frac{23}{30}$ the corresponding exact binomial limits.† The binomial probability is .9986, whereas Tchebycheff's inequality says the interval holds with probability *at least* .89 $(\frac{8}{9})$.

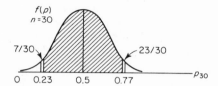

Fig. B.5

Suppose we were estimating a population mean $\mu = 15$ with the mean of a sample of size 25 from a normally distributed population with $\sigma^2 = 100$. If the sample random variables are $x_j, j = 1, \ldots, n$, with $x_j \sim N(15,100)$ for all j, then for the sample mean

$$\bar{x}_n = \frac{1}{n} \sum_{j=1}^{n} x_j, \qquad E(\bar{x}_n) = \mu, \quad \text{and} \quad \sigma_{\bar{x}_n}^2 = \frac{\sigma^2}{n},$$

so that $\bar{x}_n \sim N(15, 4)$ if sampling is accomplished by an SRS method.‡

For a confidence interval with $e = 2\sigma_{\bar{x}_n}$ Tchebycheff's inequality states the probability that μ is contained within the limits $\bar{x}_n \pm 2\sigma_{\bar{x}_n}$ is at least .75. The actual probability may easily be obtained from the standard normal tables, corresponding to the area under the $N(0, 1)$ distribution in the interval $(-2, 2)$; this probability is .9544.

It is easy to see how a probability statement from a normal sampling distribution about the (e.g.) sample mean being contained within fixed limits may be turned around to yield a statement about the fixed parameter being contained within variable limits. For the example just treated, the probability that a normally distributed n-sample mean is contained within the

† .23 and .77 are *not* possible values, so that $P(.23 \leq p_{30} \leq .77) \equiv P(\frac{7}{30} \leq p_{30} \leq \frac{23}{30})$.
‡ Note that the (continuous) normal distribution can be defined only on a population of infinite size.

limits $\mu \pm 2\sigma_{\bar{x}_n}$ is just

(B.2.3.5) $$P[\mu - 2\sigma_{\bar{x}_n} \leq \bar{x}_n \leq \mu + 2\sigma_{\bar{x}_n}] = .9544$$

and corresponds to the shaded area of Fig. B.6. In actual units of measurement $2\sigma_{\bar{x}_n} = 2\sqrt{\frac{100}{25}} = \frac{20}{5} = 4$, so that the probability above is equivalent to

(B.2.3.6) $$P(11 \leq \bar{x}_n \leq 19) = .9544.$$

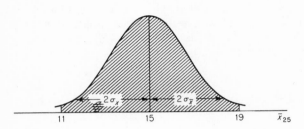

Fig. B.6

In (B.2.3.5), if we operate on the inequalities we can put $\bar{x}_n$ and μ in juxtaposition, producing the confidence interval required. Merely add $-\bar{x}_n$ and $-\mu$ to all three sides of the inequality, to obtain

(B.2.3.7) $$P[-\bar{x}_n - 2\sigma_{\bar{x}_n} \leq -\mu \leq -\bar{x}_n + 2\sigma_{\bar{x}_n}] = .9544.$$

Multiplying inside by (-1) and consequently reversing the inequalities,

(B.2.3.8) $$P[\bar{x}_n + 2\sigma_{\bar{x}_n} \geq \mu \geq \bar{x}_n - 2\sigma_{\bar{x}_n}] = .9544,$$

which is identical to

(B.2.3.9) $$P[\bar{x}_n - 2\sigma_{\bar{x}_n} \leq \mu \leq \bar{x}_n + 2\sigma_{\bar{x}_n}] = .9544.$$

For other distributions, such as the binomial and Poisson, the confidence interval or *interval estimate* of a parameter is not so easily described, and must wait for presentation later (Section B.3). The reader should also note that the examples used have involved unbiased estimates. Tchebycheff's inequality may be utilized with e being quoted in terms of MSE units, but for the normal distribution the basic unit of measure is σ, the standard deviation of the distribution. Thus if the problem situation concerns a normally distributed, *biased* estimator, then it is not true that the confidence interval may be quoted in MSE units of deviation to accomplish the required adjustment.† Our work will not deal with this problem, and we will use unbiased

---

† See, for example, W. G. Cochran, *Sampling Techniques*, 2nd ed. (New York: Wiley, 1963), pp. 12–16, for a clear demonstration of the problem.

estimators throughout (of population means), so that standard deviation measurements are appropriate in the normal case.

The relation between sample size and precision as expressed in the normal confidence interval is clear from (B.2.3.9). If we put $\sigma_{\bar{x}_n} = \sqrt{\sigma^2/n} = \sigma/\sqrt{n}$, then $n \longrightarrow \infty \Rightarrow \sigma_{\bar{x}_n} \longrightarrow 0$, which must hold since we are dealing with an unbiased and consistent estimator of μ. Thus the limits around μ may be tightened (more precise estimation) with increases in n at a given *confidence level*. Or, with given n the limits may be tightened by *lowering* the confidence level.

In either case *it is assumed that $\sigma_{\bar{x}_n}^2$ (hence σ^2) is known*. Such knowledge is not available in most instances, but the normal interval depends upon it. Our methodology must necessarily be modified to include such a situation, if possible. We return, therefore, to the now familiar circumstance of seemingly having to know what we are trying to estimate before we estimate it. The key to overcoming this obstacle is to note that σ^2 for a population may be estimated from a sample also. We turn then to an investigation of the effects of estimating σ^2 on the normal confidence interval.

B.2.4. ESTIMATION OF VARIANCE

The classical confidence interval for a normally distributed, unbiased estimator is given by

(B.2.4.1) $P[b_n - Z_{\alpha/2}\sigma_{b_n} \leq B \leq b_n + Z_{\alpha/2}\sigma_{b_n}] = 1 - \alpha,$

where b_n is the n-sample estimator, B is the population parameter of interest, σ_{b_n} is the standard deviation of b_n around B, $1 - \alpha$ is called the confidence (probability) level, and $Z_{\alpha/2}$ is the standard normal deviate that cuts off exactly $\alpha/2$ (proportion) of the area measured from the standard normal mean, zero, in each tail of the distribution. Our equation (B.2.3.9), for instance, is merely an application of this more general form, with $b_n = \bar{x}_n$, $B = \mu$, $1 - \alpha = .9544$, and $Z_{\alpha/2} = 2$.

What sort of confidence statement is available when $\sigma_{\bar{x}_n}$ is unknown? The answer may be given only after we treat the more general problem of how to estimate $\sigma_{\bar{x}_n}$. Once this is accomplished, we return to the confidence statement and attempt to analyze the effects of using an estimate (random variable) of $\sigma_{\bar{x}_n}$ rather than the parameter itself.

Equation (B.2.2.12) shows the key relationship between the variance of the sampling distribution of sample means and the population variance,

(B.2.4.2) $\sigma_{\bar{x}_n}^2 = \dfrac{\sigma^2}{n},$

under conditions of sampling *with* replacement. In other words, this relationship holds when it is possible to draw an infinite number of samples or when the population is infinitely large. From our knowledge of expected value it is clear that an unbiased estimator of σ^2 will provide an unbiased estimator of $\sigma^2_{\bar{x}_n}$. This is truly an amazing result. We may provide an estimate (and a "good" one, perhaps) of the variance of the distribution of all n-sample means from but one sample!

Using our intuition again, a possible estimator of σ^2 is its analogue in the sample†—that is,

$$(B.2.4.3) \qquad s^{*2} = \frac{1}{n} \sum_{j=1}^{n} (x_j - \bar{x}_n)^2$$

$$= \frac{1}{n} \sum_{j=1}^{n} x_j^2 - \bar{x}_n^2.$$

To evaluate (B.2.4.3) for the sampling with replacement case, we begin by taking its expected value:

$$(B.2.4.4) \qquad E(s^{*2}) = \frac{1}{n} E\left(\sum_{i=1}^{n} x_j^2\right) - E(\bar{x}_n^2)$$

$$= \frac{1}{n} \sum_{j=1}^{n} E(x_j^2) - E(\bar{x}_n^2).$$

Since we assume a sampling procedure where all random variables are independent and identically distributed, from the definition of the population variance

$$(B.2.4.5) \qquad E(x_j^2) = \sigma^2 + \mu^2,$$

so that

$$(B.2.4.6) \qquad E(s^{*2}) = \sigma^2 + \mu^2 - E(\bar{x}_n^2).$$

By definition

$$(B.2.4.7) \qquad \sigma^2_{\bar{x}_n} = E[\bar{x}_n - \mu]^2 = E(\bar{x}_n^2) - \mu^2.$$

Substituting for $E(\bar{x}_n^2)$ in (B.2.4.6):

$$(B.2.4.8) \qquad E(s^{*2}) = \sigma^2 - \sigma^2_{\bar{x}_n}.$$

Under sampling with replacement $\sigma^2_{\bar{x}_n} = \sigma^2/n$, which leads to

$$(B.2.4.9) \qquad E(s^{*2}) = \sigma^2 - \frac{\sigma^2}{n} = \frac{n-1}{n}\sigma^2,$$

† This form of the "sample variance" is also the ML estimator of σ^2 when sampling from a normal population, as the reader can determine by extending the suggested derivations at the end of Section B.2.3.

and *not* σ^2. Thus the sample value s^{*2} is *not* an unbiased estimator of σ^2 when sampling is done with replacement. But (B.2.4.9) suggests that

(B.2.4.10) $$s^2 = \frac{n}{n-1} s^{*2} = \frac{1}{n-1} \sum_{j=1}^{n} (x_j - \bar{x}_n)^2$$

is an unbiased estimate of σ^2, so that an unbiased estimate of $\sigma_{\bar{x}_n}^2$ is available from

(B.2.4.11) $$s_{\bar{x}_n}^2 = \frac{s^2}{n}.$$

The sampling-without-replacement case follows similar lines, but at step (B.2.4.9) it is *not* true that $\sigma_{\bar{x}_n}^2 = \sigma^2/n$. Instead the proper form is

(B.2.4.12) $$\sigma_{\bar{x}_n}^2 = \left(\frac{N-n}{N-1}\right) \frac{\sigma^2}{n}. \dagger$$

Inserting (B.2.4.12) into (B.2.4.8), we find

(B.2.4.13) $$E(s^{*2}) = \left[1 - \frac{N-n}{(N-1)n}\right]\sigma^2$$
$$= \frac{N}{N-1}\left(\frac{n-1}{n}\right)\sigma^2,$$

—that is, s^{*2} under sampling without replacement is again a biased estimate of σ^2. Moreover, using s^2 instead of s^{*2},

(B.2.4.14) $$E(s^2) = \frac{N}{N-1}\sigma^2,$$

and not σ^2. But this difficulty may easily be overcome by defining a new population constant (numerically indistinguishable from σ^2 if N is large):

(B.2.4.15) $$S^2 = \frac{N}{N-1}\sigma^2.$$

Then s^2 is an unbiased estimate of S^2, and we may rewrite (B.2.4.12) in terms of S^2 to get

(B.2.4.16) $$\sigma_{\bar{x}_n}^2 = \left(\frac{N-n}{N}\right) \frac{S^2}{n}$$

under sampling without replacement. Another common form for (B.2.4.16) is

(B.2.4.17) $$\sigma_{\bar{x}_n}^2 = \left(1 - \frac{n}{N}\right) \frac{S^2}{n}.$$

$\dagger$ We state this relationship here without proof. Cf. Cochran, *Sampling Techniques*, pp. 22–23.

The multiplier $[1 - (n/N)]$ is called the *finite population correction*, and is equal to the fraction of the population *not* sampled.

To obtain an unbiased estimate of $\sigma_{\bar{x}_n}^2$ under sampling without replacement, therefore, we use

(B.2.4.18)
$$s_{\bar{x}_n}^2 = \left(1 - \frac{n}{N}\right)\frac{s^2}{n}.$$

If n/N is small, (B.2.4.18) will closely approximate (B.2.4.11) numerically. (B.2.2.18) *becomes* (B.2.4.11) as $N \rightarrow \infty$.

As an illustration of such calculations in practice, suppose a sample of five individuals from a population consisting of students in a large statistics class was drawn using sampling with replacement, and their heights measured. If the observed heights in inches were: 63, 72, 78, 68, 69, the relevant sample statistics would be: $\bar{x}_5 = 70$ in., $s^2 = 30.5$ sq in., $s_{\bar{x}_5}^2 = 6.1$ sq in., $s_{\bar{x}_5} = 2.47$ in. One way of presenting the results would be to quote the estimated mean as 70 in. with a standard ("average") deviation of 2.47 in.

Before turning to the question of effects on a normal confidence interval of the use of an estimated variance, consider the implementation of a normal approximation to the binomial or hypergeometric problems of estimating a population proportion. As we shall see in the following section, our methods of inference are easily applied to these cases, using the exact distributions. But from a practical point of view it may sometimes be appropriate and much easier to use the normal approximation to these discrete distributions, which requires the expression of the estimated variance of the sample proportion, σ_p^2.

To give a one-to-one correspondence to our previous development, let the measured quantity X_i be defined over the population of N elements by the familiar zero-one variable. Then the population proportion is $\tilde{P}$ and the population variance is given by

(B.2.4.19)
$$\sigma^2 = \frac{1}{N}\sum_{i=1}^{N}(X_i - \tilde{P})^2$$

$$= \frac{1}{N}\sum_{i=1}^{N}X_i^2 - \tilde{P}^2$$

$$= \tilde{P} - \tilde{P}^2, \quad \text{since } \sum_{i=1}^{N}X_i = \sum_{i=1}^{N}X_i^2,$$

$$= \tilde{P}\tilde{Q}.$$

Thus the (population) variance of the sample proportion, p_n, under sampling with replacement (binomial) is as in (B.2.4.2) with $\tilde{P}\tilde{Q}$ substituted for σ^2:

(B.2.4.20)
$$\sigma_{p_n}^2 = \frac{\tilde{P}\tilde{Q}}{n}.$$

The analogous form for sampling without replacement is from (B.2.4.12):

(B.2.4.21)
$$\sigma^2_{p_n} = \left(\frac{N-n}{N-1}\right)\frac{\tilde{P}\tilde{Q}}{n}.$$

Following the development of (B.2.4.11), when sampling is accomplished with replacement and the population variance $\tilde{P}\tilde{Q}$ is estimated with the sample variance s^2, we see that

(B.2.4.22)
$$s^2 = \frac{1}{n-1}\sum_{j=1}^{n}(x_j - \bar{x}_n)^2$$
$$= \frac{1}{n-1}\left(\sum_{j=1}^{n}x_j^2 - n\bar{x}_n^2\right)$$
$$= \frac{1}{n-1}[np_n - np_n^2]$$
$$= \frac{n}{n-1}p_n q_n,$$

which provides an unbiased estimate of $\tilde{P}\tilde{Q}$ in (B.2.4.20), and results in the estimator

(B.2.4.23)
$$s^2_{p_n} = \frac{p_n q_n}{n-1}.$$

We know from our previous work that s^2 is also an unbiased estimate of $[N/(N-1)]\sigma^2$ for sampling without replacement. Substituting (B.2.4.22) into (B.2.4.21) for $[N/(N-1)]\sigma^2$, we get

(B.2.4.24)
$$s^2_{p_n} = \left(1 - \frac{n}{N}\right)\frac{p_n q_n}{n-1},$$

when sampling is without replacement (hypergeometric).

As an illustration of the use of the normal approximation to a binomial sampling situation, suppose $n = 10$ and that 5 of the selected individuals possess the noteworthy characteristic. Then $p_{10} = .5$ and by (B.2.4.23) $s^2_{p_{10}} = (.25)/10 = .025$, $s_{p_{10}} = .158$, and the 95 percent confidence interval for $\tilde{P}$ is approximately

(B.2.4.25) $P[.5 - (1.96)(.158) \le \tilde{P} \le .5 + (1.96)(.158)] \doteq .95$

or
$$P[.190 \le \tilde{P} \le .810] \doteq .95,$$

which states that this interval contains $\tilde{P}$ with probability .95. We shall return to this example in the next section for purposes of evaluating how good the normal approximation is to the actual binomial confidence interval.

This normal interval may likewise be used to produce confidence statements about a Poisson mean, λ. If in a sample interval of 24 hours the local post office received three special delivery letters, what is a 95 percent confidence interval around λ, the average number of special delivery letters received every 24 hours? Again, as in the binomial case, we are not yet prepared to give an answer to this question in terms of the exact distribution. But we may use the normal approximation with an estimated variance.

Recalling that the Poisson has both its mean *and* variance equal to λ, we may easily produce the required approximation:

$$(B.2.4.26) \quad P[3 - (1.96)(\sqrt{3}) \leq \lambda \leq 3 + (1.96)(\sqrt{3})] \doteq .95.$$

In this particular instance the lower interval bound $(-.39)$ has little meaning. λ cannot, by definition, be either negative or zero. Thus a more precise statement would read:

$$(B.2.4.27) \qquad P[0 < \lambda \leq 6.39] \doteq .95.$$

B.2.5 THE "*t*" DISTRIBUTION

If the sampling distribution of n-sample means is *known* to be normally distributed (for example, when the population distribution is normal), but the variance of the sampling distribution is *not* known, and is estimated by $s_{\bar{x}_n}^2$, then the statistic

$$(B.2.5.1) \qquad\qquad t = \frac{\bar{x}_n - \mu}{s_{\bar{x}_n}}$$

does not follow the standard normal distribution. This is to say that the probability statement

$$(B.2.5.2) \qquad\qquad P[\bar{x}_n - 2s_{\bar{x}_n} \leq \mu \leq \bar{x}_n + 2s_{\bar{x}_n}]$$

holds with probability *less* than .9544 as under the normal distribution. Or, saying it another way, at a probability .9544 and using $s_{\bar{x}_n}$ instead of $\sigma_{\bar{x}_n}$ the confidence limits $\bar{x}_n \pm 2s_{\bar{x}_n}$ are *too narrow*.

The basis for this discussion lies in three theorems about probability distributions.

THEOREM 1

IF y_i $(i = 1, \ldots, n)$ ARE NORMALLY AND INDEPENDENTLY DISTRIBUTED RANDOM VARIABLES WITH MEANS $E(y_i) = \theta_i$ AND VARIANCES $E[y_i - \theta_i]^2 = \sigma_i^2$, THEN THE WEIGHTED SUM $\sum_{i=1}^{n} w_i y_i$, WHERE NOT ALL $w_i = 0$, IS NORMALLY DISTRIBUTED WITH MEAN $\sum_{i=1}^{n} w_i \theta_i$ AND VARIANCE $\sum_{i=1}^{n} w_i^2 \sigma_i^2$.

THEOREM 2

IF $z_j (j = 1, \ldots, m)$ ARE INDEPENDENT STANDARD NORMAL RANDOM VARIABLES, THEN $\sum_{j=1}^{m} z_j^2$ IS DISTRIBUTED ACCORDING TO *chi-squared* (χ^2) WITH m DEGREES OF FREEDOM; $\sum_{j=1}^{m} z_j^2 \sim \chi_m^2$.

THEOREM 3

IF Z IS NORMAL $(0, 1)$ AND x IS χ_m^2 AND INDEPENDENT OF Z, THEN

$$t = \frac{Z}{\sqrt{\dfrac{x}{m}}}$$

HAS THE "t" DISTRIBUTION WITH m DEGREES OF FREEDOM.

We shall not attempt to prove any of these theorems, nor shall we give the mathematical forms of the χ^2 or t distributions. In particular, Theorem 2 is included to provide the necessary prerequisites to demonstrate that (B.2.5.1) possesses a t distribution, which like the normal is symmetric around the mean. Tables of t, like the standard normal tables, are expressed in units of standard deviation around a zero mean.

The notion of *degrees of freedom* is important in theoretical statistics and, as stated in Theorems 2 and 3 above, is a parameter of both the t and χ^2 distributions. The key to the term's meaning lies in Theorem 2: degrees of freedom is the number of independent normally distributed variables in the sum $\sum_{j=1}^{m} z_j^2$. Interpreted for our purposes then, degrees of freedom relates to the number of observations used in a given calculation that are *unrestricted*. For example, in computing

$$\bar{x}_n = \frac{1}{n} \sum_{j=1}^{n} x_j$$

there are no "restrictions" placed on the x_j's; they are indeed independent random variables and we have not altered that fact by combining them as $\bar{x}_n$.

Consider, then, the random variables $(x_j - \bar{x}_n)$, with $\bar{x}_n$ defined as usual $(j = 1, \ldots, n)$. Only $(n - 1)$ of these variables are independent, since the "last" one must be such to meet the restriction

$$\sum_{j=1}^{n} (x_j - \bar{x}_n) = 0.$$

So, for example, the number of independent variables in the statistic

(B.2.5.3) $$s^2 = \frac{1}{n-1} \sum_{j=1}^{n} (x_j - \bar{x}_n)^2$$

is $(n - 1)$. Another useful interpretation of degrees of freedom in this context is as the number of observations less the number of parameters estimated prior to any subsequent computation. For computing s^2 we need to have already calculated $\bar{x}_n$, the sample mean. Thus the number of degrees of freedom in s^2 is $(n - 1)$.

We are now in position to utilize the theorems given to discover the distribution of "t" as given in Eq. (B.2.5.1). Given any normally distributed random variable, say $x \sim N(\mu, \sigma_x^2)$, it can easily be transformed into standard normal form as

$$(B.2.5.4) \qquad Z = \frac{x - \mu}{\sigma_x}.$$

Now if the population in question possesses a normal distribution, by Theorem 1

$$(B.2.5.5) \qquad \bar{x}_n \sim N(\mu, \sigma_{\bar{x}_n}^2),$$

so that

$$(B.2.5.6) \qquad Z = \frac{\bar{x}_n - \mu}{\sigma_{\bar{x}_n}} \sim N(0, 1).$$

Under sampling with replacement† $\sigma_{\bar{x}_n}^2 = \sigma^2/n$ and we use s^2 as an unbiased estimate of σ^2. We may use Theorem 2 to ascertain the distribution of $\sum (x_j - \bar{x}_n)^2$ only if each $(x_j - \bar{x}_n)$ has first been transformed to an $N(0, 1)$ basis. For the $(x_j - \bar{x}_n)$, $\bar{x}_n$ is a constant in the sample such that the variance of each $(x_j - \bar{x}_n)$ given the sample $\bar{x}_n$ is σ^2, the population variance.‡ Viewed now as a conditional variance (conditional on $\bar{x}_n$), we deduce that the variance of $(x_j - \bar{x}_n)$ is σ^2 no matter what $\bar{x}_n$ *is actually chosen*. Thus, the conditional variance is also unconditional (that is, independent of $\bar{x}_n$). The expected value of $(x_j - \bar{x}_n)$ is zero by the following reasoning: given $\bar{x}_n$, $E(x_j - \bar{x}_n) = \mu - \bar{x}_n$. Now taken over all possible samples of size n, $E(\mu - \bar{x}_n) = \mu - \mu = 0$. Thus to correspond to the requirements of Theorem 2, we must use the transformed variables $\{(x_j - \bar{x}_n)/\sigma\}$. Then by Theorem 2,

$$(B.2.5.7) \qquad \frac{\sum_{j=1}^{n} (x_j - \bar{x}_n)^2}{\sigma^2} = \frac{s^2(n - 1)}{\sigma^2} \sim \chi_{(n-1)}^2.$$

Using Z of (B.2.5.6) in conjunction with (B.2.5.7) and invoking Theorem 3, we have

---

† Or, sampling without replacement from an infinite population.

‡ The variance of a constant is surely zero. Thus the variance of $(x_j - \bar{x}_n)$ with $\bar{x}_n$ fixed is $\sigma_{\bar{x}_i}^2 = \sigma^2$.

(B.2.5.8)
$$\frac{Z}{\sqrt{\dfrac{\sum_{j=1}^{n} (x_j - \bar{x}_n)^2}{\sigma^2(n-1)}}} \sim t_{(n-1)}$$

or

$$\frac{\dfrac{\bar{x}_n - \mu}{\sigma_{\bar{x}_n}}}{\sqrt{\dfrac{s^2(n-1)}{\sigma^2(n-1)}}} \sim t_{(n-1)}$$

from (B.2.5.7). Now, using $\sigma_{\bar{x}_n} = \sigma/\sqrt{n}$,

$$\frac{\dfrac{\bar{x}_n - \mu}{\sigma/\sqrt{n}}}{\dfrac{s}{\sigma}} \sim t_{(n-1)},$$

and finally,

(B.2.5.9)
$$\frac{\bar{x}_n - \mu}{\dfrac{s}{\sqrt{n}}} \sim t_{(n-1)}.$$

A general confidence interval for μ, analogous to (B.2.4.1) but under the assumption that $\sigma_{\bar{x}_n}$ is estimated, is therefore available, and takes the form

(B.2.5.10) $P[\bar{x}_n - t_{\alpha/2, n-1} s_{\bar{x}_n} \leq \mu \leq \bar{x}_n + t_{\alpha/2, n-1} s_{\bar{x}_n}] = 1 - \alpha.$

Using the data on heights of Section B.2.4, where $\bar{x}_5 = 70$ in., $s_{\bar{x}_5} = 2.47$ in., a 95 percent confidence interval for μ is derived from cut-off points $t_{.025, 4} = 2.77$ from Appendix Table C-2. For the specific case,

(B.2.5.11) $P[63.16 \leq \mu \leq 76.84] = .95.$

This interval is indeed wider than the analogous normal interval (with $Z_{\alpha/2} = 1.96$), or, conversely, for a given interval obtains a smaller probability. An important observation to note is that the t distribution becomes essentially described by the normal law when d.f. > 120.

To reiterate, the t distribution applies *only* when the underlying distribution is normal. If, for example, we were using the (approximate) normal confidence interval for a population proportion, even with n (or degrees of freedom) small, we would *not* use t.

Finally, from (B.2.5.10) it is clear that if the underlying distribution of $\bar{x}_n$ is normal and we give a "point" estimate of μ with an accompanying estimated standard deviation as an indicator of the precision of our estimate, this presentation implicitly connotes a confidence level corresponding to $\bar{x}_n \pm 1 s_{\bar{x}_n}$. For the example used above, the estimate of μ given by 70 in. $\pm$ 2.47 in. implies (from a confidence interval based on the t distribution) a confidence level of approximately 60 percent (68 percent under normal assumptions).

B.3   CLASSICAL HYPOTHESIS TESTING

A *statistical hypothesis* is merely a hypothesis about some population parameter or parameter set that influences the behavior of an observed random variable (a statistic). Thus if the statistic in question is an n-sample mean and the population mean is a parameter of interest, its value determines, through the frequency function $f(\bar{x}_n)$, the probability behavior of $\bar{x}_n$ either explicitly or implicitly.

The previous section makes reference to the probability that the observed difference between $\bar{x}_n$ and μ (in absolute-value terms) is no larger than some arbitrarily small number—or, as in the case of confidence intervals, the probability that certain (variable) limits contain μ. In this section we shall discuss statistical inference also, but in terms of formal tests of hypotheses about population parameters. As will become apparent, the two methods differ only in their orientation to problem-solving and not in substance.

B.3.1   STATISTICAL HYPOTHESES AND CONFIDENCE INTERVALS

Suppose we had taken a sample and computed interval limits for a given confidence probability. For a concrete example, let us use the earlier sample of five heights, where the 95 percent confidence interval for μ based on the t distribution was

(B.3.1.1) $P[63.16 \leq \mu \leq 76.84] = .95.$

The probability that the interval (63.16, 76.84) contains μ is .95. Of course, μ *could* be just about anything. That is, our sample of five observations *could* have been generated from a distribution with $\mu = 60$ in. or $\mu = 80$ in., and so on. If μ is either of these values, the interval above obviously does not contain them. In fact any values of $\mu < 63.16$ or $\mu > 76.84$ are *inconsistent* with the interval above, where inconsistency has a probabilistic definition: *if we judge* the values $\mu < 63.16$ and/or $\mu > 76.84$ to be inconsistent with the observed sample interval at a 95 percent level of confidence, then the probability that this judgment is incorrect is 5 percent. Thus, to reject any hypothetical mean in these ranges as inconsistent with the observed sample information implies a concomitant acceptance of a risk of error of rejecting such hypothetical values *when they are true* (called a type I error) of .05.

To elaborate, let us turn the argument around slightly and consider the probability distribution of 5-sample means from normally distributed population heights where $\mu = 78$ in. This distribution is shown in Fig. B.7.

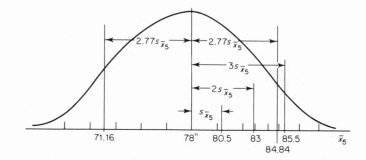

Fig. B.7

t Distribution of 5-Sample Mean Heights with
$\mu = 78$ in., $s_{\bar{x}_5} = 2.47$ in.

The analogue of a 95 percent confidence statement about μ in this situation is simply a probability statement concerning the values of 5-sample means distributed around $\mu = 78$ in.—that is,

(B.3.1.2) $$P[\mu - 2.77s_{\bar{x}_5} \leq \bar{x}_5 \leq \mu + 2.77s_{\bar{x}_5}] = .95,$$

or, substituting the proper values for μ and $s_{\bar{x}_5}$:

(B.3.1.3) $$P[71.16 \leq \bar{x}_5 \leq 84.84] = .95.$$

Ninety-five percent of 5-sample means from such a population would fall between these limits.

Suppose we decide to *reject* $\mu = 78$ in. as inconsistent with an observed sample result whenever a 5-sample mean falls outside the above limits. Then clearly the probability that our rejection decision is incorrect *given* that $\mu = 78$ in. is .05, simply the probability that sample means falling in this *rejection region* are observed under the hypothesis $\mu = 78$ in. Using this decision rule with the example result $\bar{x}_5 = 70$ in., we would reject $\mu = 78$ in. as a tenable hypothesis, realizing that μ *could* be 78 in. and accepting the probability of .05 being wrong in this respect.

Consider now replicating the above procedure for other possible hypotheses of the simple form $\mu = \mu_0$. Forming similar 95 percent probability statements about 5-sample means generated from populations with μ taking on various values and $s_{\bar{x}_5} = 2.47$ in., we would find that the observed sample result of $\bar{x}_5 = 70$ in. causes rejection (that is, lies in the rejection regions) for all hypothetical population means $\mu < 63.16$ or $\mu > 76.84$. The important implication is that a simple hypothesis about μ ($\mu = \mu_0$) may be tested at given confidence level or *level of significance* merely by constructing the confidence interval for μ based on the sample information and checking to see whether the hypothetical μ_0 is contained within the interval. If it is, then at the given confidence level (set level of type I error probability) μ_0 should not be rejected as being inconsistent with the sample result. Conversely, if μ_0 lies outside the interval, it should be rejected.

Here, then, is the bridge between statistical inference via an estimate (and some accompanying statement about its precision) and statistical inference in the form of a formal "test" of a hypothetical value of a parameter.

B.3.2 CONFIDENCE INTERVALS FOR DISCRETE SAMPLING DISTRIBUTIONS

Confidence intervals for the discrete binomial and Poisson distributions may now be interpreted and constructed from exactly the above procedure of (1) considering the distribution under a particular parameter value; (2) finding the corresponding $(1 - \alpha)$ limits; (3) observing whether or not the sample result falls between the limits. The process is continued until the confidence limits are constructed. Of special note, however, is the fact that since these are discrete distributions one may not, in general, arbitrarily set α as we did for the continuous normal and t distributions.

To illustrate, consider the example of the previous section, where the observed sample proportion was $p_{10} = \frac{5}{10} = .5$. If we hypothesize that $\tilde{P} = .2$, set $\alpha \le .05$, and attempt to split the total allowable type I error probability (.05) equally into the two tails of the distribution (allowing no more than .025 in each), the resulting probability statement is

(B.3.2.1) $$P[0 \le p_{10} \le .50] = .9936,$$

which indeed does meet the $\alpha \le .05$ condition but not at equality.† (Changing the upper boundary to $p_{10} = \frac{4}{10}$ would have increased $\alpha/2$ to .0328.) For the observed result $p_{10} = .5$ we would not reject $\tilde{P} = .2$.

Proceeding in a similar fashion, we find that the smallest $\tilde{P}$ for which our sample result would *not* have caused rejection at $\alpha \le .05$ is $\tilde{P} = .19$ and the largest is $\tilde{P} = .81$. Thus the "at least" 95 percent confidence interval for $\tilde{P}$ based on a sample of ten and an observed sample proportion of five is

(B.3.2.2) $$P[.19 \le \tilde{P} \le .81] \ge .95.$$

---

† Here we have made use of binomial tables, which are *not* included in Appendix C.

These exact limits compare very favorably with the interval (.19, .81) that was available from the normal approximation to the binomial interval at *exactly* a confidence probability of .95 (c.f. Section B.2.4). And fortunately for users of statistics such exact confidence intervals for the mean of both the binomial and Poisson cases have been constructed ad nauseum, so that computations such as those accomplished above need not be repeated nor use made of an approximate interval in most cases.†

B.3.3 DECISION RULES AND ERRORS IN DECISIONS

We shall call a fixed rule of behavior such as that used in the previous sections a *decision rule*. Decision rules cause the rejection of a hypothesis about some population parameter when the observed sample statistic falls in certain regions in its range, called rejection regions or *critical* regions, which control the probability of commiting an error of the sort: reject $\mu = \mu_0$ when true.

The risk of rejecting a true hypothesis about a parameter like μ is only half the story, however. Consider *ex post* that the sample statistic for testing a hypothesis about μ did not fall in the rejection region at a given α-level. Our adopted decision rule says not to reject such a hypothesis. But as it was *possible* for any particular sample result to be generated for the hypothesized value of μ, so is it possible that a sample result that does not dictate rejection comes from a population with some other governing parameter. In brief, another type of decision error (type II) derives from *not* rejecting a hypothetical value for a parameter when it is *not* correct.

To formalize these ideas, let us represent a hypothesis about some parameter in a population as H. We shall also limit ourselves to discussing hypothesis tests about a mean μ, although the principles involved may easily be extended to tests about any population parameter or a set of parameters tested simultaneously. For instance, a hypothesis about the mean height from before is $H: \mu = 78$ in. Since the parameter is hypothesized to have a single value, 78 in., this is called a *simple* hypothesis. Any hypothesis that contains more than one simple hypothesis is a collection of them and termed *composite*. $H: \mu > 78$ in. is an example of a composite hypothesis about μ.

Suppose $H: \mu = 78$ in. is a relevant hypothesis to test, and that as an estimator of μ we use, as before, $\bar{x}_n$. Given that observations come from a normally distributed population in terms of height, then $\bar{x}_n$ theoretically follows a normal distribution also if $\sigma_{\bar{x}_n}^2$ (from σ^2) is known. Since in the example we used before, $\sigma_{\bar{x}_n}^2$ was estimated (as will be the usual case in actuality),

† For the binomial, "Confidence limits for p in Binomial Sampling," Tables 41 and 42 (pp. 204–5), and for the Poisson, "Confidence Limits for the Expectation of a Poisson Variable," Table 40 (p. 203) in *Biometrika Tables for Statisticians*, Vol. I (2nd ed.) (Cambridge: Cambridge University Press 1958).

we know therefore that the t distribution governs the distribution of n-sample means around μ, although empirically we may revert to the normal as an approximating distribution if n is large enough. Finally, it is known that μ is the expected value of $\bar{x}_n$, so that the variance of $\bar{x}_n$ is the proper precision measure. With these preliminaries completed we are ready to discuss the hypothesis testing problem from another angle, that of $H: \mu = 78$ in. being false.

If H is false, then some other value of μ is obviously the true one—that is, $\mu \neq 78$ in. Thus, if H is rejected, $\mu \neq 78$ in. is the adopted or implied alternative hypothesis. Many possible alternative hypotheses might be used as the datum for a particular problem, but for now we shall look specifically at the general alternative hypothesis $H_A: \mu \neq 78$ in., which corresponds to the analogous test from the constructed two-sided confidence interval for μ. The important thing to note is that a statistical test of a hypothesis H is always made *relative* to *some* alternative H_A.

What values for $\bar{x}_n$ are inconsistent with H as compared to H_A? As earlier, the decision-maker may easily control α, the probability of rejecting H when it is true. But what of the chances of "accepting" H when it is false? The confidence-interval approach to the problem described inconsistency at some α-level in terms of the sample mean deviating by more (absolutely) than some amount from μ. If H is false, however, the confidence interval has little to say concerning this second sort of error.

Let H be assumed false; that is, μ has some value other than 78 in. For any single value of μ, say $\mu = 76$ in., we can compute the probability that $H: \mu = 78$ in. will be rejected.[†] Choosing $\alpha = .05$ as before, the t-rejection regions for a 5-sample mean are $\bar{x}_5 < 71.16$ and $\bar{x}_5 > 84.84$. Now if μ *really* is 76 in., we can compute β, the probability that $\bar{x}_5$ falls in (71.16, 84.84), which by our fixed rule does not cause rejection of $H: \mu = 78$ in. when (by assumption) $\mu = 76$ in. Pictorially the required probability is between 71.16 and 84.84 on a t distribution with $s_{\bar{x}_5} = 2.47$ in., $\mu = 76$ in., and 4 d.f. Converting to standard deviation units and zero mean, these limits become

$$\text{(B.3.3.1)} \qquad t_l = \frac{71.16 - 76}{2.47} = -1.96,$$

$$t_u = \frac{84.84 - 76}{2.47} = 3.57.$$

The probability that t will lie within these bounds is approximately .925, roughly interpolating the Appendix C table for 4 d.f. Thus, if $\mu = 76$ in.,

---

† Strictly speaking, this computation requires the use of a "noncentral" t distribution. For our purposes we shall assume the "central" t is an adequate approximation (which it likely is not in this case) and proceed to view our results as suggestive rather than exact.

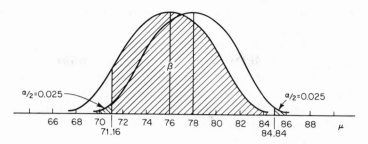

Fig. B.8

Computation of β, the Probability of "Accepting" a False
Hypothesis for the Case $H: \mu = 78$ in. vs. $H_A: \mu \neq 78$ in., at
$\mu = 76$ in., $s_{\bar{x}_5} = 2.47$ in., t Distribution, 4 d.f., $\alpha = .05$

the probability that our test (decision rule) will err in *not* rejecting $H: \mu = 78$ in. is $\beta \doteq .925$.

Of course, this probability will clearly change as other *particular* values of μ in the alternative range are considered. As μ is shifted further left (from 76 in.) in Fig. B.8, *less* area will be contained within the rejection limits, and as μ comes closer to 78 in., the opposite reaction of β is noted. As μ *becomes* 78 in., the probability of nonrejection of a false hypothesis has no meaning since $\mu = 78$ in. is the main hypothesis being tested. The probability of not rejecting it when it is true is just $1 - \alpha$, the confidence probability.

Since the sampling distribution, t, is symmetric, like calculations for $\mu > 78$ in. are mirror images of those just contemplated. The results of such calculations, covering *all* values $\mu \neq 78$ in., are summarized in Fig. B.9, where β is tabulated for the fixed decision rule: reject $H: \mu = 78$ in. in favor of $H_A: \mu \neq 78$ in. whenever $\bar{x}_s < 71.16$ in. or > 84.84 in.

We may evaluate the a priori performance of the fixed rule at least tentatively by interpreting this figure. Essentially the fixed rule—at the given sample size—performs well if the true μ is 8 in. or so away from 78 in. "Performs well" needs further definition, which will be given in the next

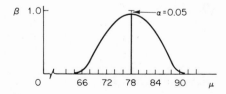

Fig. B.9

Graph of β, Probability of "Accepting"
$H: \mu = 78$ in. When It Is False, $n = 5$,
t Distribution

section; for now we shall take it to mean "small" β for the already arbitrarily small α.

Is it possible to design a rule for which $\beta = 0$ at some α-level and for a given sample size? From the figure, to obtain $\beta = 0$ requires that there be a zero probability that sample means in the "acceptance" region will be produced from any other μ than $\mu = 78$ in. Of course, this state of affairs is unattainable. But if we allow α to change (increase), we may influence β at a given sample size. Increasing α implies *less* confidence in any particular interval containing μ; or for hypothesis testing, increasing α implies narrower rejection limits to the extreme that when $\alpha = 1$ the rejection interval (for the case at hand) *is no longer* an interval. Thus to obtain $\beta = 0$ we may set $\alpha = 1$ and always reject H no matter what the sample result. Logically, of course, if we always reject H, we most certainly will *never* be guilty of not rejecting it when H_A is true.

Conversely, we may design a rule for fixed n that will allow $\alpha = 0$. This rule, by an argument similar to that above, would dictate "acceptance" of H *always*. Thus, we would definitely not err in rejecting H when true, but would always err in "accepting" it when H_A is true. How to best design a rule that takes into consideration the weights to be applied to making such errors —that is, their consequences to the decision-maker—is the climax to the present development and is treated in the next section. However, there is another variable in the design procedure to consider first, which may be adjusted to reduced β probabilities over the range of μ *without* altering α; that variable is sample size.

B.3.4 THE EFFECTS OF SAMPLES SIZE ON THE PROBABILITIES OF ERROR IN DECISIONS

Consider exactly the same test as before under the changed condition that a sample of 25 height observations is to be taken rather than 5. And, instead of assuming a hypothetical set of values, computing an estimated population variance, and finally estimating $\sigma_{\bar{x}_{25}}^2$, let us also assume for convenience that the estimated population variance for these 25 heights turns out to be the same as for the five.† So, we assume $s^2 = 30.5$ in. as the estimate of σ^2 in the population, and thus $s/5 = 1.1$ in. is the estimate of $\sigma_{\bar{x}_{25}}$.

For purposes of generating the rejection regions for a test of $H: \mu = 78$ in. versus $H_A: \mu \neq 78$ in. at $\alpha = .05$ we shall also assume that the normal distribution yields a satisfactory approximation to the t distribution. The .05-level rejection points are, therefore, given as $78 \pm (1.1)(1.96)$ in. $= 78 \pm 2.16$ in.

---

† While there is, most definitely, an inverse relationship between $\sigma_{\bar{x}_n}^2$ and n, there is no such a priori relationship between s^2 and n. Thus, while we should expect the population variance σ^2 to be estimated *more precisely* with larger n, the *actual* point estimate may not be much different for large n than for small n.

To construct the β function for this test we proceed as before. Let $\mu = 76$ in. Then the rejection points in terms of this distribution occur at $(75.84 - 76)/1.1 = -0.15$ and $(80.16 - 76)/1.1 = +3.78$. The area contained under the standard normal in this interval is .5596, as compared to a β-probability of .925 with $n = 5$. Similar calculations for other values of μ yield Fig. B.10, and the resultant effect of an increase in sample size from $n = 5$ to $n = 25$ is clear as we superimpose the previous β-function on that for $n = 25$.

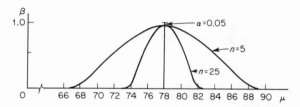

Fig. B.10

Graph of β, Probability of "Accepting" $H: \mu = 78$ in.
When It Is False, $n = 25$, Normal Distribution

Such behavior is consistent with a previous observation concerning sample-size effects on confidence intervals about μ. For given confidence probability $1 - \alpha$ we noted that an increase in sample size accomplished a tightening of the confidence limits, which here corresponds to a decrease in β-probability over the entire range of the alternative hypothesis.

The decision-maker's optimization problem, therefore, concerns discovering the "best" test of a given hypothesis vs. an alternative hypothesis about μ in the sense of balancing, according to some a priori system of weights, α and β probabilities in *conjunction* with sample-size determination, assuming it "costs" something to sample. And, while in this section we will concern ourselves solely with questions of "bestness" given a sample size, the decision-maker's choices in reality are broader than this limited analysis suggests, since a decision to sample or not *is* a realistic alternative action.

B.3.5 THE NOTION OF A "BEST" TEST

While it is intuitively appealing to reject $H: \mu = \mu_0$ vs. $H_A: \mu \neq \mu_0$ for extreme sample values, intuition cannot provide the objectivity required to make the methods of statistical inference generally usable and unambiguous. Moreover, intuition often may be a poor guide in questions dealing with random events and random variables.

To illustrate how intuition based on the actual problem situation may imply a particular rejection region for a test, suppose a garment maker wishes to discover whether the average height of American males has increased over its previous value of ten years ago, estimated at 68 in., for the purpose that if sufficient evidence can be produced to refute the hypothesis of status quo in favor of an increased average, the garment maker will add greater proportions of long suits to his output.

Intuitively, no matter what sample size might be used, a sample result will be inconsistent with the status quo hypothesis versus $H_A: \mu > 68$ in. only if the sample mean is "too large." If $\bar{x}_n$ is observed at 65 in., for example, it would be "unreasonable" to reject $H: \mu = 68$ in. in favor of $H_A: \mu > 68$ in. For many distributions of heights—for example, the normal—this intuition may be reinforced logically from the development of a notion of what constitutes a desirable or "best" rejection region (test) for a given sample size.

The classical criterion of "bestness" is simple. First, to reduce the number of variables in the problem, the α-level is kept constant in comparing alternative critical regions. Then, the criterion is defined as follows: a critical region CR_1 is judged superior to an alternative CR_2 if for given α, $\beta_1(\mu) \leq \beta_2(\mu)$; that is, if the β-function for CR_1 is always on or below the corresponding β-function for CR_2 over the range of H_A.

Use of the criterion implies that the testing problem may be reduced to a simple hypothesis test only, so that α is a single value and may, indeed, be held constant. If this is not the case, the classical criterion is ineffective in determining which of the many possible alternative critical regions to use in a particular problem. This impasse forms the focal point for the final section of this review.

To illustrate how the classical criterion is utilized, let us suppose that a very good estimate of the variance of heights of American males is available, that heights are normally distributed, and that a sample of 100 persons is contemplated. The "reliable" value for σ^2 is 100, so that $\sigma_{\bar{x}_n}^2 = \frac{100}{100} = 1$. In this case the finite population correction may certainly be neglected. Finally, we *assume* an α-level of .10.

The basic alternative critical regions for a test of $H: \mu = 68$ in. versus $H_A: \mu > 68$ in. are three: $\bar{x}_{100} \geq c$, $\bar{x}_{100} \leq c$, or a combination of the two, $\bar{x}_{100} \leq c_1$ and $\bar{x}_{100} \geq c_2$. We shall explicitly treat a comparison of the first two cases and argue the nonoptimality of the last from those results.

At $\alpha = .10$ the standard normal cut-off point is 1.28; thus the "intuitive" test suggests a critical region $\bar{x}_{100} \geq (1.28)(1) + 68$, or $\bar{x}_{100} \geq 69.28$ in. The "opposite" test is $\bar{x}_{100} \leq 66.72$ in., and the two-tailed test is some double critical region like $c_1 > 66.72$ in. and $c_2 < 69.28$ in. (symmetric, based on $\alpha/2$).

By calculating the β-functions for the first two tests we can hopefully apply the classical criterion to determine which test is best. Figure B.11 shows the relevant β-functions, where it is clear that the critical region $\bar{x}_{100} \geq 69.28$ in. is superior. For a fixed $\alpha = .10$, it provides smallest probability of "accepting" H when *any* μ in H_A is true.

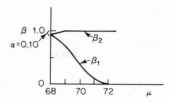

Fig. B.11

If we construct a two-sided critical region, keeping $\alpha = .10$, it is also clear that $\bar{x}_{100} \geq 69.28$ in. would remain superior. The argument is as follows: Beginning with the upper region only, we have β_1 of Fig. B.11 as the governing description of type II error probability behavior over μ in H_A. To include a lower region is tantamount to increasing the total β over all μ in H_A, since the lower region possesses an increasing β-function over μ. Any substitution of lower region for upper region, therefore, encompasses a combination of the β_1 and β_2 functions that will lie somewhere between them. For the "well-behaved" normal distribution, then, our intuitive critical region is also best in the classical sense.

As there are methods for producing estimators with certain properties, there are techniques for generating tests that likewise possess desirable properties, such as "bestness" (as defined herein). While we shall not discuss these methods at any length here, the reader should note that they too depend on the ability to control α, the probability of committing a type I error.

B.4 COSTS OF DECISION ERRORS AND THE OPTIMAL DECISION RULE

The classical approach to two-action testing problems, while providing a logical framework for decision-making, cannot always give us a "best" rule for a particular problem in terms of error probabilities alone. Thus when such errors are evaluated also in terms of the cost of their consequences, it is not surprising that the classical method meets a similar impasse, whether the costs of errors be stated merely as relative or implicit, in monetary or other terms.

When the decision problem can be stated with a simple hypothesis and a simple alternative, obviously the classical method will produce a best rule, since we may equate α-probabilities (weighted or unweighted) and look for the rule that possesses smallest β (again, either weighted or unweighted). There may be more than one rule that provides minimum β under the conditions stated, but we will be able to find an optimum decision rule to follow.

When the alternative hypothesis becomes composite, our ability to find an optimum rule is impaired by the fact that the criterion of bestness must be altered from what it was for the simple alternative case: the best rule now must provide minimum β for all values of the alternative hypothesis. Restated, the type II error function for the optimum rule must lie on or beneath all other such functions (corresponding to all other competing tests). Again, the matter of weighting α and β by costs to indicate their relative importance is straightforward but not helpful in solving this dilemma, since the weights will affect the error functions in a similar manner.

If we take the final step and look at the composite-hypothesis composite-alternative case, we must consider varying consequences of a type I error for parameter values in the range of the main hypothesis. So if application under cost considerations is our primary goal, apparently the classical approach leaves something to be desired.

One might consider making some choice of a rule by value considerations. That is, faced with a graph of the type II error functions under the simple-hypothesis composite-alternative case, for example, where, for the sake of argument, clearly no best rule exists under the classical criterion, one might reason thus: "Even though A is not best by classical standards over all values of the alternative, it is best over those values which I feel are most relevant—most likely to be the values of the *true* parameter in question—so I will use rule A." Wait a minute! One of the major premises of the classical framework is that there is a *parameter*—an unknown, *single-valued* function of the random variable in question or argument in its density function. How then can we even consider discussing *values* of a parameter as if one value were more likely than another, and so on, giving the parameter a frequency interpretation? Doesn't such an interpretation void the classical framework?

These are the questions we shall attempt to answer in this section. The most important results (in terms of impact on the methodology of decision-making under uncertainty) yielded by an investigation of these questions derive from a change in the classical interpretation of a parameter. What evolves from such a change is an addition to our logical framework, not a destruction of it. In fact, the new interpretation provides a synthesis of classical methods and their relation to how decisions are really made. The net result is a simulation of the decision process and, necessarily, a basis for making normative statements about how decisions should be made.

B.4.1 THE PARAMETER AS A RANDOM VARIABLE

Suppose we conceptualize that a parameter is not, as the classical interpretation would dictate, a *fixed* but unknown value in a defined population. Rather, the parameter itself is a random variable: it has a probability distribution, a mean, variance, and so forth.

Many arguments may be offered to support the premise that "the" parameter is a variable, among them the fact that even though a population may be "well-defined," its basic structure may be subject to change, so that at any instant of time the parameter in question has a fixed value, but in a dynamic context the parameter can actually take on a variety of values simply because the population is subject to change over time.

Another fruitful way of looking at the parameter concept is to consider problems of measurement. Even though the meaning of the term parameter may be adhered to in its classical interpretation conceptually, do measurement errors exist? Suppose we sampled an entire population and calculated some parameter. Is this value really the parameter? Are our techniques of measurement so precise as to preclude the possibility of error? Hardly. Even the most naive interpretations of the characteristics of measurement error suffice to enforce a probabilistic interpretation of a parameter. Specifically, this parameter that exists may never be measured exactly; hence we should be concerned, as a practical matter, with the *observed* value of the parameter, which is a random variable if measurement error is considered random.

Other, more sophisticated arguments surround the issue of interpretation, both supporting and opposing the probabilistic view; we shall not go into these arguments here. Most importantly, the student should note that this issue is *the significant difference* between the classical and "modern" schools of thought, and, as we shall see, a modern interpretation opens many doors to the resolution of previously "unsolvable" problems in statistical decision-making.

Moreover, it is contended that decision-makers do indeed act as if the parameters of their decision problems were variables, and make value statements like that posed in the introduction to this section; hence the modern interpretation of a parameter is really a step toward the explanation of real-world decision-making, with two definite ramifications: First, the modern interpretation of a parameter, if it holds as a premise for decision-making under uncertainty, leads to the formulation of a theory of decision-making. In turn this theoretical structure provides a logical framework that we may then use to make normative judgments about decision-making.

As will be made clear in what follows, the modern interpretation does not destroy the classical theory that preceded it. On the contrary, with only a small amount of redefinition and some new terminology the result is an almost complete absorption of classical methodology into a new logical scheme.

As with many conceptual "revelations," however, new problems arise concomitantly with a modern interpretation. These problems are primarily of application, and they are concerned with the "value" of information, type of information, and so on about the parameter in question. Succinctly, how does one go about stating the distribution of the parameter from available information? And, suppose no a priori information is available—then what? These, among other questions, are most critical in practice.

B.4.2 THE SETTING:
ESTABLISHING COSTS OF DECISION ERRORS

We shall consider a simple problem in decision-making for the purpose of developing general concepts in the modern approach. As with many applications of statistical methods, both classical and otherwise, one of the most difficult jobs is the translation of the real-world problem into terms by which a statistical model may be constructed to analyze the problem. Our approach is to build "models"; that is, by assumptions, simplifications of reality, and so on, we produce simulators of reality. When we solve a decision-making problem involving the normal distribution for a particular statistic, we first assume the normal distribution. If you were to confront a real problem that corresponded to all the other conditions and assumptions made in our exercise, you still would need to assess the correspondence of your sampling distribution to the normal curve.

Perhaps some other distribution is appropriate on theoretical grounds, such as the binomial distribution for a coin-tossing problem. Or perhaps the distribution must be approximated by fitting a known curve to some sample data. In any case, the point to be made is that each time a problem is encountered, a new "model" must be constructed. Very rarely do "textbook" examples occur.

When we previously spoke of weighting decision errors by the "costs" of making such errors, we passed over a difficult practical problem, because monetary costs usually do not describe a particular situation adequately, and in some situations monetary costs are not directly involved at all. For example, the loss of ten dollars to a millionaire would likely be of less consequence to him than the same loss to a pauper. The same sort of difference in the "value" of money probably explains why some people play poker for pennies and others play for dollars.

Since money obtains its value through the goods and services it represents (at least it used to), a given sum will have different "value" to different people, just as the possession of certain goods will have different value to the same people. The dilemma we must face involves those situations where dollar amounts and their "values" do not bear a proportional relationship to one another, for clearly if a proportional relationship exists it will not matter whether we have monetary or "value" measures to assess the *relative* costs of type I and type II errors.

How do we discover that this proportional relationship does or does not exist over the relevant dollar range for the problem at hand; how do we construct the necessary value, or, as it is more commonly referred to, *utility* scale for money? Again, here is a prerequisite to a textbook application that may not be (indeed, most probably is not) met in a real-world problem. Hence, before using any method of analysis that treats the weighting of decision errors, we must produce another model to handle the money-utility inequality that may exist.

A suggested method for constructing the individual's utility scale for money in a given decision problem is available in Schlaifer's *Introduction to Statistics for Business Decisions*,† and since our method of analysis for the "best" decision rule is independent of the measure used to assess decision errors, the reader is referred there. In the material that follows, therefore, monetary costs will be assumed to hold as "real" costs. When necessary we shall annotate the development to include any pertinent analogies to the decision problem with a utility rather than monetary cost valuation.

B.4.3 AN EXAMPLE

Suppose a prospective entrepreneur is considering embarking on a career as a pearl dealer. This fellow is very scientific in his outlook toward decision-making, having taken a meaty course in statistics in college; however, he has requested that we assist him in the analysis. To this end he gives us the following information: the oyster bed in question contains 500 oysters (counted by scuba divers, each using an abacus adapted for underwater use). It would cost our operator-friend $200 in fixed costs to set up his equipment; average variable costs amount to $1 per oyster for gathering, opening, and so on. The operator can sell pearls for an average of $4 per pearl, but cannot sell the oysters themselves at all.

By doing some arithmetic we discover that if there are more than 35 percent of the oysters with pearls, the operator will make a profit; at exactly 35 percent he breaks even, and if the proportion with pearls, say $\tilde{P}$, is less than .35, he loses money. In his estimation the time he will spend digging up 500 oysters could be used selling newspapers, for which he would receive $300. So, he is primarily interested in ascertaining whether or not his endeavors in the oyster game will reward him at least as well as selling newspapers. If the proportion of oysters with pearls is at least .50, he will make $300 or more; hence this seems to be the relevant hypothesis to test.

We now face two problems: the determination of sample size, and the choice of a decision rule for testing the hypothesis. To begin with we shall arbitrarily select a sample size of $n = 20$ and assume it costs nothing to obtain the sample. Later both these assumptions will be relaxed and included as part of our total analysis. As to the hypothesis to test, we have already

† (New York: McGraw-Hill, 1961), Chap. 2.

indicated that the region $\tilde{P} \geq .50$ is relevant as against $\tilde{P} < .50$, where the operator definitely loses money, either as a direct loss ($\tilde{P} < .35$), or an opportunity loss ($.35 \leq \tilde{P} \leq .50$). At this point we shall further assume that our friend's utility scale for money is linear, so that monetary costs and profits do indeed describe his valuation of all losses and gains.†

Our task is to determine a decision rule for testing $H: \tilde{P} \geq .50$ against $H_A: \tilde{P} < .50$ for $n = 20$ that on the average provides smallest losses from making decision errors.‡ Clearly, the pertinent considerations for selecting the rule involve incorrect decisions and the losses resulting from them. For example, suppose $\tilde{P}$ is .50 but we reject H. Our costs from making this error (type I) will be zero, since the opportunity loss of not "digging" when it is profitable to do so is $300, but he can sell newspapers for $300. The other sort of incorrect decision we could make is not to reject H when, in fact, H_A is true (type II error). Again, as an example, our losses (direct) from this incorrect decision would amount to $100 plus $300 in opportunity losses from not selling newspapers, for a total of $400, if $\tilde{P}$ were really .3. In fact, we can generate relationships that will describe these total losses as a function of $\tilde{P}$: losses $= \$2000\tilde{P} - \$1000$ if $\tilde{P} \geq .5$, and losses $= \$1000 - \$2000\tilde{P}$ if $\tilde{P} \leq .5$. Obviously such losses are precisely determined by the value that $\tilde{P}$ actually attains in the population of 500 oysters, and hence could be called "conditional" losses, conditional on $\tilde{P}$.

We shall use a concept analogous to the frequency definition of probability in choosing our best decision rule. For us a "trial" consists of taking a sample of 20 from the population of 500 and either rejecting or not rejecting the null hypothesis on the basis of this sample. What we require is a decision rule that would guarantee that if we repeated the same test, each time drawing a new sample of 20 and either rejecting or not according to our fixed rule, the losses from making incorrect decisions would be at a minimum. As we shall see, to meet this criterion requires the modern interpretation of a parameter.

B.4.4 DETERMINING THE SAMPLING DISTRIBUTION OF THE TEST STATISTIC

How should the sample be selected? This question again poses the problem of adherence to assumptions, in the sense that (1) the methodology of statistical testing requires a probability sampling method, and (2) in any real application the appropriate sampling design must be selected by cost considerations in relation to the required precision of results. When we discussed

---

† If this function were not linear (proportional) in money, all the calculations would be carried out in terms of utility measure.

‡ Since the equality $\tilde{P} = .50$ represents a breakeven point, it could be included in either the main or the alternative hypothesis.

sampling problems in dealing with classical testing problems, we only considered simple random sampling methods and merely indicated that somehow the costs of obtaining a given size sample should be considered in deciding what particular sampling method to use. There are reams of literature on the subject of sample design, and for our purposes here we must limit alternatives, so simple random sampling will be stressed again in this example. The important thing to observe is that no matter what probability sampling method is used, the inherent nature of the method will have different implications for the sampling distribution of a given test statistic. But they all will have one basic thing in common—that of assigning to each possible combination of n items from the population a definite probability of selection.

What are the effects of each simple random method on the distribution of a given test statistic? To return to our specific case, since we are concerned with losses resulting from the proportion of oysters being small, it should be clear that our decision rule will be formulated to tell us when the observed sample proportion is so small as not to be consistent with the main hypothesis. That is, the rule will state that we should reject H whenever the observed number of oysters with pearls in the sample of 20, say y, is smaller than some number c, where c is some possible value of y.

The distribution of our test statistic, y, will depend on the method of sampling used. As long as the probability that any oyster contains a pearl remains constant as we take our sample, the resulting distribution of the total number of oysters with pearls in the sample will theoretically follow the binomial distribution. But the requirement that $\tilde{P}$ remains constant as we sample is only met when we sample with replacement, where on each "trial" (or draw) the population is unchanged; previous oysters are always replaced into the population before a new selection is made; thus, $\tilde{P}$ (in the sampling sense) will remain constant throughout the entire process of selecting 20 items from the 500. Moreover, the proportion $p_n = y/n$, the sample proportion of oysters with pearls, will also follow the binomial distribution, since y and p_n differ only by a constant factor of proportionality, n. That is to say, if the probability that y has the value 10 is .1762 for a sample of 20, then the probability that p_{20} is .5 ($\frac{10}{20}$) is also .1762.

When sampling is done without replacement, the situation is slightly altered by the fact that at each stage of the sampling procedure the probability that the oyster selected has a pearl is *dependent* upon the results of previous selections. In the present example, once an oyster is opened its physical nature is somewhat "destroyed"; it really isn't the same object as the oysters that remain unopened. Thus, to sample with replacement would require some change in definition for the population. Similar, but more obvious situations where the type of sampling method is dictated by the nature of the objects sampled occur in testing firecrackers or the like, where the object is indeed destroyed by the sampling procedure.

For this hypothetical example it would appear that sampling without replacement is called for, which implies the hypergeometric distribution as the frequency function for y. But for our purposes we shall limit ourselves to the binomial as the sampling distribution of y, which implies either: (1) sampling with replacement, or (2) use of the binomial as an approximation to the hypergeometric, if we sample without replacement.

B.4.5 OBTAINING A BEST TEST

Consider adopting the rule: Reject $H: \tilde{P} \geq .5$ in favor of $H_A: \tilde{P} < .5$ whenever y is less than or equal to 6 in a sample of 20. For sake of brevity, we shall adopt the following notation for the above statement: $[y \leq 6, n = 20]$ will imply rejection of H.

For each value of $\tilde{P}$ in the range of either the hypothesis or the alternative a different binomial distribution holds; hence the probabilities for $y \leq 6$ change accordingly. As a result the chain of losses from decision errors is viewed as conditional on the value that $\tilde{P}$ actually assumes in the population. For example, using $[y \leq 6, n = 20]$ when $\tilde{P} = .1$ can only result in a type II error: if we reject H (that is, observe $y \leq 6$), we make a correct decision, but if we observe $y > 6$, our rule would cause us to accept H—obviously an error. The probability that in using $[y \leq 6, n = 20]$ when $\tilde{P} = .1$ we make this error is just $P[y > 6 | \tilde{P} = .1, n = 20] = .0024$ from binomial tables. Corresponding to this probability is a monetary loss of $1000 - 2000(.1) = 800$. On the other hand, under these circumstances if we make the correct decision, and reject H when $\tilde{P} = .1$, we do not suffer loss from a decision error. The probability that we make the correct decision is $P[y \leq 6 | \tilde{P} = .1, n = 20] = .9976$. The net effect, in terms of losses, may be viewed as a problem in determining an expected value for a random variable, monetary loss, with possible values $800 and $0 and probabilities .0024 and .9976, respectively. The resulting expected loss, $1.92, is then the amount we may expect to lose, on the average, by using the rule $[y \leq 6, n = 20]$ when $\tilde{P} = .1$.

$\tilde{P}$, of course, is not restricted to a value of .1. Indeed, as far as we know, $\tilde{P}$ may be any value between zero and one. It should be clear at this point that for $\tilde{P} < .5$, the only decision errors accruing to our fixed rule will be type II errors. If $\tilde{P} \geq .5$, then type I errors occur.

Consider the case for $\tilde{P} = .5$. A type I error will occur if we use the rule $[y \leq 6, n = 20]$ and observe $y \leq 6$. This outcome has probability $P[y \leq 6 | \tilde{P} = .5, n = 20] = .0577$ of occurring, and corresponding to its occurrence we stand to lose nothing by this error, since .5 is a break-even point. A "correct" decision, to accept H when $\tilde{P} = .5$, in reality is made whenever $y > 6$, which will happen with probability .9423. The net effect of this particular circumstance is an expected monetary loss of $0·.0577 + $0·.9423 = $0.

For $\tilde{P} = .6$, and reasoning as above, we obtain an expected loss of $200· (.0065) + $0·(.9935) = 1.30. Listed below are identical calculations for other values of $\tilde{P}$.

(a) $E_{\text{loss}} (\tilde{P} = .2) = \$52.02$.
(b) $E_{\text{loss}} (\tilde{P} = .3) = \$156.80$.
(c) $E_{\text{loss}} (\tilde{P} = .4) = \$150.00$.
(d) $E_{\text{loss}} (\tilde{P} = .7) = \$.12$.

By classical standards, our best rule (if it exists) will be one that provides minimum losses over all values of $\tilde{P}$. Carrying out the calculations for some other rules, we obtain the entries in Table B.1. These values are also graphed in Fig. B.12, where we note that no rule provides minimum losses over all values for $\tilde{P}$.†

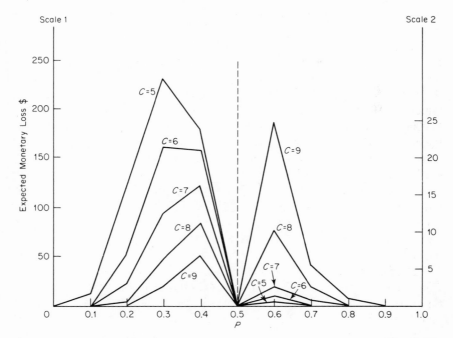

Fig. B.12

Loss Characteristics

† We have used computations for selected values of $\tilde{P}$. In the example, $\tilde{P}$ changes by increments of $1/500 = .002$, and actually the graph (and the entire analysis) should involve all 501 possible values for $\tilde{P}$.

Table B.1

Expected Loss Calculations for the Rules $c = 5$, $c = 6$, $c = 7$, $c = 8$, $c = 9$, $n = 20$; Complex-Hypothesis, Complex-Alternative Case

			REJECTION POINT: c								
		5		6		7		8		9	
$\tilde{P}$	Error Loss ($)	Pr. of Loss	E_{loss} ($)	Pr. of Loss	E_{loss} ($)	Pr. of Loss	E_{loss} ($)	Pr. of Loss	E_{loss} ($)	Pr. of Loss	E_{loss} ($)
.1	800	.0113	9.04	.0024	1.92	.0004	.32	.0001	.08	≐ 0	≐ 0
.2	600	.1958	117.48	.0867	52.02	.0321	19.26	.0100	6.00	.0026	1.56
.3	400	.5836	233.44	.3920	156.80	.2277	91.08	.1133	45.32	.0480	19.20
.4	200	.8744	174.88	.7500	150.00	.5841	116.82	.4044	80.88	.2447	48.95
.5	0	.0207	≐ 0	.0577	≐ 0	.1316	≐ 0	.2517	≐ 0	.4119	≐ 0
.6	200	.0016	.32	.0065	1.30	.0210	2.40	.0565	11.30	.1275	25.50
.7	400	≐ 0	≐ 0	.0003	.12	.0013	.52	.0051	2.04	.0171	6.84
.8	600	≐ 0	≐ 0	≐ 0	≐ 0	≐ 0	≐ 0	.0001	.06	.0006	.36

Rows .1–.4: Type II. Rows .5–.8: Type I.

We should note at this stage of the development that since α errors are *valued* differently in the range of the hypothesis, we *cannot* proceed to deduce the best rule merely by controlling α and looking for the rule that produces minimum β (weighted) over the alternative. Yet so far we have only extended our discussion of classical testing to cover this case: the appropriate criterion would call for a rule that produced (weighted) minimum β and α over $\tilde{P} <$ .5 and $\tilde{P} \geq .5$, respectively.

With a strict classical definition of the term parameter, we cannot hope to resolve the problem that now faces us. There is no way to choose between alternative rules except by either some value judgment or the introduction of new criteria, since none of the rules in Fig. B.12 meets the classical standard. But if we give credence to a modern interpretation (and I think the distinction implied by the use of *classical* and *modern* is extreme), note that the conditional expected losses associated with each rule can be viewed as random variables that take on their particular values with variations in $\tilde{P}$. Hence, we can introduce the notion of *expected losses* from a given rule over all values of $\tilde{P}$, which will result in a *single* expected loss from incorrect decisions for each rule. That there must be a rule (or rules) yielding a minimum for such losses will be argued intuitively below.

B.4.6 THE "BAYESIAN" CONTRIBUTION

Suppose we were able to obtain some idea of the probable values for $\tilde{P}$. That is, from some source we obtain information regarding the probability distribution of $\tilde{P}$, say in the form of a historical frequency distribution. This distribution, the "prior" distribution of $\tilde{P}$, might look like:

$\tilde{P}$	$P(\tilde{P})$
.2	.1
.3	.1
.4	.1
.5	.1
.6	.4
.7	.2
	1.0

How can we incorporate such information into our analysis of the best decision rule to follow? Let us not, at this point, raise the issue of the value of such information, but accept the prior distribution without question.

Then each expected loss in Table B.1 should be interpreted as a *conditional loss;* for example, for the rule [$y \leq 6$, $n = 20$] the expected loss of $52.02 is conditional on $\tilde{P}$'s taking the value .2, which it does, according to our prior distribution, with probability .1. Hence, the (joint) expected loss from using this rule with $\tilde{P} = .2$ is simply $(.1)(.0867)(\$600) = (.1)(\$52.02) = \$5.20$. Proceeding similarly for the remaining possible values of $\tilde{P}$, we obtain

$$E_{\text{loss}}[y \leq 6, 20] = (.1)(\$52.02) + (.1)(\$156.80) + (.1)(\$150.00)$$
$$+ 0 + (.4)(\$1.30) + (.2)(\$.12)$$
$$= \$41.10.$$

Identical calculations for the rules $c = 5$, $c = 7$, $c = 8$, $c = 9$ yield

$$E_{\text{loss}}[y \leq 5, 20] = \$52.71,$$
$$E_{\text{loss}}[y \leq 6, 20] = \$41.10,$$
$$E_{\text{loss}}[y \leq 7, 20] = \$23.78,$$
$$E_{\text{loss}}[y \leq 8, 20] = \$18.15,$$
$$E_{\text{loss}}[y \leq 9, 20] = \$18.54.$$

The rule $[y \leq 8, 20]$, which apparently yields minimum expected loss under our assumed prior distribution, is called a Bayesian decision rule, so characterized because we make use of a weighted average of expectations to obtain the ultimate expected losses accruing to our set of possible decision rules, the weights being the probabilities in our prior distribution of $\tilde{P}$.† The selection of the rule $[y \leq 8, 20]$ as the "best" rule to use is, of course, conditioned on the assumption that our friend's utility for money is linear; hence, a minimization of expected monetary loss is appropriate. If this is not the case, an appropriate utility scale must be constructed first; the analysis then proceeds to deduce the rule that yields minimum disutility.

It should be clear, simply by studying Table B.1, that a minimum will exist for expected total loss over alternative rules. If more rules were included, one would see a complete spectrum of movement—from rules where the expected losses from making type I errors are essentially zero, with very high expected losses from type II errors (c small), to the other extreme, where the type I and type II expected losses are in juxtaposition. So long as the prior distribution assigns some nonzero probabilities to the occurrence of both error types, a minimum will exist.

B.4.7 SAMPLE-SIZE DETERMINATION

At the outset of our discussion we made two assumptions, regarding sample size and the cost of sampling, which we shall now relax.

---

† The roots of this procedure are contained in "Bayes' theorem," which has to do with computing conditional probabilities in cause-effect problems. For those readers unfamiliar with the theorem, we present it in Section B.4.10.

If, in fact, sample size is fixed, the cost of sampling is obviously fixed over all decision rules; hence the optimal rule remains unchanged. The necessary change in our analysis would be to add to the expected loss from incorrect decisions the cost of obtaining the sample to obtain an expected total loss. The only situation that realistically portrays the fixed-sample problem occurs when the sample already has been taken, where the costs of sampling have already been incurred.

The question arises, however, how we should treat the sample information. In classical statistics whether or not the sample has already been taken is a moot point. The decision rule would be constructed as if no sample had been taken.

From the modern point of view the sample already taken constitutes additional information which should be incorporated as evidence *before* the optimum rule is determined. In point of fact, all the analysis up to this point of our discussion and the following treatment of sample size determination should proceed with the distribution which results from a combination of the prior distribution and the sample information. The resultant distribution, formed by applying Bayes' theorem, is known as a *posterior* distribution; we shall give an example of such a computation in Section B.4.10. Thus, sample-size determination, *including a decision to sample or not*, is a problem that arises even when a sample has already been taken.

To begin, we shall assume that sampling costs are known and may be represented as a function of n, which for most cases will be an increasing function. Suppose we assume a very simple linear function to represent sampling cost:

$$\text{Sampling cost} = a + bn,$$

where a is a fixed cost, incurred regardless of the sample size, and b is the per unit or per observation cost. Then we may combine the sampling costs for each n with the expected losses from incorrect decisions for the *optimum* decision rule for each n to determine an expected optimal total loss function over all values of n. What will this function look like?

It can be shown mathematically that the locus of optimum expected losses from decision errors is decreasing over n, so that if sampling were free, the decision-maker could reduce his expected losses from decision errors to zero merely by taking a large enough sample. Another algebraic proof gives the following fact: if a rule (c, n) is optimum for some n, when n is incremented by one, if the expected loss from errors $E_{\text{loss}}(c, n + 1) \leq E_{\text{loss}}(c, n)$, then the rejection point c is optimal for $n + 1$, and if $E_{\text{loss}}(c, n + 1) > E_{\text{loss}}(c, n)$, then the optimal rule is $(c + 1, n + 1)$.

Loosely interpreted, the foregoing statement says we may proceed to derive the locus of optimum points by incrementing sample size by one, testing for optimality, and either incrementing c by one or proceeding to increment sample size by one. This procedure has no direct bearing on our analysis, but it saves us from completing the set of calculations in Table B.1 for each n. Moreover, if sampling cost is an increasing function of n and the expected loss from errors is a decreasing function of n, a saddle point will exist on the expected optimal total-loss function that is the sum of these two; hence we can be sure there is an optimum n.

The three functions are shown in Fig. B.13 for our example with an assumed sampling cost of $20 + \$4n$. Note at the bottom of the graph that the optimum rules are indicated for all values of n between zero and 20.

The value for $n = 0$ is the expected loss from decision errors when no sample is taken.† How is this loss determined? Before a sample is taken, our friend may either reject or not reject the hypothesis *solely* on the evidence of the prior (or posterior) distribution of $\tilde{P}$. If he rejects H and $\tilde{P} = .5$, .6, or .7, he errs. If he "accepts" H and $\tilde{P} = .2, .3,$ or $.4$, he errs. The expected losses from such decision errors can be calculated as

$$E_{\text{loss}}(\text{accept}) = (.1)(\$600) + (.1)(\$400) + (.1)(\$200)$$
$$+ (.1)(\$0) + (.4)(\$0) + (.2)(\$0)$$
$$= \$120,$$

whereas

$$E_{\text{loss}}(\text{reject}) = (.4)(\$200) + (.2)(\$400) = \$160.$$

If our friend does not sample, the optimum decision to make is to dig up all 500 oysters. He can expect to lose $120, on the average, from incorrect decisions.

Next we attempt to answer the questions: should a sample be taken, and if so, how large should it be? We find the answers by inspecting Fig. B.13. Given the assumed sampling-cost function, the optimum n occurs at $n = 6$, where, with the rule ($y \leq 2$), expected total loss amounts to $89.25. Since this loss is smaller than the $120 loss when no sample is taken, our friend should take $n = 6$ and reject $H: \tilde{P} \geq .5$ if the number of oysters with pearls in the sample is two or less. This, according to our analysis, is the best procedure to follow (again assuming a linear utility-money relation). This cost may also be interpreted as the *cost of uncertainty* from the decision-maker's point of view.

Note that the expected total loss function in Fig. B.13 exhibits some

† Or no additional sample if working with a posterior distribution of $\tilde{P}$.

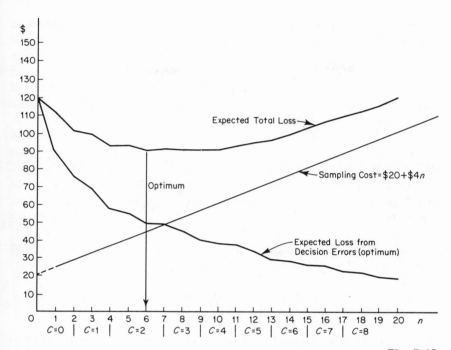

Fig. B.13

Expected Total Loss and Optimum Sample Size

strange behavior. For example, from $n = 3$ to $n = 4$ expected total loss decreases, but from $n = 4$ to $n = 5$ losses increase slightly, even though the trend in the function from $n = 0$ to $n = 6$ is downward. This behavior is due to the shape of the expected-loss function of decision errors, which exhibits a continuous downward trend but is "kinked." That is to say, at those values of n where a different rule becomes optimum the decrease in the E_{loss} function overshadows the increase in sampling cost; hence the expected total loss function shows a decrease. Until this changeover point is reached, the decrease in E_{loss} may be less than the increase in sampling cost, which causes expected total loss to increase. This behavior is not peculiar to an underlying discrete distribution.

As a final topic in the analysis of optimum sample size, it may not be possible to specify in advance the cost of sampling. An example of this situation would arise if we considered the possibility that our friend could sell the pearls obtained from the sample for $4 each. For a sample of size n the sampling cost would be $20 + $4n ($n > 0$), but for every oyster that contained a pearl we could recover $4 by selling the pearl. According to the prior distribution of $\tilde{P}$, we could expect 20 percent of the oysters to contain pearls 10 percent of the time, and so on, so that for any $n > 0$ our expected revenue from the sale of pearls would be

$$E_{\text{revenue}} = \$4[(.1)(.2)n + (.1)(.3)n + (.1)(.4)n + (.1)(.5)n$$
$$+ (.4)(.6)n + (.2)(.7)n]$$
$$= \$4(.52)n$$
$$= \$2.08n.$$

Thus, under these circumstances our sampling cost—now *expected* sampling cost—would be

$$E_{\text{sampling cost}} = \$20 + \$4n - \$2.08n$$
$$= \$20 + \$1.92n.$$

This function would replace the sampling-cost function of Fig. B.13, a new optimum n and decision rule being determined.

B.4.8 FURTHER GENERALIZATIONS

While we have concentrated the development of the basic ideas of modern decision theory on an example that utilizes a discrete distribution, the methods can equally well be applied to the continuous case—for example, where the sampling distribution is normal.† The importance of the normal distribution to both classical and modern statistical decision-making primarily derives from the fundamental central limit theorem, which demonstrates that many sampling distributions tend to the normal distribution for large sample sizes, including the binomial and hypergeometric of our example.

Also, while the test of our example is one-sided (rejection for very small values of the sample statistic), problems may arise that call for a one-sided test for the upper tail of the sampling distribution, or two-sided tests where both very large and very small values of the sample statistic may be inconsistent with a null hypothesis. Extensions of the basic methodology to these situations should be obvious.

There remain some rather serious questions regarding the practicality and limitations of the methodology presented, as well as additional conceptual problems that have not as yet been answered to the satisfaction of many. We shall treat only the more significant of these here.

Earlier we mentioned the possibility that actual cost figures for decision errors might not be obtainable. Certainly these costs play a major role in

† For an illustration the reader is referred to Schlaifer, *Introduction to Statistics for Business Decisions*, pp. 269–315.

the assessment of decision rules for both the classical and modern approaches, but their absence would not detract from the conceptual advantage of the modern interpretation. As to practical advantages of the modern method when cost figures are not available, one might assume, as is often done in practice, that type I and type II errors are equally distasteful; thus our analysis would proceed merely by minimizing the *probabilities* of making errors. Or, as many representatives of the modern school contend, one should proceed to "determine" the costs of errors in terms of utilities, by presenting the decision-maker with various pairs of alternative "bets" for which he will judge a preference for one over the other, or indifference.† In this way a utility scale depicting the decision-maker's preference patterns with respect to risk may be constructed.‡

This latter suggestion entails two difficulties that deserve consideration. First, suppose the decision-maker has no vested interest in his decision. That is to say, it is conceivable that a research worker would be completely divorced from any personal attachment to some statistical test he wished to perform. Then what sort of utility scale could be constructed for the costs of decision errors?

Second, it is also inconceivable that anyone could make *precise* judgments between these so-called alternative "bets," which must be assumed to obtain the unique utility scale required in lieu of monetary costs. How do these errors in judgment affect the modern approach?

Another practical disadvantage that presently permeates the modern approach cannot, I think, be classified as a criticism. If it is a criticism, then it applies to all sciences in their infancy. The point is that many important classical tests concern more than one parameter simultaneously. As yet little research has appeared dealing with conceptual bridges between the classical and modern methods of inference for these problems.

Finally, and perhaps most important, is the matter of prior information. In the classical view it is relatively easy to assess the relative importance of objective (sample) information. That is, the results of a sample of 500 are more reliable than those from a sample of 50, given random sampling and so on. But how reliable are the subjective estimates of a businessman, for example, about the probability distribution of a "parameter"? And, how does one assess this reliability? And then, if reliability cannot be measured, how can we be sure that the results of our analyses have any meaning whatsoever?§

To point out specifically how sample information may be readily

† See Schlaifer, *Introduction to Statistics for Business Decisions*, Chap. 2.

‡ It may not be long before every statistician has a couch in his office to aid in analyzing his "patients."

§ This problem is not unique to the modern approach. Its classical counterparts are assumptions about the underlying distribution being, say, normal, and so on.

subsumed in the analysis of Sections B.4.6 and B.4.7, consider our example again, but suppose that in addition to the prior distribution a sample of size 10 had already been taken, and that 4 of the 10 oysters were found to contain pearls. Intuitively, we might reason that this observation tends to refute $H: \tilde{P} \geq .5$ in favor of $H_A: \tilde{P} < .5$. The question is: how much "weight" should be placed on this information—or, in other words, how should we modify the prior distribution to reflect these results? A moment's reflection should suggest that we are actually asking a question of the form: given the observed result, what are the probabilities that it was produced by the various values of $\tilde{P}$ under consideration? This question is precisely the sort for which Bayes' theorem yields answers.

Bayes' theorem is developed in most elementary probability and statistics books, so we shall present only the main result here. For $H_1, \ldots, H_k$ a set of k mutually exclusive and exhaustive regions of a sample space, and A an event in this same sample space,

$$P(H_r \,|\, A) = \frac{P(A\,|\,H_r)P(H_r)}{\sum_{j=1}^{k} P(A\,|\,H_j)P(H_j)}.$$

The required inputs for an answer to our problem, therefore, are the prior probabilities for the values of $\tilde{P}$ and conditional probabilities for the sample outcome given these values. Calculations for the hypothetical situation are given in Table B.2, where we note that the prior distribution has been adjusted to show the effects of the sample result; accordingly, each conditional probability that $\tilde{P}$ has value .2, .6, or .7 has been adjusted downward, and the converse for the probabilities of $\tilde{P} = .3, .4,$ or .5. Each entry in the last column is a result of an application of Bayes' formula. As mentioned previously, the discovery of a "best" decision rule would now follow using the posterior distribution for $\tilde{P}$.

Still, the calculations just carried out depend on a statement of prior

Table B.2

Calculation of a Posterior Distribution

Value of $\tilde{P}$	$P(\tilde{P})$ "prior"	$P[y = 4\,|\,n = 10, \tilde{P}]$ (binomial)	Joint Probability $P[y = 4\,|\,n = 10, \tilde{P}][P(\tilde{P})]$	Revised Probability $P(\tilde{P})$ "posterior"
.2	.1	.0881	.00881	.070
.3	.1	.2001	.02001	.158
.4	.1	.2508	.02508	.199
.5	.1	.2051	.02051	.162
.6	.4	.1114	.04456	.353
.7	.2	.0367	.00734	.058
			$\sum = .12631$	1.000

probabilities, and these, in turn, may be of a subjective rather than objective nature. Obviously our complete analysis of the best decision rule is based upon the prior distribution to at least some degree.†

Two points are to be made concerning this last statement. If our analysis purports to be a model of the decision-making process under uncertainty, then these subjective probabilities are simply quantitative representations of a decision-maker's subjective judgment about a given random outcome. Thus, given that such judgments are made, the prior distribution is nothing more than a formal statement of them. Finally, if the subjective judgment we are speaking of is one of "no information," then its counterpart for us is a rectangular prior distribution of the parameter in question—that is, an assumption that every possible value of the parameter is equally likely.

The classical confidence interval has its modern counterpart, defined through an analysis similar to that used for developing the binomial and Poisson intervals (Section B.3.2) and based on a hypothesis test of the form $H: \mu = \mu_0$ versus $H_A: \mu \neq \mu_0$. The modern analogy to the classical estimator of the population mean is the mean of the posterior distribution. The posterior variance has a connotation as a measure of the amount of "information" contained in the sample.

Extensions of the modern analysis, including the specification of continuous prior and sampling distributions, are possible but not always easy to accomplish. Exceptions include the normal-prior normal-sampling distribution and uniform‡ (rectangular) prior cases.

B.4.9 FORMALIZATION OF BAYESIAN HYPOTHESIS TESTING AND ESTIMATION

In the previous subsections we were content with a heuristic presentation of the process by which an optimum decision rule for given n may be selected. Here, and (as will become apparent) with only a little more work, the problem is formalized and solved more rigorously.

As inputs to the solution process we have the following; for given n:

$f(y \mid \tilde{P}) = B(n, \tilde{P})$—the sampling distribution of y, a binomial for our example.

$f(\tilde{P})$—the prior distribution on the parameter $\tilde{P}$, assumed to be continuous, but left unspecified.

---

† If we carried on the process of taking samples, and used Bayes' theorem to produce new posterior distributions from old ones by a sequential incorporation of sample information, we would, under ideal circumstances, eventually arrive at a posterior distribution in which a single value of the parameter in question had probability one of being the actual parameter no matter what the prior probability distribution (as long as it allowed all values of $\tilde{P}$ to be possible). We might liken this phenomenon to that of consistent estimation.

‡ Where each value of the random variable possesses the same density.

$l_{\text{I}}(\tilde{P}) = \$2000\tilde{P} - \$1000$—the loss function for type I decision errors
($\tilde{P} \geq .5$).
$l_{\text{II}}(\tilde{P}) = \$1000 - \$2000\tilde{P} = -l_{\text{I}}(\tilde{P})$—the loss function for type II decision errors ($\tilde{P} < .5$).

We may conveniently represent conditional expected losses ("risks")
for the two sorts of decision errors in terms of these functions as follows:

Conditional Expected-Loss (Risk) Function	Range of $\tilde{P}$	Error Type
$l_{\text{I}}(\tilde{P}) \sum\limits_{0}^{c} B(n, \tilde{P})$	$\tilde{P} \geq .5$	I
$l_{\text{II}}(\tilde{P}) \sum\limits_{c+1}^{n} B(n, \tilde{P})$	$\tilde{P} < .5$	II

Note that for each decision rule $[y \leq c]$ there are, just as before, conditional
expected losses for each value of $\tilde{P}$. The representation above is just a general
specification of exactly the sort of computations carried out in Table B.1.

Next, we take the conditional expected-loss function into an overall
expected-loss function for the rule $[y \leq c]$ by calculating an expected value
over $\tilde{P}$. If $\tilde{P}$ is assumed to be continuous, we have

$$(B.4.9.1) \qquad E_{\text{loss}}(c) = \int_{.5}^{1} l_{\text{I}}(\tilde{P}) \sum_{0}^{c} B(n, \tilde{P}) f(\tilde{P}) \, d\tilde{P}$$

$$- \int_{0}^{.5} l_{\text{I}}(\tilde{P}) \sum_{c+1}^{n} B(n, \tilde{P}) f(\tilde{P}) \, d\tilde{P}.$$

In mathematical notation (B.4.9.1) represents the process of computation
indicated on *p. 272*.

The optimization required is to find the value of c that minimizes
(B.4.9.1). Conceptually this could be accomplished with the calculus if c
were a continuous variable (that is, if the sampling distribution of y were
continuous). Of course that is not the case here. If it were, we would see
an integral sign replacing each capital sigma in (B.4.9.1). Practically speaking,
however, the required calculation (B.4.9.1) is not even then generally easy
analytically unless $f(\tilde{P})$ is an extremely simple distribution (such as the
uniform). The usual procedure is to do the computations and perform the
search for an optimum c by computer—that is, using numerical methods. The
final step, the choice of an optimum n, is also easily adapted to computer
solution for a given sampling-cost function.

Bayesian estimation can be formalized to even a further extent. For ease
of presentation we will likewise limit ourselves to a single-parameter problem,
now stated in terms of some arbitrary parameter θ.

The necessary ingredients for the analysis are the distribution of sample observations, $f(x_1, \ldots, x_n | \theta)$, the prior distribution of θ, $f(\theta)$, and a loss function, say $l(\hat{\theta} | \theta)$, which describes losses in terms of the (to be) chosen estimator $\hat{\theta}$ conditional on θ. To collate this notation with our example, $f(x_1, \ldots, x_n | \theta)$ is equivalent to the binomial distribution on y (given $\tilde{P}$), $f(\theta)$ is $f(\tilde{P})$, and the loss function $l(\hat{\theta} | \theta)$ is the analogue in $\hat{\theta}$ of the loss function for decision errors presented in the table above.

The *risk function* (conditional expected losses) is computed just as it was before; in this notation it appears as

$$(B.4.9.2) \qquad R(\hat{\theta} | \theta) = \int \cdots \int l(\hat{\theta} | \theta) f(x_1, \ldots, x_n | \theta) \, dx_1 \cdots dx_n,$$

assuming continuous random variables $x_1, \ldots, x_n$. The objective is to find the $\hat{\theta}$ that minimizes the expected value of $R(\hat{\theta} | \theta)$ over θ, corresponding to the minimization of (B.4.9.1) over c for our hypothesis-testing problem. That is, we wish to find the minimum of

$$(B.4.9.3) \qquad E[R(\hat{\theta} | \theta)] = \int R(\hat{\theta} | \theta) f(\theta) \, d\theta$$

over $\hat{\theta}$, assuming θ to be continuous. Again, in general this will not be an easy problem to solve with the calculus, and numerical methods will likely be necessary.

Some additional insights are gained by reconsidering the problem slightly. If (B.4.9.3) is written out in detail, we have

$$(B.4.9.4) \qquad E[R(\hat{\theta} | \theta)] = \int \cdots \int \left\{ \int l(\hat{\theta} | \theta) f(x_1, \ldots, x_n | \theta) f(\theta) \, d\theta \right\}$$
$$\times \, dx_1, \ldots, dx_n,$$

reversing the order of integration. Now, $f(x_1, \ldots, x_n | \theta) f(\theta)$ is the *joint* distribution of the $\{x_i\}$ and θ. Also, the marginal distribution of the x_i's is

$$(B.4.9.5) \qquad f(x_1, \ldots, x_n) = \int f(x_1, \ldots, x_n | \theta) f(\theta) \, d\theta,$$

so that the conditional distribution of θ—the Bayesian posterior distribution—is just

$$(B.4.9.6) \qquad f(\theta | x_1, \ldots, x_n) = \frac{f(x_1, \ldots, x_n | \theta) f(\theta)}{f(x_1, \ldots, x_n)}.$$

Rewriting (B.4.9.4),

$$(B.4.9.7) \qquad E[R(\hat{\theta} | \theta)] = \int \cdots \int f(x_1, \ldots, x_n) \left\{ \int l(\hat{\theta} | \theta) f(\theta | x_1, \ldots, x_n) \, d\theta \right\}$$
$$\times \, dx_1 \cdots dx_n.$$

Expected risk will be minimized if a $\hat{\theta}(x_1, \ldots, x_n)$ can be found that minimizes $\{\int l(\hat{\theta}|\theta)f(\theta|x_1, \ldots, x_n) \, d\theta\}$ over all $\{x_i\}$. Usually, however, the Bayesian estimation problem is conceived of in the more limited sense of minimizing $\int l(\hat{\theta}|\theta)f(\theta|x_1, \ldots, x_n) \, d\theta$ over $\hat{\theta}$. In effect, the sample is taken as given and we act to minimize a *posterior risk function*. Note that if $l(\hat{\theta}|\theta) = (\hat{\theta} - \theta)^2$, the optimal value of $\hat{\theta}$ turns out to be the *mean* of the posterior density of θ. A "confidence interval" on θ is thus obtained directly from the posterior density function. Unlike its classical counterpart, it is a probability statement about θ directly.

To apply these ideas to our current example, suppose that our loss function is $(p_n - \tilde{P})^2$ and that the prior distribution on $\tilde{P}$ is uniform. Then the posterior density is proportional to the binomial density (recall the calculation of Table B.2), and the Bayesian estimator for $\tilde{P}$ is the mean of this density function, namely $p_n = y/n$, exactly the classical estimator. Indeed, often the least-squares estimator appears as a Bayesian estimator under the assumptions of a quadratic loss function and a uniform prior.

While with sufficient expertise in numerical integration Bayesian estimators can be computed in most applications, there nevertheless remain some difficulties in carrying over the methodology we have just considered to multiparameter problems. These we will not discuss here. The primary application of Bayesian ideas that is of interest to us here is the description of conditions under which the Bayesian framework yields either the classical estimator (in an estimation problem) or critical region (in a testing problem).

C Tables

Table C.1

Normal Distribution Function

$$\phi(z) = \frac{1}{\sqrt{2\pi}} \int_{-\infty}^{z} e^{-x^2/2} \, dx \quad \text{for} \quad 0.00 \leq z \leq 4.99.$$

z	.00	.01	.02	.03	.04	.05	.06	.07	.08	.09
.0	.5000	.5040	.5080	.5120	.5160	.5199	.5239	.5279	.5319	.5359
.1	.5398	.5438	.5478	.5517	.5557	.5596	.5636	.5675	.5714	.5753
.2	.5793	.5832	.5871	.5910	.5948	.5987	.6026	.6064	.6103	.6141
.3	.6179	.6217	.6255	.6293	.6331	.6368	.6406	.6443	.6480	.6517
.4	.6554	.6591	.6628	.6664	.6700	.6736	.6772	.6808	.6844	.6879
.5	.6915	.6950	.6985	.7019	.7054	.7088	.7123	.7157	.7190	.7224
.6	.7257	.7291	.7324	.7357	.7389	.7422	.7454	.7486	.7517	.7549
.7	.7580	.7611	.7642	.7673	.7703	.7734	.7764	.7794	.7823	.7852
.8	.7881	.7910	.7939	.7967	.7995	.8023	.8051	.8078	.8106	.8133
.9	.8159	.8186	.8212	.8238	.8264	.8289	.8315	.8340	.8365	.8389
1.0	.8413	.8438	.8461	.8485	.8508	.8531	.8554	.8577	.8599	.8621
1.1	.8643	.8665	.8686	.8708	.8729	.8749	.8770	.8790	.8810	.8830
1.2	.8849	.8869	.8888	.8907	.8925	.8944	.8962	.8980	.8997	.90147
1.3	.90320	.90490	.90658	.90824	.90988	.91149	.91309	.91466	.91621	.91774
1.4	.91924	.92073	.92220	.92364	.92507	.92647	.92785	.92922	.93056	.93189
1.5	.93319	.93448	.93574	.93699	.93822	.93943	.94062	.94179	.94295	.94408
1.6	.94520	.94630	.94738	.94845	.94950	.95053	.95154	.95254	.95352	.95449
1.7	.95543	.95637	.95728	.95818	.95907	.95994	.96080	.96164	.96246	.96327
1.8	.96407	.96485	.96562	.96638	.96712	.96784	.96856	.96926	.96995	.97062
1.9	.97128	.97193	.97257	.97320	.97381	.97441	.97500	.97558	.97615	.97670
2.0	.97725	.97778	.97831	.97882	.97932	.97982	.98030	.98077	.98124	.98169
2.1	.98214	.98257	.98300	.98341	.98382	.98422	.98461	.98500	.98537	.98574
2.2	.98610	.98645	.98679	.98713	.98745	.98778	.98809	.98840	.98870	.98899
2.3	.98928	.98956	.98983	$.9^20097$	$.9^20358$	$.9^20613$	$.9^20863$	$.9^21106$	$.9^21344$	$.9^21576$
2.4	$.9^21802$	$.9^22024$	$.9^22240$	$.9^22451$	$.9^22656$	$.9^22857$	$.9^23053$	$.9^23244$	$.9^23431$	$.9^23613$
2.5	$.9^23790$	$.9^23963$	$.9^24132$	$.9^24297$	$.9^24457$	$.9^24614$	$.9^24766$	$.9^24915$	$.9^25060$	$.9^25201$
2.6	$.9^25339$	$.9^25473$	$.9^25604$	$.9^25731$	$.9^25855$	$.9^25975$	$.9^26093$	$.9^26207$	$.9^26319$	$.9^26427$
2.7	$.9^26533$	$.9^26636$	$.9^26736$	$.9^26833$	$.9^26928$	$.9^27020$	$.9^27110$	$.9^27197$	$.9^27282$	$.9^27365$
2.8	$.9^27445$	$.9^27523$	$.9^27599$	$.9^27673$	$.9^27744$	$.9^27814$	$.9^27882$	$.9^27948$	$.9^28012$	$.9^28074$
2.9	$.9^28134$	$.9^28193$	$.9^28250$	$.9^28305$	$.9^28359$	$.9^28411$	$.9^28462$	$.9^28511$	$.9^28559$	$.9^28605$
3.0	$.9^28650$	$.9^28694$	$.9^28736$	$.9^28777$	$.9^28817$	$.9^28856$	$.9^28893$	$.9^28930$	$.9^28965$	$.9^28999$
3.1	$.9^30324$	$.9^30646$	$.9^30957$	$.9^31260$	$.9^31553$	$.9^31836$	$.9^32112$	$.9^32378$	$.9^32636$	$.9^32886$
3.2	$.9^33129$	$.9^33363$	$.9^33590$	$.9^33810$	$.9^34024$	$.9^34230$	$.9^34429$	$.9^34623$	$.9^34810$	$.9^34991$
3.3	$.9^35166$	$.9^35335$	$.9^35499$	$.9^35658$	$.9^35811$	$.9^35959$	$.9^36103$	$.9^36242$	$.9^36376$	$.9^36505$
3.4	$.9^36631$	$.9^36752$	$.9^36869$	$.9^36982$	$.9^37091$	$.9^37197$	$.9^37299$	$.9^37398$	$.9^37493$	$.9^37585$
3.5	$.9^37674$	$.9^37759$	$.9^37842$	$.9^37922$	$.9^37999$	$.9^38074$	$.9^38146$	$.9^38215$	$.9^38282$	$.9^38347$
3,6	$.9^38409$	$.9^38469$	$.9^38527$	$.9^38583$	$.9^38637$	$.9^38689$	$.9^38739$	$.9^38787$	$.9^38834$	$.9^38879$
3.7	$.9^38922$	$.9^38964$	$.9^40039$	$.9^40426$	$.9^40799$	$.9^41158$	$.9^41504$	$.9^41838$	$.9^42159$	$.9^42468$
3.8	$.9^42765$	$.9^43052$	$.9^43327$	$.9^43593$	$.9^43848$	$.9^44094$	$.9^44331$	$.9^44558$	$.9^44777$	$.9^44988$
3.9	$.9^45190$	$.9^45385$	$.9^45573$	$.9^45753$	$.9^45926$	$.9^46092$	$.9^46253$	$.9^46406$	$.9^46554$	$.9^46696$
4.0	$.9^46833$	$.9^46964$	$.9^47090$	$.9^47211$	$.9^47327$	$.9^47439$	$.9^47546$	$.9^47649$	$.9^47748$	$.9^47843$
4.1	$.9^47934$	$.9^48022$	$.9^48106$	$.9^48186$	$.9^48263$	$.9^48338$	$.9^48409$	$.9^48477$	$.9^48542$	$.9^48605$
4.2	$.9^48665$	$.9^48723$	$.9^48778$	$.9^48832$	$.9^48882$	$.9^48931$	$.9^48978$	$.9^50226$	$.9^50655$	$.9^51066$
4.3	$.9^51460$	$.9^51837$	$.9^52199$	$.9^52545$	$.9^52876$	$.9^53193$	$.9^53497$	$.9^53788$	$.9^54066$	$.9^54332$
4.4	$.9^54587$	$.9_54831$	$.9^55065$	$.9^55288$	$.9^55502$	$.9^55706$	$.9^55902$	$.9^56089$	$.9^56268$	$.9^56439$
4.5	$.9^56602$	$.9^56759$	$.9^56908$	$.9^57051$	$.9^57187$	$.9^57318$	$.9^57442$	$.9^57561$	$.9^57675$	$.9^57784$
4.6	$.9^57888$	$.9^57987$	$.9^58081$	$.9^58172$	$.9^58258$	$.9^58340$	$.9^58419$	$.9^58494$	$.9^58566$	$.9^58634$
4.7	$.9^58699$	$.9^58761$	$.9^58821$	$.9^58877$	$.9^58931$	$.9^58983$	$.9^60320$	$.9^60789$	$.9^61235$	$.9^61661$
4.8	$.9^62067$	$.9^62453$	$.9^62822$	$.9^63173$	$.9^63508$	$.9^63827$	$.9^64131$	$.9^64420$	$.9^64696$	$.9^64958$
4.9	$.9^65208$	$.9^65446$	$.9^65673$	$.9^65889$	$.9^66094$	$.9^66289$	$.9^66475$	$.9^66652$	$.9^66821$	$.9^66981$

Example: $\phi(3.57) = .9^38215 = 0.9998215.$

From A. Hald, *Statistical Tables and Formulas* (New York: Wiley, 1952), with permission of the publisher.

Table C.2

Percentage Points of the t-Distribution

v	$Q = 0.4$ $2Q = 0.8$	0.25 0.5	0.05 0.1	0.025 0.05	0.005 0.01	0.0025 0.005	0.001 0.002
1	0.325	1.000	6.314	12.706	63.657	127.32	318.31
2	.289	0.816	2.920	4.303	9.925	14.089	22.326
3	.277	.765	2.353	3.182	5.841	7.453	10.213
4	.271	.741	2.132	2.776	4.604	5.598	7.173
5	0.267	0.727	2.015	2.571	4.032	4.773	5.893
6	.265	.718	1.943	2.447	3.707	4.317	5.208
7	.263	.711	1.895	2.365	3.499	4.029	4.785
8	.262	.706	1.860	2.306	3.355	3.833	4.501
9	.261	.703	1.833	2.262	3.250	3.690	4.297
10	0.260	0.700	1.812	2.228	3.169	3.581	4.144
11	.260	.697	1.796	2.201	3.106	3.497	4.025
12	.259	.695	1.782	2.179	3.055	3.428	3.930
13	.259	.694	1.771	2.160	3.012	3.372	3.852
14	.258	.692	1.761	2.145	2.977	3.326	3.787
15	0.258	0.691	1.753	2.131	2.947	3.286	3.733
16	.258	.690	1.746	2.120	2.921	3.252	3.686
17	.257	.689	1.740	2.110	2.898	3.222	3.646
18	.257	.688	1.734	2.101	2.878	3.197	3.610
19	.257	.688	1.729	2.093	2.861	3.174	3.579
20	0.257	0.687	1.725	2.086	2.845	3.153	3.552
21	.257	.686	1.721	2.080	2.831	3.135	3.527
22	.256	.686	1.717	2.074	2.819	3.119	3.505
23	.256	.685	1.714	2.069	2.807	3.104	3.485
24	.256	.685	1.711	2.064	2.797	3.091	3.467
25	0.256	0.684	1.708	2.060	2.787	3.078	3.450
26	.256	.684	1.706	2.056	2.779	3.067	3.435
27	.256	.684	1.703	2.052	2.771	3.057	3.421
28	.256	.683	1.701	2.048	2.763	3.047	3.408
29	.256	.683	1.699	2.045	2.756	3.038	3.396
30	0.256	0.683	1.697	2.042	2.750	3.030	3.385
40	.255	.681	1.684	2.021	2.704	2.971	3.307
60	.254	.679	1.671	2.000	2.660	2.915	3.232
120	.254	.677	1.658	1.980	2.617	2.860	3.160
∞	.253	.674	1.645	1.960	2.576	2.807	3.090

$Q = 1 - P(t|v)$ is the upper-tail area of the distribution for v degrees of freedom, appropriate for use in a singletail test. For a two-tail test, $2Q$ must be used.

From *Biometrika Tables for Statisticians*, Vol. I, ed. E. S. Pearson and H. O. Hartley (Cambridge: Cambridge University Press, 1958), with permission of the Biometrika Trustees.

Table C.3

Percentage Points of the F-Distribution

Upper 5% points

v_2 \ v_1	1	2	3	4	5	6	7	8	9	10	12	15	20	24	30	40	60	120	∞
1	161.4	199.5	215.7	224.6	230.2	234.0	236.8	238.0	240.5	241.9	243.9	245.9	248.0	249.1	250.1	251.1	252.2	253.3	254.3
2	18.51	19.00	19.16	19.25	19.30	19.33	19.35	19.37	19.38	19.40	19.41	19.43	19.45	19.45	19.46	19.47	19.48	19.49	19.50
3	10.13	9.55	9.28	9.12	9.01	8.94	8.89	8.85	8.81	8.79	8.74	8.70	8.66	8.64	8.62	8.59	8.57	8.55	8.53
4	7.71	6.94	6.59	6.39	6.26	6.16	6.09	6.04	6.00	5.96	5.91	5.86	5.80	5.77	5.75	5.72	5.69	5.66	5.63
5	6.61	5.79	5.41	5.19	5.05	4.95	4.88	4.82	4.77	4.74	4.68	4.62	4.56	4.53	4.50	4.46	4.43	4.40	4.36
6	5.99	5.14	4.76	4.53	4.39	4.28	4.21	4.15	4.10	4.06	4.00	3.94	3.87	3.84	3.81	3.77	3.74	3.70	3.67
7	5.59	4.74	4.35	4.12	3.97	3.87	3.79	3.73	3.68	3.64	3.57	3.51	3.44	3.41	3.38	3.34	3.30	3.27	3.23
8	5.32	4.46	4.07	3.84	3.69	3.58	3.50	3.44	3.39	3.35	3.28	3.22	3.15	3.12	3.08	3.04	3.01	2.97	2.93
9	5.12	4.26	3.86	3.63	3.48	3.37	3.29	3.23	3.18	3.14	3.07	3.01	2.94	2.90	2.86	2.83	2.79	2.75	2.71
10	4.96	4.10	3.71	3.48	3.33	3.22	3.14	3.07	3.02	2.98	2.91	2.85	2.77	2.74	2.70	2.66	2.62	2.58	2.54
11	4.84	3.98	3.59	3.36	3.20	3.09	3.01	2.95	2.90	2.85	2.79	2.72	2.65	2.61	2.57	2.53	2.49	2.45	2.40
12	4.75	3.89	3.49	3.26	3.11	3.00	2.91	2.85	2.80	2.75	2.69	2.62	2.54	2.51	2.47	2.43	2.38	2.34	2.30
13	4.67	3.81	3.41	3.18	3.03	2.92	2.83	2.77	2.71	2.67	2.60	2.53	2.46	2.42	2.38	2.34	2.30	2.25	2.21
14	4.60	3.74	3.34	3.11	2.96	2.85	2.76	2.70	2.65	2.60	2.53	2.46	2.39	2.35	2.31	2.27	2.22	2.18	2.13
15	4.54	3.68	3.29	3.06	2.90	2.79	2.71	2.64	2.59	2.54	2.48	2.40	2.33	2.29	2.25	2.20	2.16	2.11	2.07
16	4.49	3.63	3.24	3.01	2.85	2.74	2.66	2.59	2.54	2.49	2.42	2.35	2.28	2.24	2.19	2.15	2.11	2.06	2.01
17	4.45	3.59	3.20	2.96	2.81	2.70	2.61	2.55	2.49	2.45	2.38	2.31	2.23	2.19	2.15	2.10	2.06	2.01	1.96
18	4.41	3.55	3.16	2.93	2.77	2.66	2.58	2.51	2.46	2.41	2.34	2.27	2.19	2.15	2.11	2.06	2.02	1.97	1.92
19	4.38	3.52	3.13	2.90	2.74	2.63	2.54	2.48	2.42	2.38	2.31	2.23	2.16	2.11	2.07	2.03	1.98	1.93	1.88
20	4.35	3.49	3.10	2.87	2.71	2.60	2.51	2.45	2.39	2.35	2.28	2.20	2.12	2.08	2.04	1.99	1.95	1.90	1.84
21	4.32	3.47	3.07	2.84	2.68	2.57	2.49	2.42	2.37	2.32	2.25	2.18	2.10	2.05	2.01	1.96	1.92	1.87	1.81
22	4.30	3.44	3.05	2.82	2.66	2.55	2.46	2.40	2.34	2.30	2.23	2.15	2.07	2.03	1.98	1.94	1.89	1.84	1.78
23	4.28	3.42	3.03	2.80	2.64	2.53	2.44	2.37	2.32	2.27	2.20	2.13	2.05	2.01	1.96	1.91	1.86	1.81	1.76
24	4.26	3.40	3.01	2.78	2.62	2.51	2.42	2.36	2.30	2.25	2.18	2.11	2.03	1.98	1.94	1.89	1.84	1.79	1.73
25	4.24	3.39	2.99	2.76	2.60	2.49	2.40	2.34	2.28	2.24	2.16	2.09	2.01	1.96	1.92	1.87	1.82	1.77	1.71
26	4.23	3.37	2.98	2.74	2.59	2.47	2.39	2.32	2.27	2.22	2.15	2.07	1.99	1.95	1.90	1.85	1.80	1.75	1.69
27	4.21	3.35	2.96	2.73	2.57	2.46	2.37	2.31	2.25	2.20	2.13	2.06	1.97	1.93	1.88	1.84	1.79	1.73	1.67
28	4.20	3.34	2.95	2.71	2.56	2.45	2.36	2.29	2.24	2.19	2.12	2.04	1.96	1.91	1.87	1.82	1.77	1.71	1.65
29	4.18	3.33	2.93	2.70	2.55	2.43	2.35	2.28	2.22	2.18	2.10	2.03	1.94	1.90	1.85	1.81	1.75	1.70	1.64

Table C.3 (continued)

Upper 5% points

v_1 v_2	1	2	3	4	5	6	7	8	9	10	12	15	20	24	30	40	60	120	∞
30	4.17	3.32	2.92	2.69	2.53	2.42	2.33	2.27	2.21	2.16	2.09	2.01	1.93	1.89	1.84	1.79	1.74	1.68	1.62
40	4.08	3.23	2.84	2.61	2.45	2.34	2.25	2.18	2.12	2.08	2.00	1.92	1.84	1.79	1.74	1.69	1.64	1.58	1.51
60	4.00	3.15	2.76	2.53	2.37	2.25	2.17	2.10	2.04	1.99	1.92	1.84	1.75	1.70	1.65	1.59	1.53	1.47	1.39
120	3.92	3.07	2.68	2.45	2.29	2.17	2.09	2.02	1.96	1.91	1.83	1.75	1.66	1.61	1.55	1.50	1.43	1.35	1.25
∞	3.84	3.00	2.60	2.37	2.21	2.10	2.01	1.94	1.88	1.83	1.75	1.67	1.57	1.52	1.46	1.39	1.32	1.22	1.00

$F = \dfrac{s_1^2}{s_2^2} = \dfrac{S_1/v_1}{S_2/v_2}$, where $s_1^2 = S_1/v_1$ and $s_2^2 = S_2/v_2$ are independent mean squares estimating a common variance σ^2 and based on v_1 and v_2 degrees of freedom, respectively.

Upper 1% points

v_1 v_2	1	2	3	4	5	6	7	8	9	10	12	15	20	24	30	40	60	120	∞
1	4052	4999.5	5403	5625	5764	5859	5928	5982	6022	6056	6106	6157	6209	6235	6261	6287	6313	6339	6366
2	98.50	99.00	99.17	99.25	99.30	99.33	99.36	99.37	99.39	99.40	99.42	99.43	99.45	99.46	99.47	99.47	99.48	99.49	99.50
3	34.12	30.82	29.46	28.71	28.24	27.91	27.67	27.49	27.35	27.23	27.05	26.87	26.69	26.60	26.50	26.41	26.32	26.22	26.13
4	21.20	18.00	16.69	15.98	15.52	15.21	14.98	14.80	14.66	14.55	14.37	14.20	14.02	13.93	13.84	13.75	13.65	13.56	13.46
5	16.26	13.27	12.06	11.39	10.97	10.67	10.46	10.29	10.16	10.05	9.89	9.72	9.55	9.47	9.38	9.29	9.20	9.11	9.02
6	13.75	10.92	9.78	9.15	8.75	8.47	8.26	8.10	7.98	7.87	7.72	7.56	7.40	7.31	7.23	7.14	7.06	6.97	6.88
7	12.25	9.55	8.45	7.85	7.46	7.19	6.99	6.84	6.72	6.62	6.47	6.31	6.16	6.07	5.99	5.91	5.82	5.74	5.65
8	11.26	8.65	7.59	7.01	6.63	6.37	6.18	6.03	5.91	5.81	5.67	5.52	5.36	5.28	5.20	5.12	5.03	4.95	4.86
9	10.56	8.02	6.99	6.42	6.06	5.80	5.61	5.47	5.35	5.26	5.11	4.96	4.81	4.73	4.65	4.57	4.48	4.40	4.31
10	10.04	7.56	6.55	5.99	5.64	5.39	5.20	5.06	4.94	4.85	4.71	4.56	4.41	4.33	4.25	4.17	4.08	4.00	3.91
11	9.65	7.21	6.22	5.67	5.32	5.07	4.89	4.74	4.63	4.54	4.40	4.25	4.10	4.02	3.94	3.86	3.78	3.69	3.60
12	9.33	6.93	5.95	5.41	5.06	4.82	4.64	4.50	4.39	4.30	4.16	4.01	3.86	3.78	3.70	3.62	3.54	3.45	3.36
13	9.07	6.70	5.74	5.21	4.86	4.62	4.44	4.30	4.19	4.10	3.96	3.82	3.66	3.59	3.51	3.43	3.34	3.25	3.17
14	8.86	6.51	5.56	5.04	4.69	4.46	4.28	4.14	4.03	3.94	3.80	3.66	3.51	3.43	3.35	3.27	3.18	3.09	3.00

Table C.3 (continued)

Upper 1% points

v_2 \ v_1	1	2	3	4	5	6	7	8	9	10	12	15	20	24	30	40	60	120	∞
15	8.68	6.36	5.42	4.89	4.56	4.32	4.14	4.00	3.89	3.80	3.67	3.52	3.37	3.29	3.21	3.13	3.05	2.96	2.87
16	8.53	6.23	5.29	4.77	4.44	4.20	4.03	3.89	3.78	3.69	3.55	3.41	3.26	3.18	3.10	3.02	2.93	2.84	2.75
17	8.40	6.11	5.18	4.67	4.34	4.10	3.93	3.79	3.68	3.59	3.46	3.31	3.16	3.08	3.00	2.92	2.83	2.75	2.65
18	8.29	6.01	5.09	4.58	4.25	4.01	3.84	3.71	3.60	3.51	3.37	3.23	3.08	3.00	2.92	2.84	2.75	2.66	2.57
19	8.18	5.93	5.01	4.50	4.17	3.94	3.77	3.63	3.52	3.43	3.30	3.15	3.00	2.92	2.84	2.76	2.67	2.58	2.49
20	8.10	5.85	4.94	4.43	4.10	3.87	3.70	3.56	3.46	3.37	3.23	3.09	2.94	2.86	2.78	2.69	2.61	2.52	2.42
21	8.02	5.78	4.87	4.37	4.04	3.81	3.64	3.51	3.40	3.31	3.17	3.03	2.88	2.80	2.72	2.64	2.55	2.46	2.36
22	7.95	5.72	4.82	4.31	3.99	3.76	3.59	3.45	3.35	3.26	3.12	2.98	2.83	2.75	2.67	2.58	2.50	2.40	2.31
23	7.88	5.66	4.76	4.26	3.94	3.71	3.54	3.41	3.30	3.21	3.07	2.93	2.78	2.70	2.62	2.54	2.45	2.35	2.26
24	7.82	5.61	4.72	4.22	3.90	3.67	3.50	3.36	3.26	3.17	3.03	2.89	2.74	2.66	2.58	2.49	2.40	2.31	2.21
25	7.77	5.57	4.68	4.18	3.85	3.63	3.46	3.32	3.22	3.13	2.99	2.85	2.70	2.62	2.54	2.45	2.36	2.27	2.17
26	7.72	5.53	4.64	4.14	3.82	3.59	3.42	3.29	3.18	3.09	2.96	2.81	2.66	2.58	2.50	2.42	2.33	2.23	2.13
27	7.68	5.49	4.60	4.11	3.78	3.56	3.39	3.26	3.15	3.06	2.93	2.78	2.63	2.55	2.47	2.38	2.29	2.20	2.10
28	7.64	5.45	4.57	4.07	3.75	3.53	3.36	3.23	3.12	3.03	2.90	2.75	2.60	2.52	2.44	2.35	2.26	2.17	2.06
29	7.60	5.42	4.54	4.04	3.73	3.50	3.33	3.20	3.09	3.00	2.87	2.73	2.57	2.49	2.41	2.33	2.23	2.14	2.03
30	7.56	5.39	4.51	4.02	3.70	3.47	3.30	3.17	3.07	2.98	2.84	2.70	2.55	2.47	2.39	2.30	2.21	2.11	2.01
40	7.31	5.18	4.31	3.83	3.51	3.29	3.12	2.99	2.89	2.80	2.66	2.52	2.37	2.29	2.20	2.11	2.02	1.92	1.80
60	7.08	4.98	4.13	3.65	3.34	3.12	2.95	2.82	2.72	2.63	2.50	2.35	2.20	2.12	2.03	1.94	1.84	1.73	1.60
120	6.85	4.79	3.95	3.48	3.17	2.96	2.79	2.66	2.56	2.47	2.34	2.19	2.03	1.95	1.86	1.76	1.66	1.53	1.38
∞	6.63	4.61	3.78	3.32	3.02	2.80	2.64	2.51	2.41	2.32	2.18	2.04	1.88	1.79	1.70	1.59	1.47	1.32	1.00

$F = \dfrac{s_1^2}{s_2^2} = \dfrac{S_1}{v_1} \Big/ \dfrac{S_2}{v_2}$, where $s_1^2 = S_1/v_1$ and $s_2^2 = S_2/v_2$ are independent mean squares estimating a common variance σ^2 and based v_1 and v_2 degrees of freedom, respectively.

Table C.4

95% Significance Points, d_L and d_U, for the Durbin-Watson Test
of Serial Correlation, d

	$k = 1$		$k = 2$		$k = 3$		$k = 4$		$k = 5$	
n	d_L	d_U	d_L	d_U	d_L	d_U	d_L	d_U	d_L	d_U
15	0.95	1.23	0.83	1.40	0.71	1.61	0.59	1.84	0.48	2.09
16	0.98	1.24	0.86	1.40	0.75	1.59	0.64	1.80	0.53	2.03
17	1.01	1.25	0.90	1.40	0.79	1.58	0.68	1.77	0.57	1.98
18	1.03	1.26	0.93	1.40	0.82	1.56	0.72	1.74	0.62	1.93
19	1.06	1.28	0.96	1.41	0.86	1.55	0.76	1.72	0.66	1.90
20	1.08	1.28	0.99	1.41	0.89	1.55	0.79	1.70	0.70	1.87
21	1.10	1.30	1.01	1.41	0.92	1.54	0.83	1.69	0.73	1.84
22	1.12	1.31	1.04	1.42	0.95	1.54	0.86	1.68	0.77	1.82
23	1.14	1.32	1.06	1.42	0.97	1.54	0.89	1.67	0.80	1.80
24	1.16	1.33	1.08	1.43	1.00	1.54	0.91	1.66	0.83	1.79
25	1.18	1.34	1.10	1.43	1.02	1.54	0.94	1.65	0.86	1.77
26	1.19	1.35	1.12	1.44	1.04	1.54	0.96	1.65	0.88	1.76
27	1.21	1.36	1.13	1.44	1.06	1.54	0.99	1.64	0.91	1.75
28	1.22	1.37	1.15	1.45	1.08	1.54	1.01	1.64	0.93	1.74
29	1.24	1.38	1.17	1.45	1.10	1.54	1.03	1.63	0.96	1.73
30	1.25	1.38	1.18	1.46	1.12	1.54	1.05	1.63	0.98	1.73
31	1.26	1.39	1.20	1.47	1.13	1.55	1.07	1.63	1.00	1.72
32	1.27	1.40	1.21	1.47	1.15	1.55	1.08	1.63	1.02	1.71
33	1.28	1.41	1.22	1.48	1.16	1.55	1.10	1.63	1.04	1.71
34	1.29	1.41	1.24	1.48	1.17	1.55	1.12	1.63	1.06	1.70
35	1.30	1.42	1.25	1.48	1.19	1.55	1.13	1.63	1.07	1.70
36	1.31	1.43	1.26	1.49	1.20	1.56	1.15	1.63	1.09	1.70
37	1.32	1.43	1.27	1.49	1.21	1.56	1.16	1.62	1.10	1.70
38	1.33	1.44	1.28	1.50	1.23	1.56	1.17	1.62	1.12	1.70
39	1.34	1.44	1.29	1.50	1.24	1.56	1.19	1.63	1.13	1.69
40	1.35	1.45	1.30	1.51	1.25	1.57	1.20	1.63	1.15	1.69
45	1.39	1.48	1.34	1.53	1.30	1.58	1.25	1.63	1.21	1.69
50	1.42	1.50	1.38	1.54	1.34	1.59	1.30	1.64	1.26	1.69
55	1.45	1.52	1.41	1.56	1.37	1.60	1.33	1.64	1.30	1.69
60	1.47	1.54	1.44	1.57	1.40	1.61	1.37	1.65	1.33	1.69
65	1.49	1.55	1.46	1.59	1.43	1.62	1.40	1.66	1.36	1.69
70	1.51	1.57	1.48	1.60	1.45	1.63	1.42	1.66	1.39	1.70
75	1.53	1.58	1.50	1.61	1.47	1.64	1.45	1.67	1.42	1.70
80	1.54	1.59	1.52	1.62	1.49	1.65	1.47	1.67	1.44	1.70
85	1.56	1.60	1.53	1.63	1.51	1.65	1.49	1.68	1.46	1.71
90	1.57	1.61	1.55	1.64	1.53	1.66	1.50	1.69	1.48	1.71
95	1.58	1.62	1.56	1.65	1.54	1.67	1.52	1.69	1.50	1.71
100	1.59	1.63	1.57	1.65	1.55	1.67	1.53	1.70	1.51	1.72

From J. Durbin, and G. S. Watson, "Testing for Serial Correlation in Least Squares Regression," *Biometrika* **38**: 1-2 (1951), pp. 159–177. Reprinted with permission of the Biometrika trustees and the authors.

n = number of observations; k = number of regressors (not including constant).

Table C.5

Critical Points for the Mean Square Error Test
for a Linear Restriction

$T - K$ ╲ α	.05	.10	.25	.50
1	340.34	86.15	12.65	2.29
2	37.38	17.50	5.53	1.56
3	19.93	11.16	4.33	1.38
4	14.96	9.04	3.88	1.31
5	12.66	8.06	3.62	1.26
6	11.36	7.44	3.47	1.23
7	10.57	7.05	3.37	1.21
8	9.96	6.79	3.30	1.20
9	9.58	6.57	3.24	1.19
10	9.25	6.41	3.20	1.18
11	9.04	6.30	3.16	1.17
12	8.83	6.20	3.13	1.16
13	8.68	6.13	3.11	1.16
14	8.54	6.05	3.09	1.15
15	8.41	5.98	3.07	1.15
16	8.31	5.93	3.05	1.15
17	8.23	5.88	3.04	1.15
18	8.18	5.84	3.03	1.15
19	8.10	5.82	3.02	1.14
20	8.05	5.78	3.01	1.14
21	7.98	5.75	3.00	1.14
22	7.96	5.71	3.00	1.14
23	7.91	5.69	2.99	1.14
24	7.83	5.68	2.98	1.14
25	7.82	5.66	2.98	1.13
30	7.65	5.60	2.95	1.13
40	7.52	5.49	2.92	1.12
60	7.33	5.40	2.89	1.12
120	7.14	5.31	2.86	1.11

$T - K =$ degrees of freedom $(n - k - 1)$.

From C. Toro-Vizcarrondo, and T. D. Wallace, "A Test of the Mean Square Error Criterion for Restrictions in Regression," *Journal of the American Statistical Association*, Vol. 63 (June 1968), pp. 558–72. Reprinted with permission of the American Statistical Association and the authors.

Index